D1223712

DURATION ANALYSIS

DURATION ANALYSIS
Managing Interest Rate Risk

GERALD O. BIERWAG

BALLINGER PUBLISHING COMPANY
Cambridge, Massachusetts
A Subsidiary of Harper & Row, Publishers, Inc.

Copyright © 1987 by Ballinger Publishing Company. All rights reserved. No part of this publication may be reproduced, stored in a retrieval system, or transmitted in any form or by any means, electronic, mechanical, photocopy, recording or otherwise, without the prior written consent of the publisher.

International Standard Book Number: 0-88730-116-9

Library of Congress Catalog Card Number: 86-28745

Printed in the United States of America

Library of Congress Cataloging-in-Publication Data

Bierwag, Gerald O.
  Duration analysis.

  Includes index.
  1. Investments — Mathematics. 2. Bonds. 3. Mortgage
banks. 4. Interest rates. 5. Rate of return. I. Title.
HG4515.3.B54 1987   332.8′2   86-28745

ISBN 0-88730-116-9

LIBRARY
ALMA COLLEGE
ALMA, MICHIGAN

CONTENTS

LIST OF FIGURES

LIST OF TABLES

PREFACE

Within the last 10 years, duration-based investment strategies have been intensively developed and implemented. Professional managers, using duration concepts, manage investment funds worth billions of dollars in fixed income securities. Duration analysis has come of age. It represents a methodical approach to prudent investments in bonds and mortgages. Whether duration analysis appeals to all investment managers or not, it will likely continue into the twenty-first century.

The formal development of duration analysis is scattered over a large part of the finance literature. Published summaries are usually very casual nontechnical developments that exclude many relevant and interesting applications of duration analysis. This book, *Duration Analysis,* contains

- a complete development of the fundamentals,
- a detailed description of leading applications,
- technical appendixes,
- an up-to-date summary of published empirical research on duration analysis,
- some caveats dealing with callability and credit risk, and
- some indications of the direction of future research.

The book is intended to be a guide to the many-splendored wrinkles of duration analysis as well as an accessible exposition of the fundamentals and their applications.

Duration Analysis has taken over three years to produce. I have received much assistance and encouragement along the way. George G. Kaufman, who has been instrumental in the development of many duration concepts and applications, has contributed enormously to this book with valuable suggestions and with endless discussions. Robert Rogowski used portions of the first four chapters in a class at Washington State University. His suggestions helped to improve these chapters immensely. I have also used much of this work in seminars for doctoral candidates at the University of Arizona. I am particularly indebted to Mahamood Hassan, Wu-Hsiung Lin, and Sung-Ky Min, doctoral students at the University of Arizona, for many helpful, line-by-line suggestions. My wife also assisted in many ways and made many helpful suggestions. All errors and ambiguities remaining are strictly the fault of the author, who didn't accept all suggestions. Finally, the staff at Ballinger Publishing Company, particularly Carolyn Casagrande, has been very supportive and patient in awaiting the completion of this work. I am grateful for the assistance and encouragement received from everyone mentioned.

Gerald O. Bierwag
Tucson, Arizona
July 1986

DURATION AND CHANGES IN VALUATION

1 INCOME STREAMS, DISCOUNT FUNCTIONS, YIELD TO MATURITY

INCOME STREAMS

Debt instruments, created by contracts between borrowers and lenders, usually promise specific cash flows at future dates.[1] Financial instruments that promise these fixed flows are called *fixed-income securities*. For a specific financial instrument these cash flows can be represented as

$$(F_1, F_2, ..., F_t, ..., F_M), \tag{1.1}$$

where F_t, $t = 1, 2, ..., M$, is the cash flow promised at the end of period t, and where M is the last period in which a flow is promised. Most bonds promise a flow at the end of every 6-month period. Most mortgages promise a flow at the end of every month. U.S. Treasury bills promise only one cash flow at some future dates. For some of these bills the future date may be 1 week away and for others it may be as long as 12 months.

The pattern of the cash flows over time can vary considerably from one financial instrument to another. Mortgages, for example, conventionally promise cash flows that are constant over time; that is, $F_1 = F_2 = \cdots = F_t = \cdots = F_M$. Bonds typically promise a constant flow through time up to the last period, but then F_M, the last payment, called the *balloon payment*, is much larger. The cash flow at each date in time is often divided into components. Each cash flow on a mortgage, for example, is traditionally divided into two parts. One part represents a fractional repayment of principal

3

which is a reduction in the *unpaid balance,* and the other part represents an *interest payment.* The early flows on a bond are called *coupon* payments and the last flow (the balloon payment) consists of a coupon payment and the *face value* of the bond. The division of the flows into parts is useful for several reasons. First, the magnitudes of these components are often directly useful in the valuation or pricing of the financial instrument. Second, the laws on the income and capital gains taxes may apply differently to different components. For example, the interest payments on mortgages are deductible from gross income to determine the borrower's taxable income.

The income stream on any financial instrument can be regarded as a combination of many different more fundamental income streams. The income stream, $(F_1, F_2, ..., F_t, ..., F_M)$, is a summation of the M single-payment income streams:

$$(F_1, 0, 0, ..., 0)$$
$$(0, F_2, 0, ..., 0)$$
$$(0, 0, F_3, ..., 0) \tag{1.2}$$
$$\vdots$$
$$(0, 0, 0, ..., F_M),$$

A lender or investor who acquires the income stream $(F_1, F_2, ..., F_t, ..., F_M)$ can be regarded as acquiring this package of M income streams in (1.2). If the markets for these assets are sufficiently developed, the investor might as well separately buy each of these M simple income streams as buy the single composite income stream of (1.1). The investor acquires the same promised cash flows in either case.

Each of the single-payment income streams of (1.2) is also the summation of many single-payment income streams. For example, the income stream $(F_1, 0, 0, ..., 0)$ consists of F_1 units of the income stream $(1, 0, 0, ..., 0)$. These one-dollar income streams,

$$(1, 0, 0, ..., 0)$$
$$(0, 1, 0, ..., 0)$$
$$(0, 0, 1, ..., 0) \tag{1.3}$$
$$\vdots$$
$$(0, 0, 0, ..., 1)$$

are the basic building blocks of all income streams. If the markets for financial assets are sufficiently developed, an investor can purchase any desired income stream by purchasing combinations of the one-dollar income streams. However, regardless of how well developed the markets are, the analyst can regard any income stream as consisting of a set of the one-dollar single-payment income streams. For purposes of valuation it is useful to think of any income stream as consisting of combinations of these basically simple income streams.

DISCOUNT FUNCTIONS

Income streams considered here represent dollars to be received at prespecified future dates. A discount function transforms an income stream into current or present value. If a discount function is chosen appropriately, this present value represents the current market value of an income stream.

Let d_t be the discount function that transforms \$1.00 to be received at the end of t periods into current dollars. That is, d_t is the current or present value of \$1.00 to be received t periods later. For example, if \$1.00 is promised to a lender at the end of one month, a borrower might be willing to accept \$0.95 now. In this case d_t is \$0.95 and t is one month. If an investor acquires the income stream, $(0, 0, \ldots, F_t, \ldots, 0)$, the current value of this income stream may be regarded as $F_t d_t$. In other words, it is assumed that an investor who buys F_t one-dollar single-payment income streams pays exactly the same price for each of them. The price d_t of the one-dollar single-payment income stream is assumed to be independent of the number of such units purchased. The situation is similar to buying cans of peas in a grocery store. If one can of peas costs \$0.49, then the purchase of 10 cans costs $10 \times \$0.49 = \$4.90$. The one-dollar income stream is analagous to one can of peas and F_t is analogous to 10, the number of such cans purchased. If this idea is extended to all of the components of the income stream $(F_1, F_2, \ldots, F_t, \ldots, F_M)$, the current or present value of this income stream can be expressed as

$$V = \sum_{t=1}^{M} d_t F_t = d_1 F_1 + d_2 F_2 + \cdots + d_M F_M. \qquad (1.4)$$

This valuation formula reflects the assumption of *value additivity*. The value of one component of the stream, say $d_1 F_1$, is not affected by the value of some other component, say $d_M F_M$. If the *value additivity* assumption were violated, other terms would have to be added to the right-hand side of (1.4) to reflect the interactions of the flows F_t on the value of the stream. Value additivity reflects the assumption of competitive pricing of income streams, an assumption most often made implicitly. If investors can acquire the flows

F_t independently from different borrowers or markets, then the value of the package of flows is the sum of the value of its components. Imperfectly competitive pricing features (like "tie-in sales," in which a flow F_k may be bought at a price lower than d_k provided an investor also acquired the flow F_s at a price higher than d_s) are assumed not to be possible. In other words, as is typical in the valuation of income streams, it is assumed that each flow F_t, $t = 1, 2, ..., M$, is sold in separate competitive markets at the price of d_t per dollar in each market. Thus, the value of an income stream with M future payments is regarded as the aggregate value of M different flows, each of which has implicitly a separate market.

The discount function, d_t, $t = 1, 2, ..., M$, is sometimes called a discount factor, and it is often expressed as a function of one or more interest rates. It is important to realize what a discount function does. The expression of it as a function of one or more interest rates involves additional assumptions about the nature of valuation. However, simply expressed as d_t, $t = 1, 2, ..., M$, the discount function or set of discount factors represents prices of the basic building blocks of the income streams.

Although markets may not exist for the various simple income streams comprising a modern mortgage, bond, or other financial instruments, modern valuation of these financial assets proceeds on the assumption that these basic streams do have independent markets or can be created by simultaneous transactions in different markets.

Some general properties of d_t, $t = 1, 2, ..., M$, are often postulated. Most certainly $d_t > 0$. The current value of a future dollar is surely positive. Future dollars, under most conditions, can neither be regarded as "free goods" nor as "bads." If d_t were negative, this would mean that an investor is willing to pay someone else to take over a contract that promises a positive future cash inflow. Evidently the promised future cash flow is like garbage for which an investor is willing to pay now in order to have it taken away. It is reasonable to assume that $d_t > 0$. Under most circumstances, it is also reasonable to assume that $d_t < 1$. Investors are not normally willing to give up one dollar or more now in order to acquire just one dollar in the future. That is, investors, are regarded as having positive time preference; they would prefer to have one dollar now to spend than one dollar later on to spend, and, hence, if they give up d_t dollars now they must be compensated by the return of the d_t dollars later plus an increment of $(1 - d_t)$ dollars to compensate for the current sacrifice in spending. For example, if \$0.90 is given up now, an investor must be compensated by receiving an increment to the \$0.90 of (\$1.00 − \$0.90) = \$0.10, say. Moreover, one would also expect that $d_t < d_{t-1}$. The farther into the future that a dollar is promised, the less the investor is willing to pay for it now. This is another aspect of the investor's time preference and shows that such investors or lenders prefer to have dollars in the near term to spend rather than in the far term. These assumptions imply that d_t is a monotonic decreasing function of t and that it is bounded within the interval $0 < d_t < 1$. These properties of the discount function provide a wide scope for a variety of such possible functions. Figure 1-1 shows the graphs of two very different discount functions, each of which is consistent with the three properties noted here. In each of the two diagrams, d_t is a positive number less than unity and it always decreases as the date of the future payment moves farther into the future. The valuation of a given income

Figure 1-1.   Discount Functions: Appropriately Decreasing and Bounded

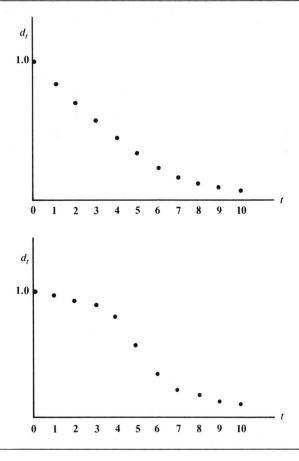

stream with these two discount functions can be considerably different. The reasonable restrictions here imposed on the discount functions are very weak ones. An enormous variety of such functions are consistent with the three properties assumed here.

THE INTEREST RATE AS AN INDEX NUMBER

In the markets for debt instruments, each of the discount factors is often expressed as a function of a single number called the interest rate. In this case, the discount factor may be defined as

$$d_t = (1+r)^{-t}, \quad t = 1, 2, 3, \ldots, M, \tag{1.5}$$

where r is the rate of interest that is assumed to be some positive number that does not depend upon t. In this way every discount factor in the set $(d_1, d_2, \ldots, d_M)$ is a function of the same number r. Instead of requiring knowledge of every d_t, $t = 1, 2, \ldots, M$, all one needs to know is the value of r. For every value of r one can easily compute the value of every discount factor by use of equation (1.5). The interest rate r is thus an "indicator" or an "index" of all the discount factors. Table 1-1 shows various values of d_t for a selected set of r's. This is a common table that appears in most undergraduate textbooks in finance. In Table 1-1, for example, when $r = .08$, d_t decreases from 0.926 for $t = 1$ to 0.463 for $t = 10$. For every given interest rate, it is seen that

Table 1-1. Values of d_t for Various Values of the Rate of Interest r

				r		
t	.08	.09	.10	.11	.12	.13
1	.926	.917	.909	.901	.893	.885
2	.857	.842	.826	.812	.797	.783
3	.794	.772	.751	.731	.712	.693
4	.735	.708	.683	.659	.636	.613
5	.681	.650	.621	.593	.567	.543
6	.630	.596	.564	.535	.507	.480
7	.583	.547	.513	.482	.452	.425
8	.540	.502	.467	.434	.404	.376
9	.500	.460	.424	.391	.361	.333
10	.463	.422	.386	.352	.322	.295

$$d_t > 0,$$
$$d_t < 1, \text{ and}$$
$$d_t < d_{t-1}.$$

The discount factor defined in (1.5) has all three of the desired properties previously noted. Table 1-1 illustrates the use of the interest rate r as an index number, or as an indicator of all of the discount factors. For any r, the relevant column in Table 1-1 gives all the discount factors. Equation (1.5) is a very special function. There are many alternative ways to define a discount function that will be consistent with the three properties noted above. An advantage of using equation (1.5) is clear, however, One can calculate the value of any income stream by knowing only the components of the income stream and the value of r, the interest rate.

THE INTEREST RATE AS A RATE OF RETURN

The interest rate, r, as used in equation (1.5) is usually interpreted as a rate of return. For example, suppose that an investor acquires the simple income stream $(1, 0, 0, \ldots, 0)$ for the price of $d_1 = (1+r)^{-1}$ dollars. The investor gives up d_1 dollars now in order to acquire one dollar one period from now. If we multiply d_1 by $(1+r)$ we obtain one dollar. Thus, the return of one dollar can be written as $d_1(1+r) = d_1 + rd_1$. At the end of one period the investor gets back the initial investment of d_1 dollars plus the additional amount rd_1, which is called the interest on the investment. This increment expressed as the ratio $rd_1/d_1 = r$ is the rate of interest and is often expressed in percentage terms. In Table 1-1 $r = 0.08$ represents a percentage rate of return of 8 percent. That is, 8 percent of d_1 is \$0.074; this is the increment to d_1 ($= \$0.926$) received as interest in one period.

One can also interpret r as the rate of growth of an investment. This is particularly apparent when the investment is for more than one period. For example, suppose the investor acquires the simple income stream $(0, 1, 0, 0, \ldots, 0)$ for the price of $d_2 = (1+r)^{-2}$ dollars. Multiplying d_2 by $(1+r)^2$ gives us the one-dollar return at the end of two periods. This is equivalent to investing d_2 dollars for one period to acquire the return $d_2(1+r)$ for one period and then reinvesting that amount for an additional period to acquire the return $d_2(1+r)(1+r) = d_2(1+r)^2$. The rate of return is said to be r per period, and it is the same as the growth rate of the investment d_2 for two periods. The same idea extends to any number of periods. Notice that after one period the reinvestment of the amount $d_2(1+r)$ involves a reinvestment of the interest rd_2. The return over the last period, written as

$$d_2(1+r)^2 = d_2(1+r) + rd_2(1+r),$$

includes the term $rd_2(1+r)$, which is the interest on the reinvestment of the interest return from the first period. This interest on interest is sometimes called *compound interest*.

Usually interest rates are expressed as annual rates. This is a standard that is in common use. It is the method of specifying discount factors appropriate for evaluating flows, F_t, which are one year apart. If the flows are one month apart, the monthly rate is conventionally expressed as $r/12$. If the flows are three months apart, the 3-month or quarterly rate is expressed as $r/4$. In general, if the flows occur at intervals of equal length, the rate per period is expressed as r/n where n is the number of such intervals in a year. The daily rate is expressed as $r/360$ on the assumption of 360 days in a year. These conventions make the calculations of the relevant discount factors very simple. However, compounding effects make investment comparisons not quite precise. For example, one dollar invested for two 6-month periods grows to $[1+(r/2)]^2$ over a year, but one dollar invested for 1 year accumulates to just $(1+r)$ dollars in one year and $(1+r) < [1+(r/2)]^2 = 1+r+(r/2)^2$. The compounding effect of $(r/2)^2$ is often ignored when making such comparisons conventionally.

The annual interest rate r is often broken down into units called *basis points*. A basis point is one hundredth of a percentage point. For example, if r increases from 8% to 8.01%, it is said that r has increased by 1 basis point. Thus an increase in the rate of interest from 8% to 9% would be regarded as an increases of 100 basis points. In equation (1.5), r is always expressed in decimal form. Thus, in that expression where the rate of interest is 8% we would write $r = .08$. Hence, if the rate of interest increases from 8% to 8.01%, we would note this as an increase of r from .08 to .0801 in equation (1.5).

A CONSTANT TIME PRICE FOR MONEY

If r remains constant as time passes and if d_t is the discount factor as defined in equation (1.5), then the current price or present value of $1.00 to be received t periods later does not change with the passage of time. For example, if $r = .08$, then the price as of January 1, 1983 of $1.00 to be received on January 1, 1984 is $d_1 = \$0.926$; and if r remains unchanged, then the price as of January 1, 1984 of $1.00 to be received on January 1, 1985 is $d_1 = \$0.926$. If the interest rate r does not change with the passage of time, the discount function so defined implies a *constant time price for money*.

The cost of a future dollar depends only on the length of the time interval between the date the flow is purchased and the date that it is received. A constant time price for money has an important implication. If d_t is the current price of \$1.00 to be received on date t, then $(1+r)d_t = d_{t-1}$ is either (a) the current price of \$1.00 to be received at time $t-1$ or (b) the price one period from now of receiving \$1.00 at date t. In other words, the price of \$1.00 to be received $(t-1)$ periods ahead is the same regardless of when we compute it provided r does not change through time. This property of the discount function has very specific implications for evaluating any given income stream over time.

Using the discount function in equation (1.5), the present value of the income stream $(F_1, F_2, ..., F_M)$ is

$$V = \sum_{t=1}^{M} d_t F_t = \sum_{t=1}^{M} F_t (1+r)^{-t}. \tag{1.6}$$

After 1 year passes, the investor receives F_1 dollars in cash and then owns the income stream $(F_2, F_3, ..., F_M)$, where F_2 is to be received 1 year later, F_3 is to be received 2 years later, and so forth. The total value of the investment after one year is F_1 plus the value of the remaining income stream. If the time price for money is constant the value of the investment after one period can be expressed as

$$V_1 = F_1 + \sum_{t=2}^{M} d_{t-1} F_t = F_1 + \sum_{t=2}^{M} F_t (1+r)^{-(t-1)}. \tag{1.7}$$

If V in equation (1.6) is multiplied by $(1+r)$, it can be observed

$$(1+r)V = \sum_{t=1}^{M} F_t (1+r)^{-(t-1)} = F_1 + \sum_{t=2}^{M} F_t (1+r)^{-(t-1)} = V_1. \tag{1.8}$$

The initial investment of V dollars grows to the value of $(1+r)V$ in one period. The rate of return for 1 year is r. The rate of return, r, is totally independent of the components of the income stream F_t. The accumulation depends only on the initial investment V and on the rate of return r. This result occurs because of a constant time price for money. In equation (1.7), the value of the income stream yet to be received is

$$\sum_{t=2}^{M} d_{t-1} F_t = d_1 F_2 + d_2 F_3 + \cdots + d_{M-1} F_M.$$

After one period has passed, the component F_t of this income stream represents a flow to be received in $(t-1)$ periods. Each such flow is valued at the price that prevailed one period earlier for flows to be received in $(t-1)$

periods. If they were valued at an alternative set of prices, there would be no assurance that equations (1.7) and (1.8) would be equivalent. Finally, it may be noted that if $V_1 = (1+r)V$ independently of the flows F_t so that as long as V dollars is initially invested, the accumulation is the same regardless of what income stream is acquired. In other words, income streams of equal value are perfect substitutes if the time price of money is constant.

The development in equations (1.6)–(1.8) can be extended to any number of years. After one period, if the cash flow F_1 can be invested in any income stream because they are perfect substitutes, then it follows that $(1+r)V_1 = V_2$, the accumulated value of the investment after 2 years. It is apparent that

$$V_2 = (1+r)^2 V = (1+r)F_1 + F_2 + \sum_{t=3}^{M} F_t(1+r)^{-(t-2)}, \qquad (1.9)$$

where $(1+r)F_1$ is the accumulated value from investing F_1 for one year, F_2 is the cash received in two years, and the remainder is the value of the income stream yet to be received after 2 years have passed.

Thus, if d_t is specified as a function of r as in equation (1.5), and if the interest rate r does not change over time, then all financial instruments are perfect substitutes and they will all accumulate over time at the same rate.

THE YIELD TO MATURITY
(INTERNAL RATE OF RETURN)

The *maturity* of an income stream is the length of the time interval from the date of purchase to the date that the last cash flow is received. The income stream $(F_1, F_2, ..., F_M)$ has a maturity of M periods. If

> V is the initial present value of the income stream,
> the rate of interest, r, does not change as time passes, and
> all cash flows are reinvested as they are received,

then the terminal or accumulated value of the initial investment at maturity is $V_M = (1+r)^M V$. This result follows from the last section because all securities are perfect substitutes and there is a constant time price for money. In this context the rate of interest r is called the *yield to maturity*. The yield to maturity measures the rate of growth of the investment over time when interest rates do not change and there is a constant time price for money. This yield can be viewed as the interest return per period for the life of the income stream. Many investors view the yield to maturity as a measure of the earning power of an asset even though the cash flows are not reinvested and even though the time price for money is not constant. Much of this book is concerned with investment accumulation when interest rates are not constant over time and when the time price for money is not constant.

The yield to maturity is also called the *internal rate of return*. Given an income stream $(F_1, F_2, \ldots, F_M)$, and its value V, the internal rate of return is formally defined as that rate of interest r which discounts the former to the latter. The discounted value of the income stream is

$$\sum_{t=1}^{M} F_t(1+r)^{-t}.$$

This sum of terms varies inversely with the interest rate r or the discount rate. Picking the tth term in this sum,

$$\frac{F_t}{(1+r)^t},$$

it is easy to see that its value decreases as r rises and that its value increases as r falls. Since this is true for every term in the sum, it follows that the sum varies inversely with r. Given V, the rate of interest, r, is that rate which makes the value of the sum equal to the given value of V. By definition this value is the yield to maturity, but in this context of finding r so as to equate the discounted sum to the value V, it is also called the internal rate of return.

Consider an example for calculating r. Suppose a debt instrument promises a single cash flow of $100 at the end of two periods and that it currently sells for $81. The internal rate of return is that value of r for which

$$81 = \frac{100}{(1+r)^2}.$$

The value of r that solves this equation is 0.1111. It is not always arithmetically easy to find r — given V and the cash flows — but fortunately there are many calculators and computer programs that can do this with great ease.

NOTE

1. Loan contracts often contain provisions that permit the borrower and the lender to modify the income streams at later dates. These options to change the form of the contract have a value too. Here, however, we consider only simple contracts in which such options are not in effect.

2 BONDS AND MORTGAGES

Bonds and mortgages are the most commonly traded debt securities in the United States. These securities have standardized income streams that permit the development of specific formulas that express the price of the security in terms of the yield to maturity and other properties of the income stream. Bond and mortgage traders and analysts of financial markets frequently utilize these formulas. Assorted price/interest rate tables and special calculator programs are now very widely available so that the price/interest rate relationships are literally at the fingertips of their users.

BONDS

General Valuation

Bonds typically promise a cash payment to their holders or owners every six months. This periodic cash payment depends on the *face value* and the *coupon rate* of the bond. The face value of the bond is included only in the last payment the holder receives on the maturity date of the bond. It is called the face value because it is printed in very large letters on the face of the bond contract or indenture.[1] The face value is usually $1,000, $5,000, $10,000, or multiples of $10,000. Denote the face value of a bond by F. The coupon rate, like the yield to maturity, is expressed as an annual rate of return. Let the coupon rate expressed in decimal form be denoted as c. The annual cash flow on the bond is found by multiplying the face value by the coupon rate. The annual cash flow is hence cF. This cash payment is normally made in two installments; one half of it is paid every 6 months. Thus, $cF/2$ is the cash flow or "coupon income" paid every 6 months until maturity. The entire income stream on a typical bond can then be represented as

$$\left(\frac{cF}{2}, \frac{cF}{2}, \frac{cF}{2}, ..., \frac{cF}{2} + F\right),$$

where the final payment at maturity includes F. Thus, the stream is "flat" up to the maturity date at which time a big leap in the stream occurs. For example, a 10%, $1,000 bond would have the income stream:

$$(\$50, \$50, \$50, ..., \$1,050).$$

The income stream of a bond that promises a cash flow every 6 months is completely described by its maturity date, annual coupon rate, and face value. If any two bonds differ with respect to any one of these three characteristics, their pattern of promised future cash flows will also differ.

For some bonds the face value can be regarded as the initial amount borrowed or *principal,* and the coupon income as the periodic *interest* on the principal. For these bonds, the cash flows prior to maturity represent interest and the final payment includes repayment of the principal. In this context, the coupon rate is often called "the interest rate," but it may *not* be the same as the yield to maturity or the internal rate of return. There are many bonds, noted in this chapter, for which the face value *does not* represent the principal and for which the coupon income *does not* represent the interest.

The coupon rate refers to the fact that most bonds at one time had pieces of paper called coupons physically attached to them. At the prespecified interest payment dates, the holder could clip the coupons and cash them in for dollars. Bonds having these physical coupons attached were called "bearer" bonds. The issuers of these bonds did not keep records as to who was the owner of each of them. Presentation of the coupons and the bond at maturity was sufficient to indicate ownership and entitlement to the coupon payment and face value on the specified dates. This practice is no longer in effect in the United States on newly issued bonds, but there remain extant many municipal and other local government securities that have coupons that physically can be clipped on the prespecified coupon payment dates. Today most securities are registered so that the bond issuer knows who is the owner of record of the bonds and the issuer pays the value of the coupons by bank draft on the prespecified dates.

If r is the annual rate of interest or yield to maturity then, as indicated in the last chapter, the 6-month rate of interest is $r/2$. Thus, the discount function is $d_t = (1 + r/2)^{-t}$, where t is measured in 6-month periods. The price of a bond maturing in M years is then

$$P = \sum_{t=1}^{2M} d_t F_t = \sum_{t=1}^{2M} F_t \left(1 + \frac{r}{2}\right)^{-t}$$

$$= \frac{cF/2}{1+r/2} + \frac{cF/2}{(1+r/2)^2} + \cdots + \frac{cF/2}{(1+r/2)^{2M}} + \frac{F}{(1+r/2)^{2M}} \qquad (2.1)$$

$$= \left(\frac{cF}{2}\right) \sum_{t=1}^{2M} \left(1 + \frac{r}{2}\right)^{-t} + F\left(1 + \frac{r}{2}\right)^{-2M},$$

where there are $2M$ 6-month intervals in an M-year period. Equation (2.1) represents a special application of equation (1.6) of Chapter 1. That equation is simply specialized so as to account for 6-month intervals between cash flow dates. The cash flow is $cF/2$ on every 6-month payment date and F is paid as well on the last date while the interest rate used in the discount function is the 6-month rate calculated by convention as the annual rate divided by 2. Equation (2.1) shows that the value of the bond is divisible into two parts. The first part involving the sum of the discount factors multiplied by $cF/2$ is the current value of the coupon payments. The second part is the current value of the face value F to be received on the maturity date.

For long maturities the use of equation (2.1) may require a considerable number of calculations. If $M = 25$ years, for example, there would be 51 terms on the right-hand side to sum. Fortunately, the sum of the discount factors can be simply expressed as

$$\sum_{t=1}^{2M} \left(1 + \frac{r}{2}\right)^{-t} = \frac{2}{r}\left[1 - \left(1 + \frac{r}{2}\right)^{-2M}\right]. \qquad (2.2)$$

The derivation of this result is shown in Appendix 2A (at the end of this chapter). Equation (2.2) gives the value of $1.00 to be received on each of $2M$ future payment dates which are spaced 6 months apart. The income stream so evaluated is said to be flat. This income stream is sometimes called an *annuity*. Originally an annuity was an income stream promising equal cash flows spaced one year apart, but in current usage an annuity is any "flat" income stream. Multiplication of (2.2) by $cF/2$ gives the value of an annuity that promises $cF/2$ dollars every 6 months. The formula in (2.2) is widely used and tabulated in many financial handbooks and textbooks.

Substitution of equation (2.2) into (2.1) shows that the value of the bond can be expressed as

$$P = \frac{cF}{r}\left[1 - \left(1 + \frac{r}{2}\right)^{-2M}\right] + F\left(1 + \frac{r}{2}\right)^{-2M}. \tag{2.3}$$

This formula is easier to use than equation (2.1) because it requires far fewer computations. This formula is the one used in most hand calculators.

In order to standardize the price for bonds having different face values, P in equation (2.3) is usually divided by F and expressed as a percentage. In this way, the standardized price is

$$p = 100\frac{c}{r}\left[1 - \left(1 + \frac{r}{2}\right)^{-2M}\right] + 100\left(1 + \frac{r}{2}\right)^{-2M}. \tag{2.4}$$

Here, $p = 100P/F$. In this way, the price of a bond is expressed as a percentage of its face value. Given the price p, one can then easily calculate the price P by multiplying p by $F/100$. Bonds that differ only in having different face values consequently have identically the same price p, or standardized price. Bonds selling at a price of $p = 89$ in effect are selling at 89% of their face value. Bonds for which $p = 100$ are called *par bonds*. If $p > 100$, the bonds are called *premium bonds,* and if $p < 100$, the bonds are called *discount bonds.*

The prices of bonds are quoted in terms of the standardized prices above. Table 2-1 shows a partial list of price quotations on U.S. Treasury securities for May 31, 1985. There are seven columns in this table. The first column indicates the coupon rate of a bond and the second and third columns indicate the year and month of maturity. Thus, "the 14's of June 1985," as used in common parlance, means the 14% coupon securities to mature in June of 1985. The "n" following the month indicates that the security is a Treasury note. Treasury notes have maturities no longer than 10 years and they have a cycle of coupon and principal payments over the year that is different from bonds. Treasury securities are normally bought and sold in secondary markets through government bond dealers in money market centers. The prices quoted indicate the prices at which they are willing to sell securities (the "asked" prices) and the prices at which they are willing to buy securities (the "bid" prices). The difference between the "asked" and "bid" prices is intended to cover dealer costs and to provide a margin of profit. All prices are quoted as a percentage of face value, and are expressed in 32's of a dollar. For example, the "asked" price on the "10's of June 1985" is $100 plus 9/32's of a dollar. This a convention in bond markets. In this book, however, all prices will be stated in terms of dollars and cents. The next column indicates the change in the "bid" price from the previous business day. Finally, the last column shows the annual yield to maturity corresponding to the "asked" price. Fabozzi and Pollack (1983) is an excellent source of more information on the securities markets and other conventions.

Par Bonds

Equation (2.4) can be rewritten as

$$p = \frac{c}{r}100 + 100\left(1 - \frac{c}{r}\right)\left(1 + \frac{r}{2}\right)^{-2M}. \tag{2.5}$$

It is easily seen that $p = 100$ when $c = r$. Such bonds are called *par bonds*. The price of this bond cannot vary with maturity M as long as $c = r$. Given that $p = 100P/F$, it follows that $P = F$. The price of a par bond is always equal to its face value. For par bonds the face value F is the invested principal and the coupon income, $cF/2 = rF/2$, is the interest earned over a 6-month period. As time passes, the price of the par bond will always remain at 100 as long as the rate of interest stays unchanged and equal to the coupon rate. If that is the case, the initial investment remains at F dollars throughout the life of the bond and the periodic cash flows comprise the interest payments.

Discount Bonds

If $c < r$, the bond is a discount bond for which $p < 100$. To show this, subtract both sides of equation (2.5) from 100. This gives

$$d = 100 - p = 100\left(\frac{c}{r} - 1\right)\left[\left(1 + \frac{r}{2}\right)^{-2M} - 1\right]. \tag{2.6}$$

If $c < r$, the right-hand side must be positive because $(1 + r/2)^{-2M} - 1 < 0$ and $c/r - 1 < 0$. Therefore, $d = 100 - p$ is a positive number. Here, d is called the *discount*. It is the number of dollars subtracted from the face value of 100 to determine the price. Bonds selling at a discount must then sell at a price that is less than the face value.

In the most extreme case of a discount bond, $c = 0$. The income stream for the standardized bond then becomes

$$(0, 0, 0, \ldots, 0, 100).$$

A bond for which this is so is called a *zero coupon bond* or a *pure discount bond*. These bonds promise no periodic cash flow at all; no periodic interest

Table 2-1. Price Quotations for U.S. Securities, May 31, 1985

Treasury Bonds, Notes, and Bills

Friday, May 31, 1985

Representative mid-afternoon Over-the-Counter quotations supplied by the Federal Reserve Bank of New York City, based on transactions of $1 million or more.

Decimals in bid-and-asked and bid changes represent 32nds; 101.1 means 101$\frac{1}{32}$. a—Plus $\frac{1}{64}$. b—Yield to call date. d—Minus $\frac{1}{64}$. k—Non U.S. citizens exempt from withholding taxes. n—Treasury notes. p—Treasury note; non U.S. citizens exempt from withholding taxes.

Treasury Bonds and Notes

Rate	Mat.	Date	Bid	Asked	Bid Chg.	Yld.
14s,	1985	Jun n	100.14	100.18	−.1	5.79
10s,	1985	Jun n	100.5	100.9	....	5.82
10⅝s,	1985	Jul n	100.15	100.8	....	6.58
8¼s,	1985	Aug n	100.4	100.8	....	6.81
9⅝s,	1985	Aug n	100.13	100.17	....	6.72
10⅝s,	1985	Aug n	100.20	100.24	....	7.23
13⅛s,	1985	Sep n	101.2	101.6	−.1	6.80
10⅞s,	1985	Sep n	101.1	101.5	....	7.07
15⅞s,	1985	Sep n	102.19	102.23	−.1	7.05
10½s,	1985	Oct n	101.3	101.7	....	7.33
9¾s,	1985	Nov n	100.28	101	+.1	7.39
10½s,	1985	Nov n	101.8	101.12	−.1	7.58
11¾s,	1985	Dec n	101.23	101.27	+.2	7.43
10⅞s,	1985	Dec n	101.23	101.27	+.1	7.53
14⅛s,	1986	Jan n	103.18	103.22	+.2	7.43
10½s,	1986	Feb n	101.23	101.27	+.2	7.70
10⅞s,	1986	Feb n	102.1	102.5	+.1	7.83
13⅛s,	1986	Feb n	103.28	104	+.2	7.54
9⅝s,	1986	Feb n	101.7	101.11	+.1	7.87
14s,	1986	Mar n	104.24	104.28	....	7.78

Rate	Mat.	Date	Bid	Asked	Bid Chg.	Yld.
11⅛s,	1987	Sep n	104	104.4	+.3	9.12
7⅝s,	1987	Nov n	97.8	97.16	+.6	8.78
11s,	1987	Nov p	103.25	103.29	+.4	9.18
12⅝s,	1987	Nov n	107.10	107.14	+.5	9.16
11¼s,	1987	Dec n	104.13	104.17	+.4	9.23
12⅝s,	1988	Jan n	107.2	107.6	+.4	9.22
10⅛s,	1988	Feb n	101.29	102.1	+.4	9.26
10⅞s,	1988	Feb p	102.17	102.19	+.5	9.27
12s,	1988	Mar n	106.11	106.15	+.5	9.34
13¼s,	1988	Apr n	109.16	109.24	+.5	9.30
8¼s,	1988	May n	97.17	97.25	+.5	9.13
9⅞s,	1988	May n	101.11	101.15	+.6	9.29
10s,	1988	May p	101.28	102	+.7	9.21
13⅜s,	1988	Jun n	110.24	110.28	+.5	9.46
14s,	1988	Jul n	111.24	112	+.6	9.37
10½s,	1988	Aug n	102.26	103.2	+.4	9.53
15⅜s,	1988	Oct n	116.8	116.16	+.5	9.53
11⅜s,	1988	Sep p	105.3	105.7	+.6	9.51
8¾s,	1988	Nov n	98.10	98.18	+.5	9.25
11¾s,	1988	Nov n	106.9	106.13	+.8	9.53

11½s,	1986	Mar n	102.22	102.26	+ .1	7.91
11¾s,	1986	Apr n	103.4	103.8	+ .2	7.96
7⅞s,	1986	May n	99.25	99.29	+ .1	7.98
9⅜s,	1986	May n	101.5	101.9	+ .2	7.94
12⅝s,	1986	May n	104.3	104.7	+ .3	8.10
13¾s,	1986	May n	105.5	105.9	+ .2	7.85
13s,	1986	Jun n	104.24	104.28	+ .3	8.16
14⅞s,	1986	Jun n	106.20	106.24	+ .3	8.18
12⅝s,	1986	Jul p	104.18	104.22	+ .2	8.30
8s,	1986	Aug n	99.19	99.23	+ .1	8.25
11⅜s,	1986	Aug n	103.8	103.12	+ .3	8.36
12⅜s,	1986	Aug p	104.12	104.16	+ .2	8.48
11⅞s,	1986	Sep p	104	104.4	+ .3	8.52
12¼s,	1986	Sep n	104.13	104.17	+ .3	8.56
11⅝s,	1986	Oct p	103.28	104	+ .3	8.55
6⅛s,	1986	Nov	97	98	+ .2	7.61
10⅜s,	1986	Nov p	102.7	102.11	+ .3	8.66
11s,	1986	Nov n	103.1	103.5	+ .1	8.63
13⅞s,	1986	Nov n	106.30	107.2	+ .2	8.58
16⅛s,	1986	Nov n	109.29	110.1	+ .3	8.60
9⅞s,	1986	Dec p	101.16	101.20	+ .2	8.75
10s,	1986	Dec n	101.22	101.26	+ .3	8.74
9¾s,	1987	Jan p	101.8	101.12	+ .3	8.84
9s,	1987	Feb n	100.8	100.12	+ .3	8.76
10s,	1987	Feb p	101.20	101.24	+ .3	8.89
10⅞s,	1987	Feb n	102.31	103.3	+ .2	8.88
12¾s,	1987	Feb n	105.30	106.2	+ .3	8.83
10¼s,	1987	Mar n	102.5	102.9	+ .5	8.87
10¾s,	1987	Mar p	102.29	103.1	+ .2	8.91
9¾s,	1987	Apr p	101.10	101.12	+ .4	8.95
9⅛s,	1987	May p	100.12	100.14	+ .7	8.88
12s,	1987	May n	105.14	105.18	+ .3	8.83
12½s,	1987	May n	106.6	106.10	+ .1	8.90
14s,	1987	May n	108.30	109.2	+ .2	8.83
10½s,	1987	Jun n	102.25	102.29	+ .3	8.93
12⅜s,	1987	Aug p	106.9	106.13	+ .3	9.10
13¾s,	1987	Aug n	109	109.4	+ .3	9.08
10⅝s,	1988	Dec p	103.3	103.7	+ .7	9.54
14⅝s,	1989	Jan n	114.14	114.18	+ .4	9.75
11⅜s,	1989	Feb n	105.6	105.10	+ .5	9.63
11¼s,	1989	Mar p	105.7	105.9	+ .9	9.57
14⅜s,	1989	Apr n	114.7	114.15	+ .5	9.79
9¼s,	1989	May n	99.20	99.28	....	9.29
11¾s,	1989	May n	106.10	106.14	+ .4	9.75
14½s,	1989	Jul n	115.5	115.13	+ .5	9.86
13⅞s,	1989	Aug n	113.6	113.10	+ .6	9.92
11⅞s,	1989	Oct n	106.31	107.7	+ .7	9.80
10¾s,	1989	Nov n	103.18	103.26	+ .5	9.67
12¾s,	1989	Nov p	109.30	110.2	+ .5	9.90
10½s,	1990	Jan n	102.14	102.18	+ .6	9.80
3½s,	1990	Feb	94.13	95.13	+ .4	4.60
11s,	1990	Feb p	104.4	104.8	+ .3	9.85
10½s,	1990	Apr n	102.14	102.18	+ .6	9.82
8¼s,	1990	May	96.2	96.18	+ .8	9.13
11⅜s,	1990	May p	105.25	105.29	+ .7	9.84
10¾s,	1990	Jul n	103.14	103.18	+ .9	9.85
10¾s,	1990	Aug n	103.14	103.18	+ .7	9.86
11½s,	1990	Oct n	106.11	106.15	+ .9	9.92
13s,	1990	Nov n	112.3	112.7	+ .9	10.03
11¾s,	1991	Jan n	107.6	107.10	+ .10	10.02
12⅜s,	1991	Apr	109.26	109.30	+ .11	10.09
14½s,	1991	May n	118.21	118.29	+ .9	10.18
13¾s,	1991	Jul n	115.20	115.24	+ .11	10.22
14⅞s,	1991	Aug n	120.19	120.27	+ .8	10.25
12¼s,	1991	Oct p	109.15	109.19	+ .11	10.17
14¼s,	1991	Nov n	118.16	118.24	+ .11	10.21
11⅝s,	1992	Jan p	106.24	106.28	+ .12	10.17
14⅝s,	1992	Feb n	120.20	120.28	+ .10	10.24
11¾s,	1992	Apr	107.27	107.31	+ .17	10.11
13¾s,	1992	May n	116.23	116.27	+ .11	10.30
4¼s,	1987–92	Aug	94.24	95.24	+ .8	4.96
7¼s,	1992	Aug	86.10	86.26	+ .8	9.85
10½s,	1992	Nov n	102.4	102.20	+ .14	10.04

Source: *Wall Street Journal,* June 3, 1985, page 31.

is paid in cash. The accumulated interest is received entirely on the maturity date. Using equation (2.4), we observe that the pure discount bond has the price

$$p = 100\left(1 + \frac{r}{2}\right)^{-2M}.$$ (2.7)

Pure discount bonds have a built-in reinvestment process. For example, if 6 months pass and the interest rate does not change, the price of the bond becomes

$$p' = 100\left(1 + \frac{r}{2}\right)^{-(2M-1)}$$ (2.8)

because there now remain $(2M-1)$ 6-month periods before maturity. Note that

$$p' = \left(1 + \frac{r}{2}\right)p = p + \left(\frac{r}{2}\right)p,$$ (2.9)

so that the appreciation in value is exactly equal to the 6-month interest, $p(r/2)$. The interest is not received in cash, however, because there are no cash payments prior to maturity. It is consequently unnecessary for the investor to reinvest the cash flows; the interest is automatically reinvested at the annual rate r and is included in the price appreciation. Savings accounts or certificates of deposits (CDs) at depository institutions (commercial banks, savings and loan associations, and credit unions) are examples of zero coupon bonds. If interest is not received in cash, it accumulates as part of the appreciation of the investment. Savings accounts, in addition, have maturity dates that are given as an option to the investor; the investor can withdraw a part or all of the investment at any time, possibly subject to notice of a given number of days. Some zero coupon bonds, such as those issued by corporations, must be held until maturity before the investor can receive interest in cash unless the bonds are sold in secondary markets.

A discount bond having periodic coupon payments ($c>0$, $c<r$) is a bond on which some of the interest is reinvested automatically and some is not. If the bond is purchased for p dollars, then the interest earned in the first 6 months is $rp/2$. The amount of coupon income received is $100c/2$. The interest earned exceeds the coupon income received by the amount $(rp-c100)/2$. This excess amount can be expressed as

$$\frac{rp-c100}{2} = \frac{c100}{2} + 100\left(\frac{r-c}{2}\right)\left(1 + \frac{r}{2}\right)^{-2M} - \frac{100c}{2}$$
$$= 100\left(\frac{r-c}{2}\right)\left(1 + \frac{r}{2}\right)^{-2M} > 0$$ (2.10)

using equation (2.4). This portion of the interest earned but not received in cash represents the appreciation in the value of the bond and can be regarded as interest that is automatically reinvested. Examples of this partition of interest into cash flows and into appreciation of the value of the security are presented in the subsection titled Amortization.

Premium Bonds

If $c > r$, the bond is a premium bond. In this case, as can be seen from equation (2.6), $p - 100 > 0$, and so its price exceeds the face value of the security. This additional amount paid for the bond is called the *premium*.

Premium bonds promise coupon payments that exceed the interest earned. The interest earned over a 6-month period is $rp/2$, but the coupon income received by the investor is $100c/2$. The coupon income exceeds the interest earned. This is easily seen to be the case in equation (2.10), where the expression on the right-hand side is clearly negative when $c > r$. The cash flow exceeds the interest. This excess can be regarded as a partial repayment of the initial amount borrowed so that the price of the bond is reduced. This result is exactly the opposite of the case of discount bonds. For discount bonds, the interest earned but not received can be regarded as an automatic reinvestment. For premium bonds the coupon income received in excess of interest earned can be regarded as an automatic disinvestment.

Amortization

As time passes, the value of a bond can change because either the yield to maturity changes or the remaining time to maturity changes or both. The coupon rate and the face value of the security are fixed as a part of the loan contract between the borrower and the lender. Hence, the value of the security in the market is determined strictly by M and r.[2] Any change in the value of a security over time can consequently be divided into two parts. The value of the bond as would be determined if the yield to maturity did not change is called the *amortized value* of the bond. Changes in the amortized value of a bond differ depending on whether the bond is a par bond, a discount bond, or a premium bond. In order to illustrate these differences, Table 2–2 shows the amortized value of three bonds each having a yield of 10%. The discount bond has a coupon rate of 8% and the premium bond has a coupon rate of 12%. Each bond is assumed to have an initial maturity

Table 2-2.   The Price of a Discount, Par, and a Premium
Bond as a Function of Maturity Only

Maturity (years)	Discount Bond	Par Bond	Premium Bond
10.0	$ 87.54	$100.00	$112.46
9.5	87.92	100.00	112.08
9.0	88.31	100.00	111.69
8.5	88.73	100.00	111.27
8.0	89.16	100.00	110.84
7.5	89.62	100.00	110.38
7.0	90.10	100.00	109.90
6.5	90.61	100.00	109.39
6.0	91.14	100.00	108.86
5.5	91.69	100.00	108.31
5.0	92.28	100.00	107.72
4.5	92.89	100.00	107.11
4.0	93.54	100.00	106.46
3.5	94.21	100.00	105.79
3.0	94.92	100.00	105.08
2.5	95.67	100.00	104.33
2.0	96.45	100.00	103.55
1.5	97.28	100.00	102.72
1.0	98.14	100.00	101.86
0.5	99.05	100.00	100.95
0.0	100.00	100.00	100.00

Note: The yield to maturity of each bond is 10 percent. The coupon rates are respectively
8, 10, and 12 percent for the discount, par, and premium bonds.

of 10 years, but as time passes the maturity becomes shorter. The maturity of each bond is indicated in column 1. The amortized value of the discount bond increases as it approaches maturity. The amortized value of the par bond does not change as it approaches maturity. The amortized value of the premium bond decreases as it approaches maturity. These different patterns of the amortized value reflect the differing compositions of the income streams. Since $r = c$ for par bonds, the coupon payments received in cash are exactly equal to the interest payments; the value of the initial investment or principal never changes because it always remains invested; only the interest payments are withdrawn in cash. Since $r > c$ for discount bonds, the coupon payments are less than the interest payments; the automatically reinvested interest is effectively added to the issuer's outstanding debt and this is why the amortized value of the security increases over time. For example, initially the discount bond has a value of $87.54. In 6 months the interest earned is $(.05)(87.54) = \$4.38$. The coupon payment in 6 months is $(.04) \times (100) = \$4.00$. The interest that is not paid thus amounts to $0.38 and is automatically added to the outstanding debt, which grows to $87.92. Since $r < c$ for premium bonds, the coupon payments exceed the interest and this excess is subtracted from the outstanding value of the debt and hence it decreases with time. For example, initially the premium bond has a value of $112.46. In 6 months the interest earned is $(.05)(\$112.46) = \$5.62$. The coupon payment in 6 months is $(.06)(100) = \$6.00$. The coupon payment exceeds the interest by $0.38. This reduces the amortized value of the outstanding debt by $0.38 to $112.08. The issuer of premium bonds reduces the outstanding debt with every coupon payment. The value of all of the bonds approaches the face value at maturity. For discount bonds unpaid interest is added to the amortized value of the bond. For premium bonds the excess of the coupon payment over the interest reduces the amortized value of the bond. For par bonds, the coupon payment exactly equals the interest so that there is no change in the amortized value of the bond.

Figure 2–1 shows the graph of the amortized values of these three bonds. The amortized value of the discount bond increases over the 10-year period at an increasing rate from $87.54 to $100.00. In the first 6 months, the increase in value is $0.38, but in the last 6 months the increase in value is $0.95. This increase in the increments to the amortized value occurs because the coupon payments are constant but the unpaid interest increases as the amortized value of the bond increases. In other words, as the unpaid interest is compounded and added to the amortized value of the bond, the interest owed in later years must be larger. The opposite effect occurs for premium bonds. The excess of the coupon payment over interest owed increases because the interest owed decreases with the amortized value of the bond. Thus, larger amounts must be subtracted from the amortized value in later years.

As time passes, most often the yield to maturity also changes because changes in the demand and supply in the markets may affect the prices and yields of all securities. A change in the yield also has an impact on the value of a bond. For example, as shown in Table 2–2, the value of the illustrated discount bond rises in value in its first year from $87.54 to $88.31, if the yield to maturity is unchanged at 10%. If the yield to maturity had fallen to 9%, the bond would have a value of $93.92 at the end of its first year. The total change in value is $93.92 - \$87.54 = \$6.38$. However, a portion of this change is due only to a shortening of the maturity of the bond. The change in the amortized value is $88.31 - \$87.54 = \$0.77$. Consequently the change in value of $6.38 can be decomposed as

Figure 2-1. Bond Price–Maturity Relationship: Coupons and Yields Fixed

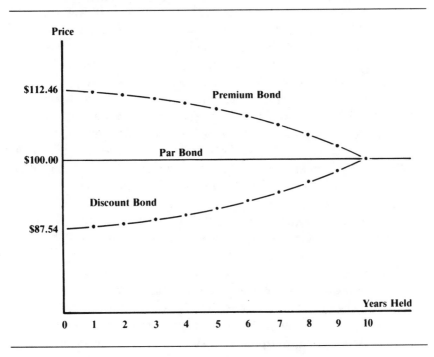

$0.77   change because of shorter maturity
+ $5.61   change because of lower yield
$6.38   total change in value.

Value as a Function of Yield to Maturity

Bonds having identical maturities and coupon rates can differ in price only if they differ in yields to maturity. Equation (2.4), the bond pricing equation, indicates that p is solely a function of r only if c and M are constants. Table 2-3 illustrates how the price can change as only the yield to maturity changes. The table shows that the price is inversely related to the yield to maturity. As can be easily seen from equation (2.1), this inverse relationship holds for all bonds because an increase in the yield to maturity reduces the discount factor multiplied by each periodic cash flow. Graphs of the price/

Table 2-3.   Prices of Two Bonds as a Function of Only the Yield to Maturity

Yield to Maturity	Price of Bond #1	Price of Bond #2
6.0%	$129.76	$117.06
6.5	125.44	114.74
7.0	121.32	112.48
7.5	117.37	110.27
8.0	113.59	108.11
8.5	109.97	106.01
9.0	106.50	103.96
10.0	100.00	100.00
10.5	96.95	98.09
11.0	94.03	96.23
11.5	91.22	94.41
12.0	88.53	92.64
12.5	85.95	90.91
13.0	83.47	89.22
13.5	81.10	87.57
14.0	78.81	85.95

Note: Both bonds have coupon rates of 10 percent. Bond 1 has a maturity of 10 years. Bond 2 has a maturity of 5 years.

yield relationship for the two bonds are illustrated in Figure 2-2. Each of the curves decreases at a decreasing rate. That is, an increment of 50 *basis points* (for example, an increase from 6.00% to 6.50%) has a smaller decrement to the value of a bond at high yields than it has at low yields. All bonds with the same coupon rate of 10% will pass through the same point on this diagram. Similarly, all bonds with a coupon rate of 11% will pass through the point consisting of a price of $100 and a yield to maturity of 11%. Bond 1 has a steeper slope at the point where they cross than Bond 2. This feature will be explained in Chapter 3.

The curves in Figure 2-2 are nonlinear. This nonlinearity accounts for the difficulty of quickly computing the price of a bond for a given yield to maturity. Before the development of advanced calculators, traders and others consulted "bond books." A bond book consists of a large set of tables organized by coupon rate and maturity. For every given coupon rate and maturity, one could quickly find a table that would allow one to pick off the points on curves like those of Figure 2-2.

Figure 2-2. Bond Price-Yield Relationship: Coupon Rate = 10%; Bond 1 Maturity Greater Than Bond 2 Maturity

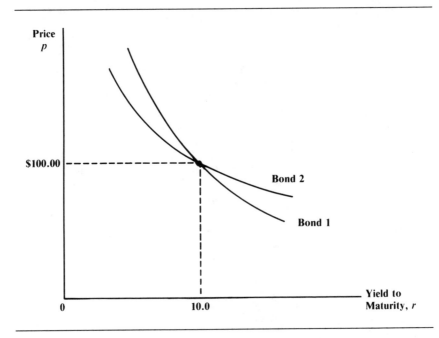

MORTGAGES

General Valuation

Mortgages are loan contracts that are utilized primarily to finance the purchase of residential, commercial, or other real estate. Typically mortgages have flat income streams. Each of the periodic cash flows is the same. This implies that some portion of every cash flow or payment is interest and some portion may be a reduction in the amortized value of the debt. Mortgages typically require monthly payments so that the monthly rate of interest is $r/12$, where r is the annual rate of interest. If Y is the monthly payment the value of a mortgage is

$$V = Y \sum_{t=1}^{12M} \left(1 + \frac{r}{12}\right)^{-t}, \tag{2.11}$$

where M is the number of years to maturity. Here, the income stream is $(Y, Y, Y, ..., Y)$ so that (2.11) simply discounts each of the cash flows by the appropriate discount factor where Y has been factored out of the summation. The expression

$$\sum_{t=1}^{12M}\left(1+\frac{r}{12}\right)^{-t}$$

is the value of an annuity that promises a $1.00 cash flow each month. A similar annuity was evaluated for the coupon income stream for a bond, and is developed in Appendix 2A. Using that method of development it follows that the value of a mortgage can be expressed as

$$V = Y\frac{12}{r}\left[1-\left(1+\frac{r}{12}\right)^{-12M}\right]$$

$$= AY,$$

(2.12)

where

$$A = \frac{12}{r}\left[1-\left(1+\frac{r}{12}\right)^{-12M}\right] = \frac{V}{Y}.$$

(2.13)

The variable A is the *mortgage factor,* which is equal to the ratio of the mortgage value to the monthly payment Y. Equivalently, it is also the value of a mortgage that pays $1.00 (that is, $Y = 1$) per month for M years. Knowing the mortgage factor one can always calculate Y if V is known or conversely. The value of a mortgage is always proportional to the monthly payment, but the factor of proportionality is a function of only the annual rate of interest r and the number of years M to maturity. Table 2-4 gives the mortgage factors for a selection of yields r and years M to maturity. Several examples on how such a table can be used follow.

Example 1. $100,000 is borrowed at 10% for 30 years. The monthly payment is

$$\left(\frac{100,000}{113.951}\right) = \$877.57 = Y,$$

where 113.951 is the mortgage factor.

Example 2. $100,000 is borrowed at 15% for 30 years. The monthly payment is

$$\left(\frac{100,000}{79.086}\right) = \$1,264.45 = Y,$$

where 79.086 is the mortgage factor.

Table 2–4. Mortgage Factors for a Selected Set of Annual Yields r and Years to Maturity M

Annual Yield	Years to Maturity					
	25	26	27	28	29	30
10.0%	110.047	110.991	111.845	112.618	113.317	113.951
10.5	105.912	106.743	107.492	108.166	108.774	109.321
11.0	102.029	102.761	103.418	104.006	104.534	105.006
11.5	98.380	99.025	99.601	100.114	100.572	100.980
12.0	94.947	95.515	96.020	96.466	96.866	97.218
12.5	91.713	92.215	92.657	93.048	93.393	93.698
13.0	88.665	89.107	89.495	89.836	90.136	90.400
13.5	85.785	86.175	86.519	86.817	87.077	87.305
14.0	83.073	83.416	83.715	83.975	84.201	84.397
14.5	80.505	80.807	81.069	81.296	81.492	81.662
15.0	78.074	78.341	78.571	78.769	78.939	79.086
15.5	75.772	76.007	76.209	76.382	76.350	76.657
16.0	73.590	73.797	73.974	74.124	74.253	74.363

Example 3. The monthly payment on a 30-year 12% mortgage is $500. What is the value of the mortgage?

$$V = (500)(97.218) = \$48,609.00,$$

where 97.218 is the mortgage factor.

Example 4. The monthly payment on a 30-year 16% mortgage is $500. What is the value of the mortgage?

$$V = (500)(74.363) = \$37,181.50,$$

where 74.363 is the mortgage factor.

Example 5. $100,00 is to be borrowed for 30 years. Calculate the monthly payments corresponding to interest rates of 10, 11, 12, 13, 14, 15, and 16% and indicate the percentage increase in monthly payment as the interest rate rises by each percentage point.

Interest Rate	Monthly Payment	Percentage Increase
10%	$ 877.57	—
11	952.33	8.5%
12	1,028.62	8.0
13	1,106.20	7.5
14	1,184.88	7.1
15	1,264.45	6.7
16	1,344.76	6.4

In the last example it may be noticed that the percentage increase in the monthly payment decreases at the higher levels of the rate of interest.

Many institutions, particularly savings and loan associations, hold enormous proportions of their asset portfolios in mortgages. The market value of these mortgages are subject to fluctuations in mortgage rates. Table 2–5 shows how the value of a mortgage, initially issued at 8%, changes as interest rates rise above 8%. In the absence of options that can change the income stream at future dates, the monthly payments on a mortgage are fixed at the time of issuance. As interest rates increase, the market values of these fixed income streams must, therefore, decrease as the table shows. During the early 1980s, many savings and loan associations suffered an enormous loss in the market value of their mortgages that had been issued in earlier years at much lower interest rates.

Table 2–5.　The Value of a $100,000 30-Year Mortgage Issued at 8%

Interest Rate	Value
8%	$100,000.00
9	91,193.06
10	83,612.55
11	77,049.46
12	71,334.92
13	66,331.62
14	61,927.38
15	58,030.25

Amortization

The income stream on a mortgage is flat up to its maturity date, at which time the loan balance goes to zero. The constant monthly payment over time not only pays interest as it accrues but also contributes toward a gradual repayment of the loan balance. Figure 2–3 illustrates the partition of the monthly payment into interest and the contribution toward reducing the loan balance. In the early months of the mortgage life almost the entire monthly payment constitutes interest, but as time passes, an increasing amount goes toward reducing the loan balance. A rearrangement of equation (2.12) shows this partition algebraically. Multiply both sides of equation (2.12) by $r/12$ and then add $Y(1+r/12)^{-12M}$ to both sides. This produces

$$\frac{r}{12}V + Y\left(1+\frac{r}{12}\right)^{-12M} = Y, \tag{2.14}$$

which is the monthly payment. The first term on the left is the portion of Y comprising interest and the second term is the portion going toward a reduction of the loan balance. Equation (2.12) gives a very easy interpretation of the partition. Let V be the loan balance at the beginning of a month when there are $12M$ months remaining to maturity. Over the month the interest owed on the loan balance is the monthly interest rate ($r/12$) multiplied by the beginning loan balance. The remaining portion must then be the contribution toward reducing the loan balance. After the payment of Y, the loan balance is reduced to $V - Y(1+r/12)^{-12M}$, a smaller value so that the contribution toward the interest in the next month is reduced and the contribution toward the reduction in the loan balance increases. Notice that M is reduced

Figure 2–3. Division of Mortgage Payment into Interest and Payment on Unpaid Balance

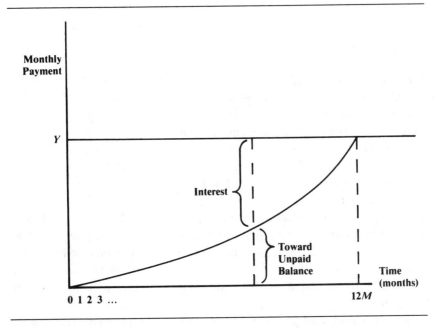

as time passes. This means that $(1+r/12)^{-12M}$ gets larger. Tracing $(r/12)V$ as V is reduced over time produces the curve in Figure 2–3.

The loan balance is called the *amortized* or *book* value of the mortgage. This value at any future time in the life of a mortgage can be computed as a function of the monthly payment and the interest rate which is initially given at the time the mortgage is created. As time passes, market interest rates may change, but the monthly payment remains fixed on a traditional mortgage. This means that the market value of the mortgage can change over time with every change in interest rates, but the book value changes over time according to a fixed schedule determined by the initial interest rate. Institutions or other investors who wish to sell portions of their mortgage portfolios may find that the market price is not the same as the amortized or book value of the mortgages. It is an accepted accounting practice to list the values of mortgages held at their book values. When market interest rates rise, the market values of mortgages decrease because the discount factors, $(1+r/12)^{-t}$, must decrease as r rises. During periods of rising interest rates the value of mortgage assets may, indeed, fall below their book values. The value of an institution's assets during such periods may be well below the book values reported on the balance sheets and the institution's net worth may consequently be much overstated.

Mortgage Points

Financial institutions often offer mortgages with *points,* which is essentially a way to discount a mortgage below its amortized value at the time of issue. The mortgage contract specifies V as the initial unpaid balance and the monthly payment Y is calculated using the mortgage factor, as in equations (2.12) and (2.13); but the borrower receives only L dollars, which is less than V. The difference, $V - L$, can be regarded as a discount at time of issue. In effect, the borrower makes a payment on the loan at time zero. It is as though the mortgagor borrows V dollars but instantly pays $V - L$ dollars ("up front") in interest to the lender, and the amortized value of the loan is unaffected. For example, suppose \$100,000 is borrowed at 10% for 30 years. Suppose the borrower receives \$98,000 instead of \$100,000, the amount borrowed. The borrower is said to be giving up 2 points or 2% of the loan value at the time of issue. The amortized value or loan balance remains \$100,000, however.

For such mortgages, the rate of return to the investor (lender) exceeds the interest rate used to calculate the monthly payment. Let r_m be the interest rate used to calculate the monthly payment. Then,

$$V = \frac{12 \cdot Y}{r_m} \left[1 - \left(\frac{r_m}{12} \right)^{-12M} \right]. \tag{2.15}$$

If the borrower gives up k points (expressed as a decimal, that is, $k = .02$ represents 2 points) so that $L = V - kV$ is the amount received, then the rate of return on the mortgage is r, where

$$L = (1-k)V = \frac{12 \cdot Y}{r} \left[1 - \left(1 + \frac{r}{12} \right)^{-12M} \right]. \tag{2.16}$$

The right-hand side of the expression discounts the monthly cash flows so that their present value is equal to L which is less than V. To do this r must be larger than r_m. Recall that the discount factors are inversely related to the rate of interest. For fixed cash flows the interest rate must therefore be larger in order to reduce the present value of the cash flows. In equation (2.15), r_m discounts the flows so that their present value is V, but in equation (2.16) r ($> r_m$) discounts the same cash flows so that their present value is L ($< V$). Table 2-6 shows the effective interest rates for selected 30-year mortgages

Table 2-6. The Effective Interest Rate on Mortgages with Points, 30-Year Maturities

Mortgage Rate	Points (%)				
	1	2	3	4	5
8	8.11	8.21	8.32	8.44	8.55
8.5	8.61	8.72	8.83	8.95	9.07
9	9.11	9.23	9.34	9.46	9.58
9.5	9.62	9.73	9.85	9.98	10.10
10	10.12	10.24	10.37	10.49	10.62
10.5	10.62	10.75	10.88	11.01	11.14
11	11.13	11.26	11.39	11.52	11.66
11.5	11.63	11.76	11.90	12.04	12.18
12	12.13	12.27	12.41	12.55	12.70
12.5	12.64	12.78	12.92	13.07	13.22
13	13.14	13.29	13.44	13.59	13.74
13.5	13.65	13.80	13.95	14.10	14.26
14	14.15	14.30	14.46	14.62	14.78
14.5	14.66	14.81	14.97	15.14	15.31
15	15.16	15.32	15.49	15.66	15.83
15.5	15.66	15.83	16.00	16.17	16.35
16	16.17	16.34	16.51	16.69	16.88

with different points. Each point adds about 10 to 12 basis points to the interest rate at relatively low interest rates of 8% to 10%; and each point adds about 15 to 19 basis points to the interest rate at relatively high interest rates of 14% to 16%.

Clearly two rates of interest are associated with a mortgage having points. The contracted rate of interest, r_m, discounts the cash flows back to the amortized value of the loan. The yield to maturity or internal rate of return, r, discounts the cash flows back to the actual amount received.

Mortgages with points primarily protect the interests of the lender. Most mortgage contracts allow the borrower to prepay their mortgages. Borrowers who sell their mortgaged property (the collateral) often collect cash from a buyer who has found his or her own financing. This cash can be used to pay off the mortgagee (lender) prior to maturity. This is called *prepayment*. Moreover, if interest rates should decline after the issuance of a regular mortgage, the borrower may advantageously prepay and refinance the debt at a lower rate of interest. The time of prepayment is often unpredictable. The lender may unexpectedly have to reinvest funds. If there are points on the mortgage, the borrower is less disposed toward refinancing when interest rates drop slightly because the amortized value (V) to be paid exceeds the amount of the loan initially acquired (L). The cost of refinancing to the borrower includes the points so that interest rates must decline by enough so that refinancing will permit a recovery of these costs. A mortgage with points also implies that the lender has a claim on the collateral that exceeds the initial cash commitment comprising the loan. The collateral position of the investor is slightly larger than otherwise.

Adjustable Rate Mortgages

In recent years (1984 and 1985) about 50 percent or more of all new mortgages issued were *adjustable rate mortgages* (ARMs). These are mortgages on which the interest rate and monthly payments are periodically adjusted so that the rates reflect current market rates more closely. The impetus to issue such mortgages originated primarily with depository financial institutions like savings and loan associations. These institutions borrow (receive deposits) on primarily a short-term basis. The interest rates offered on these deposits consequently are adjusted frequently so as to coincide with current market conditions. These deposits are the principal sources of funds for mortgage investments for many depository institutions. Regular mortgages (*fixed rate mortgages,* FRMs) tend to be relatively long-term mortgages ranging in maturity from 15 to 30 years. If the financial institution is able to anticipate the movement of short-term rates on deposits reasonably well, it can establish long-term rates on FRMs so that it makes a profit on the average as it borrows at short rates and lends at long rates. If there are unexpected upward movements in interest rates that persist over a long period, the financial institution may find its cost of funds rising faster than its interest revenues. These unexpected movements in rates can create liquidity and solvency problems for financial institutions. Kaufman and Erdevig (1981) describe this development very well and show that ARMs, among other mortgage instruments, represent a way by which the depository institution can substantially reduce the risks of unexpected interest rate movements.

An ARM is a mortgage contract in which the lender (mortgagee) is permitted at specified intervals to adjust the interest rate on the mortgage so as to keep it in line with some underlying interest rate index. For example, the mortgage contract may allow for a single annual change on specific future dates so that the mortgage rate is some precise number of basis points above the prime rate or the one-year U.S. Treasury rate. Consider an example of how this may work. Suppose a \$100,000, 30-year mortgage is initially issued at 10%. The mortgage factor in Table 2-4 is 113.951, which implies that the monthly payment is \$877.51 (= 100,000/113.951). Suppose that interest rates over the next 3 years do not change enough to trigger an interest rate adjustment, but that in the fourth year the interest rates change so that the rate on the mortgage is allowed to go up to 12% at the beginning of the fifth year. After 4 years have passed the amortized value of the mortgage will be \$97,402.05 and the mortgage factor at 12% will be 95.515. This implies an upward movement in the monthly payment to \$1,019.76 (= 97,402.05/95.515). In response to the interest rate change the monthly payment has increased from \$877.51 to \$1,019.76. The ARM contract usually includes other provisions such as a maximum interest rate that can ever be charged (a so-called *cap*) and a limitation on the frequency and magnitude of any specific adjustment. Effectively an ARM passes to the borrower the risk of unexpected interest rate changes. The financial institution acquires some protection from unexpected interest rate movements.

Since the adjustability provisions of the mortgage generally benefit the lender at the expense of the borrower, competition compels the interest rates on ARMs to be generally less than on comparable FRMs. If a borrower can acquire an FRM and an ARM at the same initial rate, most assuredly the borrower would choose the FRM unless he or she is very confident that interest rates would fall in the future. Acquiring an ARM exposes the borrower to the risk of increasing interest rates. Most investors or borrowers cannot predict accurately the movement of interest rates over the long term. Consequently the ARMs tend to sell or be issued in the market only at rates that are less than the rates on comparable FRMs.

Analytically, one can view the value of an ARM as

$$V_{ARM}(Y, M) = V_{FRM}(Y, M) + \text{Prem.} \tag{2.17}$$

The value of the ARM with monthly payment Y and maturity M is equivalent to the value of an FRM with monthly payment Y and maturity M plus a premium, Prem, which reflects the value of the adjustability provision. An investor having the opportunity to acquire the monthly income Y for M years by either buying an FRM or an ARM will value the ARM more highly because of the adjustability provision, which reduces the risk that interest rates will rise. Both mortgages in this case offer the same income stream, but if $V_{ARM}(Y, M) > V_{FRM}(Y, M)$, the discount factors for the ARM must exceed those for the FRM. This can only imply that the mortgage interest rate on the FRM exceeds that of the comparable ARM.

Equation (2.17) is a way to represent the value of two financial contracts that are identical in every respect except for a single provision. If that provision benefits the lender (or investor in the instrument), then Prem > 0 and if it benefits the borrower, then Prem < 0. This is another way of concluding that lenders will offer lower rates of return if they are compensated by some other benefit or that borrowers must be compensated for a potentially costly provision by paying interest at a lower rate. Empirically there are many problems in estimating Prem for various financial instruments because it is difficult to find two debt contracts that differ in only one respect and that are bought and sold under comparable market conditions. As a conceptual construction, equation (2.17) and the above interpretation of Prem are useful in devising a theoretical explanation of the spread—the interest rate differences for two financial instruments.

Other Mortgages

High interest rates in the period 1980–1984 spawned a variety of new types of mortgages designed to keep monthly payments from rising to levels that would seriously threaten the home-building industry and the "American dream" of homeownership. Kaufman and Erdevig (1981) analyze the market implications of many of these mortgages. Technical and institutional features of many of these mortgages are contained in Senft (1983).

Rollover Mortgages. These are short-term mortgages with balloon payments occurring at the end of five years or so. The balloon payment is the amortized value of the mortgage at the maturity date and it is due and payable at that time. Most home buyers would be compelled to refinance their mortgages on the maturity date when the balloon payment is due. If high interest rates are a temporary phenomenon and decrease within a few years, a rollover mortgage enables a borrower to reduce monthly payments after refinancing at lower rates. The monthly payment as specified in the rollover mortgage may include little or no amortization of the loan balance. In this way the monthly payment required may be less than that required on FRMs or other mortgages.

The borrowers' main attraction to the rollover mortgage is that the monthly payment may be slightly less than on comparable instruments and it provides the opportunity to refinance later on at lower rates of interest. In many ways the rollover mortgage is comparable to the ARM. At the end of the specified maturity date, the refinancing implies that the monthly payment is adjusted to reflect current market rates, but the refinancing need not be undertaken with the same initial issuer. The borrower still bears the risk that interest rates may increase. During periods of extremely high interest rates, lenders may be unwilling to issue long-term mortgages. During such periods, lenders often have a strong demand for more secure, less default-prone, and more liquid investments.

The rollover mortgage, except for monthly rather than semiannual payments, is just like a bond. If there is no amortization, the borrower only pays the interest as it accrues monthly. The loan balance is unaffected. Such a mortgage is exactly comparable to a par bond the book value of which always remains fixed through time so that the loan balance is unchanged and becomes due and payable at maturity. If there exists some amortization, the bond is comparable to a premium bond. With every monthly payment, part of the loan balance is reduced, but then at the specified maturity, the remaining loan balance is due and payable. If the monthly payment is smaller than the interest, then the unpaid interest is added to the loan balance. This is called *negative amortization*. Such mortgages behave like discount bonds that appreciate in value to maturity. In practice most rollover mortgages were not of this type. With the loan balance conceivably rising relative to the value of the collateral (the financed property), the lender's collateral position can become progressively weaker and riskier.

Graduated Payment Mortgages.   GPMs are mortgages on which the monthly payments gradually become larger as time passes. There is no fundamental reason, other than simplicity, perhaps, why monthly payments should be constant over time as with the FRM. The GPM is designed so that young families with modest but growing incomes can purchase a home on which the monthly mortgage payments would be a roughly constant proportion of their income. Early in the life of the mortgage the monthly payments are relatively small, but later in the life of the mortgage the payments are relatively large. The income or payment stream on the mortgage contract is thus "tilted." Most GPM plans, as reported in Senft (1983) consist of annual percentage increases of from 2% to 7.5% in the monthly payments for 5 to 10 years with a level income stream after that. The value of the level payment stream after a specified number of years can be computed in the same way as the traditional FRM mortgage, but the years in which the payments are increasing must be separately treated. For example, suppose the monthly payment Y increases at a rate of 5% per year for 10 years and that thereafter it remains constant until 30 years have passed from the date of issue. Let Y_1 be the first monthly payment. Then $Y_2 = (1 + .05/12) Y_1$ is the second, $Y_3 = (1 + .05/12)^2 Y_1$ is the third, and so forth until $(1 + .05/12)^{119} Y_1$ is the 120th. Thereafter, the monthly payment is constant at $(1 + .05/12)^{119} Y_1$. The present value of this income stream is

$$V = Y_1 \left[\sum_{t=1}^{120} \left(1 + \frac{.05}{12}\right)^{t-1} \left(1 + \frac{r}{12}\right)^{-t} + \left(1 + \frac{.05}{12}\right)^{119} \sum_{t=121}^{360} \left(1 + \frac{r}{12}\right)^{-t} \right]$$ (2.18)

$$= AY_1,$$

where A is the long expression in brackets. Equation (2.18) simply discounts each monthly payment back to the present to determine the current present value of the monthly payments. The computation reduces to the computation of the "mortgage factor" A just as in the case of FRMs, but given V and r, equation (2.18) determines the first monthly payment and all others are determined by the GPM plan. Appendix 2C shows how the computation of the factor A may be computed. It is a worthwhile exercise in discounting methodology. As shown in Appendix 2C for this example, $A = 132.18585$. The first monthly payment on a 12%, $100,000 mortgage would be $756.51, and the monthly payments would rise steadily until it becomes $1,240.81 for the 120th month and would remain level thereafter. An FRM at 12% would require a level monthly payment of $1,028.61. In the early years, the payment of $756.51 is less burdensome than $1,028.61 for the FRM, but then after the 10th year the payment of $1,240.81 is relatively more burdensome. During some of the early years in the life of the GPM, the monthly payments may be less than the interest owed. The unpaid interest is then added to the loan balance. This negative amortization continues until the monthly payments have increased by enough to cover monthly interest costs; thereafter, positive amortization gradually reduces the loan balance.

GPMs were first authorized by the FHA in 1976. By 1978, GPMs represented about 25 to 30% of newly issued mortgages insured by the Federal Housing Administration (FHA). After 1979 with higher and more volatile market interest rates, the popularity of GPMs subsided. The values of these mortgages, like the FRMs, are very sensitive to interest rate changes.

Pledged Account Mortgages.   PAMs are mortgages with a variation of some features of the GPM. Borrowers who are able to make large down payments in purchasing a home, but who have a relatively small income out of which to make monthly payments, may find this mortgage attractive. A portion of the down payment is placed in a bank savings account that earns interest at current rates. The borrower's monthly payment is graduated as in a GPM plan, but the payment to the lender is level as it would be for an FRM. The amount received by the lender in excess of the borrower's payment is drawn from the savings account which is "pledged" or set aside for this purpose. This process continues until the savings account is exhausted or until the monthly payments can cover the level payment to the lender after which time the monthly payment is equal to the required level payment. From the perspective of the borrower it is a GPM, but from the perspective of the lender it is an FRM. This mortgage is more complex than the GPM for two reasons. First, the interest earned on the savings account may change with time so as to require an adjustment in the borrower's monthly payment. Second, lenders will usually lend only some proportion of the value of the collateral. Here, the collateral outstanding is the value of the house plus the value of the savings account. The savings account may decrease faster than the loan balance, so that the borrower's net worth and capacity to repay the loan balance may decline.

The home buyer may, instead, consider utilizing the savings account as an initial down payment that would reduce the loan required to purchase a home. Since the interest rate on the mortgage is likely to exceed the interest rate on the savings account, the monthly payment required may be reduced relative to a PAM. When coupled with attractive features of a GPM, however, the PAM may be attractive to the borrower.

Buydown Mortgages.   A buydown mortgage is like a PAM except that the initial savings or escrow account is provided by the seller of a piece of property. Such "buydowns" are most common for newly constructed homes. It makes the home purchase attractive to many home buyers because it reduces the monthly payments in the early life of the mortgage. Most important, the buydown may permit a buyer to qualify for a mortgage that would not otherwise be available. The buydown adds to the collateral security of the mortgagee or lender. The seller cannot always recoup the buydown costs by raising the price of the home. A higher price can jeopardize the potential buyer's qualification for purchase. The seller may be motivated to offer a buydown because it reduces his inventory costs. It can be costly for the seller to keep a home on the market while advertising it and waiting for a qualified buyer to turn up.

An example of a buydown is the 3-2-1 plan. If the FRM mortgage is set at 15%, say, the borrower pays 12% in the first year, 13% in the second year, 14% in the third year, and finally 15% thereafter. The seller contributes to an escrow account that makes up the difference of 3% in the first year, 2%

in the second year, and 1% in the third year. For example, suppose the borrower acquires a $100,000, 15%, 30-year mortgage. At 15% the monthly payment is $1,264, but at 12% the monthly payment is $1,029. The seller contributes the difference of $235 per month for the first year. At the start of the second year the amortized value of the mortgage is $99,814. This amount financed for 29 years at 13% implies a monthly payment of $1,107. The difference of $157 is paid by the seller in the second year. At the start of the third year the amortized value of the loan is $99,599. This amount financed for 28 years at 14% implies a monthly payment of $1,186. The difference of $78 per month is paid by the seller. Thereafter, the borrower pays the full amount of $1,264 per month. The total cost to the seller is $235 per month for the first year, $157 per month for the second, and $75 per month for the third year. This adds up to $5,640. If the escrow account pays interest at 10%, say, then the present value of the seller's commitment is $5,346.

In 1983–1984 many homeowners who had purchased homes under buydown agreements were shocked to find their monthly payments increasing. Many homeowners went into default and foreclosure procedures were undertaken. The increase in the monthly payments for a buydown is considerably larger than under GPMs, but the adjustments of the monthly payments may not be larger than can be expected under ARMs. Apparently, many home buyers did not fully understand the nature of the buydown agreement, and many home buyers were probably not qualified for the mortgages to which they were committed. Borrowers who accept buydown mortgages or ARMs must be prepared to make higher monthly payments eventually.

Shared Appreciation Mortgages (SAMs).   High interest rates are often associated with a high rate of inflation. In order to reduce the interest costs and monthly payments to potential home buyers, many lenders offered SAMs. These are mortgages in which the lender shares in the appreciation in the value of the collateral property in compensation for a reduction in the interest rate on the mortgage. In this way many home buyers would qualify for mortgages that otherwise would be unavailable. As pointed out by Kaufman and Erdevig (1981), there are many problems with SAMs. The lender faces uncertainty as to how much the appreciation will be and when it will be received. This can create liquidity problems especially for depository institutions who must meet relatively short-term outflow commitments. If the appreciation in value is recouped before the sale of the property, the financing of it can be a major problem for the borrower. Moreover, disputes can arise between borrower and lender as to what portion of the increment in home value constitutes appreciation and what constitutes home improvement.

Mortgage contracts can also be indexed to the rate of inflation. These *price-level adjusted mortgages* (PLAMs) essentially require that the monthly payments rise by some portion of the recently realized inflation rates. Such mortgages tend to arise when the inflation rate is very high and persists for many years. Few mortgages of this type have been issued in the United States. Kaufman and Erdevig (1981) discuss the features of these mortgages at length.

APPENDIX 2A
THE VALUE OF AN ANNUITY

In the text, the price of a bond is given as

$$P = \frac{cF}{2} \sum_{t=1}^{2M} \left(1+\frac{r}{2}\right)^{-t} + F\left(1+\frac{r}{2}\right)^{-2M} \tag{2A.1}$$

where c is the coupon rate, F is the face value, M is the number of years to maturity, and r is the annual yield to maturity. It was asserted that

$$\sum_{t=1}^{2M} \left(1+\frac{r}{2}\right)^{-t} = \frac{2}{r}\left[1-\left(1+\frac{r}{2}\right)^{-2M}\right]. \tag{2A.2}$$

In this appendix, it is proven that equation (2A.2) holds.

Let $x = (1+r/2)^{-1}$. Then (2A.2) can be expressed as

$$\sum_{t=1}^{2M} \left(1+\frac{r}{2}\right)^{-t} = \sum_{t=1}^{2M} x^t = x+x^2+x^3+\cdots+x^{2M}. \tag{2A.3}$$

Multiply this expression by x to get

$$x \sum_{t=1}^{2M} \left(1+\frac{r}{2}\right)^{-t} = \sum_{t=1}^{2M} x^{t+1} = x^2+x^3+\cdots+x^{2M+1}. \tag{2A.4}$$

Subtract (2A.4) from (2A.3). This gives

$$(1-x) \sum_{t=1}^{2M} \left(1+\frac{r}{2}\right)^{-t} = x-x^{2M+1}. \tag{2A.5}$$

Dividing by $(1-x)$, it follows that

$$\sum_{t=1}^{2M} \left(1+\frac{r}{2}\right)^{-t} = \frac{x-x^{2M+1}}{1-x}. \tag{2A.6}$$

Given that $x = (1+r/2)^{-1}$, it follows that

$$1-x = 1-\frac{1}{1+r/2} = \frac{r/2}{1+r/2}. \tag{2A.7}$$

Substituting for x and $1-x$ in (2A.6), we have

$$\sum_{t=1}^{2M}\left(1+\frac{r}{2}\right)^{-t} = \frac{(1+r/2)^{-1}-(1+r/2)^{-2M-1}}{(r/2)(1+r/2)^{-1}}. \qquad (2A.8)$$

Multiply the numerator and denominator of the latter ratio by $(1+r/2)$. This implies that

$$\sum_{t=1}^{2M}\left(1+\frac{r}{2}\right)^{-t} = \frac{1-(1+r/2)^{-2M}}{r/2}$$

$$= \frac{2}{r}\left[1-\left(1+\frac{r}{2}\right)^{-2M}\right], \qquad (2A.9)$$

which was to be shown. This formula makes it very easy to compute the sum of a set of discount factors and is the standard basis for computing the value of a flat income stream or an annuity.

APPENDIX 2B
THE BOND PRICE ON DATES
BETWEEN COUPON PAYMENT DATES

The price of a bond specified in the text is written as

$$P = \frac{cF}{r}\left[1-\left(1+\frac{r}{2}\right)^{-N}\right]+F\left(1+\frac{r}{2}\right)^{-N}, \qquad (2B.1)$$

where N is the number of 6-month periods to maturity. This is the formula for computing the bond price when the first coupon payment date is exactly 6 months away. When the bond is purchased between payment dates, certain conventions are used to determine the price.

Consider, first, the case in which the bond is purchased at exactly K months prior to the first coupon payment date, where K is any integer from 1 to 5. Let us suppose that there are exactly N future coupon payment dates, but that the first one occurs in K months and the remaining occur evenly at 6-month intervals thereafter. Under current convention, we first calculate the price of the bond on the next coupon date just after the coupon payment has been made. This price is given by equation (2B.1) with $N-1$ substituted for N because there then will be $N-1$ coupon payments remaining and they all occur at 6-month intervals. Let P_{N-1} be this price. Next, we add the cash value of the next coupon payment to this price to get $(cF/2)+P_{N-1}$. This must then be the price of the bond just before the next coupon payment to occur in K months. This value is discounted back to the present for K months to determine the price. In this way, the price is determined to be

$$P_{NK} = \left(1 + \frac{r}{2}\right)^{-K/6} \left(P_{N-1} + \frac{cF}{2}\right). \tag{2B.2}$$

The first subscript on P_{NK} indicates the number of coupon payments and the second subscript indicates the number of months to the first coupon payment. For example, if $N = 18$, $c = 10\%$, $r = 11\%$, and $F = 100$, then $P_{N-1} = \$94.57$, which is the price of the bond with seventeen 6-month periods to maturity. Let $K = 5$ months to the first coupon payment date; then the discount factor is $(1 + r/2)^{-5/6} = (1.055)^{-5/6} = .95636$. The value of the bond, using (2B.2), is then

$$P_{18, 5} = (.95636)(94.57 + 5) = \$95.22.$$

It is customary to divide the price P_{NK} into two parts. One part represents the *accrued coupon interest* over the $(6 - K)$ months since the last coupon payment, and the other is called the *principal value* of the bond. The notion here is that the seller of the bond regards a portion of P_{NK} as interest earned since the last coupon date. This accrued coupon interest on the bond is calculated as $[(6 - K)/6](cF/2)$. In this calculation $(6 - K)$ is the number of months that have passed since the last coupon payment. The remaining portion of the price P_{NK} is the *principal value*.[3] In the example, above, the decomposition would be tabulated as

Principal Value	$94.39
+ Accrued Interest	.83
Bond Price (P_{NK})	$95.22

It is important to realize that the principal value is calculated as a residual in this decomposition. The bond price, P_{NK}, given by formula (2B.2) and the accrued interest is $(6 - K)cF/2 \cdot 6$, so that the principal value is computed as the difference. The principal value is the base price that the buyer utilizes to compute any capital gain that is applicable when the bond is sold at some future date or reaches maturity.

If the bond is purchased on a date within a month, the computation of the price takes into account the number of months and days to the first coupon payment date. Let there be K months plus D days to the first coupon payment date. It is assumed that there are 30 days in a month so that D ranges from 1 to 30.[4] Let P_{NK}^{B} be the base price or principal value for a bond having N future coupon payments with the first occurring in exactly K months,

$K = 1, 2, 3, 4$, or 5. Let P_{NKD}^B be the base price or principal value of a bond with K months and D days to the first coupon payment date. This price is computed as a linear interpolation of P_{NK}^B and $P_{N,K+1}^B$. That is,

$$P_{NKD}^B = \frac{30-D}{30} P_{NK}^B + \frac{D}{30} P_{N,K+1}^B. \tag{2B.4}$$

Thus, for example, if $D = 0$, $P_{NKD}^B = P_{NK}^B$ and if $D = 30$, $P_{NKD}^B = P_{N,K+1}^B$, as expected. The price, P_{NKD}, of the bond is then calculated by adding the accrued interest to the base price. The accrued interest, computed on the basis of a 30-day month, is

$$\left(1 - \frac{30K+D}{180}\right)\frac{Fc}{2}. \tag{2B.5}$$

The number $[1-(30K+D)/180]$ is the proportion of the time period which has passed since the last coupon payment date. Thus, the price of the bond is

$$P_{NKD} = \left(1 - \frac{30K+D}{180}\right)\frac{Fc}{2} + P_{NKD}^B. \tag{2B.6}$$

Example. A bond has a yield to maturity of 11%, a coupon rate of 10%, and 18 coupon payment dates to maturity. There are 4 months and 16 days to the first coupon date. To calculate the price of the bond we first compute the base prices as

$$P_{18,4}^B = (1.055)^{-4/6}(P_{17}+5) - \left(\frac{2}{6}\right)\cdot 5 = \$94.41, \quad \text{and}$$

$$P_{18,5}^B = (1.055)^{-5/6}(P_{17}+5) - \left(\frac{1}{6}\right)\cdot 5 = \$94.39.$$

The base price then becomes

$$P_{18,4,16}^B = \frac{14}{30}P_{18,4}^B + \frac{16}{30}P_{18,5}^B = \$94.40.$$

Finally, we add the accrued coupon interest of

$$\left(1 - \frac{30\cdot 4+16}{180}\right)5 = \frac{44}{180}5 = \$1.22$$

to the base price to determine the actual price as

$$P_{18,4,16} = \$94.40 + \$1.22 = \$95.62.$$

Although these calculations may seem tedious, they are very easily programmed so that in practice these prices can be determined quickly.

When there are fewer than 6 months to maturity, market convention treats the security as a zero coupon bond that pays $(1+c/2)F$ dollars on the designated maturity date. If there are exactly K months to maturity ($K = 1, 2, 3, 4,$ or 5) then the price of the bond is

$$P_{1,K} = \left(1 + r\left(\frac{K}{12}\right)\right)^{-1}\left(1 + \frac{c}{2}\right)F.$$

Note that the discount factor is now specified as $(1 + rK/12)^{-1}$ rather than as $(1+r/2)^{-K/6}$. Although the two expressions are very close, they are not equal. Such, such is the nature of market convention. Accrued interest, base prices, and the computation of midmonth prices are computed in the same manner.

APPENDIX 2C
THE VALUE OF A GPM

Consider a GPM plan in which the monthly payment increases at $x\%$ per year for 10 years and then remains level for the next 20 years. Let the first monthly payment be Y_1. The second is then $(1+x/12)Y_1$, the third is $(1+x/12)^2Y_1$, and so forth, until the 120th is $(1+x/12)^{119}Y_1$. Thereafter, the monthly payment is constant at $(1+x/12)^{119}Y_1$. If r is the mortgage interest rate, we can discount these monthly cash flows to determine the value of the mortgage as

$$V = Y_1\left[\sum_{t=1}^{120}\left(1+\frac{x}{12}\right)^{t-1}\left(1+\frac{r}{12}\right)^{-t} + \left(1+\frac{x}{12}\right)^{119}\sum_{t=121}^{360}\left(1+\frac{r}{12}\right)^{-t}\right],$$

$$= AY_1,$$

(2C.1)

where A is the mortgage factor, which is the long expression in brackets. Let us rewrite (2C.1) as

$$A = \left(1+\frac{x}{12}\right)^{-1}\sum_{t=1}^{120}\left(\frac{1+r/12}{1+x/12}\right)^{-t}$$
$$+ \left(1+\frac{x}{12}\right)^{119}\left(1+\frac{r}{12}\right)^{-120}\sum_{t=1}^{240}\left(1+\frac{r}{12}\right)^{-t}$$

(2C.2)

so that known discounting formulas can be used. Next, note that we can write

$$\frac{1+r/12}{1+x/12} = 1 + \frac{z}{12},$$

(2C.3)

where, as is easily solved, $z = (r-x)/(1+x)$. Thus,

$$A = \left(1 + \frac{x}{12}\right)^{-1} \sum_{t=1}^{120} \left(1 + \frac{z}{12}\right)^{-t}$$
$$+ \left(1 + \frac{x}{12}\right)^{119} \left(1 + \frac{r}{12}\right)^{-120} \sum_{t=1}^{240} \left(1 + \frac{r}{12}\right)^{-t}. \tag{2C.4}$$

Noting that

$$\sum_{t=1}^{120} \left(1 + \frac{z}{12}\right)^{-t} = \frac{12}{z} \left[1 - \left(1 + \frac{z}{12}\right)^{-120}\right], \tag{2C.5}$$

and

$$\sum_{t=1}^{240} \left(1 + \frac{r}{12}\right)^{-t} = \frac{12}{r} \left[1 - \left(1 + \frac{r}{12}\right)^{-240}\right], \tag{2C.6}$$

it follows that

$$A = \left(1 + \frac{x}{12}\right)^{-1} \left(\frac{12}{z}\right) \left[1 - \left(1 + \frac{z}{12}\right)^{-120}\right]$$
$$+ \left(1 + \frac{x}{12}\right)^{119} \left(1 + \frac{r}{12}\right)^{-120} \left(\frac{12}{r}\right) \left[1 - \left(1 + \frac{r}{12}\right)^{-240}\right]. \tag{2C.7}$$

For example, when $x = .05$ and $r = .12$, then $A = 132.185585$. As shown in the text, if $V = 100,000$, then $Y_1 = \$756.51$ is the first monthly payment and subsequent payments steadily rise until the monthly payment is $1,240.81 for the 20th month and it stays at that level thereafter. An FRM at 12% for 30 years would require a monthly payment of $1,028.61.

NOTES

1. Many bonds, like marketable U.S. Treasury securities, exist only as a bookkeeping entry. In these modern times, bookkeeping entries have reduced the cost of transferring, recording, and storing securities.
2. As in previous sections, the analysis here is strictly applicable to bonds having income streams fixed by the loan contract. Options of either party (the lender or borrower) to modify the income stream at future dates are assumed not to be a part of the loan contract.
3. Homer and Leibowitz (1972) utilize this expression and present numerical examples of its calculation.
4. For Treasury securities, the exact number of days between coupon payment dates is utilized.

REFERENCES

Homer, Sidney, and Martin L. Leibowitz. 1972. *Inside the Yield Book* (Englewood Cliffs, N.J.: Prentice-Hall).

Kaufman, George G., and Eleanor Erdevig. 1984. "Improving Housing Finance in an Inflationary Environment: Alternative Residential Mortgage Instruments." *Economic Perspectives,* Federal Reserve Bank of Chicago, July/August 1981. Reprinted in *Financial Institutions and Markets in a Changing World,* edited by D.R. Fraser and P.S. Rose (Plano, Tex.: Business Publications).

Senft, Dexter. 1983. "Mortgages." In *The Handbook of Fixed Income Securities,* edited by F.J. Fabozzi and I.M. Pollack (Homewood, Ill.: Dow Jones-Irwin).

3 DURATION AND CHANGES IN PRICES AND YIELDS TO MATURITY

The price of a security is an inverse nonlinear function of the yield to maturity. The impact on the price of a change in the yield to maturity depends on (1) the level of the yield to maturity, (2) the coupon rate, and (3) the maturity of the security. How it is that these features exactly affect a corresponding change in the price is not obvious, because of the nonlinearities in the relationship. Many investors who purchase bonds and mortgages, however, have a strong interest in knowing how the value of their investments is likely to fare for various scenarios of changes in the yield to maturity that may arise in the future. For example, suppose that an investor considers holding either a 15-year par bond or a 5-year par bond at a 10% yield to maturity. Suppose the investor believes that the yield to maturity will be 8% in one year. For equal investments in these bonds, which bond will have the greater value in one year? In short, the investor is interested in those characteristics of the securities which can affect the future value of the investment. Only then can the investor wisely select appropriate investments.

The next three sections show with examples how each of the three factors — the yield to maturity, the coupon rate, and the maturity — exactly affect the percentage changes in prices for given changes in the yield to maturity. A subsequent section shows that there is an index number called *duration* of the security which can be used in devising a single rule for calculating these percentage price changes regardless of the characteristics of the security.

51

YIELD TO MATURITY AND PRICE CHANGES

To show the nonlinear relationship between yield to maturity and price, Table 3–1 shows the price of a 15-year, 10 percent coupon bond for various yields to maturity. All the prices in the table have been calculated for bonds having semiannual coupon payments. The yields to maturity change in increments of 25 basis points from 8% to 12%. The corresponding prices change from $86.24 (at 12%) to $117.29 (at 8%). The third column in the table indicates the corresponding change in the price for each decrease of 25 basis points in the yield to maturity. The relationship has two main characteristics. First, the bond price and the yield to maturity are inversely related. Second, the change in price is larger the lower the level of the yield to maturity. A graph of this relationship in Figure 3–1 describes very well these two main characteristics. The curve is downward sloping depicting the inverse relationship, and the slope of the curve increases with the yield to maturity indicating larger price changes for lower yields to maturity. Table 3–1 contains other relevant information. Suppose the yield to maturity is at 8.25% and decreases

Table 3–1. Prices of a 15-Year 10% Coupon Bond for Various Yields to Maturity

Yield to Maturity	Price	Price Change
8.00%	$117.29	—
8.25	114.90	$2.39
8.50	112.58	2.32
8.75	110.33	2.25
9.00	108.14	2.19
9.25	106.02	2.12
9.50	103.96	2.06
9.75	101.95	2.01
10.00	100.00	1.95
10.25	98.11	1.89
10.50	96.26	1.85
10.75	94.47	1.79
11.00	92.73	1.74
11.25	91.04	1.69
11.50	89.39	1.65
11.75	87.79	1.60
12.00	86.24	1.55

Figure 3-1.   Bond Price-Yield Relationship

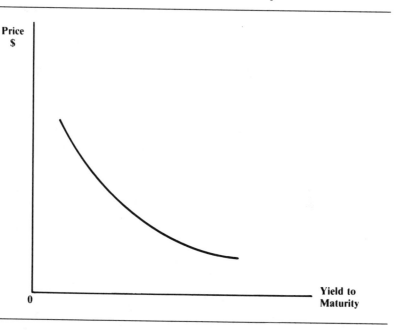

to 8.00%. The price increases from $114.90 to $117.29; this constitutes a 2.08% increase in price. On the other hand, if the yield to maturity is at 11% and decreases to 10.75%, the price increases from $92.73 to $94.47; this constitutes a 1.88% increase in price. Evidently the higher the yield to maturity the smaller the percentage increase in price for a decrease of 25 basis points in the yield to maturity. Table 3-2 shows the percentage increase in price as a function of the initial yield to maturity. Here, it is very clear that a given decrease in the yield implies a larger percentage change in the price the smaller the initial yield to maturity. This is a very basic and general relationship that holds for all bonds and mortgages. The rule can be stated as follows:

Given a fixed income stream, the percentage change in its value for a given change in the yield to maturity is larger the smaller the initial yield to maturity.

In understanding this rule, it is important to realize that the cash flows promised by the security must be fixed. There are only two changes in the valuation of the security that are occurring. The yield to maturity changes and the price changes. The rule allows the investor to conclude that given changes in

Table 3-2. Percentage Changes in Price of a 15-Year 10% Coupon Bond for Equal Decreases in the Yield to Maturity

Initial Yield to Maturity	Percentage Price Increase (25 Basis Points)	Percentage Price Increase (50 Basis Points)	Percentage Price Increase (100 Basis Points)
8.00%	—	—	—
8.25	2.08%	—	—
8.50	2.06	4.02%	—
8.75	2.04	3.98	—
9.00	2.02	3.94	7.80%
9.25	2.00	3.91	7.73
9.50	1.99	3.87	7.66
9.75	1.97	3.84	7.60
10.00	1.95	3.81	7.53
10.25	1.93	3.76	7.46
10.50	1.91	3.74	7.41
10.75	1.89	3.71	7.34
11.00	1.88	3.67	7.27
11.25	1.86	3.63	7.21
11.50	1.84	3.60	7.14
11.75	1.82	3.57	7.07
12.00	1.81	3.52	7.00

the yield to maturity have larger percentage impacts on price the lower the level of the yield to maturity. When interest rates are high, as in the early 1980s, a given drop in the yield to maturity will have a smaller impact on the percentage price change than when interest rates are low.

THE COUPON RATE AND PRICE CHANGES

The prices of bonds having different coupon rates, but identical maturity dates and yields to maturity, respond differently to a given change in the yield to maturity. To show this, consider bonds having a maturity of 15 years. Table 3-3 shows the corresponding prices of a set of bonds with coupon rates ranging from 0% to 15%. The price of each bond is calculated for yields to maturity of 10% and 8%. As the yield decreases, the price of each bond increases. The last column in the table shows the percentage increase. The percentage increase in the price decreases for the bonds as the coupon rates on them become larger. This rule holds generally for all bonds regardless of coupon rates or yields to maturity. The rule may be stated as follows:

Table 3–3.   Percentage Changes in Prices of 15-Year Bonds with Varying Coupon Rates for a Decrease in the Yield to Maturity from 10% to 8%

Coupon Rate	Bond Price @ 10% Yield	Bond Price @ 8% Yield	Percentage Price Change
0.0%	$ 23.14	$ 30.83	33.2%
1.0	30.82	39.48	28.1
2.0	38.51	48.12	25.0
3.0	46.20	56.77	22.9
4.0	53.88	65.42	21.4
5.0	61.57	74.06	20.3
6.0	69.26	82.71	19.4
7.0	76.94	91.35	18.7
8.0	84.63	100.00	18.2
9.0	92.31	108.65	17.7
10.0	100.00	117.29	17.3
11.0	107.69	125.94	16.9
12.0	115.37	134.58	16.7
13.0	123.06	143.23	16.4
14.0	130.74	151.88	16.2
15.0	138.43	160.52	16.0

Given a fixed income stream with a given maturity and yield to maturity, the percentage change in its value is smaller the larger the coupon rate for any given change in the yield to maturity.

For mortgages the coupon rate corresponds to the initially contracted rate of interest. The rule applies to mortgages also.

MATURITY AND PRICE CHANGES

Holding coupon rates and yields to maturity fixed, percentage changes in bond prices vary with the maturity of the bonds for a given change in the yield to maturity. With the exception of a few discount bonds, the percentage price change increases with the maturity of the bond. Thus, bond prices with the exception of some discount bonds tend to be more sensitive to given yield changes the longer the maturity.

To illustrate this relationship, let us first consider par bonds having a coupon rate of 9%. Table 3–4 exhibits for various maturities the percentage price increases corresponding to a decrease in the yield of 100 basis points.

Table 3-4. Percentage Change in Price of 10% Par Bonds for a Decrease in the Yield to Maturity to 9%

Maturity (Years)	Price @ 9%	Percentage Increase in Price
5	$103.96	3.96%
10	106.50	6.50
15	108.14	8.14
20	109.20	9.20
25	109.88	9.88
30	110.32	10.32
35	110.60	10.60
40	110.78	10.78
⋮	⋮	⋮
∞	111.11	11.11

Clearly, as maturity increases, the percentage change in price increases. For a 5-year bond the percentage change is only 3.96%, and as the maturity tends to infinity, the percentage change tends to the maximum of 11.11%.[1]

Next, consider the percentage price changes for 4% coupon bonds for which the yield to maturity drops from 13% to 12%. As shown in Table 3-5,

Table 3-5. Percentage Change in Price of 4% Coupon Bonds for a Decrease in the Yield to Maturity from 13% to 12%

Maturity (Years)	Price @ 13%	Price @ 12%	Percentage Increase in Price
5	$67.6503	$70.5597	4.401%
10	50.4167	54.1203	7.346
15	41.2360	44.9407	8.984
20	36.3451	39.8148	9.547
21	35.6853	39.1018	9.574
22	35.1035	38.4673	9.582
23	34.5906	37.9025	9.575
24	34.1384	37.3999	9.554
25	33.7397	36.9526	9.523
30	32.3517	35.3543	9.281
35	31.6122	34.4618	9.014
⋮	⋮	⋮	⋮
∞	30.7692	33.3333	8.333

Table 3–6. Percentage Change in the Prices of Zero Coupon
Bonds for a Decrease in the Yield to Maturity from 13% to 12%

Maturity (Years)	Price @ 13%	Price @ 12%	Percentage Increase in Price
5	$53.2726	$55.8395	4.818%
10	28.3797	31.1805	9.869
15	15.1186	17.4110	15.163
20	8.0541	9.7222	20.711
25	4.2906	5.4288	26.528
30	2.2857	3.0314	32.625
35	1.2177	1.6927	39.015
40	0.6487	0.9452	52.734
45	0.3456	0.5278	60.094

the percentage increase in price increases with maturity to 9.58% with the
22-year bond; but, thereafter, the percentage increase in price decreases to
8.333% on the "perpetuity." Table 3–6 shows the results for zero coupon
bonds. Here, the percentage increase in price increases with maturity. The
behavior of the bond prices as shown in Table 3–5 occurs only for some discount bonds. For all other bonds and mortgages the percentage increase in
price increases with maturity. There is the following general rule:

*For par or premium bonds and mortgages the percentage increase in
the price for a given decrease in the yield to maturity increases with
maturity. For some discount bonds the percentage increase in price
first increases with maturity and then decreases with maturity once
maturity is large enough.*

PERCENTAGE PRICE CHANGES AND DURATION

The rules governing percentage price changes, illustrated in previous sections, can be summarizd in one rule that relates the percentage price change
to a single property of the income stream called *duration*. The duration of a
security is a measure of the average life of a security. It is an average of the
dates on which cash flows are promised where those dates having the larger
current values of the cash flows receive the greater weight.

Macaulay (1938) first used the word "duration," and invented the first
duration formula as a measure of the average life of a security. Although

maturity is an appropriate measure of the life of a zero coupon bond that promises a single future payment, it is an ambiguous measure of the life of a security that promises cash flows at many future dates. The price behavior of a zero coupon bond is also different from that of a nonzero coupon bond with the same maturity. Macaulay reasoned that duration, which is a function of all the cash flows, would be a better measure of the life of a security. Hicks (1946) independently invented duration (but called it the "average period") as the elasticity of the bond price with respect to the discount factor $(1+r)^{-1}$ and showed that changes in the rate of interest r would not affect the relative prices of two securities each of which has the same duration. Samuelson (1945) and Redington (1952, reprinted 1982) also independently invented the duration measure in their studies of the sensitivity of the net worth of some financial institutions to interest rate changes. Fisher and Weil (1971), in extending the work of Redington, noted the usefulness of duration in developing immunization strategies for investing in bonds. Immunization as an investment strategy is discussed in Chapter 4. Hopewell and Kaufman (1973) showed the usefulness of duration in explaining the price behavior of debt securities and their work is an interesting blend and extension of the work of Macaulay and Hicks. An enormous amount of research after 1977 on the price behavior of securities and investment strategies in fixed-income securities showed that duration is an important theoretical and practical concept in the analyses of returns on fixed-income securities. Bierwag, Kaufman, and Toevs (1983) contains a survey of much of this work and an extensive bibliography of research involving the duration concept.

Duration: A Definition

A simple example will illustrate a method of determining duration. Consider a one year bond promising a coupon payment every six months. The value of this security using equation (2.9) of Chapter 2 is simply

$$p = \frac{100(c/2)}{1+r'} + \frac{100(1+c/2)}{(1+r')^2}, \qquad (3.1)$$

where $r' = r/2$, r is the annual yield to maturity, and c is the annual coupon rate. The price of the security is a function of two different cash flows. The value of the first cash flow as a proportion of the price is

$$w_1 = \frac{(c/2)(100)(1+r')^{-1}}{p}, \qquad (3.2)$$

and the value of the second as a proportion of the price is

Table 3-7. The Weights w_1 and w_2 for a One-Year Bond for Selected Values of the Coupon Rate and Yield to Maturity

Coupon Rate	Annual Interest Rate		
	8%	10%	12%
8%	$w_1 = .0385$	$w_1 = .0388$	$w_1 = .0392$
	$w_2 = .9615$	$w_2 = .9612$	$w_2 = .9608$
10%	$w_1 = 0.472$	$w_1 = .0476$	$w_1 = .0481$
	$w_2 = .9528$	$w_2 = .9524$	$w_2 = .9519$
12%	$w_1 = .0556$	$w_1 = .0564$	$w_1 = .0566$
	$w_2 = .9444$	$w_2 = .9439$	$w_2 = .9434$

$$w_2 = \frac{(1+c/2)(100)(1+r')^{-2}}{p}. \tag{3.3}$$

Both w_1 and w_2 are positive fractions and $w_1 + w_2 = 1$. These weights reflect the relative importance of the cash flows promised by the security, and the values of these weights change as the coupon rate and the yield to maturity change. Table 3-7 shows how these weights can shift for selected changes in the coupon rate and yield to maturity. The relative weights shift to the first flow as the coupon rate or the yield to maturity increase. Although each of the securities represented in Table 3-7 is a 1-year security, the investor may be interested in knowing whether the cash flows promised are to be received predominantly early or late. The weights, such as those in Table 3-7, measure the degree to which the flows are received relatively early or late. By evaluating the flows in present dollars and comparing the proportion of the value of each flow to the price of the security we can construct a method for measuring the degree of earliness or lateness, and different securities can be compared in this regard.

This example, described in equations (3.1)-(3.3), of course, can be extended to any bond maturity or to other fixed income securities like mortgages. If a bond or mortgage has a maturity of M periods, the weights corresponding to the flows can be represented as $w_1, w_2, w_3, \ldots, w_t, \ldots, w_M$, where w_t is the proportion of the price represented by the value of the tth cash flow. The weights for different securities can then be described in a diagram like that in Figure 3-2. In that diagram the weights for security 2 are relatively larger for the early cash flow dates and the weights for security 1 are relatively larger on the later cash flow dates. Each of the distributions of weights

Figure 3–2.   Present Value Weights for Two Different Securities: Different Durations

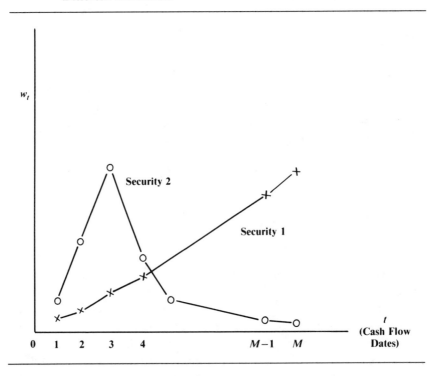

represented in Figure 3-2 can be represented by the average of the cash flow dates. This average is called the duration and it can be stated as

$$D = \sum_{t=1}^{M} tw_t. \tag{3.4}$$

Like most averages, duration lies somewhere between the earliest and the latest date and is measured in lengths of the intervals along the horizontal axis. If the cash flow dates are 6 months apart, then a D value of 8 would be eight 6-month periods or 4 years from the present.

Most persons think of an average as the sum of a set of scores or other numerically expressed values divided by the number of scores or items. Such averages involve equal weights given to each score or item. For example, if the scores received on three exams are 80, 70, and 60, the average score is

$$70 = \frac{80 + 70 + 60}{3},$$

but this average can also be written as

$$70 = \tfrac{1}{3}(80) + \tfrac{1}{3}(70) + \tfrac{1}{3}(60),$$

where the weights are $\tfrac{1}{3}$ and are multiplied by each score and the sum of the weights is unity. On the other hand, one may wish to give twice as much weight to the last score of 60, in which case one would write the average as

$$67.5 = \tfrac{1}{4}(80) + \tfrac{1}{4}(70) + \tfrac{1}{2}(60),$$

where again the weights sum to unity. The average described in equation (3.4) is similar. The greater weights correspond to the dates on which the values of the cash flows are larger. As an example, consider the 10% par bond in Table 3-7. Using those weights, the duration is

$$D = .0476(1) + .9524(2) = 1.9524$$

6-month periods or .9762 years, slightly less than the maturity of 1 year. Another example for a 6-year 10% bond is presented in Table 3B-1 in Appendix 3B to this chapter.

Duration is only one characteristic of the distribution of the w_t's over the cash flow dates. Two different distributions of the w_t's may have exactly the same durations, but have quite different shapes. In Figure 3-3, the w_t's for two different securities have exactly the same durations, but the distributions

Figure 3-3. Present Value Weights for Two Different Securities: Identical Durations

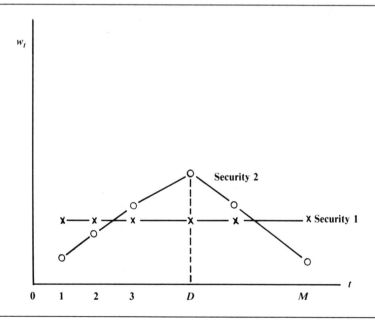

of the weights are very different. The weights for security 1 are spread out more around the duration, but the weights for security 2 are more concentrated on the duration. In some applications, characteristics of the distribution other than the duration are important to consider in investment decisions. The durations, apart from other features of the distributions, however, do provide some very useful ways to describe the percentage changes in the prices of securities for given changes in the yield to maturity.

The use of equation (3.4) to calculate the duration of securities, especially those having long maturities, is very tedious. Fairly simple formulas for calculating the durations of bonds and mortgages are developed in Appendix 3B to this chapter. The duration for bonds paying semiannual coupons can be calculated using

$$D = \frac{1+r'}{r'} - \frac{(c/2-r')M+(1+r')}{(1+r')^M(c/2)-(c/2-r')}, \tag{3.5}$$

where M is the number of 6-month periods to maturity, c is the annual coupon rate, r' $(=r/2)$ is the 6-month interest rate, and where D is expressed in 6-month intervals. The durations of mortgages having fixed monthly payments that are identically the same in each month can be calculated using

$$D = \frac{1+r'}{r'} - \frac{M}{(1+r')^M-1}, \tag{3.6}$$

where r' $(=r/12)$ is the monthly interest rate, M is the number of months to maturity, and where D is expressed in months.

Duration and Price Changes

A principal usefulness of duration stems from the equation

$$\frac{\Delta p}{p} \cong \frac{-D\Delta r'}{1+r'}. \tag{3.7}$$

Here, r' is the yield to maturity utilized to calculate the price p of the security; $\Delta r'$ is a change in the yield to maturity and Δp is the corresponding change in the price; and D is the duration. The symbol "$\cong$" means that the equality of the two sides of equation (3.7) is approximately correct. If we multiply $\Delta p/p$ by (100) we have the percentage change in the price of a security. Equation (3.7) is a very accurate representation of the percentage price change corresponding to a given change in the yield (or to a given percentage change in $(1+r')$).

The rationale underlying equation (3.7) is easily shown with some geometry. Let us begin with some specific security and consider the proportional changes in price corresponding to various given changes in yield. Holding the cash flows of the income stream fixed we can calculate exactly how $\Delta p/p$ should be related to $\Delta r'/(1+r')$. This relationship is shown as the curve inscribed as the solid line and labeled as the "true relationship" in Figure 3-4. Equation (3.7) approximates this true relationship with the dashed line in Figure 3-4. This line is tangent to the solid line at the origin and the negative of the slope of this line is duration. Utilizing equation (3.7) as an estimator of the percentage price change we can note the location and the direction of the inaccuracy resulting. When $\Delta r'$ is positive the estimated percentage decrease in the price exceeds the true percentage decrease and when $\Delta r'$ is

Figure 3-4.   Approximating Bond Price Percentage Changes with Duration

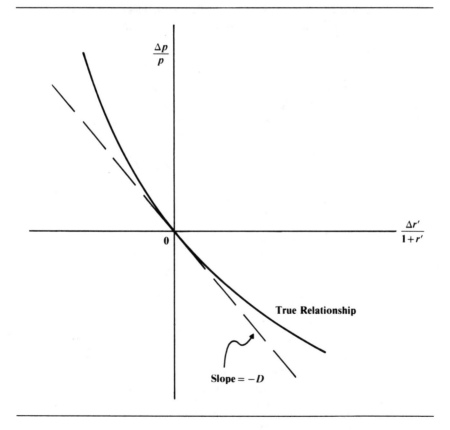

negative the estimated percentage increase in the price is less than the true percentage increase. If the changes in r' are very small, the error in estimating the true percentage price change is also very small. Notwithstanding these quantitative errors, duration can be utilized very effectively on a qualitative basis for comparing the percentage price changes of securities having different durations. The security with the larger duration will always have the larger percentage price change regardless of the errors in estimation implied by equation (3.7) used as an approximation. The remainder of this subsection contains some examples that will illustrate the magnitude of the error in utilizing equation (3.7) to estimate $\Delta p/p$ for a corresponding $\Delta r'$. In the next section we consider the attributes of the income streams — coupon rates, maturity, monthly mortgage payments — which can cause durations to differ among securities but still allow us to make qualitative comparisons on the magnitude of $\Delta p/p$ corresponding to the change in the yield.

Table 3–8. True Percentage Changes in Price of a 10%, 10-Year Par Bond versus the Estimated Percentage Price Change Using Duration

Annual Yield Change (Basis Points)	True Percentage Price Change	Estimated Percentage Price Change Using Duration	Error
+200	−11.470%	−12.433%	.963%
+175	−10.139	−10.879	.740
+150	− 8.780	− 9.325	.545
+125	− 7.392	− 7.771	.379
+100	− 5.975	− 6.217	.242
+ 75	− 4.528	− 4.663	.135
+ 50	− 3.051	− 3.108	.057
+ 25	− 1.541	− 1.554	.013
− 25	+ 1.574	+ 1.554	.020
− 50	+ 3.183	+ 3.108	.075
− 75	+ 4.826	+ 4.663	.163
− 100	+ 6.504	+ 6.217	.287
− 125	+ 8.219	+ 7.771	.448
− 150	+ 9.971	+ 9.325	.646
− 175	+11.761	+10.879	.882
− 200	+13.590	+12.433	1.157

Note: Using equation (3B.18), duration equals 13.055 6-month periods. The annual yield change is twice the 6-month yield change.

Percentage changes in prices are calculated as $(100) \cdot \Delta p/p$. The estimation error is the true percentage price change less the estimated percentage price change.

Table 3-9. True Percentage Changes in Price of a 10%, 20-Year Par Bond versus the Estimated Percentage Price Change Using Duration

Annual Yield Change (Basis Points)	True Percentage Price Change	Estimated Percentage Price Change Using Duration	Error
+200	−15.046%	−17.159%	2.113%
+175	−13.376	−15.014	1.638
+150	−11.650	−12.869	1.219
+125	− 9.866	−10.724	0.858
+100	− 8.023	− 8.580	0.557
+ 75	− 6.117	− 6.435	0.318
+ 50	− 4.147	− 4.290	0.143
+ 25	− 2.109	− 2.145	0.036
− 25	+ 2.182	+ 2.145	0.037
− 50	+ 4.441	+ 4.290	0.151
− 75	+ 6.779	+ 6.435	0.344
−100	+ 9.201	+ 8.580	0.621
−125	+11.709	+10.724	0.985
−150	+14.308	+12.869	1.439
−175	+17.001	+15.014	1.987
−200	+19.793	+17.159	2.634

Note: Using equation (3B.18), duration equals 18.017 6-month periods. See Table 3-8 for other notes.

Tables 3-8 and 3-9 show the true percentage price changes for 10-year and 20-year 10% par bonds. The exhibited percentage price changes correspond to changes in the annual yield to maturity that range from −200 basis points to +200 basis points in increments of 25 basis points; the yields on these bonds thus range from 8% to 12%. Column 3 in each of these tables shows the percentage price changes as estimated using duration in equation (3.7). Column 4 shows the error in estimation. The error is expressed as the difference between the true and estimated percentage price changes. As suggested by Figure 3-4, the errors are larger, the larger the change in the yield to maturity. Clearly, the duration-based estimation of the percentage price changes are best for small changes in the yield to maturity. For the 10-year bond (Table 3-8) the percentage price change is accurately estimated within one third of 1% for increments (or decrements) in the yield as large as 100 basis points. This means that equation (3.7) in this case may mean an error as large as 33¢ on $100 paid for the par bond. For the 20-year bond (Table 3-9), the percentage price change is accurately estimated within five eighths of 1% for increments (or decrements) in the yield as large as 100 basis points. This error constitutes approximately as much as 63¢ per $100 paid for the bond. For any given change in the yield the error in estimation increases with the duration of the bond. As long as very small yield changes are considered, the accuracy of the duration-based estimate is excellent. However, in a world of programmed calculators that are easily manipulated, there is probably little advantage to using the duration-based estimation procedure. The use of the duration procedure first requires the computation of duration itself. Although these formulas can easily be programmed for many desk calculators, it is probably just as easy to calculate the actual price changes. The value of equation (3.7) lies principally in its use as a qualitative indicator and not in its use as a quantitative estimator. As shown in the next subsection and in Appendix 3B, the characteristics of debt securities—coupon rate, maturity, monthly mortgage payment, and so on—often enable one to know instantly that the duration of one security is larger than another, and that its price consequently is more sensitive to changes in the yield to maturity. Thus, in many instances qualitative comparisons are possible. Without undertaking any computations one can often say that one security is more price sensitive than another.

Duration and Debt Characteristics

The duration of a security changes systematically with changes in the properties of the income stream and in the yield to maturity. Each weight w_i, as defined above, is a function of the pattern of the cash flows promised by a security and of the yield to maturity. Any change in the time pattern of the weights $(w_1, w_2, ..., w_i, ...)$ will affect the value of the duration.

Any change in the coupon rate on a bond affects all of the cash flows. If one bond has a higher coupon rate than another even though it has the same maturity, a greater portion of the income stream is received early. This has the effect of increasing the early weights w_i and of lowering the later weights. The duration must, therefore, be smaller, as shown in Appendix 3B. Figure 3-5 shows how the duration changes with the coupon rate holding maturity fixed. Some immediate comparisons are possible. A premium bond of the same maturity as a par bond will be less price sensitive to yield changes. A discount bond will be more price sensitive than a par bond of the same maturity.

As shown in Appendix 3B, duration increases with the maturity of par or premium bonds, zero coupon bonds, and of mortgages. For some discount

Figure 3-5. Duration and Different Coupon Rates: Yield and Maturity Fixed

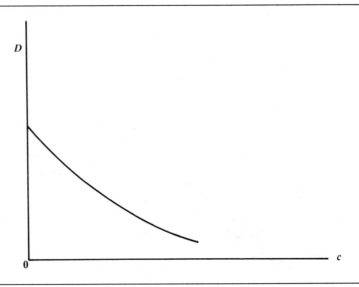

bonds, however, duration increases with maturity only up to some critical maturity and then further increases in maturity cause duration to decline. This is illustrated in Figure 3-6. The duration of a zero coupon bond is equal to its maturity and is mapped, therefore, as the straight line forming a 45° angle with the vertical axis in Figure 3-6. The perpetuity or consol has a duration of $(1+r')/r'$ as developed in Appendix 3A and is placed into Figure 3-6 as a reference line. The durations of all securities (except zero coupon bonds) asymptotically approach the duration of the perpetuity as maturity increases. The durations of par or premium bonds increase monotonically as maturity increases, but the durations of some discount bonds rise above the perpetuity duration before proceeding on their path toward the perpetuity duration. As maturity increases holding coupon rates and the yield to maturity fixed, the cash flows promised by a security occur farther in the future. This produces a positive weight beyond the initial maturity that was previously zero, and it reduces the weight which was applicable at the initial maturity date. This effect, by itself, tends to increase the duration of the security, but there are other weight changes induced by the maturity extension. The weight w_t on a nonmaturity date is given as

$$w_t = \frac{(c/2)(100)(1+r')^{-t}}{p}. \tag{3.8}$$

Figure 3-6. Duration and Maturity: Yields and Coupon Rates Fixed

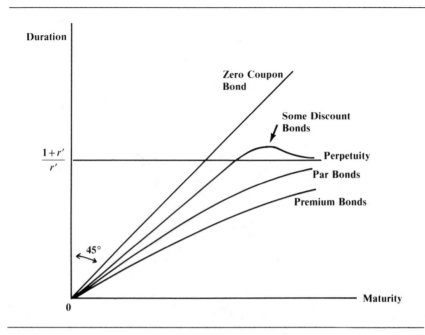

When maturity is extended, the only effect on this weight is the change induced by the change in the price of p. For premium bonds, the price increases as maturity is extended; this is illustrated in Table 3-4. For par bonds the price p is unaffected. However, as Table 3-5 shows, the prices of discount bonds decrease as maturity is extended. Thus, if the weights are given as $w_1, w_2, ..., w_M$, what we observe for par bonds as maturity is extended by one period is that w_M falls and w_{M+1} increases (where formerly $w_{M+1} = 0$); this, of course, increases duration. For premium bonds, all the weights through w_M decrease because the price increases and w_{M+1} is the only weight increasing; this causes duration to rise. For discount bonds, the weight changes are more complex. The weights w_1 through w_{M-1} must increase because the price falls as induced by the maturity extension. The weight w_M is affected by two factors; as the price falls it will tend to rise, but as a portion of the cash flow at maturity is extended, it will tend to fall. In any case the weight w_{M+1} will increase. As maturity is extended, the change in the weight patterns can actually give predominant increases to the early weights so that duration is forced down for these securities; we may refer to this as a "price effect" on duration.

Except for the anomaly of the discount bonds, the greater the maturity the more sensitive the bond price to changes in yields. For the special discount bonds, however, we may find some of them with long maturities no more price sensitive than a bond with exactly the same coupon rate but having a much shorter maturity. The example in Table 3–5 shows that the price sensitivity of a 35-year 4% coupon bond with a yield of 13% behaves very similarly to a 15-year 4% coupon bond with the same yield to maturity. Generally, however, the special "price effect" on the duration of these bonds occurs at maturities that are quite long, or at coupon rates that are quite low relative to the yield to maturity, or both.

The duration of a debt security decreases as the yield to maturity rises, holding the maturity and coupon rate constant. This occurs because of the uneven effect that price changes have on each weight, w_t. As r' increases, both the numerator and denominator of the ratio $(1 + r')^{-t}/p$ decrease; however, the decrease in the numerator will be greater the farther into the future the date t is. This has the effect of raising the early weights and lowering the later ones. Hence duration must fall as the yield to maturity increases. This relationship is depicted in Figure 3–7. Of course, the curve in that diagram shifts up (down) in response to a decrease (increase) in the coupon rate. The curve also shifts up (down) for longer (shorter) maturities except for the

Figure 3–7. Duration and Yield to Maturity: Maturity and Coupon Rate Fixed

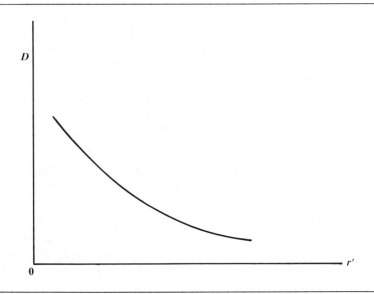

special case in which price effects dominate for discount bonds, in which case it is vice versa.

Figures 3–5 to 3–7 show how the durations change for changes in coupon rates, maturity, and yields to maturity. These curves help us to explain the observed percentage changes in price in Tables 3–2 to 3–6. In every case where the percentage change in the price for a bond exceeded that of another for a given change in the yield, the duration was greater. These relationships can be summarized in the following rule.

The larger the duration of a security, the larger the percentage change in the security price for a given change in the yield to maturity.

This duration rule can often be very useful in describing everyday events. For example, it is easy to deduce the following result without any calculations.

For any yield change, an 8% 10-year par bond has a greater percentage change in price than a 9% coupon 5-year bond selling at 8%.

The duration rule asserts this will be so because the higher coupon and lower maturity of the second bond implies it will have a lower duration. There are obvious cases, however, where the duration rule cannot provide a precise answer without calculations. For example, in comparing a 12% 15-year par bond with a 10% 10-year par bond, we observe that the duration rule cannot give a precise answer. The longer maturity of the first bond, by itself, implies a greater duration, but it also has a higher coupon rate and yield to maturity which imply a lower duration — the net effect is ambiguous. After some years of experience, many bond traders and investors acquire a "feel" for the bond markets and know with an uncanny instinct how the prices of various bonds change relative to each other for given prospective future yield scenarios. Although these traders and investors do not always think in terms of durations, the effects may often be comparable. For complicated cases like the one above, they may implicitly deduce the strength of the separate effects of different maturities, coupon rates, and yields to maturity in order to conclude which security is more price sensitive to yield changes.

Finally, one warning about duration should be expressed. Duration, as a measure of bond price volatility, may have many shortcomings. It is often contended that short-term yields change more than long-term yields. Thus, even though short-term bonds tend to have lower durations, the implied smaller effect on percentage change in prices may be offset by larger changes in yields. The role played by duration as a measure of risk or price volatility is a major underlying idea in future chapters where the development of duration in this context is systematically undertaken.

APPENDIX 3A
THE PRICE OF PERPETUITIES OR CONSOLS

A perpetuity or a consol is a security that promises a given cash flow at the end of every period forever. The length of each time period in which a flow occurs is fixed; a year, 6 months, a month, a week. Let F be the number of dollars promised as a cash flow at the end of these intervals. The present value or price of this income stream is then

$$P = \sum_{t=1}^{\infty} F(1+r')^{-t}, \tag{3A.1}$$

where r' is the interest rate for the time interval specified. Let $b = (1+r')^{-1}$. Then one can rewrite (3A.1) as

$$P = \sum_{t=1}^{\infty} Fb^{t} = F \sum_{t=1}^{\infty} b^{t} = F(b + b^2 + b^3 + \cdots). \tag{3A.2}$$

Multiply P by b to get

$$bP = F(b^2 + b^3 + b^4 + \cdots). \tag{3A.3}$$

Subtract equation (3A.3) from (3A.2). This gives

$$(1-b)P = Fb. \tag{3A.4}$$

Therefore,

$$P = Fb/(1-b). \tag{3A.5}$$

The definition of b implies that

$$1 - b = 1 - \frac{1}{1+r'} = \frac{r'}{1+r'}. \tag{3A.6}$$

Hence,

$$\frac{b}{1-b} = \frac{1}{1+r'} \frac{1+r'}{r'} = \frac{1}{r'}, \tag{3A.7}$$

and so

$$P = F/r', \tag{3A.8}$$

a very simple formula. Financial economists often prefer to use consols in their theoretical work because of the simple formula given by equation (3A.8). Often the theoretical implications derived from the use of consols extend to other securities. In this chapter some of the properties of consols can be used as "benchmarks" in deriving and comparing the properties for other securities.

APPENDIX 3B
DURATION AND ITS CALCULATION

There are a variety of different but equivalent formulas for the duration of an income stream. In this appendix, several of the most useful formulas are derived and illustrated.

Duration in General

First, we derive the general formula for duration and then we specialize it to the specific income streams represented by bonds and mortgages. If the cash flow on an income stream is generally written as S_t, for $t = 1, 2, 3, ..., M$, where the stream terminates after the Mth flow, the price of the security is

$$P = \sum_{t=1}^{M} S_t(1+r')^{-t}, \tag{3B.1}$$

where r' is the interest rate appropriate for time intervals between cash flows. If the cash flows occur annually, $r' = r$ where r is the yield the maturity expressed as an annual interest rate. If the cash flows occur semiannually as with most bonds, $r' = r/2$. If cash flows occur monthly, as with most mortgages, $r' = r/12$. The duration of the financial instrument is defined as

$$D = -\frac{1+r'}{P}\frac{dP}{dr'}, \tag{3B.2}$$

which, as was shown by Hicks (1946), is the elasticity of P with respect to $(1+r')^{-1}$. However, regardless of whether D is to be interpreted as an elasticity or not, equation (3B.2) provides the basis for numerically calculating the duration. Taking directly the derivative of the price in (3B.1), we have

$$\frac{dP}{dr'} = -\sum_{t=1}^{M} tS_t(1+r')^{-t-1}, \tag{3B.3}$$

so that upon using equation (3B.2),

$$D = \frac{\sum_{t=1}^{M} tS_t(1+r')^{-t}}{P} = \sum_{t=1}^{M} t\left\{\frac{S_t(1+r')^{-t}}{P}\right\}. \quad (3B.4)$$

If we let $w_t = S_t(1+r')^{-t}/P$, recognizing that $\sum_{t=1}^{M} w_t = 1$, and that $0 \le w_t \le 1$, for all t, then

$$D = \sum_{t=1}^{M} w_t t. \quad (3B.5)$$

Thus, D is a "weighted average" of the time periods in which the cash flows occur, and D is measured in units of the time intervals between cash payments. If the income stream represents a bond paying cash flows semiannually, then D is measured in 6-month periods. For example, $D = 5$ means that the duration is five 6-month periods or 2½ years. If the income stream represents a mortgage with monthly cash flows, D is measured in months. One can use (3B.5) easily by computing the cash flows of a financial instrument. Table 3B-1 illustrates the calculation for a 10% par bond paying cash flows semiannually for 6 years. The first four columns show the computation of w_t. Column 1 indicates the time in 6-month intervals in which the

Table 3B-1. Calculation of the Duration of a 10%, 6-Year Par Bond, Price = $100.00

Time of Payment (in 6-month Intervals)	Cash Flow S_t	$(1+r')^{-t}$	$w_t = S_t(1+r')^{-t}/100$	$w_t t$
1	$ 5.00	.95238	0.047819	0.047619
2	5.00	.90703	0.045351	0.090703
3	5.00	.86384	0.043192	0.129576
4	5.00	.82270	0.041135	0.164540
5	5.00	.78353	0.039176	0.195882
6	5.00	.74622	0.037311	0.223866
7	5.00	.71068	0.035534	0.248738
8	5.00	.67684	0.033842	0.270736
9	5.00	.64461	0.032230	0.290074
10	5.00	.61391	0.030696	0.306951
11	5.00	.58468	0.029234	0.321574
12	105.00	.55684	0.584679	7.016152
			1.000000	9.306414

Note: Because of rounding, the summations may not be exact.
$D = (9.306414/2) = 4.653207$ years or 9.306414 6-month periods.

payments are made. Column 2 indicates the value of the cash flow corresponding to the time period. Column 3 is the discount factor, and column 4 shows the corresponding weights w_t. Notice that the weights w_t add up to unity. Column 5 shows each weight multiplied by the corresponding time period. The sum of the terms in column 5 gives the duration as measured in 6-month intervals. Since duration is an average of the time periods in which cash flows occur, it follows that duration is bounded between its maturity and zero. In the example of Table 3B-1, the duration of 9.306414 6-month periods is greater than zero but smaller than 12, which is the maturity expressed in 6-month intervals.

Durations for Bonds

Computation of the duration of a security can be a tedious process if one uses the weighted average method in Table 3B-1. Thus, easier methods for its calculation have been sought. In particular, using the properties of the income stream involved, one can reduce the formula (3B.5) to a single expression not involving sums so that one can simply plug values of P, r', c, and M into the formula in order to derive the duration directly. For a bond, one can write equation (3B.1), as equation (2.1) in the text, so as to express it as

$$P = \frac{(100)c/2}{r'}[1-(1+r')^{-M}]+(100)(1+r')^{-M}. \qquad (3B.6)$$

Now, let

$$A = \frac{(100)c/2}{r'}[1-(1+r')^{-M}] \quad \text{and}$$

$$B = (100)(1+r')^{-M}. \qquad (3B.7)$$

Here, A is the value of the stream of coupon payments and B is the value of the balloon payment occurring on the Mth payment date. Thus,

$$P = A + B. \qquad (3B.8)$$

For a mortgage with no balloon payment one would regard B as zero. For a zero coupon bond, one would regard A as zero. Thus, one can think of a bond as a combination of a mortgage with 6-month payment intervals and a zero coupon bond. The value A is sometimes called an "annuity" because it is the value of an income stream that promises the same dollar flow in every period (and the sum of the flows for any year is also the same and hence the word *annuity*). Taking derivatives of A and B with respect to r', we acquire

$$\frac{dA}{dr'} = -\frac{A}{r'} + \frac{M(100)(c/2)(1+r')^{-M-1}}{r'}, \quad \text{and}$$

$$\frac{dB}{dr'} = -M(100)(1+r')^{-M-1}. \tag{3B.9}$$

Multiplying each of these expressions by $(1+r')$ gives us the result

$$-(1+r')\frac{dA}{dr'} = \frac{1+r'}{r'}A - \frac{M(c/2)}{r'}B, \quad \text{and}$$

$$-(1+r')\frac{dB}{dr'} = MB. \tag{3B.10}$$

Now, since

$$D = -\frac{1+r'}{P}\frac{dP}{dr'} = -\frac{1+r'}{P}\frac{dA}{dr'} - \frac{1+r'}{P}\frac{dB}{dr'}, \tag{3B.11}$$

it follows, using equation (3B.10), that

$$D = \frac{1+r'}{r'}\frac{A}{P} + M\left[1 - \frac{c/2}{r'}\right]\frac{B}{P}. \tag{3B.12}$$

Babcock (1984) has recommended the use of this formula. Duration is divided into two parts. If we have a par bond, then $c/2 = r'$ and the second part involving B disappears and the duration is simply $[(1+r')/r](A/P)$. If it is a premium or discount bond, the second part becomes relevant and it is an adjustment to the par bond duration to give the effect of the premium or discount on the duration. Table 3B-2 shows the duration calculations for

Table 3B-2. Durations of 6-Year Bonds with a 10% Yield to Maturity and Different Coupon Rates

Coupon Rate	Price	$\dfrac{1+r'}{r'}\dfrac{A}{P}$	$M\left[1-\dfrac{c/2}{r'}\right]\dfrac{B}{P}$	Duration (in 6-Month Periods)
0%	$ 55.68374	0.00000	12.00000	12.00000
2	64.54699	2.88361	8.28178	11.16539
4	73.41025	5.07091	5.46140	10.53231
6	82.27350	6.78693	3.24870	10.03564
8	91.13675	8.16919	1.46638	9.63557
10	100.00000	9.30641	0.00000	9.30641
12	108.86325	10.25846	-1.22760	9.03086
14	117.72650	11.06716	-2.27036	8.79680
16	126.58976	11.76261	-3.16710	8.59551

six-year bonds with a 10% yield to maturity and having different coupon rates. Notice that the duration of the par bond is the same (except for rounding errors) as the duration calculated using the weighted average method of Table 3B-1. Given that A and B can be computed easily, as it can with most calculators, the computation is much easier than the weighted average method. Using the latter method we would need a table like Table 3B-1 for each of the bonds in Table 3B-2. In Table 3B-2 the duration of the zero coupon bond is twelve 6-month periods, which is exactly equal to its maturity. Since a zero coupon bond promises only one cash payment, duration as a measure of the life of the security is equal to its maturity. In Table 3B-2 duration decreases as the coupon rate increases, holding the maturity and the yield to maturity unchanged. This occurs because at higher coupon rates a greater proportion of the cash flows promised by the security occur in the early periods and this reduces the average life of the security.

An alternative formula for duration is found by simply substituting $P - B = A$ for A in (3B.12). Doing so, and collecting terms, one can write duration as

$$D = \frac{1+r'}{r'} + \frac{B}{P}\left[(M-1) - \left(\frac{1}{r'}\right) - \frac{M(c/2)}{r'}\right]. \tag{3B.13}$$

This formula also divides duration into two parts. The first part, $(1+r')/r'$, is the duration of a perpetuity or consol that promises \$1.00 each period forever. To see this, note that the price of such a perpetuity is $p^* = 1/r'$, as calculated in Appendix 3A. Then,

$$-\frac{1+r'}{p^*}\frac{dp^*}{dr'} = \frac{1+r'}{1/r'}\left(\frac{1}{r'}\right)^2 = \frac{1+r'}{r'} = d^*, \tag{3B.14}$$

which is the duration of the stream by definition. Thus, (3B.13) takes the duration of a perpetuity and adjusts it using the second term in order to calculate the duration of the bond. Thus, one can write the duration as

$$D = d^* + (\text{Adj}), \tag{3B.15}$$

where

$$\text{Adj} = \frac{B}{P}\left[(M-1) - \left(\frac{1}{r'}\right) - \frac{M(c/2)}{r'}\right] \tag{3B.16}$$

is the adjustment. In order to illustrate this, Table 3B-3 reproduces the durations of Table 3B-2 using this partition of duration into the two parts. Exactly the same durations are produced using this partition of duration into two parts. In equation (3B.15) it is possible for the adjustment Adj to be

Table 3B–3. Durations of 6-Year Bonds with a 10% Yield to Maturity and Different Coupon Rates

Coupon Rate	d^*	Adj	$D = d^* + \text{Adj}$
0%	21.0	− 9.00000	12.00000
2	21.0	− 9.83461	11.16539
4	21.0	− 10.46769	10.53231
6	21.0	− 10.96436	10.03564
8	21.0	− 11.36443	9.63557
10	21.0	− 11.69359	9.30641
12	21.0	− 11.96914	9.03086
14	21.0	− 12.20320	8.79680
16	21.0	− 12.40449	8.59551

positive so that the duration would exceed the duration d^* on the $1.00 perpetuity. As noted in the text, this can occur for some discount bonds and arises because of the "price effect" on duration.

Utilizing the definition of P and B, one can reduce equation (3B.15) to the formula

$$D = \frac{1+r'}{r'} - \frac{M(c/2 - r') + (1+r')}{(1+r')^M(c/2) - (c/2 - r')}, \qquad (3B.17)$$

which is an easy formula to use because it does not involve a precalculation of either B or P. The second term in (3B.17) is simply the negative of the adjustment term in equation (3B.16). We may note that the denominator in the adjustment term increases faster with M than the numerator as long as the coupon rate is positive. This means that the duration of all such bonds tends closer and closer to the duration of the perpetuity as the maturity increases because the adjustment term will tend toward zero. For some discount bonds, as noted in the text, duration may increase with maturity and rise above the perpetuity duration, but eventually as maturity continues to increase the duration will decrease toward the perpetuity duration. The form of equation (3B.17) suggests that an increase in the yield to maturity reduces the duration—given a coupon rate c, and maturity M. The perpetuity duration, $(1+r')/r' = 1 + 1/r'$, clearly decreases as r' rises. The adjustment term decreases in absolute value because the denominator increases more than the numerator. This is sufficient for D to fall, although a meticulous demonstration of this is complex. In effect, an increase in r' increases the weights in equation (3B.5) on the early cash flow dates relative to the later dates and this forces the decline in duration.

For par bonds, $c/2 = r'$. In that case equation (3B.17) reduces to the easy formula

$$D = \frac{1+r'}{r'}[1-(1+r')^{-M}]. \tag{3B.18}$$

Durations for Mortgages

The duration formulas for bonds are easily modified so as to make them appropriate for mortgages. If P is the value of the mortgage and Y is the monthly payment, then

$$P = \frac{Y}{r'}[1-(1+r')^{-M}] \tag{3B.19}$$

where M is the number of monthly payments and $r' = r/12$ is the monthly interest rate. The monthly payment Y is then given as

$$Y = \frac{r'P}{1-(1+r')^{-M}} \tag{3B.20}$$

for some initial interest rate r'. Now, if we assume the monthly payments are given for some initial interest rate and do not change as the yield to maturity changes, we can regard Y as fixed in (3B.19) so that only P changes as r' changes. Thus, the mortgage is an annuity with monthly payments identically the same throughout its life. Thus, the value of the mortgage is similar to the A part of a bond's value given in (3B.7), where Y is substituted for $(100)(c/2)$ in that equation and r' is modified to reflect the monthly interest rate. Then, utilizing equation (3B.9) comparably, we have

$$\frac{dP}{dr'} = \frac{-P}{r'} + \frac{MY}{r'}(1+r')^{-M-1}, \tag{3B.21}$$

and the duration is consequently

$$D = -\frac{1+r'}{P}\frac{dP}{dr'} = \frac{1+r'}{r'} - \frac{MY}{r'}\frac{(1+r')^{-M}}{P}. \tag{3B.22}$$

Noting that P is given by (3B.19) for Y given, we can write the duration as

$$\begin{aligned} D &= \frac{1+r'}{r'} - \frac{M(1+r')^{-M}}{1-(1+r')^{-M}} \\ &= \frac{1+r'}{r'} - \frac{M}{(1+r')^M - 1}. \end{aligned} \tag{3B.23}$$

The duration of a mortgage is consequently only a function of the interest rate or yield to maturity at which the fixed flows are priced and of the matur-

Table 3B-4. Durations of Various Mortgages Having Different Maturities and Interest Rates, with Maturity and Duration Measured in Months

Maturity (Months)	Annual Interest Rate (%)							
	9.0	*10.0*	*11.0*	*12.0*	*13.0*	*14.0*	*15.0*	*16.0*
240	86.4	83.1	79.8	76.7	73.8	70.9	68.2	65.6
252	89.1	85.5	82.0	78.6	75.4	72.4	69.5	66.7
264	91.7	87.8	84.0	80.4	77.0	73.8	70.7	67.8
276	94.1	89.9	85.9	82.1	78.4	75.0	71.7	68.7
288	96.4	92.0	87.7	83.6	79.8	76.1	72.7	69.5
300	98.7	93.9	89.3	85.0	81.0	77.2	73.6	70.3
312	100.8	95.7	90.9	86.4	82.1	78.1	74.4	70.9
324	102.7	97.4	92.3	87.6	83.1	79.0	75.1	71.5
336	104.6	99.0	93.7	88.7	84.1	80.0	75.7	72.0
348	106.4	100.5	94.9	89.7	84.9	80.5	76.3	72.5
360	108.1	101.9	96.1	90.7	85.7	81.1	76.8	72.9

ity. We may note that the duration is independent of the value of the mortgage P and of the monthly payment Y as long as Y is the same for each month and does not change with the interest rate r'. Table 3B-4 gives the durations for various mortgages having different maturities and interest rates. For mortgages, we may note that duration increases with maturity holding the interest rate fixed and that duration decreases as the interest rate increases holding maturity fixed.

Summary: Durations for Bonds and Mortgages

The duration of a financial security with promised cash flows at specific dates is a function of the time pattern of those cash flows and of the yield to maturity. Duration is a measure of the average life of the security; it represents "average" maturity of the cash flows, in which greater weight in determining the average is given to the cash flow dates for which the flows have the larger values. The relationship between the duration and the various properties of the time pattern of cash flows and the yield to maturity can be summarized.

1. The duration of any bond decreases as the coupon rate rises, holding the maturity and the yield to maturity fixed.
2. The duration of any bond or mortgage decreases as the yield to maturity rises, holding the coupon rate and maturity fixed.

3. The duration of par and premium bonds and mortgages increases as the maturity increases, holding the coupon rate (or the monthly mortgage payment) and yield to maturity fixed. The durations of these bonds will always be less than the perpetuity duration.
4. The duration of all bonds and mortgages tend closer and closer to the perpetuity duration as maturity increases, holding the coupon rate (or monthly mortgage payment) and yield to maturity fixed.
5. The duration of some discount bonds will increase to a certain point and then decrease as maturity increases, holding the coupon rate and yield to maturity fixed. For these bonds duration will exceed the perpetuity duration for some maturities.
6. The duration of a zero coupon bond is equal to its maturity.

NOTE

1. A bond of infinite maturity, here, pays a coupon return of $5 every 6 months forever. The final balloon payment of $100 is never paid. Such bonds are called *consols* or *perpetuities*. Such bonds, more commonly issued in Great Britain, are rarely issued or traded in U.S. financial markets. The price of such bonds as shown in Appendix 3A consists of the flow per period (e.g., $5) divided by the interest rate per period (e.g., 0.045).

REFERENCES

Babcock, Guilford. 1984. "Duration as a Link between Yield and Value." *Journal of Portfolio Management* (Summer): 55–65.

Bierwag, G.O., George G. Kaufman, and Alden Toevs. 1983. "Recent Developments in Bond Portfolio Immunization Strategies." In *Innovations in Bond Portfolio Management: Duration Analysis and Immunization,* edited by G. Kaufman, G. Bierwag, and A. Toevs (Greenwich, Conn.: JAI Press).

Fisher, Lawrence, and Roman Weil. 1971. "Coping with the Risk of Interest Rate Fluctuations and Returns to Bondholders from Naive and Optimal Strategies." *Journal of Business* (October).

Hicks, J.R. 1946. *Value and Capital,* 2nd ed. (Oxford: Clarendon Press).

Hopewell, Michael, and George G. Kaufman. 1973. "Bond Price Volatility and Years to Maturity." *American Economic Review* (September): 749–53.

Macaulay, F.R. 1938. *Some Theoretical Problems Suggested by the Movements of Interest Rates, Bond Yields, and Stock Prices in the U.S. since 1856* (New York: National Bureau of Economic Research).

Redington, F.M. 1952. "Review of the Principle of Life Office Valuations." *Journal of the Institute of Actuaries* 18: 286–340.

Samuelson, P.A. 1945. "The Effect of Interest Rate Increases on the Banking System." *American Economic Review* (March): 16–27.

II INVESTMENT STRATEGIES, DURATION, AND RISK

4 INVESTMENT ACCUMULATION AND DURATION

Investors in fixed-income securities face two kinds of interest rate risk. Changes in interest rates over an investment period may affect (1) the value of fixed-income securities held at the end of the period and (2) the level of earnings on any reinvestments of cash flows during the period. Let us call these risks respectively *price risk* and *reinvestment risk*. A security having a maturity that is greater than the length of the investment period is subject to price risk because its value at all times before maturity depends on market yields. A security that matures exactly at the end of an investment period bears no price risk because its value at maturity is its face value, which is independent of market yields. Reinvestment risk is associated with any security that generates cash flows within an investment period. The existence and extent of either risk depends on the nature of the security as well as on the relative length of the period over which return and risk is measured.

Over a period of time in which both risks are in effect, there are some obvious offsetting tendencies. If yields rise on a particular date, the value of an investment fund decreases, but yet those higher yields imply greater interest returns from reinvestment of any future cash flows. A change in yields may be a mixed blessing. Any initial capital loss may be offset in time by greater returns from reinvestment; and any initial capital gain may be offset in time by lower returns from reinvestment. From the preceding chapter, we know that the degree of capital loss or gain from a change in yields depends on the duration of the securities held. In this chapter, we show that the time required to offset these capital gains or losses from reinvestment of the cash flows also depends on the duration of the securities held. Both price and reinvestment risk are thus related to the duration of the securities held.

DURATION OF A PORTFOLIO

Given that there is a large variety of different securities available, investors may choose to invest in many of them simultaneously, to form a portfolio of securities. Such a portfolio may produce an income stream that has a complicated cash flow pattern. For example, if an investor buys five 5-year 10% coupon bonds and eight 3-year 12% coupon bonds (all having $100 in face value), the resulting cash flow pattern for 6-month periods is

$$(\$73, \$73, \$73, \$73, \$73, \$873, \$25, \$25, \$25, \$525).$$

Of course, such flow patterns also have durations that can be calculated. The duration of the income stream corresponding to a portfolio of securities can be calculated simply as a weighted average of the durations of the respective securities comprising the portfolio. This relationship allows the investor to choose securities so that the resulting portfolio duration will be a given number. In other words, the portfolio duration can be an investor's decision variable. Analysis of the consequences of such duration decisions with respect to price and reinvestment risk is presented in the next section.

In order to derive the duration of a portfolio of two securities, let p_1 be the value of security 1 and let p_2 be the value of security 2. Let n_1 and n_2 be respectively the number of these securities held in a simple portfolio consisting of only these two securities. The total value of the portfolio is then $V = n_1 p_1 + n_2 p_2$. Let $B_1 = p_1 n_1 / V$ and let $B_2 = p_2 n_2 / V$. Thus, B_1 and B_2 are the respective proportions of V invested in the two securities. Suppose D_1 and D_2 are the respective durations of the two securities. As shown in Appendix 4A, the duration of the portfolio of these two securities is then

$$D = B_1 D_1 + B_2 D_2. \tag{4.1}$$

That is, the duration of a portfolio is a weighted average of the durations of the securities in it where the weights are the respective proportions invested in each security and where the weights add to unity; that is, $B_1 + B_2 = 1$. Some examples of how this formula can be used follow.

Example 1. Suppose $V = \$1,000$. Suppose the portfolio contains two securities. One security is a 10% 10-year par bond and the other is a 10% 20-year par bond. Using equation (2B.18) in Appendix 2B, the durations of these bonds are $D_1 = 13.085321$ and $D_2 = 18.017041$ 6-month periods. If $B_1 = B_2 = 0.5$, then the duration of the portfolio is 15.551181 6-month periods, using equation (4.1). Given that the price of each of these bonds is \$100, this implies that the number of them purchased is $n_1 = 5 = (B_1/100)(1,000)$ and similarly $n_2 = 5$.

Example 2.   Suppose in example 1, we wish to construct the portfolio so that it has a duration of sixteen 6-month periods. What must the proportions B_1 and B_2 be so that this is the case? Noting that $B_2 = 1 - B_1$, because the weights sum to unity, we can now write equation (4.1) as

$$D = 16 = B_1 D_1 + (1 - B_1)D_2 = B_1(13.085321) + (1 - B_1)(18.017041).$$

Solving for B_1 and B_2 we have $B_1 = 0.408993$ and $B_2 = 1 - B_1 = 0.591007$. Then noting that $n_1 = B_1(1,000/100) = 10B_1$ and that $n_2 = B_2(1,000/100) = 10B_2$, we have $n_1 = 4.08993$ and $n_2 = 5.91007$. The fact that n_1 and n_2 are not integers may prevent our actually achieving a portfolio of duration $D = 16$ with only \$1,000 invested and with only these two bonds. We can attempt to come only as close as possible. Note though, that if $V = \$1,000,000$, we find that $n_1 = 4,089.93$ and $n_2 = 5,910.07$, so that we obviously get much closer to the portfolio duration of 6-month periods, the larger the amount invested in the portfolio.

These examples illustrate the usefulness of equation (4.1). The duration D of the portfolio can never be larger than the larger duration of the two securities and it can never be smaller than the smaller duration of the two securities; hence D always lies somewhere between D_1 and D_2. Equation (4.1) is particularly useful in that we can always calculate the proportions B_1 and B_2 that correspond to any given duration between D_1 and D_2; and given B_1 and B_2 we can always calculate the number of units of each security that must be acquired in order to obtain the given portfolio duration D. That is, $n_1 = B_1 V/p_1$ and $n_2 = B_2 V/p_2$. The second example, above, well illustrates how n_1 and n_2 can be calculated so as to achieve a given portfolio duration D.

An investor faced with the opportunity to buy a variety of securities can form a portfolio of them so that the portfolio duration D lies anywhere between the smallest and largest durations of the available securities. The portfolio need not contain only two securities as suggested by equation (4.1). As shown in Appendix 4A, equation (4.1) can be extended so that the portfolio duration for a portfolio containing any number of securities can be similarly calculated as a weighted average.

An investor can regard the portfolio duration as a decision variable. Given the array of securities available, and their corresponding durations, the investor can choose a particular duration by investing appropriate amounts in each of a selected set of various securities. The investor can often determine the duration by investing in several different portfolios. For example, suppose three different securities have the respective durations of 3, 6, and 9 years. If 50% of an investment is allocated to each of the first two securities, a portfolio of 4.5 years is obtained. On the other hand, if 75% is allocated to the first security and 25% to the last, the same duration of 4.5 years is obtained. As long as the investor can choose from three or more securities with different durations, there are many different portfolios that can be constructed having the same duration.

Any investor who acquires a portfolio of fixed-income securities is making a duration decision, consciously or unconsciously. Let us now consider some of the consequences of that duration decision.

THE DURATION WINDOW

In Chapter 1, it was shown that any two securities with the same yield to maturity are perfect substitutes as long as the yield to maturity does not change as time passes. The yield to maturity simply becomes the rate of growth of the value of each security over time as the cash flows are reinvested at the same rate. If V dollars is invested in either of two securities having the annual yield to maturity r, then after K periods the investment grows to a value of $(1+r')^K V$ regardless of how the cash flows are reinvested, as long as they are reinvested in securities having the same annual yield to maturity r.[1] In this case, with an unchanged yield to maturity over time, the durations and other characteristics of the securities are irrelevant because the securities are perfect substitutes. If interest rates change over time, however, perfect substitutability breaks down, and the rate of growth in investment value will not be the same for each security.

In order to examine the effects of changing yields, we adopt a particular framework of analysis. First, let a portfolio of securities be initially acquired with a value of $V = V(r')$ dollars, where r' is the yield to maturity at which all the securities in the portfolio are priced and where r', as before, is measured as the interest rate over the period between cash flows. Writing $V(r')$ in this functional form means that the value of the income stream initially acquired is a function of r'. Second, let the yield to maturity change to $r^{*'}$, where $r^{*'}$ may be greater or less than r', and where the change occurs instantly after the portfolio has been acquired. Hence, if $r^{*\prime} > r'$, there will be an immediate decrease in the value of the investment to $V(r^{*\prime})$; and if $r^{*\prime} < r'$, there will be an immediate increase in the value of the investment to $V(r^{*\prime})$. Third, let the new value of the investment grow at the rate $r^{*\prime}$ per period for the remainder of the life of the portfolio. That is, we let all the cash flows as they are received be reinvested at the rate $r^{*\prime}$. After the change in rates to $r^{*\prime}$, it makes no difference how the cash flows are reinvested because if $r^{*\prime}$ remains unchanged, thereafter, all securities again become perfect substitutes. At the end of K periods, the value of the investment fund will then be

$$V_K = (1 + r^{*\prime})^K V(r^{*\prime}). \tag{4.2}$$

This development is illustrated in Figure 4-1. In that diagram $V(r')$, the initial value of the investment, is indicated on the vertical axis where time $t = 0$. If the yield to maturity remains unchanged over time, this amount will grow to $(1 + r')^K V(r')$ as indicated on the vertical line through the point on the horizontal axis where time $t = K$. If interest rates rise to $r^{*\prime}$, where $r^{*\prime} > r'$, then the value of the initial investment drops instantly to $V(r^{*\prime})$ also indicated on the vertical axis at time $t = 0$. Thereafter, however, the investment fund grows at the higher rate $r^{*\prime}$ and becomes $(1 + r^{*\prime})^K V(r^{*\prime})$, an amount

Figure 4-1. Impact of Interest Rate Changes on Growth of Investment Fund

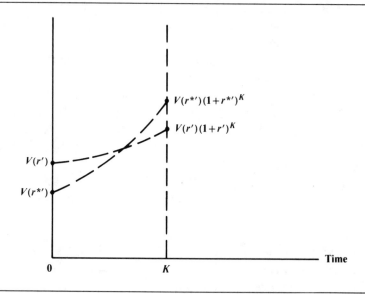

that exceeds $V(r')(1+r')^K$ for this example. This illustration shows that there are, indeed, offsetting effects produced by the change in the yield to maturity. First, there is the capital loss, $V(r') - V(r^{*'})$, produced by the initial increase in yields, and next we see that this is offset in time by reinvestment at the higher rate $r^{*'}$. We can also see these offsetting tendencies in equation (4.2) itself. As $r^{*'}$ rises, $V(r^{*'})$ falls; but $(1+r^{*'})^K$ increases. The two terms in equation (4.2) move in opposite directions in response to a change in the yield to maturity.

A numerical illustration of these offsetting tendencies and other features of the growth paths described in Figure 4-1 will pinpoint some of the major ideas involved in the description of these offsetting tendencies over time. Consider the portfolio constructed in the second example of the previous section. This portfolio consists of two par bonds with coupon rates of 10%. One bond is a 10-year bond with a duration of 13.085321 6-month periods, and the other is a 20-year bond with a duration of 18.017041 6-month periods. Suppose we invest $1,000,000 in a portfolio of these bonds having a duration of sixteen 6-month periods. As shown in the example, this requires that the portfolio contain 4,089.93 10-year bonds and 5,910.07 20-year bonds.[2] At the par price of $100 per bond, $408,993 is invested in 10-year bonds and $591,007 is invested in 20-year bonds, for a total of $1,000,000 in the investment fund. Table 4-1 shows what happens to the initial value of the portfolio as yields change instantly after the $1,000,000 is committed to these 10- and 20-year bonds, and how the investment fund grows in value at the new rate as time passes. The first row of the table for $K = 0$ gives the value of the investment fund instantly after the yield change. As expected, when yields fall the value of the fund increases and when yields rise the value of the fund decreases. Each of the columns indicates the value of the fund after K 6-month periods, where the fund grows from its base at $K = 0$ at the annual rate heading the column. For example, when interest rates fall from 10% to 7%, the initial value of the fund increases to $1,277 thousand but then grows at the annual rate of 7% per period from $1,277 thousand to $1,321 thousand in one period, to $1,367 thousand in two periods, to $1,415 thousand in three periods, and so forth. This table provides many illustrations of the two curves in Figure 4-1 where there is the initial change in the value of the investment fund and then there is continued growth thereafter at the new rate. Table 4-1 illustrates such pairs of curves for 12 different yield changes.

The most remarkable feature of the illustration in Table 4-1 is the value of the fund for every yield change after sixteen 6-month periods have passed. If interest rates do not change at all and remain at the annual rate of 10%,

Table 4-1. The Value for Various Yield Changes at 6-Month Intervals of a Portfolio with a Duration of Sixteen 6-Month Periods, an Initial Value of $1,000,000, and an Initial Yield of 10%

| Period | Annual Yield (Rounded to $000) | | | | | | | | | | | | |
K	7.0%	7.5%	8.0%	8.5%	9.0%	9.5%	10.0%	10.5%	11.0%	11.5%	12.0%	12.5%	13.0%
0	1,277	1,223	1,173	1,125	1,081	1,039	1,000	963	928	895	864	835	807
1	1,321	1,269	1,219	1,173	1,130	1,089	1,050	1,014	979	947	916	887	859
2	1,367	1,316	1,268	1,223	1,180	1,140	1,103	1,068	1,033	1,001	971	942	915
3	1,415	1,366	1,319	1,275	1,234	1,195	1,158	1,123	1,090	1,059	1,029	1,001	975
4	1,465	1,417	1,372	1,329	1,289	1,251	1,216	1,182	1,150	1,120	1,091	1,064	1,038
5	1,516	1,470	1,427	1,386	1,347	1,311	1,276	1,244	1,213	1,184	1,156	1,130	1,106
6	1,569	1,525	1,484	1,445	1,408	1,373	1,340	1,309	1,280	1,252	1,226	1,201	1,178
7	1,624	1,582	1,543	1,506	1,471	1,438	1,407	1,378	1,350	1,324	1,299	1,276	1,254
8	1,681	1,642	1,605	1,570	1,537	1,506	1,477	1,450	1,424	1,400	1,377	1,356	1,336
9	1,740	1,703	1,669	1,637	1,606	1,578	1,551	1,526	1,503	1,481	1,460	1,441	1,422
10	1,801	1,767	1,736	1,706	1,679	1,653	1,629	1,606	1,585	1,566	1,548	1,531	1,515
11	1,864	1,833	1,805	1,779	1,754	1,731	1,710	1,691	1,673	1,656	1,640	1,626	1,613
12	1,929	1,902	1,877	1,854	1,833	1,814	1,796	1,780	1,765	1,751	1,739	1,728	1,718
13	1,996	1,973	1,952	1,933	1,916	1,900	1,886	1,873	1,862	1,852	1,843	1,836	1,830
14	2,066	2,047	2,030	2,015	2,002	1,990	1,980	1,971	1,964	1,958	1,954	1,951	1,949
15	2,139	2,124	2,112	2,101	2,092	2,085	2,079	2,075	2,072	2,071	2,071	2,073	2,075
16	2,213	2,203	2,196	2,190	2,186	2,184	2,183	2,184	2,186	2,190	2,195	2,202	2,210
17	2,291	2,286	2,284	2,283	2,285	2,287	2,292	2,298	2,306	2,316	2,327	2,340	2,354
18	2,371	2,372	2,375	2,380	2,387	2,396	2,407	2,419	2,433	2,449	2,467	2,486	2,507
19	2,454	2,461	2,470	2,482	2,495	2,510	2,527	2,546	2,567	2,590	2,615	2,641	2,670
20	2,540	2,554	2,569	2,587	2,607	2,629	2,653	2,680	2,708	2,739	2,771	2,806	2,844
21	2,629	2,649	2,672	2,697	2,724	2,754	2,786	2,820	2,857	2,896	2,938	2,982	3,028
22	2,721	2,749	2,779	2,812	2,847	2,885	2,925	2,968	3,014	3,063	3,114	3,168	3,225
23	2,816	2,852	2,890	2,931	2,975	3,022	3,072	3,124	3,180	3,239	3,301	3,366	3,435
24	2,915	2,959	3,006	3,056	3,109	3,165	3,225	3,288	3,355	3,425	3,499	3,577	3,658
25	3,017	3,070	3,126	3,186	3,249	3,316	3,386	3,461	3,539	3,622	3,709	3,800	3,896
26	3,122	3,185	3,251	3,321	3,395	3,473	3,556	3,643	3,734	3,830	3,931	4,038	4,149

the investment fund grows to $2,183 thousand at the end of sixteen 6-month periods. Looking at the values of the investment fund after sixteen 6-month periods in cases where there have been yield changes, we observe that there is not a single case in which the value of the investment fund falls below $2,183 thousand in sixteen 6-month periods. In fact, in most cases the value of the fund slightly exceeds $2,183 thousand after sixteen 6-month periods. The sixteen 6-month period can be called the *duration window*. No matter what the yield change might be, after sixteen 6-month periods the accumulated value of the investment fund will *not* fall below the *threshold* level of $2,183 thousand, which is the value occurring if there are no yield changes at all. The window at sixteen 6-month periods represents an interval with a lower bound of $2,183 thousand through which *all* investment paths must pass in this illustration. Figure 4–2 shows the duration window and three of the

Figure 4–2.   Investment Accumulation and the Duration Window

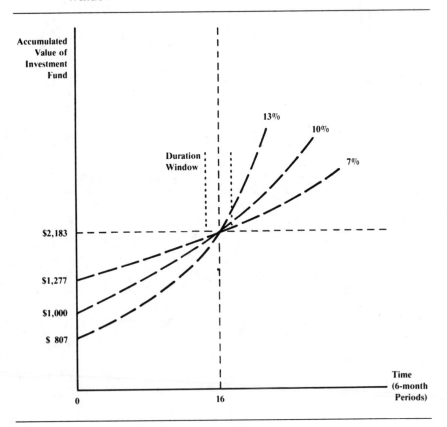

investment paths of this illustration. The diagram shows the two extreme investment paths for 13% and 7%. These can be compared with the 10% investment path. The paths not graphed would show the same characteristics when compared with the 10% path.

The offsetting tendencies suggested in Figure 4-1 and apparent in equation (4.2) can now be stated with great precision.

The time required for investment accumulation to offset any capital gain or loss from any *change in yields is exactly equal to the initial duration of the portfolio.*

Not only are the price and reinvestment effects offsetting, but the growth period over which the reinvestment occurs is exactly the same regardless of the direction or magnitude of the initial change in yields. This result holds for all portfolios so constructed. The duration window will always occur at the duration of the portfolio; virtually every investment path must pass through this window at some point no lower than the threshold level which is given by the investment path corresponding to the case in which there is no change in the interest rate. The reasons for this strong precision and the existence of the duration window lie in the convex nature of the accumulated value of the investment fund as a function of the initial yield change. Appendix 4B explains the mathematics of this result.

THE PLANNING PERIOD

Financial institutions—pension funds, life insurance companies, property and casualty insurance companies, depository financial institutions, finance companies—as well as individual households and business firms establish investment funds for a purpose. These purposes may range widely. For many of these financial entities, the investment fund is intended for particular future uses of the generated funds at particular future dates. A financial entity may convert some or all of the investment fund to cash so as to meet scheduled liability obligations, tax liabilities, the company payroll, real investment objectives, consumption expenditures, dividend commitments, or other obligations foreseen as requiring a cash dispersal at future dates. Conversion of an investment fund to cash at those dates ends the reinvestment and growth process. The length of time that the investment fund is active is called the *planning period.*

Many investors, particularly some households, may not have well-defined planning periods. Their investment fund consists of savings that is intended for expenditures on currently unknown future dates or for currently unknown contingencies that may require a cash conversion. These investors have *uncertain* planning periods. However, in formulating their investment funds, they can be viewed as currently considering the possible accumulated values of their funds at various future dates. Analytically, it may even be sensible to ascribe probabilities to possible conversion dates and to describe a household as investing so as to take into account such probabilities. For example, a household may invest a substantial portion of its assets in 6-month certificates of deposit, knowing full well that a cash conversion before the elapse of 6 months implies a penalty and hence a lower interest return, but yet the household may undertake the investment because it ascribes a low probability to the event requiring early liquidation. Knowing or having some notion of the probabilities when conversions will be required, enables an investor to array many investment funds, each with a different planning period, so as to meet the cash conversions at minimal costs. In other words, the investor is viewed as maintaining a planned liquidity position that allows meeting probable conversions from one fund or another at future dates. Although the planning periods for such investors may be uncertain, the investor may still design each investment fund as though it had a specific planning period. Although the anticipated magnitudes of cash conversions may not be the actual ones, the plan may be sufficiently close to minimize unexpected transactions costs as well as the opprobrium of default.

The length of a planning period may depend on many subjective considerations. An investor who is extremely confident that interest rates will fall in the imminent future may wish to design a fund containing par or premium bonds with extremely long maturities and with coupon rates as small as possible. From the preceding chapter, we know that such bonds have relatively long durations and any decline in interest rates will imply a maximal increase in the value of the fund. Such an investor has a planning period induced by the strong belief that interest rates will fall. The planning period for the investment fund may be only as long as the future period over which it is anticipated that rates will fall. Notice, though, that if rates should increase rather than fall, the investor could experience a considerable capital loss. The first row or two of Table 4–1 shows this plainly. One may view this investor's planning period as induced by strong beliefs as to what will happen in the financial markets, and to the investor's disposition to accept the risk of being wrong. The planning period is affected by the investor's speculative disposition.

As defined, many financial entities have many different planning periods because there may be many future dates at which cash conversions are planned. It is possible to design and manage a single portfolio of financial securities that will satisfy each of the liquidity requirements at the end of each planning period. It is *not* necessary that there be an investment fund for each planning period. However, in the remainder of this chapter, we assume that there is a single planning period corresponding to every investment fund. This not only simplifies the analysis, it forms a foundation for the study of portfolio designs to meet multiple-period cash conversion requirements.

DURATION AND THE PLANNING PERIOD

Table 4-1 contains an illustration of the relationship between the accumulated value of an investment fund, the time period for which the fund is active (the planning period), and the duration of the investment fund. In order to see the relationship, here, more clearly, the values in Table 4-1 are transformed into *realized* rates of return for various periods.

The realized rate of return is $\bar{r}'$ and it must satisfy the equation

$$(1+\bar{r}')^K(1,000,000) = (1+r^{*\prime})^K V(r^{*\prime}), \tag{4.3}$$

where, as before $r^{*\prime}$ is the new yield to maturity determined instantly after an initial investment has been made and where $r^{*\prime}$ is the rate of interest appropriate for the intervals between the cash flows. That is, $r^{*\prime} = r^*/n$ where r^* is the new annual yield and n is the number of intervals into which a year has been divided to determine the interest rate appropriate for the time between cash flows. In Table 4-1, $n = 2$ because the illustration is for bonds with semiannual coupon payments. The right-hand side of equation (4.3) gives the accumulated value of the investment fund for K, the number of periods, and $r^{*\prime}$, the new yield to maturity. The left-hand side of the equation is, of course, the same amount but it is expressed as the product of the initial investment of \$1,000,000 and of the term $(1+\bar{r}')^K$, which gives us the realized annual rate of return over K periods; that is, the annual realized rate is $\bar{r} = n\bar{r}'$ where $n = 2$. Note that $\bar{r}$ is also a function of K and r^*. It is possible to reconstruct Table 4-1 in terms of the realized rate of return $\bar{r}$. Table 4-2 gives the corresponding realized rates of return. This table would be relevant no matter what the value of the initial investment fund, and one can tell at a glance how the fund grows for every time period at every new yield to maturity r^*.

The realized rate of return incorporates the initial capital gain or loss arising when r shifts to r^* as well as the interest accumulation arising from the cash flows and their reinvestment. This is particularly apparent when we

Table 4-2. The Realized Annual Rate of Return at 6-Month Intervals for a Portfolio with a Duration of Sixteen 6-Month Periods Which Has Been Invested at an Initial Yield to Maturity of 10%

Period K	Annual Yield (r*) (%)												
	7.0%	7.5%	8.0%	8.5%	9.0%	9.5%	10.0%	10.5%	11.0%	11.5%	12.0%	12.5%	13.0%
1	64.24	53.74	43.89	34.63	25.92	17.73	10.00	2.71	− 4.16	−10.66	−16.80	−22.61	−28.11
2	33.87	29.46	25.23	21.18	17.30	13.57	10.00	6.57	3.28	0.12	− 2.92	− 5.85	− 8.65
3	24.55	21.89	19.53	16.87	14.50	12.21	10.00	7.87	5.82	3.84	1.93	0.09	− 1.69
4	20.03	18.20	16.44	14.74	13.11	11.53	10.00	8.53	7.10	5.73	4.40	3.12	1.88
5	17.36	16.02	14.73	13.48	12.28	11.12	10.00	8.92	7.88	6.87	5.90	4.96	4.06
6	15.60	14.58	13.59	12.64	11.73	10.85	10.00	9.18	8.39	7.63	6.90	6.20	5.52
7	14.35	13.55	12.78	12.05	11.34	10.66	10.00	9.37	8.76	8.18	7.62	7.09	6.57
8	13.41	12.78	12.18	11.60	11.04	10.51	10.00	9.51	9.04	8.59	8.17	7.76	7.37
9	12.69	12.19	11.71	11.25	10.82	10.40	10.00	9.62	9.26	8.92	8.59	8.28	7.99
10	12.12	11.72	11.34	10.98	10.63	10.31	10.00	9.71	9.43	9.17	8.93	8.70	8.48
11	11.65	11.33	11.03	10.75	10.48	10.23	10.00	9.78	9.57	9.38	9.20	9.04	8.89
12	11.25	11.01	10.78	10.56	10.36	10.17	10.00	9.84	9.69	9.56	9.44	9.33	9.23
13	10.92	10.74	10.56	10.40	10.26	10.12	10.00	9.89	9.79	9.71	9.63	9.57	9.52
14	10.64	10.50	10.38	10.27	10.17	10.08	10.00	9.93	9.88	9.83	9.81	9.78	9.76
15	10.40	10.30	10.22	10.15	10.09	10.04	10.00	9.97	9.95	9.95	9.95	9.96	9.98
16	10.18	10.13	10.08	10.04	10.02	10.00	10.00	10.00	10.02	10.04	10.07	10.12	10.16
17	9.99	9.97	9.96	9.95	9.96	9.98	10.00	10.03	10.08	10.13	10.19	10.25	10.33
18	9.83	9.83	9.85	9.87	9.91	9.95	10.00	10.06	10.13	10.20	10.29	10.38	10.48
19	9.68	9.71	9.75	9.80	9.86	9.93	10.00	10.08	10.17	10.27	10.38	10.49	10.61
20	9.54	9.60	9.66	9.73	9.82	9.90	10.00	10.10	10.21	10.33	10.46	10.59	10.73
21	9.42	9.50	9.58	9.68	9.78	9.88	10.00	10.12	10.25	10.39	10.53	10.68	10.84
22	9.31	9.41	9.51	9.62	9.74	9.87	10.00	10.14	10.29	10.44	10.60	10.76	10.93
23	9.20	9.32	9.44	9.57	9.71	9.85	10.00	10.16	10.32	10.48	10.66	10.84	11.02
24	9.12	9.25	9.38	9.53	9.68	9.84	10.00	10.17	10.35	10.53	10.71	10.91	11.11
25	9.03	9.18	9.33	9.49	9.65	9.82	10.00	10.18	10.37	10.57	10.77	10.97	11.18
26	8.95	9.11	9.28	9.45	9.63	9.81	10.00	10.20	10.40	10.60	10.81	11.03	11.25

consider two extreme cases in Table 4–2. Consider the tremendous drop in rates from 10% to 7%. This produces a very large capital gain relative to the interest return in 6 months' time and that is why the annual realized rate of return is 64.24% over the first 6 months. At the other extreme, suppose the yield increases from 10% to 13%. This produces an enormous capital loss, so that the annual realized rate of return after 6 months is -28.11%; the interest return in 6 months is not sufficient even to produce a net positive rate of return. Yet, after 13 years (twenty-six 6-month periods) the reinvestment of cash flows at the high rate of 13% produces an annual realized rate of return of 11.25%, thus swamping the impact of the initial capital loss.

The realized rate of return for selected time periods and yields to maturity r^* is plotted in Figure 4–3. Each line in the graph corresponds to a particular time period over which the investment fund is maintained.

The line for sixteen 6-month periods represents the annual realized rate of return described in the row of Table 4–2 for which $K = 16$. The effects of

Figure 4–3. Investment Accumulation: Different Investment Periods and Different Interest Rate Changes

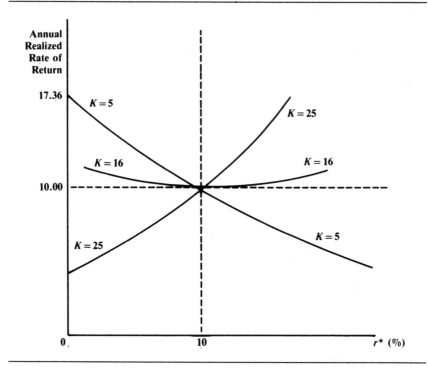

the duration window are immediately clear. The annual realized rate of return is never less than 10% for this period of time although the return can be slightly greater than 10% as Table 4-2 shows. If the portfolio is liquidated in exactly 16 months, the annual realized rate of return will not fall below 10% regardless of the direction or magnitude of change in interest rates. The portfolio of securities is said to be *immunized* because the portfolio return is immune from changes in interest rates; the realized rate of return can never fall below the threshold level of the duration window. This result holds generally and the rule can be stated as follows:

> *If a portfolio of securities is selected so that its duration is exactly equal to the length of the planning period, the portfolio is immunized so that he annual realized rate of return can never fall below the initial yield to maturity at which the securities were purchased.*

On the other hand, consider the row labeled $K = 5$. The annual realized rate of return declines steadily from 17.36% to 4.06% as the yields shift from 7% to 13%. Here, the effect of the initial capital gain or loss dominates the return over five 6-month periods. Five periods of time, even with reinvestment at 13%, is not sufficient to cover the initial losses when the yield to maturity shifted from 10% to 13%; nor is a low rate of reinvestment at 7% sufficient to dissipate the large capital gains made when the yield to maturity shifted from 10% to 7%. If the planning period were five 6-month periods, a portfolio having a duration of sixteen 6-month periods results in the capital gains or losses dominating the realized return over the planning period. If an investor constructs a portfolio of securities for which the duration exceeds the planning period, the investor can be viewed as *going long*. The illustration can be generalized to cover any planning period length or portfolio duration. The general rule can be stated as follows:

> *If the portfolio duration exceeds the length of the planning period, capital gains or losses incorporated into the annual realized rate of return and resulting from initial yield changes will dominate the reinvestment return over the planning period.*

Thus, if yields decrease, the resulting capital gain implies the annual realized rate of return will exceed the initial yield to maturity; and, if yields increase, the resulting capital losses imply the annual realized rate of return will be less than the initial yield to maturity.

Next, consider the line labeled $K = 25$. In contrast to the previous case, the annual realized rate of return is now dominated by the reinvestment return.

Enough time has passed since the initial yield change for the reinvestment effects to swamp the initial capital gains or losses. Let the planning period be twenty-five 6-month periods. Then the portfolio duration of sixteen periods is less than the planning period. Such an investor is *going short*. The general rule is the following.

If the portfolio duration is less than the length of the planning period, the reinvestment return incorporated into the realized rate of return will dominate any initial capital gain or loss resulting from yield changes.

MULTIPERIOD YIELD CHANGES AND DYNAMIC DURATION-BASED INVESTMENT STRATEGIES

The analytical framework of the previous two sections is very simple. A portfolio of securities is selected. Instantly after this selection the yields to maturity change unpredictably and do not change thereafter as the portfolio accumulates in value. Realistically, the yields on securities change frequently in response to constantly shifting demand and supply conditions in the financial markets. Although the previous framework must certainly be viewed as unrealistic in view of frequently changing yields, this framework can be extended to cover more realistic situations.

To modify the framework, we now stipulate the following sequence of events over the investor's planning period. At the beginning of each period, the investor constructs a portfolio of securities. Instantly after that portfolio is constructed, the yield to maturity on the acquired securities changes unpredictably. The process in this form continues through time to the end of the investor's planning period. In other words, this new framework allows for continual repetition, period after period, of what was previously restricted only to the beginning of the first period in the previous framework.

The consequence of the immunization strategy can easily be geometrically described within this framework. Figure 4–4 displays the results of pursuing the immunization strategy in which the duration of the portfolio at the beginning of each period is set equal to the remaining time in the planning period. Let the planning period at the start of the first period ($t = 0$) be equal to q periods, as noted on the abscissa in Figure 4–4. Following the immunization strategy the investor allocates his available funds, V_0, to securities such that the portfolio has a duration of q periods. The value V_0 is indicated on the vertical axis in the diagram. If interest rates do not change at all during the planning period, the investment fund grows to $V_q = (1 + r')^k V_0$ as

Figure 4-4.   The Dynamic Investment Accumulation Plan

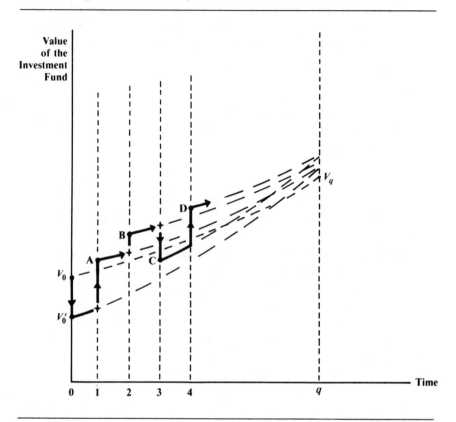

indicated by the dashed curve connecting V_0 with V_q in the diagram. Now, suppose that yields to maturity increase instantly after V_0 has been allocated. This instantly decreases the value of the portfolio to some number V_0' as indicated on the vertical axis in the diagram. If the yields to maturity do not subsequently change during the planning period, the value of the portfolio grows along a curve to a point slightly above V_q, as shown in the diagram. Since interest rates do not change until period $t = 1$ is reached, the only point on this curve that is realized is the one marked with an "×" above time period $t = 1$. This accumulated value at time period 1 is then reallocated among securities so that its duration is equal to $(q - 1)$ the remaining time to the end of the planning period. Instantly after this reallocation, suppose that interest rates decrease. This immediately results in the accumulated value rising at time period 1 to the point labeled A in the diagram. Since the portfolio is immunized it follows that if there are no subsequent changes in the yield to maturity, the value of the portfolio will grow to a point just above the previous point on the vertical line above q. This must happen because the previous point just above V_q has become the threshold of the duration window and since the portfolio is immunized for $(q-1)$ periods the curve of accumulation must pass through that window. The only point on this curve that can be realized, however, is the point marked "×" just above period 2. At this point, the portfolio is again reallocated to securities so that the duration is equal to $(q-2)$, the remaining time in the planning period. Again, instantly after this reallocation, suppose yields again decrease. This instantly increases the value of the portfolio at time period 2 to a point labeled B in the diagram. Again, if there are no subsequent changes in yields, the portfolio grows at this new yield to the point just above the last one on the vertical line above q, as shown by the dashed line extending from B to the end of the planning period. So the process continues. Allowing for an increase in rates at time period 3 after the duration adjustment and for a decrease in yields at time period 4, the realized investment growth path goes successively to point C and D, but always along a dashed curve that is headed for some point in the duration window at time period q. It follows from this description of the dynamic growth process that the final value of the investment fund will never be less than the original threshold value of V_q. In other words, the simple analysis in the previous framework still applies; the initial duration window given at the start of the process remains — although the threshold level may increase slightly — and the accumulated value of the investment fund must pass through it, regardless of the direction or magnitude of change in interest rates during the planning period.

In the dynamic process just described, adjustment of the portfolio duration at the start of each period may be necessary. If the duration at the start of a period is equal to D, it may not be $(D-1)$ at the end of the period as required in order for it to be equal to the remaining time in the planning period. This may be so for two reasons. First, as the yield changes the duration changes, as we noted in Chapter 3. This can force the initial duration up or down depending on the direction of the yield change. Second, as the bonds (or mortgages) held decrease in maturity, the duration will decrease (except for some discount bonds noted in Chapter 3), but this decrease can never be as much as the decrease in maturity. This is shown in Figure 3-6, where as maturity decreases the duration goes down but never by as much as the maturity decreases because the slope of all the duration lines there are less than unity (except for that of the zero coupon bonds).[3]

There are two ways that the duration of the portfolio can be adjusted at the end of each period. First, the cash flows received can be invested to their full extent in those securities which will bring down the portfolio duration as necessary. Second, some securities in the portfolio can be sold and others can be bought as necessary to adjust the duration.

A duration-based investment strategy other than the immunization strategy cannot easily be depicted in Figure 4–4. However, some generalizations about what can be expected from "going long" or "going short" are possible. If an investor goes long by always selecting the securities so that duration exceeds the remaining time in the planning period, then the investor secures a return greater or less than the immunized return according as the trend of interest rates is increasing during the planning period. The expected results are vice versa if the investor goes short by selecting durations less than the remaining time in the planning period.

THE DYNAMIC IMMUNIZATION STRATEGY: AN ILLUSTRATION

Figure 4–4 shows very well in a single diagram how the immunization strategy forces the terminal liquidation value of the portfolio through the duration window. Behind the scenes, however, there are continual portfolio adjustments that are necessary in order to make this possible. In this section, an illustration is presented. This illustration shows exactly, period by period, what those adjustments are.

The portfolio described in this illustration consists of only two bonds. At the start of the planning period, one of these bonds, called the "short" bond, is a 4-year 8% coupon bond; and the other, called a "long" bond, is a 10-year 8% coupon bond. The planning period is 4 years. A portfolio of the two bonds can always be formed so that the portfolio duration is always equal to the time remaining in the planning period. The yield to maturity is assumed to change every 6 months. Tables 4–3a to 4–3c give us the necessary data to show how the dynamic growth path of the investment fund will develop over the 4-year planning period. The first column in Tables 4–3a and 4–3b indicates the time period as measured in 6-month periods from the time of the initial investment. The next column gives the assumed annual yield that holds for the corresponding period. Initially the portfolio is formed when the bonds are priced at 7.5% as the yield to maturity. At the end of the first 6 months the bonds, having been reduced in maturity by 6 months, are then priced at 7.0% as the yield to maturity, and so forth. Column 3 shows the maturity of the bonds when their price is calculated. Column 4 shows the corresponding price and column 5 shows the corresponding duration in six-month periods. Table 4–3c shows the proportions B_1 and B_2 of the portfolio value which is invested in the short and long bonds in order to

Table 4–3. Information Required to Implement Immunization Strategy

a. The Price and Duration of a 4-Year 8% Coupon Bond over a 4-Year Planning Period

Time Period (in 6-Month Intervals)	Annual Yield Pattern	Bond Maturity (in 6-Month Periods)	Price	Duration (in 6-Month Periods)
0	7.5%	8	$101.70	7.01190
1	7.0	7	103.06	6.25540
2	8.0	6	100.00	5.45182
3	7.5	5	101.12	4.63226
4	8.5	4	99.10	3.77394
5	8.0	3	100.00	2.88609
6	9.0	2	99.06	1.96136
7	8.5	1	99.76	1.00000
8	9.5	0	100.00	0.00000

b. The Price and Duration of a 10-Year 8% Coupon Bond over a 4-Year Planning Period

Time Period (in 6-Month Intervals)	Annual Yield Pattern	Bond Maturity (in 6-Month Periods)	Price	Duration (in 6-Month Periods)
0	7.5%	20	$103.47	14.24506
1	7.0	19	106.85	13.85517
2	8.0	18	100.00	13.16567
3	7.5	17	103.10	12.72735
4	8.5	16	97.14	12.05326
5	8.0	15	100.00	11.56312
6	9.0	14	94.89	10.89259
7	8.5	13	97.54	10.34692
8	9.5	12	93.26	9.66719

c. Proportions B_1 and B_2 of Portfolio Value Invested, Respectively, in the 4-Year and 10-Year Bonds to Secure Duration Equal to Remaining Time in the Planning Period

Time Period K	B_1	B_2
0	.86339	.13661
1	.90202	.09798
2	.92894	.07106
3	.95457	.04543
4	.97270	.02730
5	.98687	.01313
6	.99567	.00433
7	1.00000	.00000

equate the portfolio duration to the time remaining in the planning period. Note that the proportion invested in the short bond continually increases until the entire portfolio is eventually invested in that bond at 6 months prior to the termination of the planning period. At 6 months prior to the termination date, the duration must be exactly 6 months, and this is achieved by total concentration of the investment in the short bond. The proportions invested in the short bond must increase because the portfolio duration does not decrease as fast as time passes; for example, if 6 months pass, the portfolio duration, with unchanged proportions B_1 and B_2, will decrease by less than 6 months.

Table 4-4 shows the period-by-period growth and adjustment process. Initially at $K = 0$, the value of the investment fund is \$1,000,000 distributed among the two bonds as indicated. The number of units of each bond, having a face value of \$100, is found by dividing the dollar values, V_1 and V_2, by the corresponding prices in Tables 4-3a and 4-3b. At time period $K = 1$, 6 months later, the yield to maturity has dropped to 7.0%, and the value of the bonds held, the number of units of which was determined in $K = 0$, are accordingly revalued using the prices in Tables 4-3a and 4-3b. Adding in the semiannual coupon income of \$4 per bond gives us the portfolio value after 6 months have passed. Reallocation, as shown, is accomplished by selling some long bonds and buying some short bonds. The entire amount of coupon income has gone toward the purchase of short bonds; but, in order to reduce the duration to seven 6-month periods, some long bonds must be sold. The process continues in this manner to the end of the planning period. In time period $K = 7$, the entire accumulated value of the portfolio is concentrated in short bonds. At the end of the planning period of 4 years, the portfolio is liquidated at the face value of the securities to which has been added the final coupon income. If the yield to maturity had remained constant over the planning period at 7%, the accumulation would have been slightly less than that achieved by the immunization strategy with fluctuating interest rates. That is, the immunization strategy forces the liquidation value of the portfolio through the duration window.

Notes to Table 4-4

Initially a 10-year and 4-year 8% coupon bond form a portfolio with duration equal to the 4-year planning period. The 10-year bond is the long bond; the 4-year bond is the short bond. As time passes, these bonds are bought and sold so as to keep the duration equal to remaining time in the planning period. Data used is in Table 4-3. V_1 = value of short bonds held; V_2 = value of long bonds held; n_1 = number of short bonds held; n_2 = number of long bonds held; K = time period; V = value of the portfolio. Rounding may prevent reproduction of some numbers, because original calculations carried to nine decimal places.

Table 4–4. Illustration of the Dynamic Immunization Adjustment Process

---

At $K = 0$: $V_1 = \$\ \ 863.392.90$ $n_1 = 8,489.55$
$V_2 = \$\ \ 136,607.10$ $n_2 = 1,320.21$
$V = \$1,000,000.00$

At $K = 1$:   Coupon income = $39,239.01
Buy 746.40 short bonds; sell 352.66 long bonds
Value of holdings: $V_1 = \$\ \ 951,831.85$ $n_1 = 9,235.95$
$V_2 = \$\ \ 103,387.30$ $n_2 = \ \ \ 967.55$
$V = \$1,055,219.15$

At $K = 2$:   Coupon income = $40,813.99
Buy 621.58 short bonds; sell 213.44 long bonds
Value of holdings: $V_1 = \$\ \ 985,753.20$ $n_1 = 9,857.53$
$V_2 = \$\ \ \ \ 75,410.67$ $n_2 = \ \ \ 754.11$
$V = \$1,061,163.87$

At $K = 3$:   Coupon income = $42,446.55
Buy 686.84 short bonds; sell 261.95 long bonds
Value of holdings: $V_1 = \$1,066,255.73$ $n_1 = 10,544.37$
$V_2 = \$\ \ \ \ 50,741.83$ $n_2 = \ \ \ 492.16$
$V = \$1,116,997.56$

At $K = 4$:   Coupon income = $44,146.12
Buy 614.67 short bonds; sell 171.6 long bonds
Value of holdings: $V_1 = \$1,105,837.03$ $n_1 = 11,159.04$
$V_2 = \$\ \ \ \ 31,041.83$ $n_2 = \ \ \ 319.56$
$V = \$1,136,878.86$

At $K = 5$:   Coupon income = $45,914.40
Buy 621.99 short bonds; sell 162.85 long bonds
Value of holdings: $V_1 = \$1,178,103.42$ $n_1 = 11,781.03$
$V_2 = \$\ \ \ \ 15,670.95$ $n_2 = \ \ \ 156.71$
$V = \$1,193,774.37$

At $K = 6$:   Coupon income = $47,750.97
Buy 578.43 short bonds; sell 100.64 long bonds
Value of holdings: $V_1 = \$1,224,373.32$ $n_1 = 12,359.46$
$V_2 = \$\ \ \ \ \ 5,320.04$ $n_2 = \ \ \ \ 56.07$
$V = \$1,229,693.36$

At $K = 7$:   Coupon income = $49,662.10
Buy 552.63 short bonds; sell all remaining long bonds
Value of holdings: $V = V_1 = \$1,288,112.90$ $n_1 = 12,912.09$

At $K = 8$:   Coupon income = $\ \ \ 51,648.37$
Face value of short bonds = $1,291,208.33
$V = \$1,342,857.70$
Portfolio in cash

THE DYNAMIC IMMUNIZATION STRATEGY
WITH INCOMPLETE ADJUSTMENT

In the previous two sections, the dynamic immunization strategy involved perfect synchronization of the cash flow dates and the portfolio adjustment dates. Every date at which coupon income was received was also a date at which the portfolio was adjusted so that its duration was equal to the remaining time in the planning period. In practice, large portfolios invariably have cash inflows on a very frequent basis, perhaps daily. As illustrated in the last section, the reinvestment of the cash flows only may not be sufficient to adjust fully the portfolio to its required duration. It may be necessary to sell and buy securities in the market. Frequent purchases and sales of securities in the market involve transactions costs — brokerage fees and other costs. In order to reduce these costs, the investor may choose to sell and buy securities less frequently, even though the portfolio may be temporarily out of balance. The cost in terms of not going through the duration window may be less than the transactions costs required to force the terminal portfolio value through the window.

In this section, we consider some illustrations of the dynamic immunization process with incomplete adjustment. In the first of these illustrations, consider the same illustration of the last section in which 4-year and 10-year bonds with 10% coupon rates were utilized in a portfolio to immunize the return over a planning period of 4 years. Table 4–5 shows the growth and adjustment of the investment fund when the adjustments of the duration are undertaken annually rather than semiannually. The same yield patterns, planning period, and optimal proportions are used as in Table 4–3 and 4–4. At dates $K = 1, 3, 5,$ and 7, only the coupon income is invested in the short bonds, whereas at dates $K = 0, 2, 4,$ and 6, the entire portfolio is adjusted according to the proportions required in Table 4–3c. As shown in Table 4–5, the number of long bonds is the same for periods $K = 0$ and 1, the same for $K = 2$ and 3, the same for $K = 4$ and 5, and the same for $K = 7$ and 8. The number of short bonds held increases each period as the coupon income is used to buy more of these bonds or on the annual dates long bonds are sold to buy more short bonds. At the end of the planning period, $K = 8$, the portfolio is liquidated. At that time, there will still remain some long bonds in the portfolio as determined optimally at $K = 6$, but not sold at $K = 7$. These bonds are liquidated at a yield to maturity of 9.5% as shown. The liquidation value of the portfolio is $1,338,930, which represents an annual growth rate over the four years (compounded semiannually) of 7.43%. The immu-

Table 4–5. Dynamic Immunization Illustration of Table 4–4 with Adjustments Annually Instead of Adjustments Every 6 Months, with Portfolio Values for Full Adjustment Given for Comparison

Time Period (6-Month Intervals)	Yield to Maturity	Value of Portfolio under Full Adjustment from Table 4–4	Value of Portfolio; Adjustment Every 12 Months	Number of Short Bonds Held	Number of Long Bonds Held
0	7.5%	$1,000,000	$1,000,000	8,490	1,320
1	7.0	1,055,219	1,055,219	8,870	1,320
2	8.0	1,061,164	1,059,812	9,845	753
3	7.5	1,116,998	1,115,575	10,264	753
4	8.5	1,136,879	1,134,390	11,135	319
5	8.0	1,193,774	1,191,161	11,593	319
6	9.0	1,229,693	1,226,323	12,326	56
7	8.5	1,288,113	1,284,583	12,822	56
8	9.5	1,342,858	1,338,930		
Annual realized rate of return:		7.51%	7.43%		

nization process with complete portfolio adjustment produced a liquidation value of $1,343,627 for an annual growth rate of 7.50%. Partial adjustment, therefore, produced a loss of 7 basis points in the annual growth rate. This loss does not appear to be excessive; but, in any case, this loss would have to be compared with transactions costs of securing complete relative to incomplete adjustment. Incomplete adjustment, here, implies that the investor is going long at various points during the planning period, because at times $K = 1, 3, 5,$ and 7, the duration of the portfolio after reinvesting the cash flows, exceeds the time remaining in the planning period. During periods in which the trend of interest rates is increasing, as in this illustration, the terminal value of the portfolio will tend to be less than the immunized value. If the trend in interest rates is downward, the effect of going long by partial adjustment may lift the liquidation value well into the duration window.

Other cases of incomplete adjustment are considered in Table 4-6a to 4-6c, where interest rates change according to three different scenarios. In the first of these scenarios, Table 4-6a, interest rates increase systematically from 7.5% to 15% over the 4-year period. Full adjustment of duration at each 6-month interval sends the growth path through the duration window at 7.51%. If one adjusts only every 12 months, as in Table 4-5, the realized annual rate of return is 7.45% — 5 basis points less than the minimal rate at the duration window. If one adjusts every 18 months — at dates $K = 3$ and $K = 6$ — the annual realized rate of return is even less at 7.4%. If a single adjustment occurs after 2 years, the annual realized rate of return is 7.33%. Finally if there is no adjustment at all, the realized rate of return is 7.09% — 41 basis points below the duration threshold. When the trend of interest rates is steadily upward, the failure to adjust the durations regularly can decrease the realized rate of return below the threshold of the duration window.

In Table 4-6b, interest rates increase even more dramatically. The effect is similar to that in Table 4-6a. The realized rate of return falls below the threshold of the duration window, and the less frequently adjustment occurs, the lower the realized rate of return. Compared with the interest rate scenario of Table 4-6a, the dramatic increase in rates in this example is considerably greater period by period, and yet the realized rates of return for the various adjustment periods do not appear to be significantly different. One should not attempt to generalize this result. For other bonds, other planning periods, and other increasing interest rate scenarios, the comparisons may well be different.

For contrast, Table 4-6c shows the result when interest rates fluctuate wildly. These changes are dramatically unrealistic. The only result of which we can be certain for such scenarios, however wild, is that the immunization

Table 4-6. Dynamic Immunization Illustration under Various Interest Rate Scenarios with Complete and Partial Adjustment

a. Rising Interest Rate Trend

Time Period K	Yields	Full Adjustment	12-Month Adjustment (at K = 2, 4, 6)	18-Month Adjustment (at K = 3, 6)	24-Month Adjustment (at K = 4)	No Adjustment
0	7.5%	$1,000,000	$1,000,000	$1,000,000	$1,000,000	$1,000,000
1	8.0	1,020,214	1,020,214	1,020,214	1,020,214	1,020,214
2	9.0	1,031,062	1,030,090	1,030,090	1,030,090	1,030,090
3	10.0	1,052,147	1,051,155	1,049,435	1,049,435	1,049,435
4	11.0	1,084,025	1,082,262	1,081,230	1,078,816	1,078,816
5	12.0	1,127,577	1,125,744	1,124,005	1,122,159	1,119,117
6	13.0	1,184,055	1,181,571	1,179,084	1,177,808	1,171,590
7	14.0	1,255,132	1,252,499	1,249,862	1,247,540	1,237,913
8	15.0	1,342,991	1,339,946	1,337,125	1,333,656	1,320,282
Realized annual yield		7.51%	7.45%	7.40%	7.33%	7.09%

b. Dramatically Rising Interest Rate Trend

Time Period K	Yields	Full Adjustment	12-Month Adjustment (at K = 2, 4, 6)	18-Month Adjustment (at K = 3, 6)	24-Month Adjustment (at K = 4)	No Adjustment
0	7.5%	$1,000,000	$1,000,000	$1,000,000	$1,000,000	$1,000,000
1	10.0	955,136	955,136	955,136	955,136	955,136
2	12.0	947,957	947,352	947,352	947,352	947,352
3	14.0	959,107	958,496	956,912	956,912	956,912
4	16.0	988,997	987,270	986,733	984,172	984,172
5	18.0	1,039,128	1,037,313	1,035,680	1,034,059	1,030,568
6	20.0	1,112,442	1,109,323	1,106,542	1,105,842	1,098,735
7	22.0	1,212,442	1,209,285	1,206,254	1,203,816	1,192,752
8	24.0	1,345,810	1,341,881	1,338,518	1,334,133	1,318,530
Realized annual yield		7.56%	7.49%	7.42%	7.34%	7.03%

Table 4-6 continued

c. Wildly Fluctuating Interest Rates

Time Period K	Yields	Full Adjustment	12-Month Adjustment (at K = 2, 4, 6)	18-Month Adjustment (at K = 3, 6)	24-Month Adjustment (at K = 4)	No Adjustment
0	7.5%	$1,000,000	$1,000,000	$1,000,000	$1,000,000	$1,000,000
1	10.0	955,136	955,136	955,136	955,136	955,136
2	14.0	897,417	896,336	896,336	896,336	896,336
3	6.0	1,170,147	1,168,737	1,173,524	1,173,524	1,173,524
4	14.0	1,038,344	1,018,842	1,041,340	1,018,821	1,018,821
5	10.0	1,176,442	1,154,347	1,179,704	1,154,322	1,165,486
6	20.0	1,127,073	1,098,655	1,123,061	1,098,632	1,086,395
7	16.0	1,262,848	1,231,006	1,258,353	1,234,433	1,229,355
8	6.0	1,363,875	1,333,588	1,363,213	1,351,254	1,380,642
Realized annual yield		7.91%	7.33%	7.90%	7.67%	8.23%

strategy with complete adjustment forces the realized annual rate of return through the duration window. It does so in this case at 7.91%, 41 basis points above the threshold of the duration window. For other cases of less frequent adjustment, the results are mixed. Sometimes the realized rate is above and sometimes it is below the threshold of the duration window. These mixed results occur because the portfolio duration may be larger in one case than in another at some time periods when interest rates change, so that the effects can be considerably different across the planning period.

The effects of partial adjustment may be less for some mortgage portfolios. Mortgages do not have balloon payments unless their unpaid balances are paid before maturity. In other words, the cash flows are larger relative to the size of the investment fund. This means that a reinvestment of the cash flows may secure a more complete adjustment so that the extent of the required buying and selling of mortgages in the market may be reduced.

APPENDIX 4A
DURATIONS OF PORTFOLIOS

In this chapter it was claimed that the duration of a portfolio of two different securities could be derived using the expression

$$D = B_1 D_1 + B_2 D_2, \tag{4A.1}$$

where D_1 and D_2 are the durations of the two securities held in the portfolio, and B_1 and B_2 are the proportions of the values of each represented in the portfolio. This appendix contains a proof and an indication of the generalization of this result.

Let $(F_1^1, F_2^1, ..., F_M^1)$ and $(F_1^2, F_2^2, ..., F_N^2)$ be the respective income streams of the two securities. Then, by definition, the values of each of the two securities held is

$$V_1 = \sum_t F_t^1 (1+r')^{-t}, \quad \text{and}$$
$$V_2 = \sum_t F_t^2 (1+r')^{-t}. \tag{4A.2}$$

The respective durations, by definition, are

$$D_1 = \sum_t t F_t^1 (1+r')^{-t}/V_1, \quad \text{and}$$
$$D_2 = \sum_t t F_t^2 (1+r')^{-t}/V_2. \tag{4A.3}$$

To find the duration of the portfolio, the two income streams must be added together to acquire $(F_1^1+F_1^2, F_2^1+F_2^2, F_3^2, ..., F_t^1+F_t^2, ...)$ where, if the two securities have different maturities, F_t^1 and/or F_t^2 may be zero for some of the components. The value of the portfolio is

$$V= \sum_t (F_t^1+F_t^2)(1+r')^{-t} = V_1+V_2. \qquad (4A.4)$$

The duration of the portfolio, by definition, is

$$D= \sum_t t(F_t^1+F_t^2)(1+r')^{-t}/V, \qquad (4A.5)$$

but

$$\sum_t t(F_t^1+F_t^2)(1+r')^{-t} = \sum_t tF_t^1(1+r')^{-t} + \sum_t tF_t^2(1+r')^{-t}$$

$$= V_1D_1 + V_2D_2, \qquad (4A.6)$$

using equation (4A.3). Then substituting (4A.6) into equation (4A.5) implies that

$$D = (V_1D_1+V_2D_2)/V$$

$$= \frac{V_1}{V}D_1 + \frac{V_2}{V}D_2. \qquad (4A.7)$$

However, $V_1/V=B_1$ and $V_2/V=B_2$. Hence, equation (4A.1) is the same as equation (4A.7).

To generalize this, we proceed in exactly the same way. Any number of income streams can be added together to acquire equation (4A.4) and (4A.6), so that, in a general equation (4A.7) becomes

$$D = B_1D_1 + B_2D_2 + \cdots + B_sD_s \qquad (4A.8)$$

when there are s bonds in the portfolio.

APPENDIX 4B
THE DURATION WINDOW

In the text, the illustration in Figure 4–2 and the data in Table 4–1 show that the value of an investment fund will pass through the duration window regardless of the initial and unknown change in the yield to maturity. This appendix contains a mathematical explanation of this result.

The initial value of the investment fund may be specified as

$$V(r') = \sum_t F_t(1+r')^{-t}, \qquad (4B.1)$$

where r' is the yield to maturity for the periods over which the flows are paid, and F_t is the cash flow at time t. Immediately after the acquisition of the rights to claim these cash flows, the yield changes to $r^{*'}$. This causes $V(r')$ to shift to $V(r^{*'})$. Thereafter, the investment fund grows at the rate $r^{*'}$ per period so that after K periods have passed, the value of the investment fund becomes

$$V_K(r^{*'}) = (1 + r^{*'})^K V(r^{*'}), \tag{4B.2}$$

and if there is no change in the yield to maturity this accumulated value is

$$V_K(r') = (1 + r')^K V(r'). \tag{4B.3}$$

Let D be the initial duration of the investment fund; that is, D is calculated at the rate r'. If the value of the investment fund passes through the duration window for all yield changes, then it must follow that

$$V_D(r^{*'}) \geq V_D(r'), \tag{4B.4}$$

because, with $D = K$, the value of the investment fund at $r^{*'}$ cannot fall below the threshold level $V_D(r')$.

The method of demonstrating that the duration window described in equation (4B.4) does, in fact, exist is as follows. First, we demonstrate that $V_K(r^{*'})$ is a strictly convex function of $r^{*'}$. This means that the shape of the function $V_K(r^{*'})$ for any value of K looks like the curve drawn in Figure 4B-1. Such a curve is strictly convex when given any two different points on it like A and B in the diagram, every point on the straight line connecting points A and B (excluding the points A and B themselves) lies above the curve. Second, given the curve is strictly convex, it will have a minimum point like that at point C in the diagram, if the slope of the curve at that point C is zero. This means, as is easily seen by examining the curve, that $V_K(r^{*'})$ for any value of $r^{*'}$ cannot fall below the value as determined at that minimum point. This minimum point forms the threshold of a window because all other values of $V_K(r^{*'})$ cannot be below it. Third, we show that $V_D(r^{*'})$ has its minimum point at the value where $r^{*'} = r'$, so that $V_D(r^{*'})$ can never be below the threshold level $V_D(r')$. The demonstration, thus, involves three steps.

1. *Strict Convexity.* Substituting equation (4B.1), evaluated at $r^{*'}$, into equation (4B.2) we have

$$V_K(r^{*'}) = (1 + r^{*'})^K \sum_t F_t (1 + r^{*'})^{-t}$$

$$= \sum_t F_t (1 + r^{*'})^{K-t}. \tag{4B.5}$$

Figure 4B-1.   Investment Accumulation as Convex Function of Interest Rates

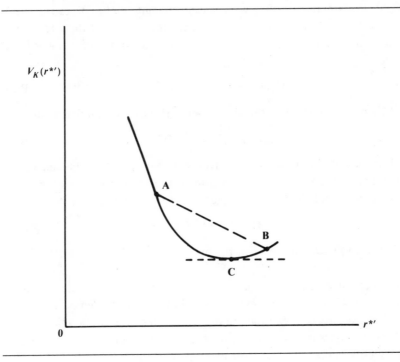

This will be a strictly convex function if the second derivative is positive, because this means that the slope of the curve $V_K(r^{*\prime})$ becomes larger as $r^{*\prime}$ increases. The first derivative of equation (4B.5) with respect to $r^{*\prime}$ is

$$V'_K(r^{*\prime}) = \sum_t F_t(K-t)(1+r^{*\prime})^{K-t-1}. \qquad (4B.6)$$

The derivative of this expression with respect to $r^{*\prime}$ gives us the second derivative. Hence,

$$V''_K(r^{*\prime}) = \sum_t F_t(K-t)(K-t-1)(1+r^{*\prime})^{K-t-2}. \qquad (4B.7)$$

This expression is always positive, except for a special case. When $t < K-1$, $(K-t)(K-t-1)$ is the product of two positive numbers and is hence positive; when $t \geq K+1$, $(K-t)(K-t-1)$ is the product of two negative numbers and is hence positive; when $t = K$ or $t = K-1$, the product $(K-t)(K-t-1)$ is zero, but this makes the expression $V''_K(r^{*\prime})$ zero only if the cash flows are concentrated on dates $K-1$ or K or both, a distribution of cash flows which we now formally assume is not the case because with portfolios of nonzero coupon bonds or mortgages this can only occur if these instruments mature in the first two periods and $K = 1$ or $K = 2$. In this latter case, the duration window is not destroyed, it simply must be developed differently.

2. *The Minimum Point.*   Given that the curve $V_K(r^{*\prime})$ is strictly convex it will have a minimum point at a value of $r^{*\prime}$ for which the first derivative as given in equation (4B.6) is zero. Rewriting equation (4B.6) on the assumption that derivative is zero implies

$$K = \sum_t F_t t (1+r^{*\prime})^{-t} / V(r^{*\prime}). \tag{4B.8}$$

The expression on the right-hand side is the duration of the cash flows, $(F_1, F_2, \ldots)$, as evaluated at the yield to maturity $r^{*\prime}$.

3. *The Duration Window.*   If $r^{*\prime} = r^\prime$, the duration on the right-hand side of equation (4B.8) is the duration as defined in the text. Hence, when $K = D$, it follows that $V_D(r^{*\prime})$ reaches its minimum point at $r^\prime$, and, therefore, the existence of the duration window as asserted in equation (4B.4) is established. Thus, given any period K for which $V_K(r^{*\prime})$ is a strictly convex function, we can make sure the return on a portfolio passes through the duration window if the cash flows or the initial choice of securities is such that $K = D$.

The Special Cases.   Suppose there is one cash flow concentrated entirely in some period — say, period K. Then, the second derivative $V_K^{\prime\prime}(r^{*\prime}) = 0$ and the first derivative $V_K^\prime(r^{*\prime})$ is also zero. This means that $V_K(r^{*\prime})$ is invariant with respect to $r^{*\prime}$ as shown in Figure 4B–2. This is the case of a zero coupon bond in which the cash flow F_K, also equal to $V_K(r^{*\prime})$, is fixed by the debt contract and is not a function of $r^{*\prime}$. The duration window for this single cash flow security, in effect degenerates to this single value and all investment paths go through this single point.

Now consider the case where there are only the positive cash flows F_K and F_{K-1}. This implies that $V_K^{\prime\prime}(r^{*\prime}) = 0$ for all $r^{*\prime}$ from equation (4B.7), and that

$$V_K^\prime(r^{*\prime}) = F_{K-1}, \tag{4B.9}$$

which is a fixed positive number independent of $r^{*\prime}$. The graph of $V_K(r^{*\prime})$ for this case is described in Figure 4B–3. The line $V_K(r^{*\prime})$ is linear with a slope $F_{K-1} > 0$. Such a curve implies that $V_K(r^{*\prime})$ reaches its minimum at nonnegative interest rates when $r^{*\prime} = 0$. Thus, as long as interest rates are nonnegative, the minimum value of $V_K(r^{*\prime})$ occurs when $r^{*\prime} = 0$. The curve

Figure 4B-2. Investment Accumulation for a Zero Coupon Bond and Interest Rate Changes

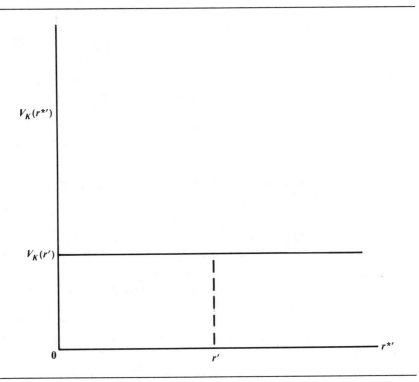

$V_K(r^{*\prime})$, therefore, has a minimum but we cannot describe it as the minimum point on a strictly convex function. This value of the intercept $V_K(0)$ forms the threshold level of the duration window in this case. Substitution of $r^{*\prime} = 0$ into the equation for $V_K(r^{*\prime})$ shows that $V_K(0) = F_K + F_{K-1}$ so that no matter which interest rate occurs as long as it is positive $V_K(r^{*\prime})$ in this case will never be less than $V_K(0)$.

A Maximin Result. We have just shown that, as long as interest rates are nonnegative, every curve $V_K(r^{*\prime})$ for any given K and every given set of cash flows has a minimum for some value of $r^{*\prime}$. For a given K and a set of cash flows, let this minimum occur at $r_K^{*\prime}$. For example, when the flows are concentrated on dates K and $K-1$, $r_K^{*\prime} = 0$ as shown in Figure 4B-3, and when the flows are such that $K = D$, $r_K^{*\prime} = r_D^{*\prime} = r'$, the initial yield to maturity. The

Figure 4B–3.   Investment Accumulation for a Special Case

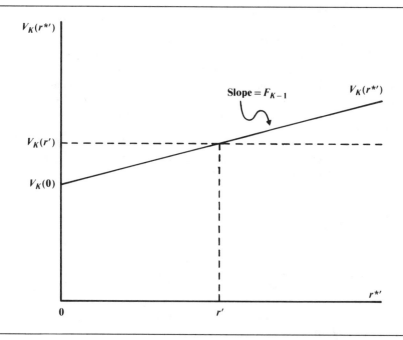

minimal value of $V_K(r^{*\prime})$ over $r^{*\prime}$ for a given set of cash flows thus occurs at $V_K(r_K^{*\prime})$. When we consider all possible distributions of positive cash flows, we acquire a large number of values of $r_K^{*\prime}$ for any given K. We may then ask the serious question: of all the distributions of cash flows for which $r_K^{*\prime}$ is calculated, which of these distributions of cash flows give the largest value of $V_K(r_K^{*\prime})$? Bierwag and Khang (1979) and Bierwag, Kaufman, and Toevs (1983) show that the distribution of cash flows for which $V_K(r_K^{*\prime})$ is largest is one for which $D = K$, to which corresponds the initial yield to maturity r'. To put it another way, imagine that K is given. Then consider portfolios of securities having different durations. Pick any one of these portfolios. The terminal value of this portfolio is $V_K(r^{*\prime})$. Find the value of $r^{*\prime}$ at which this curve reaches a minimum. Such a minimum value of $V_K(r^{*\prime})$ thus occurs for every duration we might have initially chosen. Now, choose the duration for which this minimal value is as large as possible. That duration will be K. The results in this appendix indicate that there are windows through which the investment growth path passes for every K. This maximin result says that the window having the highest threshold level is that for which $D = K$.

NOTES

1. Here, as in previous chapters, $r' = r/n$ where n is the number of periods into which a year has been divided for purposes of compounding. Hence K is the number of such periods into the future that the investment fund has grown.
2. In this illustration, the number of bonds acquired is not an integral number, but for accuracy in the illustration, we use these nonintegral units. With more invested, as shown in example 2, above, accuracy like that in this illustration can be obtained.
3. For the slope to be equal to unity, it must be parallel to the slope of the line for zero coupon bonds. As drawn in the diagram, the slopes will cross the 45° line for zero coupon bonds.

REFERENCES

Bierwag, Gerald O., George G. Kaufman, and Alden Toevs. 1983. "Recent Developments in Bond Portfolio Immunization Strategies." In *Innovations in Bond Portfolio Management,* edited by G. Kaufman, G. Bierwag, and A. Toevs (Greenwich, Conn.: JAI Press), pp. 105–58.
Bierwag, G.O., and Chulsoon Khang. 1979. "Immunization Is a Minimax Strategy." *Journal of Finance* (May).

5 MEASURING RISK AND RETURN

The immunization investment strategy is a "passive" strategy. The investor does not need to forecast or anticipate interest rates to implement the strategy. The investor simply chooses a portfolio having a duration equal to the length of time remaining in the planning period. This is a very simple decision rule. Interest rate changes during the planning period cannot reduce the accumulated investment over the planning period below the initially promised return (the return resulting if interest rates do not change). The outcome of the strategy is "immune" from interest rate changes. The active strategy is different. "Going long," for example, implies the accumulated investment return rises above (falls below) the promised return if interest rates continually fall (rise). If an investor correctly forecasts that interest rates will continually fall (rise) and if the investor goes long (short) then the acquired return will be in excess of the promised return for the planning period. Active strategies are risky strategies because forecast errors can result in a return that is less than that resulting from a passive strategy. An active strategy can perform better than a passive strategy only if interest rates generally move in the anticipated direction.

Many investors (institutional or otherwise) may intentionally pursue active strategies. These investors view the gains relative to a passive strategy as worth the risk. This is not a new idea. Not only do we observe the acceptance of risk in everyday behavior, but economic theory is replete with examples in which such behavior arises as an optimal solution to problems under uncertainty even when a risk-free solution or strategy exists. It is rare, however, that there are only two available strategies, a risky one and a risk-free one. Most often a range of risky strategies is available. Many active strategies are possible, because an investor may choose many different durations none of which are equal to the length of the planning period. In this context an investor may well ask how much more risky one strategy is than another. To answer this question one must be able to measure the risk associated with a strategy. Knowing the risk associated with a strategy an investor may be able to assess whether the possible returns from the strategy can compensate for the risk which is intentionally accepted.

In this chapter, we develop a decision framework within which the risks of the various duration strategies are measured and optimal strategy decisions are made.

EXPECTED EXCESS RETURNS AND THE VARIANCE OF RETURNS

Let $\bar{r}$ and r be respectively the realized annual and promised rate of return over a planning period. The realized rate of return is defined by

$$(1+\bar{r})^q V(r) = (1+r^*)^q V(r^*). \tag{5.1}$$

In this equation, $V(r)$ is the initial dollar amount which is invested and r is the annual yield to maturity used to discount the future cash flows of that investment as well as the promised annual rate of return over the planning period length q. Instantly after the investment of $V(r)$ is made, the annual yield to maturity changes to r^*, and the value of the investment changes to $V(r^*)$. No further changes in interest rates implies that the new value of the investment fund $V(r^*)$ accumulates to $(1+r^*)^q V(r^*)$ after q periods. The right-hand side of equation (5.1) indicates the total accumulation over the planning period. Given $V(r)$ was the initial amount invested, it must grow at some rate $\bar{r}$ so that the left-hand side of (5.1) equals the realized amount designated on the right-hand side of (5.1). Equation (5.1) defines $\bar{r}$; it is the annual rate at which the initial investment must grow in order for it to be equal to the realized value of the investment fund after q periods.[1]

Solving equation (5.1) for $\bar{r}$, we write

$$\bar{r} = (1+r^*)[V(r^*)/V(r)]^{1/q} - 1. \tag{5.2}$$

The realized rate of return is hence a function of (1) the initial yield to maturity, r, (2) the new yield to maturity, r^*, given by the market instantly after the initial investment was made, (3) q, the length of the planning period, and (4) the properties of the function $V(r)$ or $V(r^*)$. The realized rate of return, $\bar{r}$, is initially uncertain because r^* is initially uncertain; although, as seen for immunization strategies, (row 16 in Table 4–2, for example), $\bar{r}$ will be very close to r. We may view the planning period q as given. The relevant properties of $V(r)$, given r, are determined by the chosen duration strategy.

Since r^* is the uncertain or random variable in equation (5.2), it follows that any given probability distribution over r^* implies a derived probability distribution over $\bar{r}$ because $\bar{r}$ is a function of r^*, given the planning period length and the duration strategy. (Appendix 5A contains a review of the attributes of probability distributions used in the analysis in this chapter.) This extension of the probability from r^* to $\bar{r}$ can be illustrated using the data in Table 4–2 where the chosen duration of the portfolio is 8 years. Suppose the planning period is 4 years (eight 6-month periods). Then, going across the eighth row, we can arrange the realized rates, $\bar{r}$, and the yields to maturity r^* in pairs $(r^*, \bar{r})$ as

$$(.07, .1341) \quad (.075, .1278) \quad (.08, .1218) \quad (.085, .1160) \quad ... \quad (.130, .0737).$$

Any probability associated with r^*, the first number in each pair, can also be associated with the second number in the pair. For example, if .3 is the probability that $r^* = .08$, then .3 is also the probability that $\bar{r} = .1218$ over the time period of 4 years.

Given a probability distribution over values that $\bar{r}$ can take on enables us to derive the expected value and the variance of $\bar{r}$. Let r_i^*, for $i = 1, 2, 3, ..., N$, be the possible values of r^* where p_i is the probability the ith value will occur. Using equation (5.2), the expected value of $\bar{r}$ is defined as

$$E(\bar{r}) = \sum_{i=1}^{N} p_i(1+r_i^*)[V(r_i^*)/V(r)]^{1/q} - 1, \tag{5.3}$$

and the variance is defined as

$$\text{Var}(\bar{r}) = \sum_{i=1}^{N} p_i[(1+r_i^*)[V(r_i^*)/V(r)]^{1/q} - E(\bar{r})^{-1}]^2. \tag{5.4}$$

We can also define the expected excess return as

$$e = E(\bar{r} - r) = E(\bar{r}) - r, \tag{5.5}$$

and, of course, the standard deviation of $\bar{r}$ as

$$\sigma = \sqrt{\text{Var}(\bar{r})}. \tag{5.6}$$

Since the relevant properties of $V(r^*)/V(r)$ are determined by the duration strategy, it follows in the interpretation of (5.5) and (5.6) that duration affects the expected excess rate of return, e, and the standard deviation of the excess rate of return, σ. Hence, for any probability distribution over r^*, we can compute the pair (e, σ) as a function of the chosen duration.

Example.[2]   Let $N = 2$. Suppose p_1 is the probability that $r_1^* = r + \Delta r$ and that p_2 is the probability that $r_2^* = r - \Delta r$ where $\Delta r > 0$. Thus, the interest rate can move either up or down by an amount Δr. Suppose we consider two bonds, a 25-year and a 6-month bond, each having a 10% coupon rate and a 10% annual yield to maturity. The portfolio duration is $D = B_1 D_1 + (1 - B_1)D_2$ where $D_1 = 1.0000$ and $D_2 = 19.68872$ are the durations (in 6-month periods) respectively of the 6-month bond and the 25-year bond, and where B_1 is the proportion invested in the 6-month bond. We next choose a variety of B_1's so that the durations of the portfolio range from one to sixteen 6-month periods. Let the planning period be eight 6-month periods. Table 5-1 illustrates the calculations of (e, σ) for $p_1 = 0.10$ and $p_2 = 0.90$, and $\Delta r = 0.01$ (or 100 basis points). Table 5-1 shows the calculations for each probability for only $D = 1$ and $D = 2$. Notice that the expected excess rate of return is positive only for durations in excess of 7 and that when duration equals 8, the length of the planning period, the expected annual excess rate of return is only 0.000522 (or 5.22 basis points) with a standard deviation that is very small, namely, 0.000014 (or 0.14 basis points). Notice also that the standard deviations get smaller as the durations tend toward the planning period of eight 6-month periods. The expected excess rate of return is negative for durations that are less than the planning period length. Hence, only durations in excess of eight periods are efficient. No risk-averse investor would intentionally pick a duration less than eight 6-month periods, because for these small durations the standard deviation is positive and the expected annual excess rate of return is negative. The investor could always choose to immunize so as to acquire a very slightly positive expected excess rate of return having a very small standard deviation. Figures 5-1 and 5-2 show graphically the values of (e, σ) corresponding to the efficient choices of the durations. Figure 5-1 shows the relationship for the probability distributions $-(.1, .9), (.2, .8), (.3, .7),$ and $(.4, .6)$—where the first probability in these pairs is the probability that the interest rate will increase. For each of these distributions in Figure 5-1, there is an expected decrease in the interest rate. The efficient choices, here, are the durations that are greater than or equal to the planning period. In other words, investors who believe that the interest rate is more likely to decrease than increase will choose to "go long." Figure 5-2 illustrates the case for the distributions $-(.5, .5), (.6, .4), (.7, .3),$ $(.8, .2),$ and $(.9, .1)$. Except for $(.5, .5)$, these are distributions for which it is most likely that the interest rate will increase. Here, the efficient choices

Table 5-1.   Illustation of the Computation of (e, σ) for the Probability Distribution $(.1, .9)$, and for Various Duration Strategies when $\Delta r = 100$ Basis Points

$D = 1$ Prob(p)	$r^{*\prime}$	$\bar{r}'$	$p \cdot \bar{r}'$	$p \cdot (\bar{r}' - E(\bar{r}'))^2$
.1	.055	.054	.005437	6.2016×10^{-6}
.9	.045	.041	.041061	0.6891×10^{-6}

$$E(\bar{r}') = .046498; \ \text{Var}(\bar{r}') = 6.8907 \times 10^{-6}$$

$e = 2 \cdot E(\bar{r}') - 2\bar{r}' = .092996 - .1000000 = -.007004 = -70.04$ basis points.

$\sigma = 2\sqrt{\text{Var}(\bar{r}')} = .00525 = 52.5$ basis points.

$D = 2$ Prob(p)	$r^{*\prime}$	$\bar{r}'$	$p \cdot \bar{r}'$	$p \cdot (\bar{r}' - E(\bar{r}'))^2$
.1	.055	.054	.005379	4.5498×10^{-6}
.9	.045	.046	.041666	0.5055×10^{-6}

$$E(\bar{r}') = .047045; \ \text{Var}(\bar{r}') = 5.0554 \times 10^{-6}$$

$e = 2 \cdot E(\bar{r}') - 2\bar{r}' = .094090 - .1000000 = -.005910 = -59.10$ basis points.

$\sigma = 2\sqrt{\text{Var}(\bar{r}')} = .00497 = 44.97$ basis points.

$D = 3$:	$e = -48.24$;	$\sigma = 37.44$	$D = 10$:	$e = 26.21$;	$\sigma = 15.15$
$D = 4$:	$e = -37.43$;	$\sigma = 29.92$	$D = 11$:	$e = 36.62$;	$\sigma = 22.65$
$D = 5$:	$e = -26.68$;	$\sigma = 22.40$	$D = 12$:	$e = 47.00$;	$\sigma = 30.15$
$D = 6$:	$e = -15.99$;	$\sigma = 14.88$	$D = 13$:	$e = 57.28$;	$\sigma = 37.65$
$D = 7$:	$e = -5.36$;	$\sigma = 7.37$	$D = 14$:	$e = 67.53$;	$\sigma = 45.15$
$D = 8$:	$e = 5.22$;	$\sigma = 0.14$	$D = 15$:	$e = 77.22$;	$\sigma = 52.65$
$D = 9$:	$e = 15.74$;	$\sigma = 7.65$	$D = 16$:	$e = 87.87$;	$\sigma = 60.14$

Note: In the computations, $\bar{r}'_i$ is calculated as $\bar{r}_i / 2$ so that we can account for semiannual compounding, and $r^{*\prime} = (r + \Delta r)/2$. The annual excess rates of return and standard deviations are measured in basis points per annum. Semiannual compounding implies that $e = 2 \cdot E(\bar{r}') - 2 \cdot \bar{r}'$ and that $\sigma = 2\sqrt{\text{Var}(\bar{r}')}$.

are durations that are less than or equal to the planning period. The investors who believe this will choose to "go short." The results in this example give a probabilistic interpretation to active strategies. In Chapter 4 it was very clear that an investor who believed with certainty that the interest rate would decrease (increase) would go long (short). In this example, the belief with certainty is unnecessary; only a preponderance of probability in one direction or the other is required.

Figure 5-1.   Expected Excess Returns vs. the Standard
Deviation: Efficient Portfolios for Anticipated Decreases
in Interest Rates

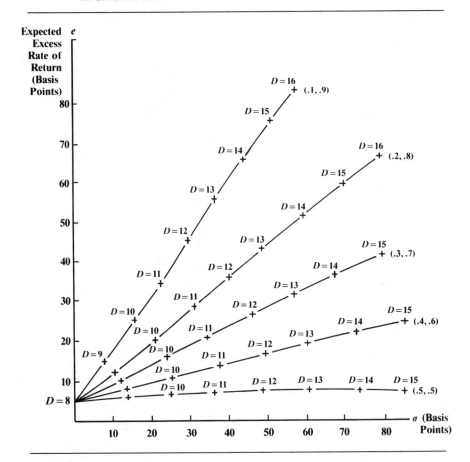

The probability distribution (.5, .5) must be treated as a special case in
this example. The expected excess rate of return relative to the standard deviation is very small. It reaches a maximum of 27.7 basis points at $D = 16$
with $\sigma = 98.21$ basis points, and only the long durations are efficient. Even
though the probabilities are 50/50 in this case, a decrease in interest rates of
50 basis points results in a larger increment to the realized return for long
durations than the impact of an increase of 50 basis points for short durations. For example, if the duration is 9 and the interest rate falls by 50 basis
points the realized excess rate of return is 9.1 basis points, but if the duration is 7 and the interest rate increases by 50 basis points the realized excess

Figure 5-2. Expected Excess Returns vs. the Standard Deviation: Efficient Portfolios for Anticipated Increases in Interest Rates

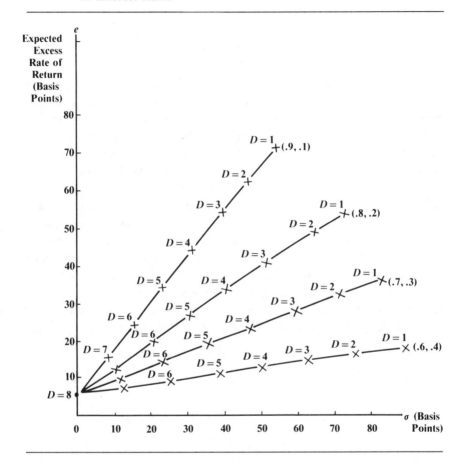

rate of return is 8.4 basis points. This asymmetric result occurs for the very technical reason that the realized rate of return as a function of the basis point change at $D = 7$ is *not* a mirror image of the function at $D = 9$.

As the probability of an increase in the interest rate increases, the slope of the efficient choice frontier in Figure 5-1 increases. In other words, for a given level of risk, as measured by σ, as it becomes more certain the interest rate will increase, the expected excess rate of return rises. Or, put another way, for a given expected excess rate of return, as it becomes more certain the interest rate will increase, the level of risk associated with that expected excess rate of return falls. Thus, the more certain the outcome the less risk there is for a given expected excess rate of return, and conversely. A similar result occurs in Figure 5–2 for the case in which the interest rate is most likely to fall.

THE OPTIMAL DURATION DECISION

Given an efficient choice frontier for some probability distribution, as in either Figure 5–1 or 5–2, the investor has the problem of choosing a particular point or duration. As in the development of liquidity preference theory or the capital asset pricing model, this decision involves the subjective attitude toward risk and return. Figure 5–3 illustrates the manner in which this decision can be made. The curves I_0, I_1, and others that could be drawn in the diagram, are indifference curves. Each indifference curve is a locus of points (e, σ) among which the investor is indifferent. Any one point on a curve is viewed as subjectively equivalent to any other on the same curve. Each curve is drawn to reflect the notion that risk is undesirable so that as more risk is added to the portfolio, the investor must be compensated by an increment to the expected excess rate of return. Moreover, as each additional unit of risk is added, the investor requires larger and larger increments in the expected excess rate of return to compensate. The points on I_1 are viewed as better than the points on I_0. Any point on I_1 involves a greater expected

Figure 5–3. An Optimal Portfolio Allocation

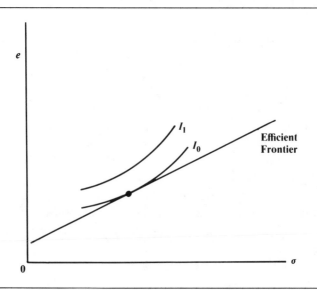

excess rate of return than for a corresponding point on I_0 for the same level of risk. Of course, every investor would like to reach the highest possible indifference curve. The efficient frontier indicates the attainable points in the diagram, given the investor's beliefs about the probability distribution. The optimal duration is then given by the point of tangency of I_0 to the efficient frontier. No other point on the efficient frontier touches a higher indifference curve.

Different investors may have different attitudes toward risk. The shape and position of the indifference curves reflect these attitudes. Some investors may have relatively flat indifference curves with very little curvature. Such investors are not very averse to risk because an increment of risk along such a curve requires very little compensation in terms of an increment to the expected rate of return. In Figure 5-3, it is not difficult to see that these investors may choose very extreme durations that are either very much larger or smaller than the planning period. Other investors may be very risk averse and have indifference curves that are relatively very steep. Such investors are likely to choose durations very close to the planning period where the risk is relatively small. In the framework described in Figure 5-3, it is easy to see that investors with exactly the same planning period and the same probabilistic beliefs may choose vastly different duration strategies.

As the future interest rate becomes more uncertain, the efficient choice frontier becomes flatter. The effect of this on the duration decision is described in Figure 5-4. There the efficient frontier has shifted downward and a new tangency with curve I_0 is obtained at a duration closer to the planning period length. It is possible, however, that the investor's lower indifference curve is the dashed line I_0', in which case the investor chooses a duration farther away from the planning period. The latter investor is a peculiar creature who has less risk aversion when there is greater uncertainty, a possibility not precluded in this framework. However, as the uncertainty approaches the probability distribution $(.5, .5)$ so that the efficient frontier is nearly flat, a risk-averse investor is most likely to reduce his risk and to choose a duration closer to the planning period length. In other words, if the future interest rate is viewed as totally uncertain, $(.5, .5)$, an active investment strategy becomes something of a "pure gamble" so that risk-averse investors will tend toward an immunization or passive strategy.

The duration decision in this simple example differs from the traditional portfolio decisions made in this framework. Here there is only one decision to make: the duration. Both the expected excess rate of return and the degree of risk depend on the duration decision. In the traditional framework with many risky assets (that is, more than two), the investor's choice of the level of risk can often be satisfied by many different portfolios from which

Figure 5–4.   Changes in an Optimal Portfolio Allocation

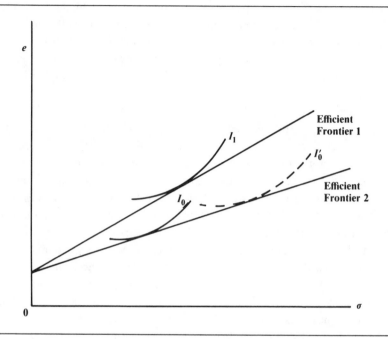

the investor may choose one that gives the largest expected return. That can happen in this framework also when there are more than two fixed income securities available. There may be many portfolios of bonds all having the same duration and level of risk. That being the case, the investor can choose a portfolio from among these so as to acquire the largest expected excess rate of return.

This framework of analysis as illustrated in this example helps to explain why investors may select active strategies rather than passive strategies; and why investors who differ from each other because of (1) different risk attitudes, (2) different planning periods, and (3) different probabilistic beliefs about the course of future interest rates may undertake different duration strategies.

APPROXIMATING THE EFFICIENT FRONTIER

Equation (5.2) gives the realized rate of return as a non-linear function of r^* and r. We can rewrite this expression as

$$(1+\bar{r})^q = (1+r^*)^q V(r^*)/V(r), \qquad (5.7)$$

which can be interpreted as the accumulated return per dollar after the passage of q periods. If we can find a good linear approximation for the right-hand side of the expression, the expected realized return per dollar and the variance can be calculated very simply. Appendix 5B shows that the right-hand side can be linearly approximated as a function of duration so that we may write (5.7) as [3]

$$\bar{r} = r + \left(1 - \frac{D}{q}\right)(r^* - r) \qquad (5.8)$$

which is a variation of the Babcock (1976) and the Babcock–Langetieg (1978) equation.[4]

It follows immediately that

$$E(\bar{r}) = r + \left(1 - \frac{D}{q}\right)(E(r^*) - r) \qquad (5.9)$$

and that

$$\mathrm{Var}(\bar{r}) = \left(1 - \frac{D}{q}\right)^2 \mathrm{Var}(r^*), \qquad (5.10)$$

or in terms of standard deviations

$$\sigma = \left|1 - \frac{D}{q}\right| \sigma(r^*). \qquad (5.11)$$

Using equations (5.9) and (5.11) to eliminate $(1 - D/q)$ we can write an approximation of the expected rate of return as

$$E(\bar{r}) = \begin{cases} r + \left(\dfrac{E(r^*) - r}{\sigma(r^*)}\right)\sigma, & D < q \\[2mm] r, & D = q \\[2mm] r - \left(\dfrac{E(r^*) - r}{\sigma(r^*)}\right)\sigma, & D > q \end{cases} \qquad (5.12)$$

or the expected excess rate of return

$$e = \begin{cases} \left(\dfrac{E(r^*) - r}{\sigma(r^*)}\right)\sigma, & D < q \\[2mm] 0, & D = q \\[2mm] \left(\dfrac{E(r^*) - r}{\sigma(r^*)}\right)\sigma, & D > q \end{cases} \qquad (5.13)$$

Table 5-2.   Error in the Linear Approximation of the
Expected Annual Rate of Return

	(.1, .9)			(.2, .8)	
Duration	*Error*	*% Error*	*Duration*	*Error*	*% Error*
8	5.22	0.52	8	5.22	0.51
9	5.74	0.57	9	5.74	0.56
10	6.21	0.60	10	6.16	0.60
11	6.62	0.64	11	6.57	0.64
12	6.98	0.67	12	6.93	0.67
13	7.28	0.69	13	7.23	0.69
14	7.53	0.71	14	7.48	0.71
15	7.72	0.72	15	7.68	0.72
16	7.87	0.72	16	7.82	0.73
	(.3, .7)			(.4, .6)	
Duration	*Error*	*% Error*	*Duration*	*Error*	*% Error*
8	5.13	0.51	8	5.08	0.51
9	5.64	0.56	9	5.90	0.55
10	6.11	0.60	10	6.06	0.60
11	6.52	0.64	11	6.47	0.64
12	6.87	0.67	12	6.82	0.67
13	7.18	0.70	13	7.13	0.70
14	7.43	0.72	14	7.38	0.72
15	7.63	0.73	15	7.58	0.74
16	7.77	0.74	16	7.72	0.75
	(.5, .5)			(.6, .4)	
Duration	*Error*	*% Error*	*Duration*	*Error*	*% Error*
8	5.03	0.50	1	−0.03	−0.0026
9	5.55	0.55	2	0.81	0.08
10	6.01	0.60	3	0.16	0.15
11	6.41	0.64	4	2.35	0.23
12	6.77	0.67	5	3.04	0.29
13	7.08	0.70	6	3.69	0.36
14	7.33	0.73	·7	4.29	0.42
15	7.53	0.75	8	4.86	0.48
16	7.68	0.76			

Table 5-2 continued

(.7, .3)			(.8, .2)		
Duration	Error	% Error	Duration	Error	% Error
1	−0.03	−0.0025	1	−0.03	−0.0025
2	0.83	0.08	2	0.82	0.08
3	1.64	0.16	3	1.60	0.16
4	2.40	0.23	4	2.37	0.23
5	3.11	0.31	5	3.08	0.30
6	3.77	0.37	6	3.73	0.37
7	4.38	0.43	7	4.34	0.43
8	4.94	0.49	8	4.89	0.49

(.9, .1)		
Duration	Error	% Error
1	−0.03	−0.0024
2	0.81	0.08
3	0.16	0.15
4	2.35	0.23
5	3.04	0.29
6	3.69	0.36
7	4.29	0.42
8	4.85	0.48

Note: The linear approximation is given by (5.12). The % error is the error as a percent of the Expected Annual Rate of Return. The probability distribution giving the efficient Expected Annual Rate of Return frontier is given by the pair (p_1, p_2). The error is expressed in basis points.

Table 5-2 illustrates the closeness of this approximation. This table continues the example given earlier. In Table 5-2 the approximation of $E(r)$ as in equation (5.12) is always within 8 basis points of the true annual expected rate of return. The percentage error, expressed as a percentage of the true expected rate of return, is always less than 1%. In the case where interest rates are expected to rise, the error is never more than 0.5%. The Babcock equation provides a good approximation to the efficient frontier. However, this illustration is for a very simple example. For more complex probability distributions, the approximation error may be larger. One must be cautious in the use of this approximation. An error analysis should be undertaken when the probability distribution is more complex.

THE FISHBURN RISK MEASURE

The variance or standard deviation of the realized rate of return is not the only risk measure that can be used. Given that a passive investment strategy is one for which the probability is zero that the realized rate of return will fall below the promised initial rate of return, one may view the passive strategy as a risk-free strategy. Thus, an appropriate risk measure is the one devised by Fishburn (1977), in a more general context, as

$$F(\bar{r}) = \sum_{r_i \leq r} p_i(\bar{r}_i - r)^2, \qquad (5.14)$$

where the inequality, $r_i \leq r$, below the summation sign means that the sum is to be taken only over i for which the inequality is true. This measure of risk is almost the same as the semivariance. If r in (5.14) is replaced by $E(\bar{r})$, we have the semivariance. One may also utilize $\sqrt{F(\bar{r})}$ as an appropriate measure of risk. The Fishburn risk index is particularly appropriate as a measure of "downside" risk. The realized rate of return appears in the formula only when it falls short of the promised rate of return. Investors who are seriously concerned that they may receive less than the promised rate of return, but who do not regard rates of return in excess of the promised rate of return as contributing to risk, may find the Fishburn risk measure appealing. Bawa and Lindenburg (1977) have extended this idea of risk to the capital asset pricing model.

The diagrams of the efficient frontiers, using the square root version of the Fishburn risk measure, are not greatly different from those in Figures 5-1 and 5-2. The efficient frontiers are very nearly linear, so that a linear approximation of the frontier will yield results just as close to the true frontier as the use of the standard deviation.

APPENDIX 5A
PROBABILITY DISTRIBUTIONS

The probability of an event can be viewed as a subjective measure of the likelihood that an event will occur. Thus, p_i is the probability that an event corresponding to the index i will occur. Probabilities are normalized (scaled) so that if $p_i = 1$ the event occurs with certainty and if $p_i = 0$ the event will not occur at all. The likelihood of the occurrence of events that are not certain but can occur have probabilities such that $0 < p_i < 1$. If the events are mutually exclusive, as in this text, the probability of either event i or event j is the sum of their probabilities, $p_i + p_j$, which also satisfies the condition $0 \leq p_i + p_j \leq 1$. In the text, if interest rate r_i^* occurs, then r_j^* does not; there can only be one prevailing interest rate. By definition $\sum_{i=1}^{N} p_i = 1$ if there are only N possible mutually exclusive events. The set of probabilities, $(p_1, p_2, \ldots, p_M)$, is called a *probability distribution*.

Probability distributions can be distinguished from each other on the basis of some of their properties. In this text the expected interest rate is defined as

$$\sum_{i=1}^{N} p_i r_i^* = E(r^*). \tag{5A.1}$$

The expected interest rate can be viewed as the average rate that will arise over time if the probability distribution does not change. It is often easy to visualize this by assuming there are N balls in a bag and that the ith ball has the number r_i^* on it. Suppose the probability is p_i that the ith ball results if one reaches into the bag and pulls out a ball. Repeating this experiment (upon replacement of every drawn ball) any number of times and averaging the interest rates that have occurred as one proceeds, it will be seen that the average will get closer and closer (converges) to $E(r^*)$. Probability distributions can also be distinguished from each other by a measure of the "dispersion" of the numbers (interest rates) that can occur. A distribution in which $N=2$, $r_1^* = .105$, $r_2^* = .095$, with probabilities $p_1 = .5$ and $p_2 = .5$ has a smaller dispersion than one for which $r_1^* = .15$, $r_2^* = .05$ with probabilities $p_1 = .5$ and $p_2 = .5$. Although both distributions have the same expected interest rate, $E(r^*) = .10$, the latter distribution corresponds to interest rates that are farther away from the expected rate. A measure of dispersion is the variance which is defined as

$$\mathrm{Var}(r^*) = \sum_{1}^{N} p_i (r_i^* - E(r^*))^2. \tag{5A.2}$$

Distributions with larger variances correspond to interest rates that, on average, are farther away from the expected value. In (5A.1), $(r_i^* - E(r^*))^2$ measures the distance of r_i^* from $E(r^*)$ and it is utilized as a measure of distance simply because it is a positive number. Often the positive square root of the variance, called the *standard deviation,* is also used as a measure of dispersion. It too is a positive number and thus suitable for measuring average distance, but it also is a measure that is expressed in the same units as the interest rate, r_i^*. Risk is often measured by the variance or the standard deviation. In the text, a measure of risk associated with a duration decision is the variance of the realized rate of return

$$\mathrm{Var}(\bar{r}) = \sum_1^N p_i(\bar{r}_i - E(\bar{r}))^2, \qquad (5A.3)$$

where the duration affects the variance by affecting the functional relationship between r_i^* and $\bar{r}_i$. It is regarded as a risk measure because it gives us a measure of the average distance or dispersion of $\bar{r}_i$ from its mean $E(\bar{r})$. If $\mathrm{Var}(\bar{r}) = 0$, then, as we observe in (5A.3), $\bar{r}_i = E(\bar{r})$ with certainty because there is only one $\bar{r}_i$ that can occur; however, when $\mathrm{Var}(\bar{r}) > 0$, there is a "risk" that the realized rate may differ from its expected value. The larger the variance the broader the length of the interval within which r_i can occur with some given probability. The realized rate can be viewed as more uncertain in such cases.

The variance or standard deviation includes all squared deviations from the expected value in the formula. If we are only interested in a dispersion measure over a portion of these deviations, some of the squared deviations can be deleted. For example, if we are interested only in the dispersion below the expected value we obtain

$$\mathrm{Semivar}(\bar{r}) = \sum_{\bar{r}_i < E(\bar{r})} p_i(\bar{r}_i - E(\bar{r}))^2, \qquad (5A.4)$$

where the inequality, $\bar{r}_i < E(\bar{r})$, written below the summation sign indicates the squared deviations are to be added only when $\bar{r}_i < E(\bar{r})$. This measure of dispersion is called the semivariance. We may be interested in the semivariance as a measure of risk when we do not care what values $\bar{r}_i$ takes on provided these values exceed the expected value. The semivariance is a measure of "downside" risk because only the negative deviations are squared in the formula.

Fishburn (1977) introduced a variation on the semivariance that is particularly appropriate for the duration decision problem. The expected realized rate of return is generally not equal to the return that results when interest rates do not change; that is, $E(\bar{r}) \neq r$. If we are interested only in cases where $\bar{r}_i < r$, then the semivariance is not the appropriate measure of downside risk. Fishburn modifies the semivariance to obtain

$$F(\bar{r}) = \sum_{\bar{r}_i < r} p_i(r_i - r)^2. \qquad (5A.5)$$

In the case of the immunization strategy $F(\bar{r}) = 0$ because none of the realized rates fall below the initially promised rate r. In this way, $F(\bar{r})$ is a measure of the risk that can be associated with an *active* strategy relative to the *passive* strategy which has a value of risk equal to zero.

APPENDIX 5B
LINEARLY APPROXIMATING THE RETURN
PER DOLLAR OVER THE PLANNING PERIOD

Equation (5.7) shows that the return per dollar over a planning period of length q can be written as[5]

$$\bar{r}' = \left[\frac{(1+r^{*\prime})^q V(r^{*\prime})}{V(r')} \right]^{1/q} - 1. \tag{5B.1}$$

Letting $r^{*\prime} = r' + \lambda$, then we can write this more generally as

$$\bar{r}' = \varphi(\lambda). \tag{5B.2}$$

In a Taylor's series expansion of $\bar{r}'$ around the value of $\lambda = 0$, equation (5B.2) can be written as

$$\bar{r}' = \varphi(0) + \lambda\varphi'(0) + \frac{\lambda^2}{2!}\varphi''(0) + \frac{\lambda^3}{3!}\varphi^{(3)}(0) + \cdots. \tag{5B.3}$$

If we use only the first two terms of this series as an approximation we can write

$$\bar{r}' \cong \varphi(0) + \lambda\varphi'(0), \tag{5B.4}$$

which expresses $\bar{r}'$ as a simple linear function of $\lambda = r^{*\prime} - r'$. We may note that when $r^{*\prime} - r' = \lambda = 0$, then

$$\varphi(0) = (1+r') - 1 = r' \tag{5B.5}$$

and that

$$\varphi'(\lambda) = \frac{1}{q}\left[\frac{(1+r^{*\prime})^q V(r^{*\prime})}{V(r')} \right]^{(1/q)-1}\left[\frac{q(1+r^{*\prime})^{q-1}V(r^{*\prime}) + (1+r^{*\prime})^q V'(r^{*\prime})}{V(r')} \right] \tag{5B.6}$$

so that when $\lambda = 0$, we have

$$\varphi'(0) = \frac{1}{q}(1+r')^{1-q}[q(1+r')^{q-1} - (1+r')^{q-1}D] \tag{5B.7}$$

because

$$\frac{V'(r')}{V(r')}\frac{1}{1+r'} = -D, \tag{5B.8}$$

the duration of the initial investment. Hence,

$$\varphi'(0) = \left(1 - \frac{D}{q}\right).$$ (5B.7')

Substitution of this result into (5B.4) implies that

$$\bar{r}' = r' + \left(1 - \frac{D}{q}\right)(r^{*'} - r').$$ (5B.9)

The reader will recognize this as the Babcock equation developed in Babcock (1976, 1984) and in Babcock and Langetieg (1978). As shown in the text, the expectation and standard deviation of r' produce very accurate approximations to the efficient frontier.

NOTES

1. Equation (5.1) assumes annual compounding. If compounding were more frequent we simply replace r, $\bar{r}$, and r^* with r', $\bar{r}'$, and $r^{*'}$ — the notation used in previous chapters.
2. This example is similar to one published in Bierwag, Kaufman, and Toevs (1983).
3. To express this for a compounding period, all one needs to do is replace $\bar{r}$, r, and r^* by their analogous primed expressions. The duration and planning period lengths can be expressed in any units of time, as long as the planning period and duration are expressed in the same units.
4. The 1976 Babcock paper and the Babcock–Langetieg (1978) paper circulated among duration aficionados for many years. A published version, appearing in 1984, was long overdue and a welcome addition to the literature.
5. For generality, the equations in this appendix are based on compounding over portions of a year. Hence interest rates are replaced by their prime values. No differences arise except that D and q must be measured in compounding periods.

REFERENCES

Babcock, Guilford C. 1976. "A Modified Measure of Duration." Working Paper, University of Southern California, Los Angeles.

Babcock, Guilford C., and Terrence C. Langetieg. 1978. "Applications of Duration in the Selection of Bonds." Working Paper, University of Southern California, Los Angeles.

Babcock, Guilford C. 1984. "Duration as a Link between Yield and Value." *Journal of Portfolio Management* (Summer): 58–65; Corrections (Fall).

Bawa, V.S., and Eric B. Lindenberg. 1977. "Capital Market Equilibrium in a Mean-Lower Moment Framework." *Journal of Financial Economics 5*, no. 2 (November): 189–200.

Bierwag, G.O., George G. Kaufman, and Alden L. Toevs. 1983. "Duration: Its Development and Use in Bond Portfolio Management." *Financial Analyst's Journal* (July/August): 3–23.

Fishburn, Peter C. 1977. "Mean–Risk Analysis with Risk Associated with Below-Target Returns." *American Economic Review 67*, no. 2 (March): 116–26.

III APPLICATIONS

6 CONTINGENT IMMUNIZATION

Contingent immunization is one of the most well-known and well-utilized active investment strategies for fixed-income securities. Weinberger and Leibowitz (1981a, b, 1982a, b, 1983) in a series of papers and memoranda, formally developed the strategy. Using this strategy, the portfolio manager or investor attempts to acquire realized returns in excess of the immunized return but, at the same time, attempts to constrain or control losses that may result from incorrect anticipations of interest rate movements. The strategy provides for a built-in floor or minimum realized rate of return below which it is very improbable the realized rate will fall. Nonetheless investors have an opportunity to exploit their prowess at forecasting the direction of interest rate movements and thus earning returns in excess of the immunized return.

If the investor initially selects an active and hence risky strategy because of confidence in the forecasted direction of interest rate movements, any error in the forecast after one period will place the value of the portfolio below what would have resulted under immunization. The impact of this error on the realized return for the planning period may be very small for two reasons. First, interest rate movements tend to be very gradual. Interest rate movements over a week are rarely more than 50 basis points on long term securities. The investor on a week-to-week basis may be alerted to any progressive trend in forecast errors. Second, the impact of one error in one period has a very small impact on the realized return over a planning period containing many such periods. The impact of changes in interest rates for other periods can swamp the impact of a single error. As errors accumulate the investor can respond by adjusting the portfolio durations and the inherent risk in an active strategy. This response can constrain or reduce the overall impact of the forecast errors on the realized return for the planning period. The investor can carefully control the degree of downside risk while pursuing the excess returns that an active strategy makes possible.

Risk control is the most important feature of contingent immunization. The investor can stipulate the degree of risk tolerance at the start of the investment plan. If a sequence of small forecast errors develops over the planning period, the investor can move the portfolio duration closer to the remaining time in the planning period and thus attempt to incur no more risk than initially regarded as tolerable. The a priori specified risk tolerance is expressed as the maximum tolerable loss in realized return for the planning period. If r is the initially promised annual rate of return, and if x is the maximum tolerable loss, then

$$r_f = r - x \qquad (6.1)$$

is the floor to the rate of return or the minimally acceptable rate of return. The maximum tolerable loss, x, is a "safety margin."

As time passes, the investor can project forward the potentially realizable rate of return for the planning period. This projection can be specified as a function of (1) previously observed rates in the planning period and (2) the current rate assuming it remains unchanged over the remaining time in the planning period. The closer is the projection to r_f, the greater the danger that the realized rate may fall below r_f. In this case, the investor may choose to set the portfolio duration closer to the remaining time in the planning period so as to reduce the likelihood that the realized return falls below r_f. If the potential realized rate falls to r_f, the immunization mode is triggered. Should the entire safety margin, x, be eroded away, immunization is the only way by which the investor can prevent the realized rate of return from falling below r_f. On the other hand, if the investor succeeds in forecasting directions of interest rate movements correctly, the projected realized return rises and the effective safety margin increases thus providing an even larger cushion for pursuing an active strategy.

In effect the safety margin, x, is the potential cost of attempting to obtain the excess returns of an active strategy. Since x is specified in advance, this potential cost is known. Many portfolio managers have shown a willingness to accept this potential cost in order to obtain the potential excess returns from an active strategy. The contingent immunization strategy is comparable to the "stop loss" strategy of investing in equity securities. In this case, if the market price of a security reaches some minimal level, or floor, the investor sells the security so as to minimize further loss. The idea is not a new one, therefore, but the application of the idea to portfolios of fixed income securities is new and far more complex.

POTENTIAL RETURN

At any point during the planning period an investor can calculate the rate of return that can be realized for the entire planning period if interest rates do not change. Let V_0 be the initial investment. Let the planning period be q years in length. Suppose that the value of the portfolio is V_t at the end of year t $(t < q)$ so that there are $q - t$ periods left in the planning period. Let the rate of interest at the end of period t be r^*, where r^* is also the yield to maturity used to discount the income stream giving the value V_t. If the interest rate does not change in subsequent periods, the investment fund will grow to a value of $(1 + r^*)^{q-t} V_t$ at the end of the planning period (assuming annual compounding). The initial investment was V_0 dollars and the projected value of the investment fund after q periods is $(1 + r^*)^{q-t} V_t$. The projected realized annual rate of return for the entire planning period must then be $\bar{r}$ where $\bar{r}$ must satisfy

$$(1 + \bar{r})^q V_0 = (1 + r^*)^{q-t} V_t. \tag{6.2}$$

Given the value of the investment fund at time t, namely V_t, the remaining time in the planning period, and the interest rate at time t, the projected realized rate of return is easily calculated using equation (6.2).

Equation (6.2) can be simplified. The realized annual rate of return through the first t periods must satisfy the condition

$$(1 + \bar{r}_t)^t V_0 = V_t, \tag{6.3}$$

where $\bar{r}_t$ is the realized annual rate for t periods. Substitution of (6.3) into (6.2) gives us

$$(1 + \bar{r})^q V_0 = (1 + r^*)^{q-t}(1 + \bar{r}_t)^t V_0 \tag{6.4}$$

or

$$(1 + \bar{r})^q = (1 + r^*)^{q-t}(1 + \bar{r}_t)^t. \tag{6.4'}$$

Using (6.4'), all that one needs to know in order to project the potential rate of return for the planning period is (1) the annual realized rate of return, $\bar{r}_t$, through the first t periods and (2) the current interest rate.

The return $(1 + \bar{r})$ in (6.4') is called the "geometric" average of $(1 + r^*)$ and $(1 + \bar{r}_t)$. Taking the logarithms of both sides of (6.4') and dividing by q, we obtain

$$\ln(1+\bar{r}) = \left(\frac{q-t}{q}\right)\ln(1+r^*) + \left(\frac{t}{q}\right)\ln(1+\bar{r}_t). \qquad (6.5)$$

Noting that the weights $(q-t)/q$ and t/q are nonnegative and add to unity shows that $\ln(1+\bar{r})$ is a simple weighted average of $\ln(1+r^*)$ and $\ln(1+\bar{r}_t)$. As an average it follows that $\ln(1+\bar{r})$ will not exceed the larger value of $\ln(1+r^*)$ or $\ln(1+\bar{r}_t)$ nor be less than the smaller of the two values. Similarly, it follows that $\bar{r}$ will also lie between the smaller and larger of the two rates r^* and $\bar{r}_t$.

Equation (6.4') can be extended so as to show that the realized return $(1+\bar{r})$ is a geometric average of all the one-period realized returns over the planning period. That is,

$$(1+\bar{r})^q = (1+\bar{r}_1)(1+\bar{r}_2)(1+\bar{r}_3)\cdots(1+\bar{r}_q). \qquad (6.6)$$

Now, suppose the promised interest rate at the start of the planning period is r, and that x, the safety margin, is initially specified so that the "floor" to the realized rate over the planning period is given as $r_f = r - x$. Suppose the realized rate after one period is $\bar{r}_1$. The projected realized rate for the planning period (using equation (6.4') with $t=1$) must then satisfy the condition

$$(1+\bar{r})^q = (1+\bar{r}_1)(1+r^*)^{q-1}, \qquad (6.7)$$

where r^* is the new interest rate given after the initial investment and presumed to prevail for the remainder of the planning period. The realized rate $\bar{r}_1$ depends upon the initial duration chosen relative to the planning period and on the new rate r^*. The basic idea underlying contingent immunization is that under the most adverse circumstances of forecast error, the realized rate $\bar{r}$ will tend toward r_f very gradually. The safety margin, x, is presumed to be large enough relative to (r^*-r) so that the investor has time to react and to shift to an immunization strategy just at the time or just before $\bar{r}$ reaches r_f. In other words, the investor believes that after one period

$$(1+r_f)^q < (1+\bar{r})^q = (1+\bar{r}_1)(1+r^*)^{q-1}$$

and that as time passes the pursuit of the active strategy will imply that the sequence of one-period realized rates $(\bar{r}_1, \bar{r}_2, \ldots)$ will be such that $\bar{r}$ will tend toward r_f at most very gradually as the most adverse scenario of new interest rates unfolds.

In the formula (6.7), the new rate r^* is assumed to be close to $\bar{r}$ because over subperiods interest rate changes are relatively small. The value of $\bar{r}_1$ may be a number occurring within a very wide range. However, the impact of the change (r^*-r) on $\bar{r}$ may be very small because r^* is given the greater weight in (6.7). The following example illustrates this phenomenon.

Table 6-1.   Illustration of the Potential Rate of Return

(1) r^*	(2) $V(r^*)$	(3) $(1+r^*/2)V(r^*)$	(4) $\bar{r}_1$	(5) $\bar{r}$
.1050	$1,136,226	$1,195,878	.3918	.1321
.1075	1,111,253	1,170,982	.3420	.1298
.1100	1,087,249	1,147,047	.2941	.1277
.1125	1,064,167	1,124,026	.2481	.1257
.1150	1,041,960	1,101,872	.2037	.1237
.1175	1,020,584	1,080,544	.1611	.1218
.1200	1,000,000	1,060,000	.1200	.1200
.1225	980,168	1,040,203	.0804	.1183
.1250	961,105	1,021,119	.0422	.1166
.1275	942,619	1,002,711	.0054	.1150
.1300	924,835	984,949	− .0301	.1134
.1325	907,670	967,803	− .0644	.1119
.1350	891,065	951,244	− .0975	.1105

Note: $1,000,000 is invested in a 30-year 12% par U.S. Treasury security. $r^* =$ the new interest rate given instantly after the investment. $V(r^*) =$ the value of the investment given r^*; $\bar{r}_1 =$ the annual realized rate after 6 months; $\bar{r} =$ the projected annual realized rate of return for a planning period of 5 years.

Example.   Let the planning period be 5.0 years in length (ten 6-month periods). An investor plunges $1,000,000 into a 30-year 12% par U.S. Treasury security. This bond has a duration of 8.566 years. The promised rate of return is 12% per annum compounded semiannually. The investor chooses a safety margin of $x = 1\%$ so that the interest rate floor is 11%. In Table 6-1, column 1 (labeled r^*) gives the new interest rate that can occur instantly after the investment of $1,000,000. Column 2 gives the value of the 30-year bond as $V(r^*)$ instantly after the new rate occurs. Multiplying the values in column 2 by $(1+r^*/2)$ gives the value of the investment fund after one 6-month period in column 3. The annual realized rate for the first 6-month period is given in column 4 as $\bar{r}_1$. This is calculated using the equation

$$1 + \frac{\bar{r}_1}{2} = \left(1 + \frac{r^*}{2}\right)\frac{V(r^*)}{1,000,000}.$$

Finally, column 5 gives the projected annual realized rate, $\bar{r}$, for the entire planning period. This rate is calculated using the equation

$$\left(1 + \frac{\bar{r}}{2}\right)^{10} = \left(1 + \frac{\bar{r}_1}{2}\right)\left(1 + \frac{r^*}{2}\right)^9.$$

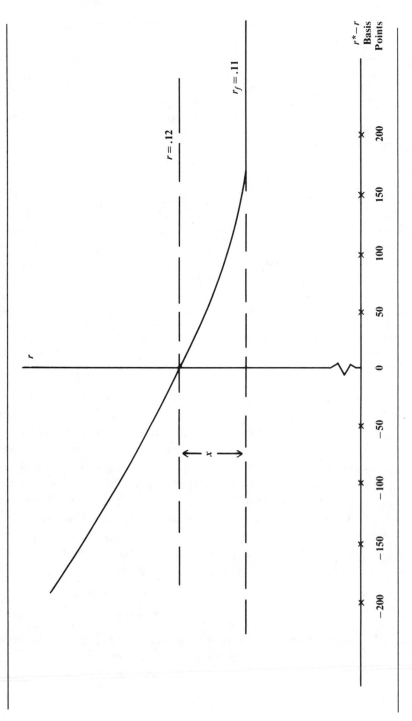

Figure 6-1. Contingent Immunization: Rate of Return $\bar{r}$ and Interest Rate Changes Given Floor Rate r_f

Looking at the last two columns, we immediately observe that the potential rate of return, $\bar{r}$, for the planning period is only slightly affected by a very wide fluctuation in the new rate, r^*, and an even wider fluctuation in the realized rate, $\bar{r}_1$, for the first 6-month period. If the annual interest rate instantly increases by 150 basis points to 0.135, the potential realized rate of return over the planning period becomes 0.1105 despite a negative rate of return over the first 6 months of -0.0975. The loss in the potential rate of return is 95 basis points $(0.1200 - 0.1105)$, still within the safety margin of 100 basis points.

This example helps us to show graphically how contingent immunization works. In Figure 6-1, $(r^* - r)$, the instant change in basis points is shown on the horizontal axis, and the potential rate of return for the planning period is measured on the vertical axis. The potential rate of return as a function of $(r^* - r)$ is then given as the solid line in the diagram. The "safety margin" of $x = .01$ is chewed up only if the increase in the interest rate is a little over 150 basis points in the diagram. If the interest rate change increases by 150 basis points, the portfolio manager shifts to an immunization strategy that "locks in" the floor rate r_f for the planning period. Therefore, the potential realized rate will not fall below 11%, yet the manager can potentially earn a rate of return well above 12% if interest rates fall as apparently anticipated because of the decision to "go long" by choosing a portfolio having a duration in excess of 5 years.

TRIGGER YIELD CONTOURS

The "trigger yield" is that annual rate of return r^* which triggers the immunization strategy. It is that rate which will wipe out the safety margin x. In Table 6-1, the trigger yield is slightly above 13.5% for the case where the investment is in a 30-year 12% par bond. The trigger yield is a function of the portfolio duration, the safety margin, and the planning period length. In the example of the previous section, all of these values were fixed so that the trigger yield r^* was slightly above 13.5%. A bond with a different duration, holding the safety margin and planning period fixed, would have a different trigger yield. The trigger yield contour relates the trigger yield to the duration initially chosen.

Figure 6-2 shows how the trigger yield varies with duration given a 1% safety margin, a 12% promised rate of return, and a 5-year planning period. In this diagram, the larger $|D - 5|$, where D is duration, the closer is the trigger yield to the promised yield and the smaller the change in interest rates,

Figure 6–2.　Contingent Immunization: Trigger Yield Contours

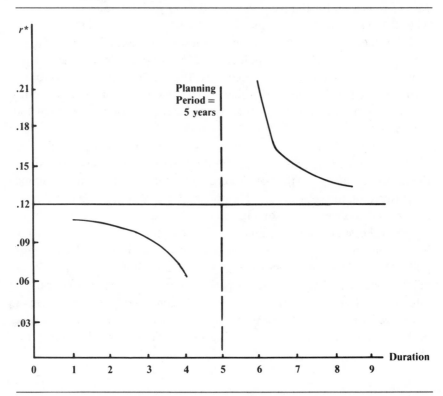

$r^* - r$, required to trigger the immunization strategy. When an investment is concentrated in a 20-year 12% par bond, the duration is 7.975 years and the trigger yield is 13.91%. If the interest rate should increase from 12% to 13.91% instantly after the initial investment, the immunization strategy would be triggered instantly. On the other hand, if the investment is concentrated in a 10-year 12% par bond, the duration is 6.079 years and the trigger yield is 21.47%. Hence, instantly after the initial investment the interest rate would have to increase from 12% to 21.47% to trigger immunization. This is an enormous increase in rates, and most unlikely. If the investor goes short by concentrating the entire investment in 1-year securities having a duration of 0.972 years, the trigger yield is 10.76%. The interest rate need only decrease from 12% to 10.76% to trigger immunization. If duration were closer to the planning period, say 3.9 years, the trigger yield drops to 7.26%.

For durations approximately between 4 and 6 years in the diagram, virtually no change in interest rates will trigger immunization. This is the "safe haven" in which the investor can be assured of earning at least the 11% floor rate. The safe haven requires an explanation. Consider the case of a 9-year bond. It has a duration of 5.739 years. For small increases (decreases) in the interest rate the potential realized yield decreases (increases) as expected when going long. However, as the interest rate increases, the duration calculated at the new rate decreases. Recall that the duration varies inversely with the interest rate. For large enough increases in the interest rate the duration can fall below 5.0 years, the planning period length. In other words, with sufficiently large increases in the interest rate, the investment shifts from a long position to a short position. Once the duration falls below 5.0 years any further increases in the interest rate will cause the potential realized rate of return to increase. By going short at the higher interest rates the potential realized return increases with the interest rate. Retracing these movements, as interest rates increase the potential realized return falls, but eventually a point is reached at which the duration is 5.0 years. A further increase in the interest rate results in the potential realized return increasing. Thus, a minimum potential realized rate of return is reached at some interest rate. For the 9-year bond with an initial duration of 5.739 years, the duration falls to 5.0 years at the very high interest rate of 19.91% with a potential realized rate of return of 11.42%. The potential realized rate can never reach the floor rate of 11.0%. This same phenomenom has occurred in previous examples. Table 4–2 contains examples of it. A similar explanation is applicable when the initial duration is less than 5.0 years. A 7-year bond has an initial duration of 4.926 years. As the interest rate decreases, the duration increases and reaches 5.0 years at an interest rate of 10.597%. Any further decrease in rates causes the potential realized return to rise. The minimum realized potential rate of return is slightly under 12%.

A trigger contour map can be drawn for the start of each period. Figure 6–2 is the contour map for the start of the very first period of the investment plan. At the start of the next period several changes must be incorporated into the diagram to reflect new circumstances. First, the planning period length is reduced by one 6-month period, given that a period is 6 months. In Figure 6–2 this means that the immunizing portfolio then has a duration of 4.5 years. Second, the promised return for the planning period changes. It is now equal to the potential realized rate for the planning period for an immunization strategy when a portfolio duration of 4.5 years is put into effect. This new promised yield will depend upon r^*, the new rate which occurred just after the initial investment was made. The floor rate, r_f, is unaffected. Third, with a new promised rate of return for the planning period, the trigger contours must shift. As an example of how the new contour map may

Figure 6-3. Contingent Immunization: Shift of Trigger Yield Contours

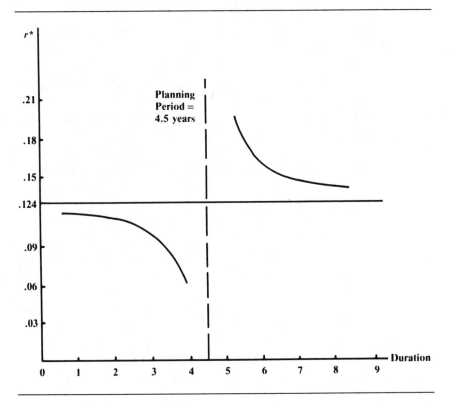

look, consider Figure 6-3. Here it is assumed that the initial investment was in a 30-year 12% par bond with a duration of 8.566 years. The investor is anticipating a decrease in interest rates. Let us suppose that this forecast is wrong and that the interest rate increases to 12.4%, an increase of 40 basis points. The annual realized rate for the first 6-month period is $\bar{r}_1 = .05734$, calculated using the formula

$$\left(1 + \frac{\bar{r}_1}{2}\right)(1,000,000) = V(r^*),$$

where $V(r^*)$ is the value of the investment after 6 months and where $r^* = .124$. The new promised annual realized rate of return $\bar{r} = .1172$ for the planning period can then be calculated using the formula

$$\left(1 + \frac{\bar{r}}{2}\right)^{10} = \left(1 + \frac{\bar{r}_1}{2}\right)\left(1 + \frac{r^*}{2}\right)^9,$$

where it is assumed that r^* will be unchanged for the remainder of the planning period. Since the floor rate, $r_f = .11$, is unchanged and since $\bar{r} = .1172 >$ .11, we see that part of the safety margin x has eroded because of the forecast error. The safety margin is now $\bar{r} - r_f = .724$. The investor must now decide the portfolio duration given these facts and a new planning period of 4.5 years. A new trigger yield contour map may be very valuable at this point because the investor can then see what the new trigger yields are for each duration that he may choose. In Figure 6–3, if the interest rate r^* stays at its level of .124 there will be no change in the realized rate for the planning period. The realized rate will remain at .1172. The contour map looks substantially the same as that occurring at the start of the period. The safe haven is now a fairly symmetric interval ranging from 3.9 to 5.3 years around the duration of 4.5 years. As a consequence of the forecast error the contours are closer to the new rate of return of .124. For example, if the investor continues to keep the investment in the 30-year 12% bond the trigger yield will be .134, only 100 basis points above .124. At the start of the period the trigger yield on this investment was .136 — 160 basis points above the starting interest rate of .12. If the investor continues the active strategy, further forecast errors will bring the contours even closer to the prevailing interest rate.

Trigger yield contour maps can be drawn at the end of each period. The investor can then visualize how close a further interest rate change may move the portfolio to a trigger point as a consequence of any chosen portfolio decision. The examples in Figures 6–2 and 6–3 show that the adverse change in the interest rate of 40 basis points only chewed up 27.6 basis points of the safety margin. Although the effect of this is to bring the contours closer to the prevailing interest rate, the example shows that changes in the prevailing rate have a smaller effect on the safety margin thus giving scope to the possibilities of an active strategy. However, there is no question that a sequence of such errors or that much larger changes in the prevailing interest rate can trigger immunization.

If there is no forecast error, the trigger yield contours move farther away from the prevailing interest rate. In this case the effective safety margin increases as the promised rate of return rises.

SOME IMPORTANT FEATURES OF CONTINGENT IMMUNIZATION

During the first 6-month period, interest rate changes are likely to be much more gradual than Figure 6–1 and the example suggest. In the example, the interest rate change took place instantly after an investment. In fact, interest rate changes may occur on a daily basis throughout a subperiod. A gradual process of change having an accumulated change as measured on the horizontal axis of Figure 6-1 has the effect of twisting the curve in Figure 6-1 counterclockwise around the intersection point on the vertical axis and of moving the intersection of this sloped line with the floor rate farther to the right. This means that the accumulated change can be much larger before the portfolio manager triggers the portfolio into the immunization mode. This also means that the portfolio manager will be observing a sequence of forecast errors over the period, so that as the safety margin is gradually eroded, the manager can begin to plan the portfolio shift into the immunization mode and can also "brake" the erosion process by gradually moving the portfolio duration closer to the planning period.

The smaller the safety margin, x, the sooner the portfolio is triggered into the immunization mode by adverse interest rate changes. In the limit when $x = 0$, any adverse change, however small, will trigger immunization. Moreover, the smaller x, the greater the likelihood that an adverse change will punch the potential realized rate $\bar{r}$ below the floor rate r_f. Given that the weekly magnitude of the yield change may be as large as 50 to 60 basis points, x should be at least 50 basis points (on a weekly basis) in order to give the manager time to react to adverse changes and to prevent the realized rate from falling through the floor rate r_f. However, the actual value of x relative to the duration of the chosen portfolio is the critical consideration. Durations closer to the planning period length may well allow for a much smaller safety margin because of the safe haven. However, the duration interval constituting the safe haven gets smaller with a smaller safety margin.

Once the immunization mode is triggered, it is essentially irreversible given the initial safety margin x. If the portfolio is returned to an active mode, any adverse change in rates, however small, would retrigger immunization.

The shorter the planning period, the greater is the impact of an interest rate change on the potential realized rate for the planning period. This is especially apparent in equation (6.6). The smaller the value of q, the greater the importance of any single realized rate for a subperiod. Given any single adverse interest rate change, there simply may be an insufficient number of successful periods in which changes may swamp the single adverse effect. Contingent immunization works best for planning periods of at least 3 years in duration.

Since risk control is one of the most important aspects of contingent immunization, the portfolio manager must continually monitor interest rate changes and calculate the impact of these changes on the portfolio. As in any active strategy, interest rate changes matter. Moreover, success with contingent immunization depends on correctly forecasting the direction of interest rate movements. Interest rate changes are extremely difficult to forecast and doing so successfully may often be happenstance. One cannot expect any particular portfolio manager to be any more consistently successful at this than investment consultants are at obtaining abnormal returns for their clients.

RISK AND RETURN UNDER CONTINGENT IMMUNIZATION

In Chapter 5 points on the efficient frontier between the expected rate of return and its standard deviation were determined by the initial portfolio duration. A random interest rate followed the initial portfolio duration decision and the new rate was maintained throughout the planning period length. The expected return and its standard deviation reflect the a priori anticipation of the outcome of the strategy. Upon continued repetition of the same initial decision with the same initial conditions, the expected rate of return would be the average rate of return. When immunization is triggered under the contingent immunization strategy, the time at which it is triggered occurs later on in the planning period. It is a dynamic strategy in which the switch to the immunization mode is *contingent* upon the random rate of interest that occurs. This switch is made after the new random rate has occurred and it is made in anticipation of further interest rate changes during the planning period. Technically, the contingent immunization strategy cannot be described in a single expected return–standard deviation diagram because of its dynamic features. One must use a sequence of diagrams. The initially chosen duration has a corresponding expected return and a standard deviation that reflects the average consequence of a new random rate that is maintained throughout the planning period. Under contingent immunization, that new random rate is used to calculate the potential realized rate of return if it stays unchanged over the remainder of the planning period. At the beginning of the next period, the planning period is shorter by one period, and some new probability distribution over the second random rate may be in effect. At the start of this next period we can redraw the expected return–risk diagram for the shorter planning period and the possibly new probability distribution. A new duration decision is made at this time within an entirely new expected return–risk framework.

Under contingent immunization, the water is never under the bridge. The investor's duration decision at the start of the second period depends on what happened during the first period. One can view the connection between the two periods in two ways. First, if there is a forecast error so large that a trigger yield is reached, the investor or portfolio manager is disposed toward modifying his or her probability distribution over future rates. This modification can be expected to produce a flatter efficient frontier. If initially a high probability is placed on interest rate increases, the error in forecast induces a readjustment toward a lower probability and a flatter efficient frontier, and conversely for a high probability on interest rate decreases. Given an unchanged shape of the indifference curves, the flatter efficient frontier implies the choice of an optimal duration closer to the remaining time in the planning period. (This assumes the perverse reaction described in Figure 5–4 cannot occur.) Second, if the portfolio manager is acting as an agent for an investor, his subjective trade-off between risk and return can change when a large forecast error is made. Large forecast errors and a deterioration in portfolio performance may induce the investors to take their accounts elsewhere and fewer new investors are likely to knock on the door of the portfolio manager. The manager may thus be induced to become more risk averse so that the indifference curves describing the manager's subjective trade-offs between risk and return develop steeper slopes. This also produces optimal durations closer to the length of the planning period.

REFERENCES

Leibowitz, Martin L., and Alfred Weinberger. 1981a. "Contingent Immunization: A New Procedure for Structured Active Management." Salomon Brothers, January 28.

———. 1981b. "The Uses of Contingent Immunization." *Journal of Portfolio Management* (Fall).

———. 1982a. "Risk Control Procedures under Contingent Immunization." Salomon Brothers, February.

———. 1982b. "Contingent Immunization, Part I: Risk Control Procedures." *Financial Analyst's Journal* (November–December): 17–32.

———. 1983. "Contingent Immunization, Part II: Problem Areas." *Financial Analyst's Journal* (January–February): 35–50.

7 FUNDING MULTIPLE LIABILITIES
Dedicated Portfolios

It is often intended that an investment fund accumulate for the purpose of discharging some future liability obligation. Pension funds are an example. In previous chapters we have regarded the planning period as the time to the date at which an obligation must be discharged; and we were interested in the liquidation value of the portfolio at the end of the planning period. In more realistic settings, there are many future dates at which liabilities are discharged. In effect, an investor (institutional or otherwise) may therefore have many simultaneous planning periods.

An obvious way to manage funds for multiple planning periods is to establish an investment fund for each one of the periods. For many investors this could require the management of thousands of different investment funds, where each has a separate planning period. This raises the issue as to whether or not the entire set of investment funds could be commingled or merged and managed as a single investment fund, yet nonetheless be managed so as to meet the objectives for each planning period. In fact, it was this problem to which Redington (1952, reprinted 1982) first applied the idea of "immunization." Redington, an insurance actuary, realized that the dates and amounts of future cash outflows required of a life insurance company could be estimated very accurately for a large life insurance company. Interest rate changes can affect the value and growth rates of the company's assets. Given the risk of interest rate changes, Redington wished to determine an asset investment strategy that would provide the insurance company with the liquidity necessary at future dates to discharge a sequence of liability obligations.

This chapter presents Redington's problem in very much the same way that he posed it. A modern solution, as devised by Bierwag, Kaufman, and Toevs (1983), is also shown.

REDINGTON'S PROBLEM

For simplicity let us consider future time intervals that are exactly one year apart. In effect we will be compounding on an annual basis, but, as in previous chapters, there is no problem in extending all results to the case of more frequent compounding.

Suppose that the liability cash outflow at the end of year t is given as L_t, where $L_t > 0$ for $t = 1, 2, 3, ..., M$. If the current interest rate is r, then the present value of these liability obligations is

$$L = \sum_{t=1}^{M} L_t (1+r)^{-t}. \qquad (7.1)$$

The investor's relevant assets are invested so as to produce the cash inflow A_t, where $A_t \geq 0$, and $t = 1, 2, 3, ..., M$. The present value of these cash inflows is then

$$A = \sum_{t=1}^{M} A_t (1+r)^{-t}. \qquad (7.2)$$

The liability obligations are said to be *fully funded* if $A \geq L$. That is, the value of the assets is sufficient to pay off the value of the liabilities instantly. If the investor liquidated the balance sheet, the value of the assets would be sufficient to pay all creditors the current value of their claims. The liability obligations are *underfunded* if $A < L$. Redington considers the case where the liability obligations are exactly fully funded so that $A = L$. Define $N = A - L$. The assumption that the liabilities are exactly fully funded means that $N = 0$. If the liabilities remain fully funded as time passes, it will always be possible to liquidate assets to pay off the claims as they come due. If there is no change in the interest rate as time passes, the liabilities will remain fully funded. In one period assets will grow to $(1+r)A$ and liabilities will grow to $(1+r)L$; hence $(1+r)(A-L) = (1+r)N = 0$. The process can continue for future periods as well. However, if interest rates change, it is possible for A to change by more or less than changes in L and possibly forcing N to be negative so that the liabilities become underfunded, and some liabilities at some future dates cannot be fully discharged if the underfunded situation persists.

Redington showed that if the assets or their cash flows were always chosen so as to satisfy two conditions, then N would never change to a negative value. Redington's two conditions are that the assets should be chosen so that

1.   the duration of the cash inflows equals the duration of the outflows, and
2.   the value of the cash inflows should be more "dispersed" around the duration than the value of the cash outflows.

If both conditions (1) and (2) are satisfied, then the liability obligations are said to be "immunized."

The first condition is a familiar one. The asset and liability durations are respectively defined as

$$D_A = \sum_1^M tA_t(1+r)^{-t}/A, \quad \text{and}$$
$$D_L = \sum_1^M tL_t(1+r)^{-t}/L. \tag{7.3}$$

To satisfy the first condition, the investor simply chooses the assets so that the inflows $A_1, A_2, ..., A_t, ..., A_M$ will give a value of D_A that is equal to the value of D_L. The liability duration, D_L, can be regarded as the "average" length of the planning period. If there were only one liability to discharge at a single future date, at time q, say, then the condition becomes $D_A = q$, the familiar immunization conditions discussed in previous chapters. However, noting that duration is a weighted average of flow dates,

$$D_L = \sum_1^M w_t^L t, \quad \text{where } w_t^L = L_t(1+r)^{-t}/L \geq 0 \text{ and } \sum_1^M w_t^L = 1,$$

it can be regarded as a weighted average of the planning periods implied by the outflow dates.

Redington's second condition, the "dispersion" condition, is a condition that is more difficult to explain. Appendix 7A contains a full technical explanation of it. The dispersion condition arises only when there is more than one planning period; it is automatically satisfied by the first condition when there is only one planning period. The dispersion condition assures us that the sequence of cash outflows can be discharged without forcing N to negative values. Although the cash flows taken as a group may satisfy the first condition, there are many time patterns of such flows that will do so. Some of the patterns may require too great a reduction in the value of assets at some dates relative to other dates in order to discharge the liability outflows. Recall that when the interest rate changes randomly, the investment accumulation depends on how quickly (slowly) initial capital losses (gains) are offset by higher (lower) growth rates in later periods. An early liquidation of some assets to meet some early obligations may prevent sufficient later growth to meet later obligations. Examples of how this can occur are presented in the next section.

The dispersion condition is similar to a variance condition in probability theory, and, as shown in Appendix 7A, it can be described in that way. The asset and liability durations can be written as

$$D_A = \sum w_t^A t, \quad \text{and}$$
$$D_L = \sum w_t^L t,$$

$$(7.4)$$

where $w_t^A = A_t(1+r)^{-t}/A$ and $w_t^L = L_t(1+r)^{-t}/L$. These weights, w_t^A and w_t^L, are like probability distributions. For example,

$$0 \le w_t^A \le 1, \quad 0 \le w_t^L \le 1, \quad \sum w_t^A = \sum w_t^L = 1.$$

If one interprets these weights as probabilities, then D_A and D_L can be regarded as the means or expected values of t which are multiplied by the weights in (7.4). In fact, Samuelson (1945), who independently devised similar formulas, called D_A and D_L the "average period" of the respective flows. In probability theory the variance is a measure of the degree to which the weights are distributed around the mean. The comparable measures of the variances, here, are defined as

$$I_A = \sum w_t^A(t - D_A)^2, \quad \text{and}$$
$$I_L = \sum w_t^L(t - D_L)^2.$$

$$(7.5)$$

In Bierwag (1979), these dispersion measures are called "inertias" because of their resemblance to similar constructs in physics. Redington's second condition, in these terms, states that the asset flows (or the w_t^A's) must be chosen so that $I_A \ge I_L$. It is in this sense that the value of the asset flows must be more "dispersed" than the value of the liability flows. If there is a single liability outflow occurring at date q, then $I_L = 0$ because then $w_q^L = 1$ and $w_t^L = 0$ for $t \ne q$, and $D_L = q$. Then, since I_A cannot be negative, it follows automatically that $I_A \ge I_L = 0$; and Redington's second condition is satisfied. If, however, there are two or more liability outflows, then $I_L > 0$, so that it is possible for $I_A < I_L$ and so violate the second condition.

Figure 7–1. Net Worth and Interest Rates: Possible Relationships

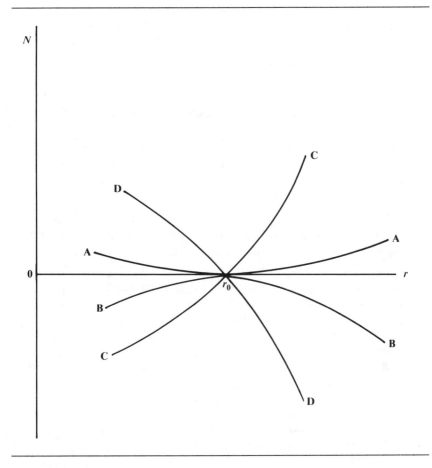

Figure 7–1 shows a diagrammatic description of the Redington conditions. In this diagram N (net worth) is chosen as a function of the rate of interest r. Let r_0 be the initial rate of interest. At the initial rate of interest $N = 0$ because the liability outflows are fully funded. If Redington's first condition is satisfied, then the slope of the curve in Figure 7–1 at the point r_0 is zero. In Figure 7–1, this occurs only for curves AA and BB. If Redington's second condition is satisfied, the curve has a slope which increases as we pass through r_0. In the diagram, this occurs only for curves AA and CC. The only curve in the diagram satisfying both conditions is AA. For this curve

we observe that $N > 0$ for $r \neq r_0$, and, hence, no change in the interest rate can result in the liabilities being underfunded. Curve DD in the diagram is one that satisfies neither of Redington's conditions.

Redington's second condition is the most difficult on for which to devise simple rules for portfolio construction. Some such rules have been worked out and are presented later in this chapter.

EXAMPLES OF REDINGTON'S CONDITIONS

Example 1.   Suppose there are two liability outflows. At the end of years 5 and 8, $10,000 and $26,620 (respectively) must be paid out. If the rate of interest is 10%, the present values of these outflows are respectively $6,209 and $12,418 so that $L = \$18,628$ (after rounding). The duration of these outflows is $D_L = 7.0$ years. The weights w_5^L and w_8^L are respectively .33 and .67. This implies that $I_L = w_5^L(5 - D_L)^2 + w_8^L(8 - D_L)^2 = 2.00 > 0$. Suppose one asset inflow of $36,300 is scheduled at the end of year 7.0. The present value of this inflow is $A = \$18,628 = L$ so that $N = A - L = 0$, and the liability outflows are fully funded. Now suppose the interest rate changes to the values given below in column 1. The corresponding values of the asset and liabilities are given in columns 2 and 3. The value of N is given in column 4. Note

(1)	(2)	(3)	(4)
r	A	L	$N = A - L$
.07	$22,606	$22,623	$ – 17.13
.08	21,181	21,188	– 7.09
.09	19,857	19,859	– 1.65
.10	18,628	18,628	0
.11	17,484	17,486	– 1.44
.12	16,420	16,426	– 5.36
.13	15,430	15,441	–11.27

that $N < 0$ for $r \neq .10$. This produces a curve like BB in Figure 7-1. We have failed to satisfy Redington's second condition because $I_A = 0 < 2.0 = I_L$, even though the first condition is satisfied.

Although the negative numbers in column 4 are not very large in absolute value relative to A or L, they could be larger in other examples, and some simple routines not involving much cost could conceivably lead to allocations that satisfy Redington's second condition.

Example 2.   Suppose we change the asset inflow dates in Example 1 so that $I_A > I_L$. Let the inflows of \$10,626 and \$27,609 occur at the end of years 3 and 10 respectively. The present value of this asset is \$18,628, the same as before, so that the liability outflows are still fully funded. Moreover, with $w_3^A = .4286$ and $w_{10}^A = .5714$, it follows that $D_A = 7.0$ years $= D_L$ so that Redington's first condition is satisfied. Reproducing the same table as in Example 1 gives us a new table as follows:

(1) r	(2) A	(3) L	(4) $N = A - L$
.07	\$22,709	\$22,623	\$85.71
.08	21,223	21,188	35.45
.09	19,867	19,859	8.26
.10	18,628	18,628	0
.11	17,493	17,486	7.18
.12	16,452	16,426	26.83
.13	15,497	15,441	56.41

Now, we note that $N > 0$ for all interest rates different from the initial rate of 10%, and the liabilities remain fully funded. We have produced a curve like AA in Figure 7-1.

Similar examples will produce the curves CC and DD in Figure 7-1.

A DECISION RULE FOR REDINGTON'S DISPERSION CONDITION

Both of Redington's conditions can be satisfied by constructing the asset portfolio systematically according to specific rules. In this section, such a systematic procedure, appearing first in Bierwag, Kaufman, and Toevs (1983), is presented. Appendix 7B contains a proof that the rules presented here do, in fact, work.

Given the liability outflows, a variety of asset portfolios will satisfy both of Redington's conditions. A large set of portfolios that will do so can be divided into groups. The simplest of these groups to describe is the *two-level asset portfolio.* Many other portfolios that will also work are built on the class of two-level asset portfolios and are called the *three-level, four-level,* ..., and *m-level* asset portfolios, classes of asset portfolios defined for any *m*, a positive integer.

Two-Level Asset Portfolios

Any potential asset portfolio that satisfies the Redington conditions has inflows that can be divided into two artibrary income streams. If the income stream promises the cash flow A_t at time t, then divide A_t into two parts, A_{t1} and A_{t2}, so that $A_{t1} + A_{t2} = A_t$. This division can be done in any way whatsoever as long as $A_{t1} \geq 0$ and $A_{t2} \geq 0$. The present values of each of the two income streams are

$$A^{(1)} = \sum A_{t1}(1+r)^{-t}, \quad \text{and}$$
$$A^{(2)} = \sum A_{t2}(1+r)^{-t}. \tag{7.6}$$

Similarly, their durations are

$$D_{A1} = \sum t A_{t1}(1+r)^{-t}/A^{(1)}, \quad \text{and}$$
$$D_{A2} = \sum t A_{t2}(1+r)^{-t}/A^{(2)}. \tag{7.7}$$

The duration of the asset portfolio is then

$$D_A = D_{A1}\left(\frac{A^{(1)}}{A}\right) + D_{A2}\left(\frac{A^{(2)}}{A}\right), \tag{7.8}$$

found in the usual way for calculating the duration of two combined income streams. To satisfy the first Redington condition we pick the asset portfolio so that $D_A = D_L$. To satisfy the second condition, we pick the asset so that

Two-Level Rule. $D_{A1} \leq t_1$ and $D_{A2} \geq t_2$,

where t_1 is the date of the earliest positive liability cash outflow and t_2 is the date of the latest positive liability cash outflow. In finding the appropriate asset composition, it is usually easiest to try to utilize at least two bonds having different durations so that one can jiggle the proportions invested in each so as to obtain the desired duration. The two-level rule works very well in the same way. We may simply pick two bonds — one having a duration less than or equal to the earliest positive cash outflow and another having a duration greater than or equal to the latest positive cash outflow. That choice, by itself, satisfies the second condition. Then, we may change the proportions invested in each bond to satisfy the first condition. Example 2, in the previous section, well illustrates this procedure. There, liability outflows are scheduled for $t = 5$ and $t = 8$. Two zero coupon bonds were chosen as assets. One had a duration of 3 years and the other had a duration of 10 years. The two-level decision rule is satisfied. Of course, it is unnecessary that the two immunizing bonds be zero coupon bonds.

There exist asset portfolios satisfying the Redington conditions that are not two-level portfolios. Suppose the cash inflows exactly match the cash outflows for three successive periods. Exact matching satisfies the Redington conditions because both the asset and liability flows have the same durations and inertias. However, no matter how we partition the asset flows into two streams, we fail to satisfy the two-level rule. If the earliest cash inflow comprises the first asset income stream and the last two cash flows comprise the second cash inflow, then the first cash flow has a duration equal to the earliest cash outflow date, but the second asset income stream has a duration less than the latest cash outflow date. If we reallocate portions of the middle cash inflow to the first asset, its duration increases and becomes greater than the earliest cash outflow date, but the second asset can never have a duration in excess of the last cash outflow date. The middle cash inflow must be allocated to either or both of the two arbitrary partitions. Doing so prevents satisfaction of the Redington second condition. Hence, this case of perfectly matched inflows and outflows is not a two-level portfolio but yet it satisfies Redington's second condition.[1] However, this perfectly matched case is a three-level asset portfolio.

Three-Level Asset Portfolios

For three-level portfolios we first arbitrarily partition the liability outflows into two income streams. Let the first have a value of $L^{(1)}$ and the second a value of $L^{(2)}$ so that $L^{(1)} + L^{(2)} = L$. Treating each liability stream as a separate liability, we then find a two-level asset portfolio for each of them, where the first asset is $A^{(1)} = L^{(1)}$ and the second is $A^{(2)} = L^{(2)}$. We then split $A^{(1)}$ into two parts $A_1^{(1)}$ and $A_2^{(1)}$ so that $A_1^{(1)} + A_2^{(1)} = A^{(1)} = L^{(1)}$. The split of the flows corresponding to $A^{(1)}$ is devised so that the duration of the first is less than or equal to the earliest outflow date in $L^{(1)}$ and the second is greater than or equal to the last outflow date in $L^{(1)}$, but so that the durations of $A^{(1)}$ and $L^{(1)}$ are equal. We split $A^{(2)}$ similarly into two parts. This approach simply represents a reapplication of two-level asset portfolios to segments of the liability outflow stream initially given. The example of three successively matched outflows and inflows is a three-level asset portfolio. In this example, the first cash outflow and half of the second can be the first liability; and the last outflow and half of the second can comprise the second liability. We then partition the asset inflows in exactly the same way. Each of the two assets is then a two-level asset portfolio relative to its liability counterpart.

m-Level Portfolios

Let m be any integer larger than 2. Partition the liabilty cash outflows into $(m-1)$ outflow streams. (Note that when $m = 3$ the liabilities are split into two parts.) This creates m liabilities. Form a two-level asset portfolio for each of them.

Asset portfolios of some level are appropriate practical ways of constructing portfolios that will satisfy Redington's conditions. However, there are asset portfolios that will work that are not in the class of m-level portfolios for any m.

One of the properties of any m-level asset portfolio is that some cash inflows must occur no later than the earliest cash outflow and some must occur no earlier than the latest cash outflow. This restriction is stronger than necessary, as is easily illustrated. Suppose the liability cash outflow stream consists of a perpetuity of $10 per year forever. An m-level asset portfolio would have to contain some flows having an infinitely large duration. There does exist an asset portfolio of only two zero coupon bonds that will satisfy the Redington conditions. Let the initial interest rate be $r = .10$. The value of the perpetuity is then $100 ($= 10/r$), its duration is 11 years ($= (1+r)/r$), and its inertia is 110 ($= (1+r)/r^2$). Choose a 1-year zero coupon bond promising $72.07 at the end of one year, and choose a 30-year zero coupon bond promising $601.70 at the end of 30 years. At $r = .10$, this income stream has a value of $100, a duration of 11 years, and an inertia of 190. Since $I_A = 190 > 110 = I_L$, it follows that the income stream satisfies Redington's condition. The following table illustrates what happens to the value of the assets A, the liabilities L, and $N = A - L$ at various interest rates:

(1) r	(2) A	(3) L	(4) $N = A - L$
.07	$146.40	$142.86	$3.54
.08	126.53	125.00	1.52
.09	111.47	111.11	0.36
.10	100.00	100.00	0
.11	91.21	90.91	0.30
.12	84.43	83.33	1.09
.13	79.16	76.92	2.24

Figure 7–2. Asset Inertia Exceeding Liability Inertia Though Having Smaller Range

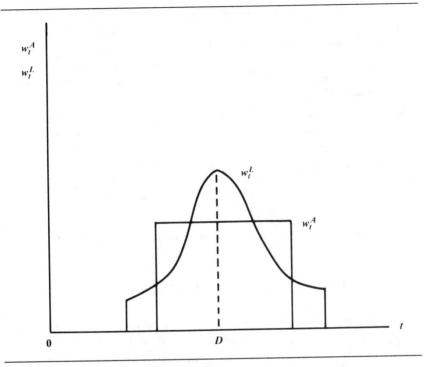

Clearly $N > 0$ at any interest rate not equal to 10%, thus illustrating satisfaction of the Redington conditions.

This last illustration indicates that the inertias are the relevant properties of the portfolio to consider when attempting to satisfy the dispersion condition. If we interpret the inertias as variances and the weights, w_t^A and w_t^L, as probabilities, it is easy to see that many non-m-level asset portfolios can satisfy the dispersion condition. Figure 7–2 illustrates the required condition $I_A > I_L$. The curves w_t^L and w_t^A show how the weights change as functions of the cash flow dates. The two curves have a common duration ("means" in a probability sense), yet the w_t^L curve is drawn so as to have a smaller inertia ("variance" in a probabilistic sense) even though some of its cash flows are earlier and some later than those promised by the asset portfolio. The equations in (7.5) show why $I_L < I_A$ here. As we move t away from D in Figure 7–2, $(t-D)^2$ increases, but note that the weights w_t^L fall below those of w_t^A, forcing I_A above I_L, and the extra weight added in the I_L formula when $w_t^L > 0$ and $w_t^A = 0$ is insufficient to recover the increments in I_A when

$w_t^A > w_t^L$. Thus, although m-level portfolios do satisfy the dispersion condition, such portfolios are not necessary in order to satisfy it.

In many situations, one can begin with an m-level portfolio, and then gradually move the early and late cash flows closer to the duration in order to find some of these non-m-level portfolios which will satisfy the dispersion conditions. Fong and Vasicek (1980) have devised a quadratic programming procedure for finding portfolios that will satisfy these conditions with the minimal possible asset inertias given the set of available bonds to which the assets may be allocated.

Two aspects of the dispersion conditions should be noted. First, from the examples presented above, it appears that the error, represented by the value of N, is small when the dispersion condition is not satisfied. This may be so in many circumstances, but the extent of it has not been subjected to a general error analysis. Second, as developed in Chapter 12, when interest rate changes satisfy "equilibrium stochastic processes," the second Redington condition is unnecessary to maintain a fully funded asset portfolio.

EXTENSIONS OF REDINGTON'S PROBLEM

Redington only considered the problem of maintaining a fully funded portfolio given it was exactly full funded at the start: $N = A - L = 0$. In a broader context one may wish to consider a financial institution for whom A, L, and N respectively represent the institution's entire assets, liabilities, and net worth N. For an economically viable institution, one would expect $N > 0$. Grove (1974) considers the problem of investing the assets so as to prevent net worth from decreasing. This problem is formally identical to Redington's problem except that net worth is initially positive rather than zero.

In Appendix 7A it is shown that the first Redington condition of identical asset and liability durations must be replaced by the condition

$$D_A = D_L(L/A). \tag{7.9}$$

When $L = A$, this reduces to the first Redington condition. When $A > L$, so that $N > 0$, then the asset duration D_A can be less than the liability duration D_L. The dispersion condition then becomes

$$I_A \geq I_L - D_L^2 + D_A^2 \tag{7.10}$$

which also reduces to the second Redington condition when $L = A$ and $D_A = D_L$. Procedures similar to those of the last section can be devised to find the asset portfolios satisfying (7.9) and (7.10).

Grove considers situations in which (7.9) is not satisfied. Satisfaction of (7.9) can be regarded as a "hedged" portfolio in the sense that net worth N is immunized against interest rate changes because N cannot decrease as interest rates change. When $D_A > D_L(L/A)$, then assets will be so more affected by interest rate changes than liabilities that net worth increases if interest rates fall and decreases if interest rates rise. Institutions that choose asset portfolios for which $D_A > D_L(L/A)$ are effectively assuming a risky posture in which they will benefit if interest rates fall but will suffer net worth losses if interest rates rise. Conversely, when $D_A < D_L(L/A)$, the institution is assuming a risky posture in which they will benefit if interest rates rise but will suffer net worth losses if interest rates fall.[2] Both risky situations, $D_A > D_L(L/A)$ or $D_A < D_L(L/A)$, can be described within the risk–return framework of Chapter 5. Moreover, institutions can also utilize the contingent immunization strategy by being willing to take a loss of a given magnitude in net worth, a loss specified a priori, in order to have the flexibility to pursue an active strategy having known consequences if forecast errors develop. Bierwag and Kaufman (1983) and Kaufman (1984) have called the difference $D_A - D_L(L/A)$ a net worth duration *gap*. The use of this "gap" and other similar gaps as measures of interest rate risk for depository institutions are discussed in Chapter 9. Many analysts have pointed out that positive net worth gaps were the main reason why so many Savings and Loan Associations were in such great trouble from 1981 to 1983 in the United States. The transition to a very high interest rate environment resulted in a dramatic loss in the market value of the net worth of these institutions. Savings and Loan Associations during this period were particularly vulnerable to increases in interest rates because it had been their practice for many years, if not their raison d'être, to engage in short-term borrowing (deposits) to finance long-term mortgages to support the U.S. housing industry.[3]

If one can extend the idea of immunization to maintaining net worth, it is natural to ask whether it can also be extended toward maintaining the value of various other meaningful target measures. Kaufman (1984) shows that we can immunize the net worth asset ratio, N/A. As shown in Appendix 7A, the two Redington conditions are exactly the ones to be satisfied in order to do this. This produces the net worth duration gap, now defined as $D_A - D_L$. Kaufman also suggests that immunization can be extended to various measures of net income, as well. Toevs (1983) develops a gap measure, which if set equal to zero, immunizes a "book" measure of income for a given accounting period.

These various gap measures indicate the sensitivity of various accounts to interest rate changes given a structure of projected asset–liability cash flows.

These institutions can thus engage in "gap management." However, the institution cannot immunize every possible target account. If it immunizes net worth, it cannot be immunizing the net worth ratio or the income accounts. The institution must decide where it wishes to bear the risk of interest rate changes as well as how much risk to bear. The prospects of gap management can be applied to a variety of institutions, not just depository institutions. Traditionally, the ideas have been applied in the life insurance industry but clearly the ideas are relevant to pension funds, business finance companies, property and casualty insurance companies, and even to nonfinancial corporations that have specific liability obligations and can meet these obligations with flexible manipulations of their asset composition which includes real assets. Chapter 9 considers some of these features of gap management in greater detail.

APPENDIX 7A
REDINGTON'S CONDITIONS AND OTHER
CONDITIONS FOR IMMUNIZATION

The value of a given stream of liability cash outflows is

$$L = \sum L_t (1+r)^{-t} \tag{7A.1}$$

and the value of a possible stream of cash inflows is

$$A = \sum A_t (1+r)^{-t}, \tag{7A.2}$$

where r is the interest rate, A_t is the cash inflow at the end of the tth year, and L_t is the cash outflow at the end of the tth year, and where annual compounding is assumed. Redington assumes $N = A - L = 0$. We are specifically interested in the behavior of N as the interest rate r changes. Taking the derivative of N with respect to r gives us

$$\frac{dN}{dr} = \sum (L_t - A_t) t (1+r)^{-t}. \tag{7A.3}$$

Noting that

$$D_L = \sum t L_t (1+r)^{-t}/L, \quad \text{and}$$
$$D_A = \sum t A_t (1+r)^{-t}/A, \tag{7A.4}$$

it follows that (7A.3) can be written as

$$\frac{dN}{dr} = (1+r)^{-1} (D_L L - D_A A). \tag{7A.5}$$

If $A = L$, it follows that $dN/dr = 0$ when $D_A = D_L$. This establishes the first Redington condition. The second Redington condition requires that $d^2N/dr^2 \geq 0$ at the point where the first condition is satisfied. This condition assures us that $N \geq 0$ when r differs from the initial rate at which $A = L$. This condition implies that the slope dN/dr gets no smaller as r passes through its initial value. Noting that

$$(1+r)\frac{d(D_A A)}{dr} = -I_A + D_A^2, \quad \text{and}$$

$$(1+r)\frac{d(D_L L)}{dr} = -I_L + D_L^2, \tag{7A.6}$$

it follows that taking the derivative of (7A.5) yields

$$\frac{d^2N}{dr^2} = (1+r)^{-2}(D_A A - D_L L - I_L + I_A + D_L^2 - D_A^2). \tag{7A.7}$$

Hence, when $A = L$, and $D_A = D_L$,

$$\frac{dN}{dr} = 0, \quad \text{and}$$

$$\frac{d^2N}{dr^2} = (1+r)^{-2}(I_A - I_L), \tag{7A.8}$$

so that Redington dispersion conditions require that $I_A \geq I_L$ in order that $d^2N/dr^2 \geq 0$.

If $A - L = N > 0$ in (7A.5) and (7A.7), then when $D_A = D_L(L/A)$ and $I_A - I_L + D_A^2 - D_L^2$, then $dN/dr = 0$ and $d^2N/dr^2 \geq 0$, thus giving us the conditions specified in equations (7.9) and (7.10) in the text.

If the ratio N/A does not decline as interest rates change, then we require that $d(N/A)/dr = 0$ and $d^2(N/A)/dr^2 \geq 0$. Taking the derivative of N/A with respect to r, we have

$$\frac{d(N/A)}{dr} = \frac{1}{A}\frac{dN}{dr} - \frac{N}{A^2}\frac{dA}{dr} = 0. \tag{7A.9}$$

Noting that $dA/dr = -(1+r)^{-1}D_A A$, and that dN/dr is given in (7A.5), it follows that

$$\frac{d(N/A)}{dr} = (1+r)^{-1}\frac{L}{A}(D_L - D_A). \tag{7A.10}$$

Next, note that

$$\frac{dD_A}{dr} = -(1+r)^{-1}I_A, \quad \text{and}$$

$$\frac{dD_L}{dr} = -(1+r)^{-1}I_L. \tag{7A.11}$$

Thus,

$$\frac{d^2(N/A)}{dr^2} = \left(\frac{L}{A}\right)(1+r)^{-2}(I_A - I_L) + (1+r)^{-1}(D_L - D_A)\frac{d(L/A)}{dr}$$

$$- (1+r)^{-2}\left(\frac{L}{A}\right)(D_L - D_A). \tag{7A.12}$$

Noting that $d(L/A)/dr = -d(N/A)/dr$, and using (7A.10), it follows that

$$\frac{d^2(N/A)}{dr^2} = \left(\frac{L}{A}\right)(1+r)^{-2}(I_A - I_L - (D_L - D_A)^2 - (D_L - D_A)). \tag{7A.13}$$

Hence, if $D_A = D_L$ and $I_A \geq I_L$, then $d(N/A)/dr = 0$ and $d^2(N/A)/dr^2 \geq 0$.

The second-order conditions $d^2N/dr^2 \geq 0$ and $d^2(N/A)/dr^2 \geq 0$ may require the strong form of the inequality, ">", in some cases, and in some cases (as when cash inflows and outflows are perfectly matched) the equality, "=", is sufficient.

APPENDIX 7B
THE m-LEVEL ASSET PORTFOLIOS

To prove that m-level portfolios satisfy Redington's dispersion condition, it is sufficient to prove it for two-level portfolios because m-level portfolios depend on two-level portfolios applied to segments of the liability outflow stream. Let the liability outflow stream be $(L_1, L_2, ..., L_K)$ where there are K different dates for positive cash flows and assume that $L_j > 0$ at time t_j, where $t_1 < t_2 < \cdots < t_K$. Let the asset inflow streams be divided into two parts and be designated as $(A_{11}, A_{12}, A_{13}, ..., A_{1t}, ...)$ and $(A_{21}, A_{22}, ..., A_{2t}, ...)$ where $A_{1t} \geq 0$, $A_{2t} \geq 0$, and $A_{1t} + A_{2t} = A_t$ for all t. Assets are chosen subject to the exact condition of fully funding the liability outflows. Thus,

$$A = \sum_t (A_{1t} + A_{2t})(1+r)^{-t} = A^{(1)} + A^{(2)} = \sum_j L_j(1+r)^{-t_j} = L, \tag{7B.1}$$

where $A^{(1)}$ and $A^{(2)}$ are the respective values of the two arbitrary inflow streams composing the aggregate cash inflows. We assume also that the assets are chosen so that the duration of the inflows equals the duration of the outflows. That is,

$$D_A = D_{A1} \frac{A^{(1)}}{A} + D_{A2} \frac{A^{(2)}}{A} = D_L, \tag{7B.2}$$

where D_{A1} and D_{A2} are the durations of the two income streams comprising the asset inflows. We assume that $D_{A1} \leq t_1$ and $D_{A2} \geq t_K$.

The method of proof is one showing that the assets so chosen can be split implicitly into K different portfolios where each of these portfolios immunizes a single liability outflow and where each outflow is immunized. The K asset portfolios are found by taking some proportion of each of the two asset inflow streams specified above. That is, we specify

$$A_t^{(j)} = \alpha_j A_{1t} + \beta_j A_{2t}, \quad j = 1, 2, \ldots, K, \text{ for all } t, \tag{7B.3}$$

where $\Sigma \, \alpha_j = 1$, $\Sigma \, \beta_j = 1$, $\alpha_j \geq 0$, and $\beta_j \geq 0$. We then prove that the stream $A_t^{(j)}$ immunizes the outflow L_j that occurs at time t_j. If this is so then we must be able to choose (α_j, β_j), $j = 1, 2, \ldots, K$, so that

$$\sum_t A_t^{(j)}(1+r)^{-t} = L_j(1+r)^{-t_j}, \quad \text{and}$$
$$\sum_t A_t^{(j)} t (1+r)^{-t} = t_j(1+r)^{-t_j}. \tag{7B.4}$$

Rewriting (7B.4), using (7B.3), we have

$$\alpha_j \sum_t A_{1t}(1+r)^{-t} + \beta_j \sum_t A_{2t}(1+r)^{-t} = L_j(1+r)^{-t_j}, \quad \text{and}$$
$$\alpha_j \sum_t A_{1t} t (1+r)^{-t} + \beta_j \sum_t A_{2t} t (1+r)^{-t} = t_j L_j(1+r)^{-t_j}, \tag{7B.5}$$

or as

$$\alpha_j A^{(1)} + \beta_j A^{(2)} = L_j(1+r)^{-t_j}, \quad \text{and}$$
$$\alpha_j A^{(1)} D_{1A} + \beta_j A^{(2)} D_{2A} = t_j L_j(1+r)^{-t_j}, \tag{7B.5'}$$

for $j = 1, 2, \ldots, K$. The first of these equations in (7B.5′) says that the value of the jth implicit income stream is $L_j(1+r)^{-t_j}$, the present value of the jth outflow to be immunized. The second equation says that the duration of the jth implicit stream is equal to the duration (maturity) of the outflow L_j. There are two equations in (7B.5′) for each j that can be solved simultaneously for α_j and β_j as

$$\alpha_j = (1+r)^{-t_j} L_j \frac{D_{2A} - t_j}{A^{(1)}(D_{2A} - D_{1A})}, \quad \text{and}$$
$$\beta_j = (1+r)^{-t_j} L_j \frac{t_j - D_{1A}}{A^{(2)}(D_{2A} - D_{1A})}. \tag{7B.6}$$

By assumption $D_{2A} \geq t_j$ for all j and $t_j \leq D_{1A}$ for all j so that $\alpha_j \geq 0$ and $\beta_j \geq 0$ for all j. Next, we show that the values of α_j and β_j given in (7B.6) add respectively to unity as required. That is,

$$\sum \alpha_j = \frac{L(D_{2A}-D_L)}{A^{(1)}(D_{2A}-D_{1A})}, \quad \text{and}$$

$$\sum \beta_j = \frac{L(D_L-D_{1A})}{A^{(2)}(D_{2A}-D_{1A})}.$$

$$(7B.7)$$

The definitions in (7B.1) and (7B.2) can be manipulated to show that

$$L(D_{2A}-D_L) = A^{(1)}(D_{2A}-D_{1A}) \quad \text{and} \quad L(D_L-D_{1A}) = A^{(2)}(D_{2A}-D_{1A}).$$

Hence, given the split of the assets into two parts with values $A^{(1)}$ and $A^{(2)}$ we can form K implicit portfolios such that each of them immunizes a single outflow and all outflows are immunized.

NOTES

1. G. Fong and O. Vasicek (1980) have provided this contrary example to show that not all portfolios satisfying the Redington conditions are two-level portfolios.
2. Samuelson (1945) goes so far as to claim that $D_A < D_L(L/A)$ is the prevailing situation for the banks *taken as a whole* because the duration of deposits is infinitely long if the banking system doesn't lose deposits by currency drains or drains of deposits to other institutions (domestic or otherwise). Hence, in the period after World War II, the fear of a bank collapse due to rising interest rates was unfounded. Samuelson did not couch his arguments in terms of duration labels; he called "duration" the average period; but, in any case, the argument is the same.
3. It is interesting to put the observations on savings and loan associations (S&Ls) into the context considered by Samuelson. There is little evidence that S&Ls lost significant deposits during the 1981–83 episode, undoubtedly because of insurance provided by the Federal Savings and Loan Insurance Corporation (FSLIC). Samuelson's proposition would suggest then that the S&L industry, *as a whole,* should not have been severely damaged by interest rate increases, and the damage would occur only to those S&Ls losing deposits to banks or other S&Ls. To understand the S&L problem during this period, one must realize that although an institution may not have lost deposits, its deposits were "turned over" in relatively short periods and reissued at higher rates while their assets were not "turned over" as quickly. This could only lead to net worth losses as income over the standard accounting periods decreased. Bierwag, Kaufman, and Toevs (1979) suggested that these "turnover periods" or the time to "repricing" of securities is the proper measure of the maturity (which affects the duration calculation).

(Samuelson does not consider the turnover rate or repricing intervals for deposits and hence exaggerates considerably the deposit durations—but we must recall that in 1945, when Samuelson was writing, most deposits carried no explicit rate of return, so that turnover rates would not matter.) Nonetheless, if interest rates peak and do not continue an upward movement, eventually the rates on assets (mortgages) will catch up and the net worth losses will cease. Meanwhile the S&Ls and perhaps other depository institutions would have to weather the transition period in order to survive.

REFERENCES

Bierwag, G.O., 1979. "Dynamic Portfolio Immunization Policies." *Journal of Banking and Finance* (April).

Bierwag, G.O., George G. Kaufman, and Alden Toevs. 1979. "Management Strategies for Savings & Loan Associations to Reduce Interest Rate Risk." In *New Sources of Capital for the S&L Industry,* Proceedings of the 5th Annual Conference, Federal Home Loan Bank of San Francisco, pp. 178–204.

———. 1983. "Immunization Strategies for Funding Multiple Liabilities." *Journal of Financial and Quantitative Analysis 18,* no. 1 (March): 113–24.

Fong, H.G., and Oldrich Vasicek. 1980. "A Risk Minimizing Strategy for Multiple Liability Immunization." Working Paper.

———. 1983. "Return Maximization for Immunized Portfolios." In *Innovations in Bond Portfolio Management,* edited by G. Kaufman, G. Bierwag, and A. Toevs. (Greenwich, Conn.: JAI Press), pp. 227–38.

Grove, M.A., 1974. "On 'Duration' and the Optimal Maturity Structure of the Balance Sheet." *Bell Journal of Economics and Management Science 5,* no. 2 (Autumn): 696–709.

Kaufman, George G. 1984. "Measuring and Managing Interest Rate Risk: A Primer." *Economic Perspective,* Federal Reserve Bank of Chicago, January–February, pp. 16–29.

Redington, F.M. 1982. "Review of the Principle of Life Office Valuations." *Journal of the Institute of Actuaries 18* (1952): 286–340. Reprinted in G.A. Hawawini, *Bond Duration and Immunization: Early Development and Recent Contributions* (New York: Garland Publishing).

Samuelson, P.A. 1945. "The Effect of Interest Rate Increases on the Banking System." *American Economic Review 35,* no. 1 (March): 16–27.

Toevs, Alden. 1983. "Gap Management: Managing Interest Rate Risk in Banks and Thrifts." *Economic Review,* Federal Reserve Bank of San Francisco, Spring.

8 DURATION AND OPERATIONS IN THE FUTURES MARKETS

For many decades commodity futures markets have been used for hedging. Commodity price hedges can substantially reduce the uncertainty of the future price of a commodity and can thus decrease a variety of risks faced by economic decision-makers. Within the last dozen years, many futures markets in a variety of financial instruments have commenced operations. These financial instruments have included U.S. Treasury bills, U.S. Treasury notes, U.S. Treasury bonds, certificates of deposit (CDs), Eurodollars, GNMAs, and commercial paper. As in commodity markets, these futures markets have also facilitated a reduction in the uncertainty of various future prices and have enabled many economic decision-makers to reduce the risks that they face in various credit markets.

Hedges, whether of commodity prices or financial prices (interest rates), involve offsetting movements through time. If an investor holds securities A and B and these securities are such that the return on A always goes up as the return on B goes down or vice versa, then these securities have returns that tend to offset one another. A perfect hedge is formed if the number of units of each of the securities held is such that the investor suffers no aggregate losses on holdings of A and B as their returns fluctuate over time. The duration of a security, as a fundamental concept, indicates how much the price of an asset will change in response to a given change in the yield to maturity. The change in the value of security A relative to that of security B may thus be indicated by the respective durations given a single yield change applicable to both assets. The durations may thus be important in forming hedges with financial instruments. This chapter explains the usefulness of duration in forming hedges with futures market instruments or in otherwise modifying the risk–return properties of an investor's financial position using futures market instruments.

FUTURES AND FORWARD CONTRACTS

When an economic agent now contracts to deliver so many units of a good to another economic agent at some particular place on a future date at some particular price, a futures or forward contract comes into being. Examples are easy to contrive.

> *On July 1, 1986, the ABC Flour Company agrees to accept delivery of 100,000 bushels of grade A Winter Wheat at its milling company in Kansas City on September 1, 1986, for $3.10 per bushel payable by bank draft. The Farmers Cooperative of Fargo, North Dakota agrees to provide delivery and to accept payment.*

Such contracts are not unusual in a business world in which one company's output is another company's input. The smooth or continuous operation of a production process may necessitate forward contracting for the appropriate materials and services.

Time and experience has shown that "good" forward or futures contracts must have certain properties. In particular, the contractual terms must be extremely precise in order that there be no doubt as to what constitutes contractual performance. In the example above, the precise quantity and quality of wheat are specified. The precise delivery date and location are indicated. The precise price and acceptable form of payment are given. The more precise the terms of the contract, the less chance that the two contracting parties will subsequently have a dispute.

When particular contracts like the example become very common in the course of normal business, systematizing the routine for forming such contracts becomes very easy. Coveys of attorneys need not work over every agreement. For example, preprinted contract forms have become common in modern business life, reflecting a systematization of business contracting.

The existence of futures markets for many goods also reflects this systematization of contracting. In a futures market, buyers and sellers essentially forge standard contracts for the delivery of a given quantity of a standardized good at a particular place and time for a specified price payable in a precisely specified way. However, in order to minimize the costs of transacting and to minimize the probability that a buyer or seller defaults or fails to perform on a contract, the contract, as given in the example, has evolved into a slightly different form on organized markets. A clearinghouse corporation operates each of the futures markets for the benefit of its members who hold "seats" on the exchange. These seats entitle the members to trade on the floor (or "in the pit") of the exchange as brokers or as traders on their own account. The corporation operates the exchange as a clearinghouse and it guarantees the performance of every contract. When trader A buys a good for future delivery from trader B, trader A in effect has agreed to buy the good from the corporation and trader B has agreed to sell the good to the corporation. On the floor of the exchange, trader A and trader B formally agree to a transaction, but that transaction is effectively a contract to sell to and to buy from the corporation. Thus, as contracts are formed during the course of trading, the corporation always agrees to sell as many units as it buys. It is said to be taking a "zero position" because it is neither a *net* buyer nor seller of the good. At the end of the trading day the "open interest" consists of the number of units of the good owed to and by the corporation. Also, at the end of the day, the corporation specifies the "settlement price." This is the price at which the good will be exchanged at the specified future date on all outstanding contracts. The "settlement price" is usually set equal to the "closing price" for the day and is expected to reflect available current information relevant to price determination. Table 8-1 shows a newspaper account of the trading of cotton futures on the New York Cotton Exchange

Table 8-1.   Futures Prices

Thursday, March 13, 1986.

Open Interest Reflects Previous Trading Day.

	Open	High	Low	Settle	Change	Lifetime High	Lifetime Low	Open Interest
COTTON (CTN) — 50,000 lbs.; cents per lb.								
May	63.59	63.60	63.15	63.30	− .33	70.00	58.80	4,217
July	64.35	64.40	63.80	64.07	− .41	70.05	56.05	5,042
Oct	43.80	43.90	43.65	43.85	+ .05	65.50	43.15	1,739
Dec	43.70	43.95	43.60	43.83	− .02	59.25	43.10	9,243
Mar87	44.60	44.69	44.50	44.50	− .25	49.50	44.29	366

Est vol 1,500; vol Wed 3,427; open int 20,693, +173.

Source: *Wall Street Journal,* March 14, 1986.

(symbolized as CTN in the table) on Thursday, March 13, 1986. As shown in the table, cotton is sold in 50,000 pound units at a price specified in cents per pound. Thus one contract consisting of 50,000 pounds has a value of $30,000 at 60¢ per pound. The prices are recorded for delivery of cotton on five different future dates (May, July, October, December, and March 1987). Each futures exchange specifies the method of delivery, the quality of the good to be delivered, and the precise time acceptable for delivery in each of the future months. The first column in the table indicates the opening price for each of the five futures contracts. The next two columns indicate the high and low prices reached during the day's trading. Finally, the "settlement price" is shown. This is the price at which all outstanding contracts are to be exercised on the future delivery dates. The next column indicates the change in the settlement price from the day before. The next two columns indicate the lifetime high and low prices for each contract. For example, cotton to be delivered in May has ranged over the life of the May contract from 58.8¢ to 70.0¢ per pound. The last column indicates the total "open interest" or the number of outstanding contracts as of the end of trading on the previous day. At the bottom of the table the estimated volume of trading in contracts on Thursday and the actual volume of trading on the previous day are given. The total open interest outstanding at the end of trading on Wednesday was 20,693 contracts, an increase of 173 from the previous day.

The clearinghouse function of the exchange is easy to understand. The exchange keeps a record of all amounts of the good that each trader owes or has coming to it on a future date. A trader can cancel any contract it has outstanding by merely forming an "opposite" transaction that "nets out" the position. For example, suppose trader A has purchased six December cotton contracts. Unless subsequently offset, trader A must be prepared to buy the cotton at the settlement price of 43.83¢ per pound on the delivery date in December. To cancel this contract, trader A can enter the market and sell six December contracts. In adding up the amounts owed to it and by it, the clearinghouse would find that trader A has as much coming for future delivery as trader A owes. The two transactions cancel each other and trader A is removed from the list of traders obligated to make or receive delivery in the future.

Given that the exchange is a guarantor of contract performance, it bears the risk that either a buyer or seller may not perform as the standardized contract requires. For example, if a seller does not deliver the good as required, the exchange must acquire the good elsewhere in order to make delivery to the buyer. The futures exchanges have established a variety of rules and procedures designed to minimize this risk and to keep it essentially at zero. In particular, all traders must establish *margin accounts*. These accounts, amounting to about 2% or 3% of the value of each contract, are close to the maximum amount by which the future price of a good is permitted to change on the exchange during the course of a trading day. If the settlement price rises above (falls below) the initially contracted price (or the settlement price from the day before) by a given increment, then that increment is subtracted from (added to) the seller's margin account and added to (subtracted from) the buyer's margin account. These amounts are effectively transferred in cash via the clearinghouse function at the close of each day's trading. This mechanism for transferring cash serves two purposes. First, it guarantees that the buyer or seller can, in fact, exchange the goods in the future at the specified price; and, second, it removes the liability of the exchange as the guarantor of the transaction. Consider each of these important points in turn. First, suppose a buyer initially agrees to acquire some goods for future delivery at the price F_0 per unit, and the settlement price rises to F_1 dollars per unit, but the buyer receives an increment of $(F_1 - F_0)$ dollars on the date that the settlement price is established. At the delivery date the buyer must now pay F_1 per unit. If the settlement price does not subsequently change, the net amount paid per unit for the goods is thus $F_1 - (F_1 - F_0) = F_0$, the initial contract price. Thus, even though up ticks and down ticks to a margin account may occur throughout the life of a contract, the initially contracted amount is the amount paid.[1] Second, as long as the margin accounts are maintained at appropriate levels, there will always be sufficient cash to be transferred; the exchange need bear no liability for the cash transfers prior to the delivery date. If the seller or buyer defaults on the delivery date, the exchange bears no risk either provided the "futures" price converges to the "spot" price. The spot price (or cash price) is the price of the good for immediate delivery. As time passes, the time to the delivery date on a futures contract gets shorter and shorter. When the time to the delivery date becomes zero, the futures contract should resemble the cash contract, and, therefore, both should sell at the same price; if this were not so, arbitragers could make immediate riskless profits by selling in one market and buying in another. If the seller defaults on the delivery date, the exchange can acquire the goods in the cash market and transfer them to the buyer at the current settlement price (which should be equal to the spot price at that time). If the buyer defaults by refusing delivery or by not paying the settlement price, the exchange can recover funds paid to the seller by selling the goods in the spot market. The system of transfers to and from the margin accounts represents an ingenious way by which (1) a contracted price remains in effect throughout the life of a contract even though the settlement price changes, and (2) the exchange corporation can minimize the liability incurred as a guarantor of all contracts.

A contract, as described above, is a *futures contract*. If differs from a *forward contract* primarily because of the daily up ticks or down ticks to the margin accounts. Forward contracts are always privately arranged by the buyer and seller or their agents, and the liability in the event of nonperformance is either established as part of the contract or by legal precedence. Commercial bank loans arranged as a funding commitment at a specific future date is an example of a forward contract. Foreign currencies are often sold by banks on the basis of a forward commitment, and the forward markets for some currencies are often larger than their corresponding futures markets.

INTEREST RATE FUTURES

In the same way as a spot price, the futures price of a financial instrument reflects the interest rate at which the cash flows promised by the instrument are discounted. For example, on Thursday, February 8, 1986, the settlement price of a 3-month (91-day) U.S. Treasury bill to be delivered in June was 93.19. This price is expressed as a percentage of face value. Each T-bill contract represents a face value of $1,000,000. The quoted price of 93.19, however, has been annualized; it reflects an annual discount rate. The "annual bank discount" rate is 6.81% (100% − 93.19%) and represents the annualized interest return expressed as a percentage of face value. The actual future delivery price implied by the quotation of 93.19 is found as

$$P = \left(100 - \frac{6.81}{4}\right) = 100 - 1.7025 = 98.2975.$$

That is, the "annual" discount of 6.81% is divided by 4 to find the relevant "quarterly" discount rate. Thus, the actual delivery price of the T-bill is $982,975. The annual rate of return on this investment compounded quarterly is $r = .06928$, as found in the equation

$$982,975\left(1 + \frac{r}{4}\right) = 1,000,000. \tag{8.1}$$

This rate — the futures rate — is an interest rate that becomes effective on the delivery date in June, approximately 4 months away. It is tempting to regard this rate as the currently expected rate to rule on 3-month bills to be selling next June. It is possible, however, for this rate to be consistently above (called a *contango*) or consistently below (called *normal backwardation*) any currently perceived market expected rate. Kolb (1985, pp. 33–39) excellently summarizes some of the reasons for a discrepancy between the futures rate and the expected spot rate.

For many financial instruments there is a strong tendency for the spot prices and futures prices to move together through time. This relationship between spot and futures prices tends to be particularly strong for U.S. Treasury securities of the same maturity. As shown in Figlewski (1986) the R^2's on these price changes are often over 90%. This means that the interest rates used as discount factors also tend to move closely together.

A strong relationship between changes in spot and futures prices facilitates the use of futures contracts for hedging. That is, it may be possible to choose futures contracts such that any change in the value of them (represented by an increase or decrease in the margin account) will offset a corresponding coincident change in the value of some other assets. Hedging in this way reduces the investor's overall risk exposure because losses or gains in one part of the portfolio are offset by gains or losses in another. To show how these offsets may occur, suppose an investor holds a 3-month $1,000,000 Treasury bill. Suppose the value of this security is $982,975 so that its yield is .06928 as in equation (8.1). For simplicity, assume that the futures price is the same and the investor sells a 3-month T-bill for future delivery. Now, suppose the 3-month interest rate on the very next day rises by 25 basis points so that the futures price also falls to $933,027. Suppose also that the futures rate on the 3-month T-bill also rises by 25 basis points so that the futures price also falls to $933,027. Since the investor is selling the bill for future delivery, there is an automatic increase in his margin account of $49,948, the incremental price change. The profit in the futures market exactly offsets the loss or decrease in value of the T-bill actually held. Similarly, if interest rates had fallen, the value of the T-bill held would have increased, but there would be a decrement or loss of the same amount in the margin account. The decrease in interest rates has produced exactly offsetting changes so that the value of the investor's overall assets has not changed.[2]

In the circumstance just described, the investor is said to have taken a *long* position in the cash market, because he or she is "long on" or holds a T-bill that can be sold for cash at any time. The investor holds a *short* position in the futures market because the investor must find the appropriate T-bill to deliver on the delivery date. In situations where the spot and futures prices tend to move together, a hedge, using a futures market instrument, is always characterized by holding a long position in one market and a short position in the other.

Consider a hedging example in which an investor holds a short position in the cash market and a long position in the futures market. Suppose an investor expects to receive $1,000,000 in 3 months from the expiration of a certificate of deposit. Currently, these funds, if available, could be invested in T-bills at 9%. The investor does not know what interest rate will prevail in 3 months, but by using the futures market, the investor may be able effectively to lock in a future 9% return. The investor buys a 3-month T-bill in the futures market. If interest rates fall, the investor's margin account increases, but the investor will earn less on the futures investment in T-bills, and conversely if interest rates rise. Here, the investor is "short" in the cash market because he or she does not currently have the dollars to be invested and has a "long" position in the futures market because the securities are to be acquired and added to the investor's holdings (even if temporarily). In this example, the investor is hedging against a decline in interest rates at which future investments are to be made.

HEDGING AND DURATION

When an investor hedges a cash portfolio (a current long position in some securities), he or she sells a given number of futures contracts. The given number of such contracts sold per unit of the cash portfolio is called the *hedging ratio*. If the hedging ratio is not properly determined, an increase in the value of the cash portfolio will not be at least offset by a decrease in the value of the futures margin account, and conversely. The duration of the securities held and of the securities to be delivered in the future can be used to determine a hedging ratio that will at least produce the offsets required under specific conditions.

To show how duration can be used for determining the hedging ratio, let us formally consider changes in the value of an investor's aggregate portfolio which includes the impact of futures operations. Let $V(r)$ be the value of a cash portfolio held, where r is the yield to maturity of the securities held. Let $F(r)$ be the futures price for delivery of a unit of some security at some future date. Let h be the number of units or contracts bought or sold for future delivery. As will be seen, it is useful to stipulate that $h > 0$ if the securities are purchased (a "long" position) and $h < 0$ if the securities are sold (a "short" position). Let r_0 be the initial rate of interest. After establishing a position in the futures market, suppose r_0 changes to r. The futures price then changes from $F(r_0)$ to $F(r)$. The increment to the margin account is then

$$h[F(r) - F(r_0)].$$

For example, suppose $h > 0$ (a "long" position is taken in the futures market) and that $r > r_0$. It follows that the futures price falls so that $F(r) - F(r_0) < 0$ and $h[F(r) - F(r_0)] < 0$; there is a decrease in the margin account. On the other hand, if h had been negative (a "short" position taken in the futures market), then $h[F(r) - F(r_0)] > 0$ and an increment to the margin account results. The aggregate value of an investor's portfolio can be written as

$$P(r) = V(r) + h[F(r) - F(r_0)]. \tag{8.2}$$

It is easy to see how the hedge works fundamentally. As r increases, $V(r)$ falls, but $h[F(r) - F(r_0)]$ increases (provided $h < 0$). And as r decreases, $V(r)$ increases, but $h[F(r) - F(r_0)]$ decreases (provided $h < 0$). If h is properly chosen, offsets will occur for each interest rate change so that $P(r)$ never falls below $V(r_0)$, the value of the cash portfolio to be hedged.

To introduce duration into the analysis, we take the derivative of (8.2) with respect to the interest rate r and we evaluate the derivative at the initial rate of interest r_0 to obtain

$$P'(r_0) = V'(r_0) + hF'(r_0). \tag{8.3}$$

As shown in previous chapters, the duration of a security is related to the derivative of its value with respect to the rate of interest. Here,

$$V'(r_0) = -DV(r_0)/(1 + r_0) \quad \text{and} \quad F'(r_0) = -D_F F(r_0)/(1 + r_0),$$

where D is the duration of the cash portfolio, D_F is the duration on the delivery date of the security sold in the futures contract, and where annual compounding is assumed. Substitution of these definitions into (8.3) gives

$$P'(r_0) = \frac{-DV(r_0)}{1 + r_0} - h\frac{D_F F(r_0)}{1 + r_0}. \tag{8.4}$$

If D^* is the duration of the aggregate portfolio, $P'(r_0) = -D^*P(r_0)/(1 + r_0)$. Substitution into (8.4) then gives

$$\frac{-D^*P(r_0)}{1 + r_0} = \frac{-DV(r_0)}{1 + r_0} - h\frac{D_F F(r_0)}{1 + r_0}. \tag{8.5}$$

Noting that $P(r_0) = V(r_0)$, this equation can be simplified to

$$D^* = D + hD_F \frac{F(r_0)}{V(r_0)}. \tag{8.6}$$

If a change in interest rates does not reduce the initial aggregate value of the portfolio, then $P'(r_0) = 0$ or $D^* = 0$. Clearly, $D^* = 0$ in equation (8.6) when

$$h = \frac{-D}{D_F} \frac{V(r_0)}{F(r_0)}. \tag{8.7}$$

The hedging ratio is thus computed as the negative of the price ratio multiplied by the ratio of durations.

Example 1.   An investor holds a 3-month T-bill having a face value of $1,000,000. The duration D is 3 months since it is a zero coupon instrument. The investor attempts to hedge the value of this investment by selling contracts in the futures market on 3-month T-bills. Again, the duration D_F is 3 months. Assuming both securities are discounted at the same rate of interest, r_0, then $V(r_0) = F(r_0)$. It follows from (8.7) that $h = -1$. If interest rates change from r_0 to r, the increment to the cash portfolio is $V(r) - V(r_0)$ and the increment to the margin account is $-[F(r) - F(r_0)]$, a perfect offset since the cash security and the underlying futures security are identical and are identically priced. Notice that the time of delivery is of no consequence.

Example 2.   An investor holds a 6-month T-bill having a face value of $1,000,000. The duration, D, is 6 months because it is a zero coupon instrument. The investor attempts to hedge by selling contracts on 3-month T-bills. The duration, D_F, is 3 months. Thus, $D/D_F = 2$. The prices of the two instruments will not be equal if discounted at the same rate. The cash portfolio has the value $V(r_0) = 1,000,000(1 + r_0/4)^{-2}$ and the 3-month T-bill has the future value $F(r_0) = 1,000,000(1 + r_0/4)^{-1}$ discounted at the annual rate r_0 quarterly compounded. The hedge ratio is, hence,

$$h = -2\left(1 + \frac{r_0}{4}\right)^{-1},$$

which is slightly less than two contracts.[3]

Example 3.   A government bond dealer holds $1,000,000 in face value of Treasury bonds that have 10% coupon rates and will mature in 12 years. The dealer attempts to hedge this inventory by selling futures contracts on 8% coupon, 10-year Treasury notes, the standard contract on the futures market for Treasury notes. Assuming the current interest rate is 9%, the current price of the 12-year bonds is $107.247739 (per $100 of face value), and the current futures price for the 10-year Treasury note is $93.4960318 (per $100 of face value). The duration of the 12-year bonds is 7.41444614 years and the duration of the 10-year notes is 6.9544963 years. Thus, the hedge ratio is

$$h = \frac{-DV(r_0)}{D_F F(r_0)} = -\frac{107.247739}{93.496032} \cdot \frac{7.41444614}{6.9544963} = -1.22224503.$$

Table 8–2.   Hedging a Bond Dealer's Inventory of 12-Year, 10% Coupon, U.S. Treasury Bonds with 10-Year, 8% Coupon, Treasury Notes at a Current Interest Rate of 9%

Interest Rate	Value of Inventory $V(r)$	Increment to Margin Account $h[F(r) - F(r_0)]$	Aggregate Portfolio Value col. 2 + col. 3
6.00%	$1,338,711	$ − 261,333	$1,077,377
6.50	1,288,546	− 212,774	1,075,772
7.00	1,240,876	− 166,350	1,074,526
7.50	1,195,560	− 121,956	1,073,604
8.00	1,152,470	− 79,494	1,072,976
8.50	1,111,481	− 38,872	1,072,609
9.00	1,072,477	0	1,072,477
9.50	1,035,351	37,206	1,072,557
10.00	1,000,000	72,824	1,072,824
10.50	966,327	106,932	1,073,259
11.00	934,242	139,600	1,073,842
11.50	903,658	170,897	1,074,555

For each $100 of face value held in inventory, the dealer wishes to sell $122.2245 of face value in the futures market. Table 8–2 shows the consequences of the hedge for various possible interest rate movements. No matter to what extent interest rates change, the aggregate value of the portfolio never falls below $1,072,477, the initial value computed at a 9% yield.[4]

THE HEDGE AND DURATION MORE GENERALLY

Several extensions and qualifications for the duration-based hedge may be noted.

Second-Order Features

Example 3, above, as illustrated in Table 8–2, exhibits a property that not all duration-based hedges have. The aggregate value of the portfolios, after the hedge is put into place and interest rates have changed, never decreases, and, in fact, it *increases* if interest rates change, whether up or down. This result may not always occur for duration-based hedges as described here.

In Appendix 8A, there is an example in which a long cash position is hedged with a short futures position and in which the aggregate portfolio value *decreases* for all nonzero interest rate changes. This latter result occurs because of a failure of the *second-order conditions* for a hedge to hold. These technical conditions are derived and described in Appendix 8A.

Two observations about these second-order conditions may be noted. First, as shown in Appendix 8A, the failure of the second-order conditions to hold does not imply a dramatic failure of the hedge to maintain the initial cash value of the portfolio. The costs of failure are minuscule relative to the value of the cash assets. Second, in practice, most hedgers attempt to hedge in a futures market in which the underlying security has a maturity close to that of the cash asset. They do this for reasons described in the next section. When the maturities are close together, the second-order conditions are either very likely to hold or the losses from failing to hold are relatively even more minuscule than described in the appendix.

Different Levels and Changes of Relative Yields

The development in the preceding section, Hedging and Duration, was based on two major assumptions. First, it was assumed that the yield to maturity on the cash or spot securities was the same as that on the security underlying the futures contract. Second, it was assumed that both yields changed by the same amount. Neither of these assumptions is generally warranted. Casual observation of these yields invariably reveals that they may differ substantially and that changes in the yields are rarely the same. Duration-based hedges can be extended to cover these more general cases.

Let r_0^c and r_0^f be the currently observed yields to maturity respectively on a cash asset and a futures security. Let $V(r_0^c)$ and $F(r_0^f)$ be the respective values of the cash asset and the future price. The aggregate value of the portfolio can then be written as

$$P = P(r^c, r^f) = V(r^c) + h[F(r^f) - F(r_0^f)], \tag{8.8}$$

where r^c is the yield on the cash asset and r^f is the yield on the futures security. The change in the futures yield is $r^f - r_0^f$ and the change in the yield on the cash asset is $r^c - r_0^c$. In general, we can now allow the yield changes to differ as well as the initial levels of the yields. As before, we wish to specify the hedging ratio, h, so that changes in interest rates will not have any effect on the aggregate value of the portfolio. Given h is fixed in advance, it is not difficult to see that there exist combinations of r^f and r^c such that the aggregate portfolio value may rise above or fall below $V(r_0^c)$ — the initial cash value of the portfolio. For example, pick a pair of values of r^c and r^f such that for a given h, $P(r^c, r^f) = V(r_0^c)$. If now, r^f is increased above this chosen level it will no longer be true that P is $V(r_0^c)$. In order for this more general approach to a duration-based hedge to work properly, the interest rate changes on different instruments must follow a predictable pattern relative to each other. Taking the total derivative of (8.8) with respect to r^c where dr^f/dr^c gives the change in r^f relative to a change in r^c, we have

$$\frac{dP}{dr^c} = V'(r^c) + hF'(r^f)\frac{dr^f}{dr^c}. \tag{8.9}$$

As in the preceding section, we may now evaluate this derivative at the initial values of the yields to determine the hedging ratio. That is, we may determine h so that

$$V'(r_0^c) + hF'(r_0^f)a = 0, \tag{8.10}$$

where a is the derivative dr^f/dr^c evaluated at the initial point (r_0^c, r_0^f). Using the definitions of duration, as before, we can write (8.10) as

$$\frac{-DV(r_0^c)}{1+r_0^c} - \frac{ahD_F F(r_0^f)}{1+r_0^f} = 0, \tag{8.11}$$

where we have assumed annual compounding and the calculation of the durations at the initial respective yields.[5] In some of the duration literature $D/(1+r_0^c) = D^M$ and $D_F/(1+r_0^f) = D_F^M$ are called the "modified" durations. Using this notation, we have

$$-D^M V(r_0^c) - hD_F^M F(r_0^f)a = 0 \tag{8.12}$$

as the equation giving the hedging ratio. Formally, we can write h as

$$h = \frac{-V'(r_0^c)}{F'(r_0^f)a} = \frac{-D^M V(r_0^c)}{D_F^M F(r_0^f)a}. \tag{8.13}$$

This determination of the hedging ratio is exactly the same as that used in the preceding section except that (1) the prices and durations of the securities are determined at different yield levels, and (2) the variable a appears in the formula to describe the relative motion of the yields to maturity.

If the cash asset has a maturity that is roughly equal to the maturity of the underlying futures security, then $a \cong 1$ because the yields on both securities will tend to move together. If the maturities tend to be far apart, then a will depart from unity. Regression analysis is one way by which a can be determined. One simply regresses r^f on r^c. The slope coefficient is then an estimate of a.

Instead of utilizing durations, prices, and yield derivatives like a, one may alternatively go back to equation (8.10) and simply note that

$$h = -V'(r_0^c)dr^c/F'(r_0^f)dr^f,$$
$$= -\Delta V/\Delta F,$$
(8.14)

which is the negative of the ratio of price changes (induced, of course, by yield changes). By regressing past spot price changes, ΔV, on the concurrent futures price changes, ΔF, the past empirical relationship between ΔV and ΔF is directly estimated. The slope coefficient in this relationship can then be used as an estimate of the hedging ratio, h. The regression of ΔV on ΔF, in effect, summarizes the historical movements of ΔV relative to ΔF. If the regression fit to past observations is a strong one and if the future values of ΔV relative to ΔF are comparable to past observations, then the regression slope estimate should be an excellent estimate of h. Figlewski (1986) discusses this approach and modifications of it. Figlewski's regressions suggest that the strongest correlations between ΔV and ΔF occur for spot and futures securities having maturities that are close to one another. As suggested in the preceding section, these are also the situations in which the second-order conditions appear least likely to fail and that if they do the consequences are of minor significance.

IMMUNIZATION AND THE FUTURES MARKET

Equation (8.6) suggests that the duration of a cash portfolio can be extended or contracted by a futures market operation. By taking a short position in the futures market, the duration D of a cash portfolio can be contracted. Indeed, the hedging objective consists of contracting the duration to zero. By taking a long position in the futures market the duration can be increased or extended. In principle, operations in the futures market can thus enhance the investment choices available to an investor. The investor can, for example, choose a cash portfolio utilizing criteria not even remotely related to the implications of duration and can then use the futures market to determine an ideal duration.

A portfolio is immunized over a planning period of length q when the portfolio is constructed so that its duration, D, is equal to q. If one allows for futures operations, the aggregate portfolio (including the futures position) may be chosen so that $D^* = q$, where D^*, as defined in equation (8.6), is the cash portfolio duration that is extended or contracted by futures positions. The only distinction between a hedging and an immunization strategy is the time period over which a riskless position is attempted to be maintained. In the hedging strategy, above, the duration of the aggregate portfolio, D^*, is set equal to zero. In an immunization strategy, D^* is set equal to q, the planning period length. Over the period of length q, the immunized portfolio grows at the "risk-free" rate. In this context, we may regard immunization as a hedge of the growth rate over a planning period of given length.

The return characteristics of an immunized portfolio containing a futures position are not the same as in the case where an immunized portfolio is maintained without a futures position. That is, the two portfolios – one in which $D = q$ with no futures position and the other in which $D^* = q$ with a futures position – need not change in value in the same way in response to a given interest rate change. The differences are of the second-order or higher effects, however. Typically the second-order conditions for immunization hold when no futures position is maintained. That is, the value of the portfolio will fail to decrease if interest rates change. However, the second-order conditions for immunization may fail to hold if a futures position is maintained. Thus, for such cases, the value of the portfolio may decline if interest rates change. Little (1986) has derived some of the second-order properties of these portfolios.

APPENDIX 8A
SECOND-ORDER CONDITIONS FOR HEDGING

Hedging so that the duration of the aggregate portfolio is zero, as in equation (8.6), is not sufficient to prevent a decrease in the value of the aggregate portfolio. Some second-order conditions must also be satisfied. Although the failure to satisfy second-order conditions may result in only very minor losses, these losses may often be simply avoided by an appropriate choice of futures instruments.

In this appendix, we specify the second-order conditions and present an example to illustrate how losses may result from a failure to satisfy these conditions. Let $(V_1, V_2, ..., V_t, ..., V_N)$ and $(F_1, F_2, ..., F_t, ..., F_M)$ be respectively the cash flows promised by a cash asset and by the asset underlying the futures instrument. The cash flow V_t occurs t periods from now, whereas F_t occurs t periods after the date of delivery of the asset. Letting r be the rate of interest per period, the value of the cash asset is

$$V(r) = \sum_{1}^{N} V_t(1+r)^{-t} \tag{8A.1}$$

and the value at delivery of the underlying futures instrument is

$$F(r) = \sum_{1}^{M} F_t(1+r)^{-t}. \tag{8A.2}$$

If r_0 is the initial rate of interest then

$$P(r) = V(r) + h[F(r) - F(r_0)] \tag{8A.3}$$

is the value of the aggregate portfolio where h is the hedging ratio. We choose h so that $V'(r_0) + hF'(r_0) = P'(r_0) = 0$. Having so chosen h, it follows that $P(r) \geq P(r_0)$ for all r, provided $P''(r) \geq 0$. Thus,

$$P''(r) = V''(r) + hF''(r) \geq 0 \tag{8A.4}$$

for all r is a sufficient condition for the hedge to work properly so that $P(r) \geq P(r_0)$. Now,

$$V''(r) = \sum_{1}^{N} t(1+t)V_t(1+r)^{-t-2}, \quad \text{and}$$

$$F''(r) = \sum_{1}^{M} t(1+t)F_t(1+r)^{-t-2}. \tag{8A.5}$$

Defining durations as a function of the interest rate r, we can write

$$D(r) = \sum_{1}^{N} tV_t(1+r)^{-t}/V(r), \quad \text{and}$$

$$D_F(r) = \sum_{1}^{M} tF_t(1+r)^{-t}/F(r). \tag{8A.6}$$

Finally, let the "inertias" (see Chapter 7) with respect to the origin be expressed as

$$I(r) = \sum_{1}^{N} t^2 V_t(1+r)^{-t}/V(r), \quad \text{and}$$

$$I_F(r) = \sum_{1}^{M} t^2 F_t(1+r)^{-t}/F(r). \tag{8A.7}$$

In this notation, (8A.5) can be rewritten as

$$V''(r) = [D(r) + I(r)](1+r)^{-2}V(r), \quad \text{and}$$

$$F''(r) = [D_F(r) + I_F(r)](1+r)^{-2}F(r). \tag{8A.5'}$$

Then, given that $h = -D(r_0)V(r_0)/D_F(r_0)F(r_0)$, it follows in (8A.4) that the second-order condition for a hedge becomes

$$[D(r)+I(r)]V(r) - \frac{D(r_0)V(r_0)}{D_F(r_0)F(r_0)}[D_F(r)+I_F(r)]F(r) \geq 0 \quad (8A.8)$$

or

$$\frac{[D(r)+I(r)]V(r)}{D(r_0)V(r_0)} \geq \frac{[D_F(r)+I_F(r)]F(r)}{D_F(r_0)F(r_0)}. \quad (8A.9)$$

This condition is extremely difficult to interpret. A much easier condition is the one for the special case in which the conditions hold locally for small interest rate movements away from r_0. This local condition is found by calculating (8A.9) for $r = r_0$ to obtain the condition

$$\frac{I(r_0)}{D(r_0)} \geq \frac{I_F(r_0)}{D_F(r_0)}. \quad (8A.10)$$

That is, the inertia around the origin relative to duration for the cash portfolio cannot be less than the inertia around the origin relative to duration for the underlying futures investment.

Many cases in which (8A.10) fails to be satisfied are those in which the maturity of the instrument underlying the futures contract greatly exceeds the maturity of the cash portfolio. Equation (8A.10) translates directly into this simple result for zero coupon bonds, but the maturity interpretation also tends to hold more widely. Consider the following example. Let the cash portfolio consist of $1,000,000 (in face value) of U.S. Treasury bonds with an 8% coupon rate and 10 years to maturity. Let us attempt to hedge this cash portfolio with a futures contract to sell h units of $1,000,000 (in face value) of Treasury bonds with an 8% coupon rate, but with 20 years to maturity. Assume that the current rate of interest is 8% so that all bonds sell at par. The duration of the 10-year bond is 7.0669697 years and the duration of the 20-year bond is 10.2922424 years. Thus, $h = -.686630709$. The aggregate value of the portfolio for various interest rates is given in Table 8-1. When interest rates change, the aggregate value always falls below the initial value at 8%. The loss tends to be very small, however. For example, when interest rates increase dramatically by 200 basis points from 8% to 10%, the loss is only $6,808, which is relatively small for $1,000,000 initially invested. Note, that in the absence of the attempt to hedge, the cash portfolio drops to $875,378, a decrease in value of $124,622, but the increment to the margin account of $117,814 covers 94.5% of this loss. Hedging in a case where the second-order conditions fail to hold does not appear to be an unattractive prospect.

Table 8A-1.   Hedging a 10-Year, 8% Coupon Bond with a
20-Year, 8% Coupon Bond at a Current Interest Rate of 8%
and Hedge Ratio of $-.6866$

Interest Rate	Value of 10-Year Bond $V(r)$	Increment to Margin Account $h[F(r)-F(r_0)]$	Aggregate Portfolio Value col. 2 + col. 3
6.00%	$1,148,775	$ − 158,706	$ 990,069
6.50	1,109,045	− 114,362	994,683
7.00	1,071,062	− 73,312	997,750
7.50	1,034,741	− 35,276	999,465
8.00	1,000,000	0	1,000,000
8.50	966,764	32,746	999,510
9.00	934,960	63,173	998,133
9.50	904,520	91,471	995,991
10.00	875,378	117,814	993,192

NOTES

1. This abstracts from interest costs and gains because the up ticks or down ticks may occur at different times. Above, for example, the increment $(F_1 - F_0)$ might have been invested at the risk-free rate so that the amount paid per unit is effectively less than F_0.
2. Notice, though, that a liquidity problem may arise. The investor may have to replenish the loss in the margin account in order for the futures contract to be retained. Replenishing the account may require that cash be transferred to the account. If this cash is not held for such purposes, it may be necessary to sell the currently held T-bill or other assets, or to borrow in order to maintain the futures position.
3. If exchange restrictions require that an integral number of contracts be exchanged, then the investor would choose two contracts. If there were 10 T-bills held in the cash portfolio, then $10h$ would be the number of futures contracts to sell. The number $10h$ taken to the closest integer may be closer to the required number of contracts than when a single T-bill was held. We can get closer to the number of futures contracts the larger the cash portfolio.
4. The prices and durations in this example have been rounded to more than the usual two to three places after the decimal in order that the results in Table 8-2 have increased accuracy.
5. If semiannual compounding had been utilized instead, then r_0^c and r_0^f would be replaced by $(r_0^c/2)$ and $(r_0^f/2)$, respectively.

REFERENCES

Figlewski, Stephen. 1986. *Hedging with Financial Futures for Institutional Investors.* Cambridge, Mass.: Ballinger.

Kolb, Robert W. 1985. *Understanding Futures Markets.* Glenview, Ill.: Scott, Foresman.

Little, Patricia K. 1986. "Financial Futures and Immunization." *Journal of Financial Research 9,* no. 1 (Spring): 1–12.

9 DEPOSITORY AND OTHER FINANCIAL INSTITUTIONS
Duration Gap Management

Fluctuations in interest rates can affect the income, liquidity, and solvency of financial intermediaries. The income of these firms may be very sensitive to interest rate changes if their cost of funds is more (or less) sensitive to interest rate changes than their revenues. The net worth of these firms may also be very sensitive to interest rate changes if the value of their assets are more (or less) sensitive to interest rate changes than the value of their liabilities. These firms may also face liquidity crises from time to time if the seasonality or cyclicity of their cash inflows relative to their cash outflows are subject to unexpected changes induced by interest rate fluctuations.

These risks stemming from interest rate fluctuations can be controlled to some degree by managing the duration gaps of the financial institution. The duration gaps measure the sensitivity of critical asset, liability, and income accounts to fluctuations in interest rates. Managerial decisions that affect the magnitudes of these duration gaps or sensitivity measures also affect the exposure of the financial institution to risk.

The measurement of interest rate risk by duration gaps is a relatively new notion, although its roots can be traced far back in the immunization lore to Redington (1952, reprinted 1982). In Federal Home Loan Bank Board (FHLBB, 1983) it was suggested that the concept of a duration gap would be useful in measuring a depository institution's degree of exposure to interest rate risk. The FHLBB study, mandated by Congress under the Garn–St. Germain Act of 1982, came on the heels of some of the highest and most volatile interest rates in the United States in this century. The extent of red ink among savings and loan associations (S&Ls) was alarming. It was typically argued that S&Ls were bearing too much interest rate risk and that federal deposit insurance was motivating S&Ls to do so.[1] In FHLBB (1983) it was argued that appropriate duration gaps could measure interest rate risk and that federal deposit insurance premiums based on these duration gaps could dampen the incentives of S&Ls and other depository institutions to bear this risk.[2]

Today, most asset and liability managerial committees in commercial banks and in other depository institutions are aware that the concept of duration may be useful in measuring and managing interest rate risk. These ideas are still relatively new, however, and detailed managerial plans for managing duration gaps are still fairly rare. This chapter reviews the meaning of duration gaps and illustrates with several examples how they may be measured and managed.

NET WORTH AND INTEREST RATE RISK

The value of a firm's net worth, relative to its assets, is a reflection or indicator of the firm's condition of solvency. If a firm's net worth, calculated as the difference between the market value of its assets and liabilities, is negative, the firm is insolvent. Liquidation of an insolvent firm would imply that some creditors must receive less than the amounts to which they are contractually entitled. Continued operation of the firm raises the prospect that the returns on its assets will be insufficient to meet the periodic contractual obligations to creditors and that there will be a further reduction in the market value of creditor claims. It is often very probable that an insolvent firm will be forced into bankruptcy so that the condition of insolvency cannot become worse. For example, federal deposit insurance agencies are obliged, under the law, to close insolvent insured depository institutions. The lower net worth drops, the greater the generally perceived risk that the firm will become insolvent. The greater the risk of insolvency the greater the likelihood that the firm will fail to survive.

The net worth of most financial institutions is subject to interest rate risk. Increases in the level and changes in the structure of interest rates can decrease the market value of assets by more than the value of liabilities, thus implying a decrease in net worth. Managers can control or manage to some degree this sensitivity of net worth to interest rate changes. In this section a measure of this interest rate risk is proposed. This measure of risk is a function of the asset and liability durations so that decisions affecting the asset or liability durations also affect the sensitivity of net worth to interest rate changes.

Denote the market value of assets by $A(r_A)$ and the market value of liabilities by $L(r_L)$. Here, r_A is the annual interest rate on assets and r_L is the annual interest rate on liabilities. These rates r_A and r_L are rates that discount the cash flows back to the market value of the assets and liabilities respectively.[3] Net worth, as a function of interest rates, can then be expressed as

$$N(r_A, r_L) = A(r_A) - L(r_L).\tag{9.1}$$

In this formulation it is easy to see that changes in interest rates can lead immediately to changes in the market value of net worth. Using the calculus, we can denote the direction of change of net worth in response to interest rate changes as

$$\frac{dN}{dr_A} = A'(r_A) - L'(r_L) \cdot \frac{dr_L}{dr_A}.\tag{9.2}$$

In this equation, $A'(r_A)$ and $L'(r_L)$ are the derivatives of the market values of the assets and liabilities respectively. Normally, we would expect that $A'(r_A) < 0$ and $L'(r_L) < 0$ because the discounting of a set of cash flows at higher rates must imply a decrease in value. The derivative dr_L/dr_A indicates the relative changes in the interest rates at which the liabilities and assets are each discounted. If $dr_L/dr_A = 1$, then both r_L and r_A change by the same amount. If $dr_L/dr_A < 1$, then r_A changes by more than r_L and conversely if $dr_L/dr_A > 1$. If $dN/dr_A > 0$, then the interest rate changes have caused net worth to increase. If $dN/dr_A < 0$, then the interest rate changes have caused net worth to decrease. If $dN/dr_A = 0$, then the interest rate changes have had an offsetting impact in which the assets have changed by as much as the liabilities. Previous chapters have made it clear that $A'(r_A)$ and $L'(r_L)$ can be written as functions of their durations as

$$A'(r_A) = \frac{-D_A}{1 + r_A} A(r_A), \quad \text{and}$$

$$L'(r_L) = \frac{-D_L}{1 + r_L} L(r_L),\tag{9.3}$$

where D_A and D_L are the respective asset and liability durations, and where annual compounding is assumed. Substitution of (9.3) into equation (9.2) gives

$$\frac{dN}{dr_A} = \frac{-D_A A(r_A)}{1 + r_A} + \frac{D_L L(r_L)}{1 + r_L} \frac{dr_L}{dr_A}.\tag{9.4}$$

If, next, it is assumed that $dr_L/dr_A = 1$, implying that the interest rates on assets and liabilities change by exactly the same amounts, then equation (9.4) can be expressed as

$$
\frac{dN}{dr_A} = \frac{A(r_A)}{1+r_A}\left(-D_A + D_L\frac{L(r_L)}{A(r_A)}\frac{1+r_A}{1+r_L}\right)
$$
$$
= -\frac{A(r_A)}{1+r_A}\,\text{GAP}_N
$$

(9.5)

where

$$
\text{GAP}_N = D_A - D_L\frac{L(r_L)}{A(r_A)}\frac{1+r_A}{1+r_L}.
$$

(9.6)

Here, GAP_N is a measure of the sensitivity of net worth to changes in interest rates. The larger the absolute value of GAP_N, the greater the net worth sensitivity.[4]

If $\text{GAP}_N = 0$, then $dN/dr_A = 0$. In this case net worth is insensitive to interest rate changes in which the borrowing rate (r_L) and lending rate (r_A) change by the same amounts.

If $\text{GAP}_N > 0$ so that

$$
D_A > D_L\left\{\frac{L(r_L)(1+r_A)}{A(r_A)(1+r_L)}\right\},
$$

then an increase in interest rates will tend to reduce net worth and a decrease in interest rates will tend to increase net worth. Most financial institutions tend to have positive GAP_N's because they borrow for short periods in order to fund longer term assets. The solvency of such institutions tends to decrease in an environment of rising interest rates.

If $\text{GAP}_N < 0$, then an increase in interest rates will tend to increase net worth.

If $dr_L/dr_A = \beta \neq 1$, then we can redefine GAP_N as

$$
\text{GAP}_N = D_A - D_L\frac{L(r_L)}{A(r_A)}\frac{1+r_A}{1+r_L}\beta
$$

(9.7)

and use it as a measure of interest rate risk.[5]

Variations and themes involving the measure GAP_N have previously appeared in the literature. Grove (1974), who bases his work on some of Redington's ([1952], 1982) contributions, considers a portion of the balance sheet in which $A(r_A)$ represents the assets funded by the liabilities $L(r_L)$. Then, under the assumption that the assets are exactly fully funded, $A(r_A) = L(r_L)$. Assuming further that $(1+r_A)/(1+r_L) = 1$ and that $\beta = 1$, then $\text{GAP}_N = D_A - D_L$.[6] This simple definition of interest rate risk is often encountered in everyday financial parlance. Later, we shall regard $D_A - D_L$ as the appropriate measure of risk of fluctuations in the net worth/asset ratio.

The risk measurement, GAP_N, is one that applies to considerations of solvency. It may be quite inappropriate to consider GAP_N as relevant to the risk of short-run changes in the values of some securities or of the institution's income. In a short-run operations context, the value of many liabilities may be viewed as insensitive to interest rate changes. For example, if the value of the CDs issued by a solvent commercial bank are fixed contractually at all times, then fluctuations in borrowing or deposit rates in the market do not affect the value of such liability obligations. Bierwag and Toevs (1982) discuss some of the management issues raised by this feature of CDs. However, if the institution itself is viewed as marketable, then the value of the assets and liabilities would be computed at their market values in order to reflect the values of identically the same future cash inflows and outflows that could be currently acquired in the market. It is important to interpret GAP_N as a risk measure that is attached to the financial institution as though it were a marketable net asset. The measure GAP_N reflects the risk of fluctuations in the market liquidation value of the institution.

THE CAPITAL/ASSET RATIO AND
INTEREST RATE RISK

The risk measurement, GAP_N, applies only to the dollar value of net worth and measures only the risk of its market value fluctuation stemming from interest rate changes. Alternatively, the financial institution may be more concerned with the sensitivity of its net worth/asset ratio. It is possible for large changes in net worth to be accompanied by large changes in assets and liabilities without substantial changes in the net worth/asset ratio. The financial institution may simply be growing or contracting in size but retaining essentially the same risk posture. In this circumstance, GAP_N may not be zero, but the institution may be bearing no *relative* interest rate risk in the sense that the net worth/asset ratio may not be sensitive to interest rate changes.

The sensitivity of the net worth/asset ratio to interest rate changes is an alternative measure of interest rate risk. This measure, denoted as $GAP_{N/A}$, may also be useful for purposes of internal management. In Appendix 9A, it is shown that

$$\frac{d[N(r_A, r_L)/A(r_A)]}{dr_A} = -\frac{L(r_L)}{A(r_A)} \frac{1}{1+r_A} GAP_{N/A}, \qquad (9.8)$$

where[7]

$$GAP_{N/A} = D_A - D_L \left(\frac{1+r_A}{1+r_L} \right). \tag{9.9}$$

If $GAP_{N/A} > 0$, as for most financial institutions, an increase in interest rates results in a decrease in the net worth ratio. If $GAP_{N/A} = 0$, then an increase in interest rates has no effect on the net worth ratio. If $GAP_{N/A} < 0$, then an increase in interest rates results in an increase in the net worth ratio. The larger the absolute value of $GAP_{N/A}$, the more sensitive is the net worth/asset ratio to changes in interest rates. The value of $GAP_{N/A}$ as a measure of interest rate sensitivity is, therefore, a measure of interest rate risk.

Comparison of $GAP_{N/A}$ and GAP_N in equations (9.6) and (9.9) shows that

$$GAP_N = GAP_{N/A} + \left(\frac{1+r_A}{1+r_L} \right) D_L \cdot \frac{N(r_A, r_L)}{A(r_A)}, \tag{9.10}$$

so that $GAP_N > GAP_{N/A}$ as long as $D_L > 0$ and $N(r_A, r_L) > 0$. In particular this means that $GAP_N > 0$ when $GAP_{N/A} = 0$. Thus, it is, indeed, possible that the institution bears no relative risk that N/A will fluctuate with interest rates but since net worth changes in these circumstances, it follows that N is sensitive to interest rate changes. It is interesting to observe that when $GAP_N = 0$, then $GAP_{N/A} < 0$. That is, although an increase in interest rates may not affect the value of net worth, it increases the net worth/asset ratio as assets decrease in value.

NET ECONOMIC INCOME AND INTEREST RATE RISK

The income of a financial institution is also a function of its asset and liability durations. Interest rate changes can obviously change an institution's income. This suggests that the institution can manage or control the risk of income fluctuations stemming from interest rate changes by managing or controlling its asset and liability durations. Measures of interest rate risk relative to income can thus, in principle, be devised.

The net economic income of a financial institution can be expressed as

$$I = r_A A(r_A) - r_L L(r_L), \tag{9.11}$$

where r_A and r_L are annual rates of interest, and where I is a "flow" of earnings arising from the asset and liability "stocks," $A(r_A)$ and $L(r_L)$. That is, I is a measure of earnings over an *interval* of time whereas $A(r_A)$ and $L(r_L)$ are measures of assets and liabilities at a *point* in time. The net economic income, I, is not necessarily a cash flow. Interest revenue, $r_A A(r_A)$, may include any appreciation in some assets (discount bonds, for example) on which the cash interest earned is less than the market return $r_A A(r_A)$ and it may exclude depreciation in some assets (such as premium bonds and mortgages) for which cash flows were received but which partially represent a return of capital and not income earned. A similar interpretation of the interest expense, $r_L L(r_L)$, is also required. Some components of interest expense may not represent cash outflows, and there may be cash outflows not included in interest expense.

Given that a "flow," such as I, is connected to "stocks" such as $A(r_A)$ and $L(r_L)$ via equation (9.11), it follows that some features of the stocks—like their durations—can affect the properties of the "flows." Comparably, equation (9.11) connects the balance sheet and its properties to the income statement. The asset and liability durations may thus affect the nature of the income flow. As shown in Appendix 9A, we may write

$$\frac{dI}{dr_A} = -I \cdot \text{GAP}_I, \tag{9.12}$$

where

$$\text{GAP}_I = \frac{-N}{I} + \frac{r_A}{1+r_A} D_A \frac{A(r_A)}{I} - \frac{r_L}{1+r_L} D_L \frac{L(r_L)}{I}, \tag{9.13}$$

and where it is also assumed that $dr_L/dr_A = 1$.

If $\text{GAP}_I = 0$, then changes in interest rates will imply no change in economic income.[8] Similarly, if $\text{GAP}_I \gtrless 0$, then increases in interest rates will respectively reduce or increase net economic income.

If $dr_L/dr_A = \beta \neq 1$, then β appears as a multiplier of $L(r_L)$ in equation (9.13) and the term $-(1-\beta)L(r_L)/I$ must be added to the right-hand side in equation (9.13). As noted before, β can be potentially estimated by regression analysis, but its estimation is also potentially complex.

It is interesting to note that $\text{GAP}_I = 0$ need not imply that the previous GAP measures are zero. It is potentially possible for a financial institution to stabilize its net economic income but have its net worth position deteriorate to the point of insolvency.

NET RETURN ON ASSETS AND INTEREST RATE RISK

The dollar income return, I, can be standardized and expressed as a return on assets as

$$i = I/A = r_A - r_L \frac{L(r_L)}{A(r_A)}. \tag{9.14}$$

As shown in Appendix 9A,

$$\frac{di}{dr_A} = -i\,\text{GAP}_{I/A}, \tag{9.15}$$

where

$$\text{GAP}_{I/A} = -\frac{N}{I} + \frac{r_A AD_A}{I(1+r_A)} - \frac{r_L LD_L}{I(1+r_L)} - \frac{D_A}{1+r_A}, \tag{9.16}$$

and where it is assumed that $dr_L/dr_A = 1$.

If $\text{GAP}_{I/A} = 0$, then changes in interest rates will imply no change in i, net income as a percent of assets. Similarly, if $\text{GAP}_{I/A} \gtreqless 0$, then increases in interest rates will respectively reduce or increase net economic income. The larger the absolute value of $\text{GAP}_{I/A}$ the greater the sensitivity of the net economic income on assets to changes in interest rates.

If $dr_L/dr_A = \beta \neq 0$, then $\text{GAP}_{I/A}$ can be modified in exactly the same way as GAP_I.

We may note that

$$\text{GAP}_{I/A} = \text{GAP}_I - D_A/(1+r_A). \tag{9.17}$$

If $\text{GAP}_I = 0$ so that the dollar value of net economic income is insensitive to interest rate changes, then $\text{GAP}_{I/A} < 0$ so that increases in interest rates that do not affect I but that reduce the value of assets will increase the net economic income on assets.

ILLUSTRATIONS OF THE IMPACT OF INTEREST RATE CHANGES

Using a hypothetical balance sheet and income statement for a depository institution, one can illustrate the consequences of having various initial values of the gaps.[9] Table 9–1 shows an initial balance sheet and income statement for a hypothetical depository institution. On the asset side, the institution is endowed with cash reserves of $100, business loans of $400, and mortgage loans of $500 for a total of $1,000 in assets. Business loans are intended to be short-term commercial loans. They are assumed to have a maturity of 2.5 years. Mortgage loans, on the other hand, have an assumed maturity of 30 years. Cash reserves, of course, have a zero maturity. The rate of return on assets (excluding cash reserves), r_A, is assumed to be 13%. Cash reserves pay a zero rate of return. On the liability side, the depository institution has a mixture of long-term and short-term deposit liabilities specified as certificates of deposits, CDs. Initially the institution has outstanding

Table 9-1. An Initial Balance Sheet and Other Characteristics
of a Hypothetical Depository Institution

Balance Sheet

Assets		Liabilities/Net Worth	
Cash reserves	$ 100	One-year CDs	$ 600
Business loans	400	Five-year CDs	300
Mortgage loans	500	Total deposits	$ 900
		Net worth	100
Total assets	$1,000	Total liability/net worth	$1,000

Maturities (years)		Durations (years)	
Cash reserves	0.0	Cash reserves	0.0
Business loans	2.5	Business loans	1.22
Mortgage loans	30.0	Mortgage loans	7.14
One-year CDs	1.0	One-year CDs	1.00
Five-year CDs	5.0	Five-year CDs	5.00
		Total liabilities	2.33

Rates of Return (%)		GAPs (years)
Cash reseves	0.0	$GAP_N = 1.96$
Business and mortgage loans	13.0	$GAP_{N/A} = 1.73$
Deposits	11.0	$GAP_I = 3.82$
Net income	$18.00	$GAP_{I/A} = 7.83$
Net income/assets	1.8%	
Net worth/assets	10.0%	

$600 worth of 1-year CDs and $300 worth of 5-year CDs for a total of $900
in deposits. Net worth is assumed to be $100. The rate of return on CDs is
11%. In all the simulations to follow it is assumed that all assets and liabilities are amortized on a monthly basis, and that interest is paid or accrued
monthly. As noted in Table 9-1, net economic income on an annual basis
(monthly income projected for 12 months) is $18.

$$r_A A(r_A) - r_L L(r_L) = .13(900) - .11(900) = .02(900) = \$18,$$

which is 1.8% of assets. Of course, net worth is 10% of assets. Table 9-1
also shows the durations of the respective accounts. The CDs are assumed
to pay interest only at maturity and hence their durations are equal to their
maturities. The asset durations are computed on the assumption of monthly
cash flows. The duration of the asset side of the balance sheet is computed
as a weighted average of the durations of the components,

$$4.06 = \left(\frac{400}{900}\right)(1.22) + \left(\frac{500}{900}\right)(7.14),$$

in accordance with standard procedures as noted in previous chapters. The duration of the deposit liabilities are similarly computed:

$$2.33 = \left(\frac{600}{900}\right)(1.00) + \left(\frac{300}{900}\right)(5.00).$$

The gaps for this initial balance sheet are also indicated on Table 9–1.[10]

Zero Gaps

In the simulations shown in Tables 9–2 through 9–5, the level of deposits in 1- and 5-year CDs is changed so as to produce zero gaps. Each of the hypothetical institutions is then bombarded with a set of possible interest rate changes in order to observe the impact on various accounts.

$GAP_N = 0.$ Table 9–2 shows the initial balance sheet when deposits are such that $GAP_N = 0$. Each of the other GAPs in this example is negative. This means that values of the net worth/asset ratio, net economic income, and the net economic income/asset ratio should increase with interest rate increases. Table 9–2 shows that this is indeed the case for increases in interest rates. For example, a 200-basis-point increase in interest rates results in the net income return on assets rising from 1.8% to 2.06% and in the net worth/asset ratio rising from 10% to 10.8%. The net worth of the institution is stabilized, however, and never falls below its initial value of $100.[11] This institution appears to be in fine condition, even though the value of the firm's assets has diminished to $927.90, a decrease of 7.21% stemming from the sharp increase in interest rates.

Since all gaps are negative except that for net worth, a decrease in interest rates will reduce the net worth/asset ratio, net income and the net income/asset ratio.[12] A sharp decrease in interest rates of 200 basis points brings about a deterioration in most of these accounts. The net worth/asset ratio falls from 10% to 9.7%, and the net income return on assets falls from 1.8% to 1.68%. Because of the large change in rates, however, net income increases from $18 to $18.32. Although there has been a deterioration in some major accounts the institution has increased in size by 9.07% as a consequence of the decrease in interest rates.

Table 9-2. Changes in Balance Sheet Accounts and Income Statement for Various Interest Rate Changes, $GAP_N = 0$

Initial Conditions

Assets		Liabilities and Net Worth		GAPs	
Cash reserves	$ 100	One-year CDs	$ 109.75	GAP_N	0.00
Business loans	400	Five-year CDs	790.25	$GAP_{N/A}$	−0.45
Mortgage loans	500	Total deposits	900.00	GAP_I	−1.14
		Net worth	100.00	$GAP_{I/A}$	−5.16
Total assets	$1,000	Total liability and net worth	$1,000.00		

Impact of Interest Rate Changes

Interest Rate Changes[a]	One-Year CDs	Five-Year CDs	Business Loans	Mortgage Loans	Total Assets	Net Worth	Net Worth/ Assets	Net Income	Net Income/ Assets
−200	$111.94	$872.64	$409.86	$580.79	$1,090.65	$106.06	9.7%	$18.32	1.68%
−150	111.39	851.26	407.36	558.52	1,065.88	103.23	9.7	18.12	1.70
−100	110.84	830.41	404.89	537.71	1,042.60	101.35	9.7	18.04	1.73
− 50	110.29	810.08	402.43	518.24	1,020.68	100.31	9.8	17.96	1.76
− 25	110.02	806.10	401.21	508.98	1,010.19	100.07	9.9	17.98	1.78
+ 25	109.47	780.53	398.71	491.31	990.10	100.10	10.1	18.02	1.82
+ 50	109.20	770.92	397.59	482.88	980.47	100.35	10.2	18.25	1.85
+100	108.66	752.07	395.20	466.80	962.00	101.26	10.5	18.37	1.91
+150	108.13	733.69	392.82	451.67	944.50	102.68	10.9	18.70	1.98
+200	107.59	715.76	390.47	437.43	927.90	104.54	11.3	19.11	2.06

a. In basis points. Rate changes apply to all initially given rates.

Table 9-3. Changes in Balance Sheet Accounts and Income Statement for Various Interest Rate Changes, $GAP_{N/A} = 0$

Initial Conditions

Assets		Liabilities and Net Worth		GAPs	
Cash reserves	$ 100	One-year CDs	$ 211.27	GAP_N	0.41
Business loans	400	Five-year CDs	688.73	$GAP_{N/A}$	0.00
Mortgage loans	500	Total deposits	900.00	GAP_I	1.32
		Net worth	100.00	$GAP_{I/A}$	−2.70
Total assets	$1,000	Total liability and net worth	$1,000.00		

Impact of Interest Rate Changes

Interest Rate Changes[a]	One-Year CDs	Five-Year CDs	Business Loans	Mortgage Loans	Total Assets	Net Worth	Net Worth/ Assets	Net Income	Net Income/ Assets
−200	$215.50	$760.53	$409.86	$580.79	$1,090.65	$114.61	10.5%	$19.09	1.75%
−150	214.44	741.90	407.36	558.52	1,065.88	109.55	10.3	18.76	1.76
−100	213.38	723.73	404.89	537.71	1,042.60	105.50	10.1	18.45	1.77
− 50	212.32	706.01	402.41	518.24	1,020.68	102.35	10.0	18.17	1.78
− 25	211.80	697.31	401.21	508.98	1,010.19	101.08	10.0	18.08	1.79
+ 25	210.75	680.25	398.79	491.31	990.10	99.10	10.0	17.92	1.81
+ 50	210.23	671.88	397.59	482.88	980.47	98.36	10.0	17.94	1.83
+100	209.19	655.45	395.20	466.80	962.00	97.36	10.1	17.89	1.86
+150	208.16	639.43	392.82	451.67	944.50	96.91	10.3	18.04	1.91
+200	207.13	623.81	390.47	437.43	927.90	96.96	10.4	18.19	1.96

a. In basis points. Rate changes apply to all initially given rates.

GAP$_{N/A}$ = 0.   Table 9-3 shows the comparable account changes when GAP$_{N/A}$ = 0. Here, the number of dollars in one year CDs has increased relative to the amounts when GAP$_N$ = 0. This is because GAP$_{N/A}$ = 0 here only when GAP$_N$ > 0 (as shown in equation 9.10). Now, however, GAP$_I$ > 0 and GAP$_{I/A}$ < 0. Thus, small increases in interest rates should result in decreases in dollar income and in increases in the net income on assets.

Table 9-3 shows that the net worth/asset ratio is, indeed, stabilized at its initial value of 10% (although it may rise slightly for either increases or decreases in interest rates due to convexities or nonlinearities). One of the objectives in setting GAP$_{N/A}$ = 0 has consequently been satisfied. The other major accounts of interest tend to change in the directions indicated by their gaps. Since GAP$_N$ > 0, increases (decreases) in interest rates result in declining (increasing) net worth. Since GAP$_{I/A}$ < 0, the net income return on assets increases (decreases) as interest rates increase (decrease). Since GAP$_I$ > 0, the dollar value of net income decreases (increases) as interest rates increase (decrease), although increases in interest rates in excess of 25 basis points may reverse this tendency because of nonlinearities.

GAP$_I$ = 0.   Table 9-4 shows the results when GAP$_I$ = 0. In this case GAP$_N$ > 0, GAP$_{N/A}$ < 0, and GAP$_{I/A}$ < 0. Thus, for small increases (decreases) in interest rates, we should expect net worth to decrease (increase), the net worth/ asset ratio to increase (decrease), and the net income return on assets to increase (decrease). This is, indeed, the case but large changes reverse some of these expected impacts in the case of the net worth/asset ratio and net worth.

With GAP$_I$ = 0, the intended effect results. Net economic income is stabilized at $18.00; in no case does net income fall below $18.00. However, the net income return on assets falls as low as 1.72% when interest rates decrease by 200 basis points. This relatively large decrease results because GAP$_{I/A}$ is relatively large in absolute value. For changes in interest rates between −200 and +200 basis points, however, the level of net worth and the net worth asset ratio change very little. This is because GAP$_N$ and GAP$_{N/A}$ are very small in absolute value. It isn't always true that GAP$_N$ and GAP$_{N/A}$ tend to be small when GAP$_I$ = 0. In other examples, the net worth gaps may be much larger.

GAP$_{I/A}$ = 0.   Table 9-5 shows the corresponding results when GAP$_{I/A}$ = 0. Here, we may observe that all the other GAPs are positive, so that there is a tendency for small increases (decreases) in interest rates to lead to decreases (increases) in net worth, the net worth/asset ratio, and net income. As expected the net income return on assets is stabilized at 1.8%; in no case does

Table 9-4. Changes in Balance Sheet Accounts and Income Statement for Various Interest Rate Changes, $GAP_I = 0$

Initial Conditions

Assets		Liabilities and Net Worth		GAPs	
Cash reserves	$ 100	One-year CDs	$ 156.79	GAP_N	0.19
Business loans	400	Five-year CDs	743.21	$GAP_{N/A}$	−0.24
Mortgage loans	500	Total deposits	900.00	GAP_I	0.00
		Net worth	100.00	$GAP_{I/A}$	−4.02
Total assets	$1,000	Total liability and net worth	$1,000.00		

Impact of Interest Rate Changes

Interest Rate Changes[a]	One-Year CDs	Five-Year CDs	Business Loans	Mortgage Loans	Total Assets	Net Worth	Net Worth/ Assets	Net Income	Net Income/ Assets
−200	$159.89	$820.74	$409.86	$580.79	$1,090.65	$110.02	10.1%	$18.75	1.72%
−150	159.09	800.63	407.36	558.52	1,065.88	106.16	10.0	18.44	1.73
−100	158.31	781.02	404.89	537.71	1,042.60	103.27	9.9	18.14	1.74
− 50	157.52	761.90	402.43	518.24	1,020.68	101.25	9.9	18.07	1.77
− 25	157.13	752.52	401.21	508.98	1,010.19	100.54	10.0	18.00	1.78
+ 25	156.36	734.11	398.79	491.31	990.10	99.63	10.1	18.02	1.82
+ 50	155.97	725.07	397.59	482.88	980.47	99.43	10.1	18.04	1.84
+100	155.20	707.34	395.20	466.80	962.00	99.46	10.3	18.18	1.89
+150	154.43	690.05	392.82	451.67	944.50	100.01	10.6	18.42	1.95
+200	153.67	673.19	390.47	437.43	927.90	101.03	10.9	18.65	2.01

a. In basis points. Rate changes apply to all initially given rates.

Table 9-5. Changes in Balance Sheet Accounts and Income Statement for Various Interest Rate Changes, $GAP_{I/A} = 0$

Initial Conditions

Assets		Liabilities and Net Worth		GAPs	
Cash reserves	$ 100	One-year CDs	$ 322.60	GAP_N	0.85
Business loans	400	Five-year CDs	577.40	$GAP_{N/A}$	0.49
Mortgage loans	500	Total deposits	900.00	GAP_I	4.02
		Net worth	100.00	$GAP_{I/A}$	0.00
Total assets	$1,000	Total liability and net worth	$1,000.00		

Impact of Interest Rate Changes

Interest Rate Changes[a]	One-Year CDs	Five-Year CDs	Business Loans	Mortgage Loans	Total Assets	Net Worth	Net Worth/ Assets	Net Income	Net Income/ Assets
-200	$329.06	$637.60	$409.86	$580.79	$1,090.65	$123.99	11.4%	$19.96	1.83%
-150	327.43	621.98	407.36	558.52	1,065.88	116.48	10.9	19.40	1.82
-100	325.81	606.75	404.89	537.71	1,042.60	110.05	10.6	18.87	1.81
- 50	324.20	591.89	402.43	518.24	1,020.68	104.59	10.2	18.37	1.80
- 25	323.40	584.60	401.21	508.98	1,010.19	102.19	10.1	18.18	1.80
+ 25	321.80	570.30	398.79	491.31	990.10	98.00	9.9	17.82	1.80
+ 50	321.00	563.28	397.59	482.88	980.47	96.19	9.8	17.65	1.80
+100	319.42	549.50	395.20	466.80	962.00	93.08	9.7	17.41	1.81
+150	317.84	536.07	392.82	451.67	944.50	90.59	9.6	17.19	1.82
+200	316.27	522.97	390.47	437.43	927.90	88.65	9.6	17.07	1.84

a. In basis points. Rate changes apply to all initially given rates.

this rate of return fall below 1.8%. On the other hand, for interest rate increases within the range, net worth drops as low as $88.65, the net worth/asset ratio falls to 9.6% and net income falls to $17.07. Moreover, the value of assets falls to $897.13 when interest rates increase by 200 basis points; this is a decrease of 10.2%.

Extremely Risky Positions

The financial institution above can take extremely risky positions with respect to some accounts by choosing the relevant gaps to be as large as possible. For example, holding exactly the same asset mixture as in all the previous zero gap simulations and reducing the 5-year CDs to $1.50 (something insignificant) increases the gaps considerably. Table 9–6 shows that GAP_N is increased to 3.55 and $GAP_{N/A}$ is increased to 3.05. The income gaps change dramatically. GAP_I rises to 17.97 and $GAP_{I/A}$ rises to 13.95. The income measures become considerably more sensitive to changes in interest rates than they were before. An increase of interest rates by 200 basis points reduces net economic income to $11.50 and reduces the net income return on assets to 1.24%. The net worth accounts are also dramatically affected. The increase of 200 basis points in interest rates reduces net worth to $45.60, a decrease of 54.4%; and it reduces the net worth/asset ratio to 4.9%, a dramatic drop from an initial 10%. The enhanced sensitivity of all of these accounts to changes in interest rates plainly increases the institution's exposure to interest rate risk.

Table 9–7 illustrates an even riskier position. Here, the deposits are entirely concentrated in 30-day CDs, assets are concentrated in 30-year mortgages, and cash reserves are maintained at $100. Then, $GAP_N = 6.35$ years, $GAP_{N/A} = 6.34$, $GAP_I = 35.51$, and $GAP_{I/A} = 29.82$. These are extremely large gaps that reflect the obvious risks faced by an institution that is funding 30-year mortgages with 30-day CDs but attempts to soften a bad turn of events with 10% of its assets in cash reserves. If interest rates should drop by 200 basis points, assets increase dramatically by 145% and net worth increases by 143.9%. Income increases from $18 to $31.86, representing an increase of the net income return on assets from 1.8% to 2.78%. The institution is in the gravy when interest rates fall. On the other hand, when interest rates increase by 200 basis points, the institution is driven into insolvency; that is, net worth becomes negative. An increase of interest rates by only 150 basis points drives net worth from 10% of assets to 2% of assets. The income of the institution, although more sensitive to interest rate changes than

Table 9-6. Changes in Balance Sheet Accounts and Income Statement for Various Interest Rate Changes

Initial Conditions

Assets		Liabilities and Net Worth	
Cash reserves	$ 100	One-year CDs	$ 898.50
Business loans	400	Five-year CDs	1.50
Mortgage loans	500	Total deposits	900.00
		Net worth	100.00
Total assets	$1,000	Total liability and net worth	$1,000.00

GAPs

GAP_N	3.16
$GAP_{N/A}$	3.05
GAP_I	17.97
$GAP_{I/A}$	13.95

Impact of Interest Rate Changes

Interest Rate Changes[a]	One-Year CDs	Five-Year CDs	Business Loans	Mortgage Loans	Total Assets	Net Worth	Net Worth/Assets	Net Income	Net Income/Assets
−200	$916.49	$1.66	$409.86	$580.79	$1,090.65	$172.49	15.8%	$24.32	2.23%
−150	911.96	1.62	407.36	558.52	1,065.88	152.31	14.3	22.81	2.14
−100	907.45	1.58	404.89	537.71	1,042.60	133.57	12.8	21.16	2.03
− 50	902.96	1.54	402.43	518.24	1,020.68	116.18	11.4	19.60	1.92
− 25	900.72	1.52	401.21	508.98	1,010.19	107.94	10.7	18.79	1.86
+ 25	896.27	1.49	398.79	491.31	990.10	92.34	9.3	17.23	1.74
+ 50	894.06	1.47	397.59	482.88	980.47	84.94	8.7	16.37	1.67
+100	889.64	1.43	395.20	466.80	962.00	70.93	7.4	14.72	1.53
+150	885.25	1.40	392.82	451.67	944.50	57.85	6.1	13.13	1.39
+200	880.88	1.36	390.47	437.43	927.90	45.60	4.9	11.50	1.24

a. In basis points. Rate changes apply to all initially given rates.

Table 9-7. Changes in Balance Sheet Accounts and Income Statement for Various Interest Rate Changes

Initial Conditions

Assets		Liabilities and Net Worth	
Cash reserves	$ 100	One-month CDs	$ 900
Business loans	0	Five-year CDs	0
Mortgage loans	900	Total deposits	900
		Net worth	100
Total assets	$1,000	Total liability and net worth	$1,000

GAPs:

GAP_N	6.35
$GAP_{N/A}$	6.34
GAP_I	35.51
$GAP_{I/A}$	29.82

Impact of Interest Rate Changes

Interest Rate Changes[a]	One-Month CDs	Mortgage Loans	Total Assets	Net Worth	Net Worth/ Assets	Net Income	Net Income/ Assets
-200	$901.49	$1,045.42	$1,145.42	$243.90	21%	$31.86	2.78%
-150	901.12	1,005.34	1,105.34	204.22	18	28.51	2.58
-100	900.74	967.89	1,067.89	167.14	16	25.07	2.34
- 50	900.37	932.84	1,032.84	132.47	13	21.57	2.09
- 25	900.19	916.16	1,016.16	116.00	11	19.79	1.95
+ 25	899.81	884.35	984.35	84.54	9	16.20	1.65
+ 50	899.63	869.19	969.19	69.56	7	14.38	1.48
+100	899.26	840.24	940.24	40.99	4	10.72	1.14
+150	898.87	813.01	913.01	14.13	2	7.03	0.77
+200	898.52	787.37	887.37	-11.15	-1	3.29	0.32

a. In basis points. Rate changes apply to all initially given rates.

in prior examples, never slips below zero, even when the firm has become insolvent. This is because the lending rate always exceeds the borrowing rate by 200 basis points, representing a prospect of positive income even when liabilities exceed assets to some extent. This illustration clearly reveals the consequences of a highly leveraged position. Relatively small changes in interest rates can have an enormous impact on the institution's financial condition.

PROSPECTS FOR DURATION GAP MANAGEMENT

Traditional Gap Management

Traditionally, gap management in commercial banks and in other depository institutions, focuses on assets and liabilities that generate interest income that is sensitive to changes in interest rates over a prospective planning period (90 days to a year). In this traditional approach, interest income is defined as "book" income and this meaning of income is different from net economic income defined above. Book income consists of contracted earnings generated on an asset/liability base that is amortized over time at initially contracted interest rates. Unless the assets or liabilities giving rise to this income are repriced or mature during the planning period, interest rate changes can have no effect whatever on the book value of income.

Example 1. A bond is purchased at par with a coupon rate of 6%. The annual interest revenue throughout the life of the bond is regarded as 6% of the purchase price regardless of what may happen to interest rates after its purchase.

Example 2. A discount bond is purchased at a yield to maturity of 6%. The bond has a coupon rate of 4%. Throughout the life of the bond the annual interest revenue is regarded as 6%. This consists of the 4% coupon rate and an increase in the amortized value of the bond of 2%. Changes in market interest rates over the period have no effect on the measured income.

Example 3. A mortgage is issued at 12%. The monthly interest revenue is regarded as 1% of the mortgage's amortized value at the beginning of the month. A portion of the monthly payment is regarded as a return of capital which reduces (or amortizes) the value of the mortgage over time. Again, changes in market interest rates have no impact on measured interest revenue.

The assets in these three examples are called rate insensitive assets (RIA) because their values on the "books" of the financial institution that holds them do not normally change with market rates. Similarly, rate-insensitive liabilities are defined. On the books, the value of all of these assets and liabilities are perfectly well defined at all future dates during the life of these assets and liabilities. The assets or liabilities are simply amortized or appreciated in value over time depending on whether the periodic cash payments exceed or are less than the interest payments as calculated using the contractual interest rates on each loan or debt contract. Similarly, the book income is fixed also throughout the life of the asset or liability. The only exception to this accounting procedure occurs when an asset or liability is terminated prior to its contracted maturity. In that case the institution may adjust its net worth account to reflect an adjustment of the asset or liability to its market value.

If an asset matures (or is sold) during the planning period, then the maturity (or market) value can be reinvested at market rates before the end of the planning period. The income generated by the asset over the entire planning period is consequently a function of changes in market rates over the period. These assets are called rate-sensitive assets (RSA). Similarly, rate-sensitive liabilities (RSL) are defined. Some assets and liabilities can be repriced during the planning period. These are assets and liabilities that represent securities on which the financial institution has the right to change the contractual interest rate so as to align it more closely with market rates. Adjustable rate mortgages (ARMs) are examples of such securities. These securities are also interest rate sensitive.

If management focuses strictly on book income or the so-called *net interest margin,* it will concentrate strictly on rate-sensitive assets and liabilities. The income generated by RIA and RIL is constant over the planning period and is not subject to management control.

In traditional management, the GAP is then defined as

$$\text{GAP\$} = \text{RSA} - \text{RSL}, \qquad (9.18)$$

the difference between the book value of rate-sensitive assets and liabilities. If GAP\$ = 0, then there is presumably no risk. As market rates change, presumably interest revenue changes by as much as interest expenses. If GAP\$ > 0, interest revenue is more sensitive to changes in market rates than interest expenses, and conversely if GAP\$ < 0. An institution can then control its exposure to risk presumably by controlling the value of GAP\$. Sinkey (1983) (and references cited there) discuss this traditional management approach. Toevs (1983) refines this approach by taking into account the different dates within the planning period at which RSA and RSL mature or are repriced.

Tables 9-2 through 9-7 illustrate some of the consequences of this approach. Suppose that the planning period is 30 days. In Table 9-7 there are no RSA or RSL for this planning period. In effect, GAP\$ = 0. Presumably this institution faces no interest rate risk. Clearly, however, the table shows that the institution is tremendously levered relative to market rates. In fact, the institution can be "wiped out" by an increase of market rates of less than 200 basis points. Similar interpretations of the other tables are also possible.

Traditional gap management ignores the impact of interest rate changes on the market value of net worth; nor is income in the traditional approach defined in a way that is consistent with the market value of balance sheet accounts. This form of management is based strictly on the book value of accounts. In a modern world in which market rates can change and can change quickly by large amounts, it is very hard to argue that the illustrations in Tables 9-2 through 9-7 have no relevance to an institution's risk exposure.

Duration Gap Management

In order to utilize the duration-based gaps of this chapter, it is necessary to compute an institution's durations. For large institutions having hundreds of millions of dollars of assets and liabilities spread over a large variety of financial securities with a broad range of characteristics, this may not be a simple task. Ideally, a computerized information system would be able to indicate in a flash exactly the value of the cash flows to occur on any future date (or in some small time interval) as a consequence of any given current stock of assets and liabilities. If the institution then had appropriate estimates of the market yield at which each cash flow should be discounted so as to give market values, it could very simply compute durations for any set of assets or liabilities. Accordingly, the GAPs could then be computed. The fact that different assets and liabilities would be discounted at different rates, contrary to the illustrations in this chapter, is no problem in the computations. Essentially, the gap formulas hold for an average of rates.

The construction of such an ideal computerized information system is likely to very costly — costly to construct and costly to maintain — relative to the normal revenue and expenses of a financial intermediary. Alternative and less expensive approaches to estimating the gaps are possible and can be utilized. Assets and liabilities can be lumped into groups based on common features — coupon rates (or comparable contractual rates), maturities, credit risk, and so forth. Finally one can derive some estimate of the implied cash flow stream and of the relevant market yields for discounting to obtain market values. Within the cells, so defined, one can then compute durations.

The durations within the cells can then be appropriately aggregated and utilized for estimating the gaps. It is also possible to organize the cells so that they conveniently coincide with an institution's managerial divisions. Divisions for commercial loans, residential mortgages, installment debt, and so forth immediately come to mind. In some schemes, financial intermediaries have connected some asset investment divisions with a source of funding on the liability side of the balance sheet. In this way, such divisions become mini-institutions within a large financial organization and may be managed independently to a large degree.

Futures market operations within managerial divisions can also become part of the overall approach to duration gap management. As illustrated in Chapter 8, one can contract or increase the duration of an asset or liability by utilizing the futures markets. In this way, the gaps can also be contracted or increased by futures market operations. Moreover, the stronger the correlation between the interest return on securities issued as a source of funding and the interest return on the invested funds, the greater the potential for hedging or reducing the effective interest rate risk. Many financial institutions have opened up futures trading divisions with the express purpose of having greater flexibility in its gap management, but the amount of hedging by financial institutions is quite small in the aggregate. The full potential use of futures markets in gap management is a long way from realization.

Market value accounting to some degree and a management framework partly based on it is likely to become more prevalent among financial institutions in years to come. The exposure to interest rate risk, made so clear in illustrations like those in the tables of this chapter, has become a matter of considerable concern in asset and liability management because of the volatility of interest rates in recent years. The concept of duration and its use is likely to become more important to management in the years ahead.

APPENDIX 9A
DERIVATION OF $GAP_{N/A}$, GAP_I, AND $GAP_{I/A}$

The derivation of these gap measures of interest rate risk are also contained in Bierwag and Kaufman (1985). The following notation is used in this appendix. Interest rates: r_A = annual interest rate on assets, and r_L = annual interest rate on liabilities. The value of assets = $A = A(r_A)$. The value of liabilities = $L = L(r_L)$. The duration of assets = D_A. The duration of liabilities = D_L. The value of net worth is $N = N(r_A, r_L)$. The derivatives of variables will often be denoted with only primes ($L' = L'(r_L)$, $A' = A'(r_A)$, and so on).

$\text{GAP}_{N/A}$

The net worth/asset ratio can be expressed as

$$n = N/A = 1 - L/A. \tag{9A.1}$$

Then,

$$dn/dr_A = -(L'/A)(dr_L/dr_A) + (L/A^2)A'. \tag{9A.2}$$

Assuming

$$dr_L/dr_A = 1,$$

$$L' = -D_L L/(1 + r_L), \quad \text{and} \tag{9A.3}$$

$$A' = -D_A A/(1 + r_A),$$

it follows that

$$\frac{dn}{dr_A} = \frac{D_L(L/A)}{1 + r_L} - \frac{D_A(L/A)}{1 + r_A}$$

$$= \frac{-(L/A)}{1 + r_A} \text{GAP}_{N/A}, \tag{9A.4}$$

where

$$\text{GAP}_{N/A} = D_A - \frac{1 + r_A}{1 + r_L} D_L \tag{9A.5}$$

is the definition of $\text{GAP}_{N/A}$ used in the text.

GAP_I and $\text{GAP}_{I/A}$

The net economic income earned by the financial institution can be expressed, as in the text, as

$$I = r_A A - r_L L. \tag{9A.6}$$

Then,

$$dI/dr_A = A - r_A A D_A/(1 + r_A) - L + r_L L D_L/(1 + r_L)$$

$$= N - r_A A D_A/(1 + r_A) + r_L L D_L/(1 + r_L). \tag{9A.7}$$

We can then write this as

$$dI/dr_A = -I\text{GAP}_I, \tag{9A.8}$$

where

$$\mathrm{GAP}_I = -(N/I) + r_A(A/I)D_A/(1+r_A) - r_L(L/I)D_L/(1+r_L). \tag{9A.9}$$

Of the many possible ways to define this gap measure so that (9A.7) is equivalent to (9A.8), the measure is defined so that as a linear approximation we can always write

$$\Delta I/I = -\mathrm{GAP}_I \cdot \Delta r_A$$

in the same manner that the percentage change in the price of a security is linearly approximated by duration multiplied by the negative of an interest rate change. The gap measure in (9A.8) is analogous to duration in the usual equations.

We may standardize the income measure by dividing economic income by the value of assets so as to give a return on assets. Letting $i = I/A$, we have

$$di/dr_A = (1/A)(dI/dr_A) - (I/A^2)(dA/dr_A). \tag{9A.10}$$

Then, using equations (9A.7) and (9A.3), it follows that

$$\frac{di}{dr_A} = 1 - \frac{r_A D_A}{1+r_A} - \frac{L}{A} + \frac{r_L D_L(L/A)}{1+r_L} + \frac{D_A(I/A)}{1+r_A}. \tag{9A.11}$$

Finally, we can write

$$di/dr_A = -(I/A)\mathrm{GAP}_{I/A}, \tag{9A.12}$$

where

$$\mathrm{GAP}_{I/A} = -\frac{N}{I} + \frac{r_A D_A(A/I)}{1+r_A} - \frac{r_L D_L(L/I)}{1+r_L} - \frac{D_A}{1+r_L}$$

$$= \mathrm{GAP}_I - \frac{D_A}{1+r_A}. \tag{9A.13}$$

NOTES

1. FHLBB (1983) and Bierwag and Kaufman (1983a, b) discuss the incentive structure that can lead to an excessive amount of interest rate risk. Buser, Chen, and Kane (1981) were among the first to perceive the adverse effects of deposit insurance on the disposition of depository institutions to bear interest rate risk.
2. Risk-sensitive federal deposit insurance premiums, their feasibility and some of their likely effects, are discussed in Campbell and Glen (1984), Horvitz (1983), Kane (1983a, b), and Peterson (1983).
3. Some assets may not be sensitive to interest rate changes. Let the value of these assets be A_{NS} and let the remaining assets be $A_S(r_A)$. Then, $A(r_A) = A_{NS} + A_S(r_A)$.

In some treatments of asset and liability management, a distinction between A_{NS} and $A_S(r_A)$ is made. Liabilities can be similarly decomposed.

4. In the literature [see, for example, Bierwag and Kaufman (1985, 1983a, b)], GAP_N is defined slightly differently. It is assumed that $(1+r_A)/(1+r_L)=1$ in equation (9.5). This ratio will tend toward unity with continuous compounding. Essentially, continuous compounding is assumed in the literature.

5. As in similar relative interest rate sensitivity measures devised in Chapter 8, the analyst can estimate β by regression analysis. That is, regress r_L, or some index of it, on r_A, or some index of it, over time. The slope coefficient is then an estimate of β. However, β may not be independent of the durations because interest rate changes may be bigger for some terms to maturity than for others. That is, β may be sensitive to factors which can affect the term structure of interest rates. Appropriate estimation procedures may accordingly be very complex.

6. In the derivation, the assumption that $(1+r_A)/(1+r_L)=1$ does not necessarily mean that $r_A=r_L$. The result in the derivation could be derived as though that were the case by simply allowing for continuous compounding. This has been noted before.

7. Upon continuous discounting, by approximation, or in the special case where $r_A=r_L$, we can let $GAP_{N/A}=D_A-D_L$.

8. In fact, income I is a nonlinear function of interest rates even when $GAP_I=0$. This statement holds only for small changes in interest rates.

9. These illustrations were devised using *Interest Rate Risk Management Game—DGAME* by G. Bierwag and G. Kaufman, a software computer game that can be used on most personal computers. Using this program one can choose the various components of an initial hypothetical balance sheet so as to be consistent with most given value of any gap. One can them bombard that balance sheet and income statement with any given interest rate change or with a random sequence of interest rate changes. In this way, a manager may observe the consequences of various gap decisions. This program is available at a nominal cost for educational purposes from Professor G. Kaufman, Department of Finance, School of Business, Loyola University, Chicago, Ilinois 60611. Further illustrations are contained in Kaufman (1983).

10. These gaps are computed assuming monthly compounding in the present value formulations. The gap formulas in the text above assume annual compounding. To go from the gaps computed on an annual compounding basis to those computed on a monthly compounding basis, one need only divide any interest rate by 12 wherever it appears in the denominators of the gaps computed on an annual basis. GAP_N and $GAP_{N/A}$ in Table 9-1 are approximated as though there were continuous compounding. All of these technical aspects do not affect any of the interpretations to follow.

11. Because of convexities, net worth may increase slightly for either increases or decreases in interest rates.

12. The sign of the GAP determines the sign of the change in the account only for small changes in interest rates. Because of nonlinearities, large changes may result in just the opposite effect. For example, a decrease of interest rates by 25 or 50 basis points reduces net income, but larger decreases result in an increase in net income.

REFERENCES

Bierwag, Gerald O., and George G. Kaufman. 1983a, b. "A Proposal for Federal Deposit Insurance with Risk Sensitive Premiums." *Bank Structure and Competition: Conference Proceedings,* Federal Reserve Bank of Chicago, May 1983a, pp. 223–242; a much more detailed version of this paper is contained in a Staff Memorandum, Federal Reserve Bank of Chicago, March 1983b.

———. 1984. *Interest Rate Risk and Management Game – DGAME,* Department of Finance, School of Business, Loyola University, Chicago.

———. 1985. "Duration Gaps for Financial Institutions." *Financial Analysts Journal* (March–April): 68–71.

Bierwag, Gerald O., and Alden Toevs. 1982. "Immunization of Interest Rate Risk for Depository Financial Institutions." *Bank Structure and Competition: Conference Proceedings,* Federal Reserve Bank of Chicago, May.

Buser, Stephen A., Andrew H. Chen, and Edward J. Kane, 1981. "Federal Deposit Insurance, Regulatory Policy, and Optimal Bank Capital." *Journal of Finance* (March): 51–60.

Campbell, Tim S., and David Glenn. 1984. "Deposit Insurance in a Deregulated Environment." *Journal of Finance* (July): 775–85.

Federal Home Loan Bank Board (FHLBB). 1983. *Agenda for Reform,* A report on deposit insurance to the Congress from the FHLBB, Washington, D.C., March.

Grove, M.A. 1974. "On 'Duration' and the Optimal Maturity Structure of the Balance Sheet." *Bell Journal of Economics and Management Science* (Autumn): 696–709.

Horvitz, Paul M. 1983. "The Case against Risk-Related Deposit Insurance Premiums." *Housing Finance Review* (July): 253–63.

Kane, Edward J. 1983a. "The Role of Government in the Thrift Industry's Net Worth Crisis." In *Financial Services,* The American Assembly, edited by George J. Benston. (Englewood Cliffs, N.J.: Prentice-Hall).

———. 1983b. "A Six-Point Program for Deposit-Insurance Reform." *Housing Finance Review* (July): 269–78.

Kaufman, George G. 1984. "Measuring and Managing Interest Rate Risk: A Primer." *Economic Perspective,* Federal Reserve Bank of Chicago, (January-February): 16–29.

Peterson, Paul T. 1983. "The Case against Risk-Related Deposit Insurance Premiums: A Contrary View." *Housing Finance Review* (July): 265–68.

Redington, F.M. [1952] 1982. "Review of the Principle of Life Office Valuations." *Journal of the Institute of Actuaries* (1952): 286–340; reprinted in G.A. Hawawini, *Bond Duration and Immunization,* (New York: Garland, 1982).

Sinkey, Joseph F., Jr. 1983. *Commercial Bank Financial Management.* (New York: Macmillan).

Toevs, Alden. 1983. "Gap Management: Managing Interest Rate Risk in Banks and Thrifts." *Economic Review,* Federal Reserve Bank of San Francisco, (Spring).

IV EMPIRICAL ESTIMATION AND SIMULATIONS

10 THE TERM STRUCTURE OF INTEREST RATES

The transformation of future value into present value is a basic feature of any analysis of the value of an asset. In Chapter 1 this transformation of value was expressed in a very simple way. The present value of a cash flow, F_t, occurring at time t, was found by multiplying F_t by d_t, a discount factor. In this way, the present value V of an income stream $(F_1, F_2, ..., F_t, ..., F_N)$ could be expressed as

$$V = \sum_1^N d_t F_t,$$ (10.1)

which is simply the sum of the present values of the cash flows of the income stream. Throughout Part I of this book, d_t, the discount factor, was expressed as a simple function of a rate of interest r. That is,

$$d_t = (1+r)^{-t},$$ (10.2)

for the case of annual compounding. The specification of d_t by such a relationship as in equation (10.2) has several agreeable properties as previously noted. First, the functional form in (10.2) implies $0 \le d_t \le 1$, so that the present value is less than the future value. Second, $d_t < d_{t-1}$ so that cash flows more remote in the future have a present value less than more immediate cash flows. The simplicity of the relationship allows one to treat r as an annual rate of growth over long period. All of these features certainly commend its use. Also, as noted earlier, the rate r in equation (10.2) is the yield to maturity and it is often used as an index of the earning power of an asset.

Casual observation reveals, however, that the relationship in (10.2) is very rarely true in the financial markets for securities. Securities with different maturity dates are generally discounted at different yields to maturity. In other words, r in equation (10.2) is rarely observed to be independent of the date t at which the cash flow occurs. In a more general analysis, the functional relationship between r and t is taken into account. To do so, and to preserve the properties of d_t as a discount factor ($0 \le d_t \le 1$ and $d_t < d_{t-1}$), the function can be modified and written as

$$d_t = \frac{1}{[1+h(0,t)]^t},$$

(10.3)

where $h(0,t)$ is now interpreted as the rate of return appropriate for discounting the cash flow F_t and where $h(0,t)$ may take on different values for different t's. The rate $h(0,t)$ is sometimes called the "holding" period yield —and this explains why the notation is h. It is a holding period yield in the sense that

$$[1+h(0,t)]^t V = F_t.$$

(10.4)

If the single cash flow is purchased now at time 0 at the value V and if the asset is *held* for t periods, it accumulates in value to F_t for the holder. The annual rate of return over that period is $h(0,t)$. The zero in the expression $h(0,t)$ indicates the date at which the investment V is made.

The set of values

$$h(0,1), h(0,2), h(0,3), h(0,4), \ldots, h(0,t), \ldots$$

(10.5)

is the *term structure of interest rates*. If $h(0,t) > h(0,t-1)$ for all t, it is an *upward sloping* term structure. If $h(0,t) < h(0,t-1)$, for all t, it is a *downward sloping* term structure. If $h(0,t) = h(0,t-1)$ for all t, the term structure is *flat*. In the latter case we may represent $h(0,t)$ by r because the interest rate in the discount function, equation (10.3), is independent of t. The date t at which the cash flow F_t occurs is also called the *term* of the cash flow. A downward sloping term structure is sometimes called an *inverted* term structure. Term structures that increase with t to a certain point and then decline as t increases are called *humped* term structures.

It is important to note that $h(0,t)$ is a rate of interest applicable to an interval of length t in calendar time. In equation (10.4) it is an annual rate of growth for t years if we use t to measure calendar time in years. On the other hand, it could also be a 6-month rate of growth for t 6-month periods if t is measured as the number of 6-month periods. Whether it is an annual rate for t years, a 6-month rate for t 6-month periods, or otherwise, it can generally be understood from the context of its use. In the financial literature there is sometimes some confusion about how these rates are to be measured and interpreted. Throughout the remainder of this book, it should be understood that $h(0, t)$ is a rate of interest or growth per period for t periods where the length of each period in calendar time is explicitly assumed.

FORWARD RATES

Suppose an investor allocates $1.00 to a one-period security. That one-period security must then promise a cash flow of $[1 + h(0, 1)] = F_1$ dollars one period later. This must be the cash flow in one period because the present value of it is $1.00 = F_1 / [1 + h(0, 1)]$, the amount initially assumed to have been invested. Suppose the cash flow F_1, upon receipt, is immediately reinvested in another one-period security. At the end of the next period, the cash flow will be F_2 dollars. Then F_1 must be the present value of F_2. This being so, it follows that we can connect F_1 and F_2 by the relationship

$$F_1 = \frac{F_2}{1 + h(1, 2)}, \tag{10.6}$$

where $h(1, 2)$ is a one-period rate of interest applicable to the time interval between the dates $t = 1$ and $t = 2$. The present value of F_1 can then be expressed as

$$1 = \frac{F_1}{1 + h(0, 1)} = \frac{F_2}{[1 + h(0, 1)][1 + h(1, 2)]}. \tag{10.7}$$

There are two one-period rates of interest in equation (10.7), but these rates, $h(0, 1)$ and $h(1, 2)$, are applicable to two different time intervals. The interest rate $h(1, 2)$ is the one-period *forward* rate spanning the time interval between $t = 1$ and $t = 2$. It is called a forward rate because at time 0 this rate is applicable to a period in the future.

Alternatively, the investor might have initially invested $1.00 in a two-period security that promised a single cash flow at the end of the second period. In equilibrium, this cash flow at the end of year 2 must be exactly the same as the cash flow received by the two successive investments in one-period securities. In equilibrium, under certainty, the return, F_2, must be exactly the same for each of these two strategies. If this were not the case, no one would invest $1.00 in one of the two strategies. Hence, as long as one- *and* two-period securities of this type are to exist in the financial markets, the interest rates must be such that the two strategies are equivalent. The present value of F_2 must, therefore, be $1.00 also. That is,

$$1 = \frac{F_2}{[1+h(0,2)]^2}. \tag{10.8}$$

Equations (10.8) and (10.7) imply that

$$[1+h(0,2)]^2 = [1+h(0,1)][1+h(1,2)]. \tag{10.9}$$

The forward rate $h(1,2)$ can thus be expressed as a function of interest rates observed in the initial term structure. That is,

$$1+h(1,2) = \frac{[1+h(0,2)]^2}{[1+h(0,1)]}. \tag{10.10}$$

The expression on the right-hand side contains only the interest rates $h(0,1)$ and $h(0,2)$. These are rates observed at time $t = 0$. The forward rates can consequently be immediately calculated given an initially observed term structure of rates.

Equation (10.9) is easy to interpret. A \$1.00 investment in a one-period security grows to a value of $1+h(0,1)$ after one period. Reinvestment of this accumulation for another period implies that it grows at rate $h(1,2)$ to the value $[1+h(0,1)][1+h(1,2)]$. On the other hand, a \$1.00 investment in a two-period security grows to $[1+h(0,2)]^2$ in two periods. Equilibration of interest rates must then be such that the accumulations for each of the two strategies are equivalent. In (10.9), we can regard $h(0,2)$ as the realized rate of return per period for two periods. In (10.9), $1+h(0,2)$ is a geometric average of $1+h(0,1)$ and $1+h(1,2)$. This geometric average arises here very much in the same way it arose in Chapter 6 on contingent immunization.

Equation (10.9) is easily extended to far more complex investment strategies. We can define the forward rate $h(\tau,t)$, for example, by the comparable equation

$$[1+h(0,t)]^t = [1+h(0,\tau)]^\tau [1+h(\tau,t)]^{t-\tau}; \quad 0 < \tau < t. \tag{10.11}$$

This equation arises in equilibrium when an investor initially allocates \$1.00 to a security having a single cash flow at the end of τ periods. After τ periods pass the accumulation $[1+h(0,\tau)]^\tau$ is then invested in a $(t-\tau)$-period security paying a single cash flow at the end of period t. Of course, the same return occurs by investing initially in a t-period security. It is in this manner that the forward rates, $h(\tau,t)$, can be defined for all τ that are less than t.

Under certainty, the forward rates become the actual future rates. Given any initial term structure from which the forward rates can be calculated, it is apparent that the future is embedded in the present. Surprising as that may be, the course of future rates is already implicitly contained in a set of currently observed rates.

Assuming all interest rates are positive, it follows that $d_t < d_{t-1}$. Given the definition of d_t in equation (10.3), it follows that

$$\frac{d_{t-1}}{d_t} = \frac{[1+h(0,t)]^t}{[1+h(0,t-1)]^{t-1}} = [1+h(t-1,t)] > 1.$$

The attributes of d_t as a discount factor are preserved by allowing the term structure to be nonflat.

Moreover, in this more general framework, it also follows that all securities are perfect substitutes under certainty. If one invests \$1.00 in a t-period security, it will accumulate to $[1+h(0,t)]^t$ dollars at the end of the tth period. After one period has passed we can discount this flow at the $t-1$ rate ruling then to determine its value. Clearly this value is

$$\frac{[1+h(0,t)]^t}{[1+h(1,t)]^{t-1}} = 1+h(0,1),$$

which is independent of t. After two periods pass, the value is $[1+h(0,2)]^2$, and so forth. All securities with the same initial value (say, \$1.00) will consequently have the same accumulated values at all future dates.

Of course, we live in a world of uncertainty. Future rates may not be equal to current forward rates that span future time intervals. In fact, considerable evidence exists to suggest that forward rates are not very good predictors of future rates. It follows, therefore, as in previous chapters, that securities may not be perfect substitutes for each other under uncertainty. Nonetheless, forward rates, as derived from the equilibrium considerations under certainty, play a major role under uncertainty because the departures of future term structures from those predicted by forward rates serve as stochastic or random components in the movement of term structures over time and they can be analyzed conveniently as such.

EXAMPLES OF FORWARD RATE COMPUTATIONS

A few examples will illustrate how forward rates behave as a function of an initially observed term structure. Table 10-1 shows all of the forward rates as calculated for a given increasing and a given decreasing term structure. Column 1 gives the term to maturity. Column 2 gives the initial term structure. Column 3 gives the term structure that will exist after one period if future rates are equal to the forward rates. The first term in this column is the one-period rate one period from the present; the second term is the two-period rate one period from the present; and so on. Column 4 gives the forward rates commencing two periods from the present, and so forth. In general the forward rates are calculated using the formula

Table 10-1. Calculation of Forward Rates for an Initially Increasing and Decreasing Term Structure of Interest Rates

a. Increasing Term Structure

t	$h(0,t)$	$h(1,t+1)$	$h(2,t+2)$	$h(3,t+3)$	$h(4,t+4)$	$h(5,t+5)$	$h(6,t+6)$	$h(7,t+7)$	$h(8,t+8)$	$h(9,t+9)$
1	.0800	.0900	.0986	.1056	.1111	.1151	.1176	.1186	.1181	.1160
2	.0850	.0943	.1021	.1083	.1131	.1164	.1181	.1183	.1171	
3	.0895	.0980	.1051	.1106	.1146	.1171	.1181	.1176		
4	.0935	.1013	.1076	.1124	.1156	.1174	.1176			
5	.0970	.1040	.1096	.1136	.1161	.1171				
6	.1000	.1063	.1111	.1143	.1161					
7	.1025	.1080	.1121	.1146						
8	.1045	.1093	.1126							
9	.1060	.1100								
10	.1070									

b. Decreasing Term Structure

t	$h(0,t)$	$h(1,t+1)$	$h(2,t+2)$	$h(3,t+3)$	$h(4,t+4)$	$h(5,t+5)$	$h(6,t+6)$	$h(7,t+7)$	$h(8,t+8)$	$h(9,t+9)$
1	.1000	.0900	.0816	.0746	.0691	.0651	.0626	.0616	.0755	.0606
2	.0950	.0858	.0781	.0718	.0671	.0639	.0621	.0685	.0680	
3	.0905	.0820	.0751	.0696	.0656	.0631	.0666	.0659		
4	.0865	.0788	.0726	.0679	.0646	.0662	.0651			
5	.0830	.0760	.0706	.0666	.0668	.0651				
6	.0800	.0738	.0691	.0681	.0657					
7	.0775	.0720	.0700	.0670						
8	.0755	.0725	.0688							
9	.0740	.0711								
10	.0730									

$$[1+h(\tau, t+\tau)]^t = \frac{[1+h(0, t+\tau)]^{t+\tau}}{(1+h(0,\tau))^\tau},$$

where τ is the period at which the forward rate commences. This formula is a variation of equation (10.11).

For the increasing term structure, we note that interest rates over the same term to maturity tend generally but not always to increase as time passes. Consider the one-period rates. These are displayed in the first row. Initially the one-period rate is 8%. In one period it rises to 9%; in the next period it rises to 9.86%; and so forth. The one-period rate rises as time passes until the eighth period. Thereafter, the one-period rate decreases. The one-period rates increase at a decreasing rate until the eighth period. The two-period rate increases at a decreasing rate until the seventh period. The three-period rate increases at a decreasing rate until the sixth period. The initial term structure is increasing at a decreasing rate. This causes the term structures in subsequent periods to rise generally and to become flatter. There are exceptions, however. The term structure at the start of period 6 is humped and the term structure is decreasing thereafter. If the initial term structure increases over several periods, then the short-term rates will most certainly increase in subsequent periods.

For an initially decreasing term structure, the forward rates behave in just the opposite manner. The one-period rates decrease systematically until the eighth period. The term structures after the first period tend to be at lower levels. Eventually, however, a kind of "inverted" hump appears as in the fourth period, and the term structures begin to have irregular patterns. Generally, however, the short-term rates will tend to decrease in the first few periods following time $t = 0$.

Flat term structures have forward rates identically equal to the initial rate. If $h(0, t) = .09$ for all t, then $h(\tau, t) = .09$ for all $\tau < t$.

Under certainty in equilibrium, the course of future rates is completely revealed in the initial term structure, insofar as they can be calculated. The future pattern of rates may follow irregular patterns at remote periods ahead, but in the immediate future, rates will tend to increase (decrease) if the initial term structure is increasing (decreasing).

YIELD CURVES

Even though the discount factor in equation (10.3) is well defined for non-flat term structures, the yield to maturity still plays a major role in portfolio analysis. The price of an M year, $c\%$ coupon bond, using the discount factors in (10.3) can be expressed as

$$p = 100\left(\frac{c}{2}\right)\sum_{t=1}^{2M}[1+h(0,t)]^{-t}+100[1+h(0,2M)]^{-2M}, \quad (10.12)$$

where $h(0,t)$ is now a 6-month rate, $100(c/2)$ is the semiannual coupon payment in dollars, and 100 is the face value of the bond. There is nothing preventing us from writing the same expression for the price as

$$p = 100\left(\frac{c}{2}\right)\sum_{t=1}^{2M}\left(1+\frac{r}{2}\right)^{-t}+100\left(1+\frac{r}{2}\right)^{-2M}, \quad (10.13)$$

where $r/2$ is the 6-month yield to maturity (and where r is the annual yield to maturity). Given c, M, and the term structure, one can easily calculate p in equation (10.12). Given c, M, and this price p, one can then calculate r in equation (10.13). In this way we can see that equation (10.12) implies some yield to maturity as implicitly expressed in equation (10.13).

Often in reported statistics only the yields to maturity on available bonds are reported. Since zero coupon bonds are not widely available in all maturities, direct observations of the rates $h(0,t)$ are not available. Salomon Brothers regularly publishes an index of the annual yields to maturity on *par* U.S. Treasury bonds.[1] Given a complete range of yields across maturities for these bonds one can determine the underlying term structure of interest rates. Let $r'_1, r'_2, ..., r'_t, ...$ be the 6-month yields to maturity on par U.S. Treasury securities observed at time $t=0$. The corresponding set of prices can then be expressed as

$$100 = p_1 = 100r'_1(1+r'_1)^{-1}+100(1+r'_1)^{-1}$$
$$100 = p_2 = 100r'_2[(1+r'_2)^{-1}+(1+r'_2)^{-2}]+100(1+r'_2)^{-2}$$
$$100 = p_3 = 100r'_3[(1+r'_3)^{-1}+(1+r'_3)^{-2}+(1+r'_3)^{-3}]+100(1+r'_3)^{-3} \quad (10.14)$$
$$\vdots$$
$$100 = p_{2M} = 100r'_{2M}\sum_1^{2M}(1+r'_{2M})^{-t}+100(1+r'_{2M})^{-2M}.$$

This series of equations merely repeats equation (10.13) for various maturities. Since all of the bonds are par bonds, they each have the same price of 100, and the 6-month coupon rate $c/2$ is always equal to the 6-month yield to maturity, r'_t. The expression of r'_t as a function of term to maturity is called a *par yield curve*.

The 6-month par bond with price $p_1 = 100$ has a yield to maturity of r'_1. Since this is a zero coupon bond, it follows that $h(0,1) = r'_1$. The one-year bond with a price $p_2 = 100$ is *not* a zero coupon bond. Given r'_2, however, we can calculate $h(0,2)$. We know that the price p_2 can be expressed as

$$100 = p_2$$
$$= 100r'_2[(1+h(0,1))^{-1}+(1+h(0,2))^{-2}]+100(1+h(0,2))^{-2}. \quad (10.15)$$

Given r_2' and $h(0, 1)$ we can solve for the unknown value of $h(0, 2)$ in equation (10.15). The procedure can also be extended to the third equation, which can be written as

$$100 = p_3 = 100r_3' \sum_1^3 (1 + h(0, t))^{-t} + 100(1 + h(0, 3))^{-3}, \qquad (10.16)$$

where now given r_3', $h(0, 1)$ and $h(0, 2)$, we can calculate the value of $h(0, 3)$. Of course, the procedure can be extended until the entire term structure, $h(0, 1), h(0, 2), h(0, 3), \ldots, h(0, 2M)$, is determined from the par yield curve.

Table 10-2 gives an example of the relationship between the par yield curve and the term structure of interest rates. The most important feature of this table to note is that the term structure lies entirely above the par yield curve except for the first 6-month rate. The difference between the term structure

Table 10-2. The Transformation of a Par Yield Curve into the Term Structure of Interest Rates

Maturity (in 6-Month Periods) t	Annual Yield to Maturity r	Term Structure (in Annual Rates) $2h(0, t)$	Coupon Bias (in Basis Points)
1	.0900	.0900	0
2	.0940	.0941	1
3	.0970	.0972	2
4	.0990	.0993	3
5	.1000	.1004	4
6	.1005	.1009	4
7	.1010	.1014	4
8	.1015	.1020	5
9	.1020	.1025	5
10	.1025	.1031	6
11	.1030	.1037	7
12	.1033	.1041	8
13	.1036	.1044	8
14	.1039	.1048	9
15	.1042	.1052	10
16	.1045	.1056	11
17	.1047	.1058	11
18	.1049	.1061	12
19	.1051	.1064	13
20	.1054	.1068	14

Note: $h(0, t)$ is the 6-month yield to the term to maturity t and $2h(0, t)$ is the annual representation of this yield.

rate and the par yield for any given term to maturity is called the *coupon bias*. For upward sloping yield curves, the bias gets larger with the term to maturity.[2] Livingston and Jain (1982) have shown that the yield curve flattens out and approaches an upper limit even if the term structure is unbounded from above. In such cases the coupon bias could get infinitely large with maturity.

For downward sloping yield curves, the coupon bias is negative. The term structure will lie entirely below the yield curve with the exception of the first 6-month rate. The relationship between the coupon bias and the yield curve is technically elaborated in Appendix 10A.

Yield curves may also exist for other classes of bonds. One might choose all premium bonds selling at $105, for example, and again develop the yield curve expressing the relationship between the yield to maturity and the term to maturity. In general, the coupon bias is larger, the larger the coupon rate. In the limit as the coupon rate approaches zero the yield curve will approach the term structure of interest rates.

Mortgages also have coupon biases. The price of a mortgage is

$$p = F \sum_{1}^{M} (1+r')^{-t}, \tag{10.17}$$

where F is the monthly payment, M is the number of months to maturity, and r' is the monthly yield to maturity. Of course, equation (10.17) can also be written as

$$p = F \sum_{1}^{M} [1+h(0,t)]^{-t}, \tag{10.18}$$

where $h(0,t)$ is the monthly rate of return in the term structure spanning the interval up to t months. Given the term structure, and the monthly payment F, one can use (10.18) to calculate the price p. Then given the price p, one can use (10.17) to compute r'. The coupon bias is then $h(0,M) - r'$, expressed in monthly rates. Kaufman and Morgan (1980) have shown that the coupon bias for mortgages tends to be larger than the coupon biases for bonds. This is because the balloon payment on a bond makes it more closely resemble a zero coupon bond. In addition Morgan (1978) has shown that the coupon bias for mortgages increases with the level of the term structure.

In order to illustrate the coupon bias on a mortgage, note that the two equations (10.17) and (10.18) imply that

$$\sum_{1}^{M} (1+r')^{-t} = \sum_{1}^{M} [1+h(0,t)]^{-t}. \tag{10.19}$$

Given the term structure, $h(0,t)$, $t = 1, 2, \ldots, M$, as expressed on the right-hand side of the equation, the yield to maturity can be calculated as on the

Table 10-3.   Coupon Biases for Mortgages Given a Monthly
Term Structure

Term to Maturity (in 6-Month Periods) t	Annual Term Structure Rates $2h(0,t)$	Annual Yield to Maturity; Mortgage; Monthly Cash Flows r	Coupon Bias; Mortgages; Monthly Cash Flows (in Basis Points)	Coupon Bias; Mortgages; 6-Month Cash Flows (in Basis Points)
1	.0900	.0900	0	0
2	.0941	.0919	22	14
3	.0972	.0940	32	23
4	.0993	.0959	34	28
5	.1004	.0972	32	27
6	.1009	.0982	27	23
7	.1014	.0989	25	22
8	.1020	.0995	25	22
9	.1025	.1000	25	23
10	.1031	.1005	26	24
11	.1037	.1009	28	26
12	.1041	.1013	28	26
13	.1044	.1016	28	26
14	.1048	.1020	28	27
15	.1052	.1023	29	28
16	.1056	.1026	30	29
17	.1058	.1028	30	28
18	.1061	.1031	30	29
19	.1064	.1033	31	30
20	.1068	.1035	33	32

Note: The term structure in the table, taken from Table 8–2, is modified by linear interpolation to acquire a monthly term structure. For each of the first 6 months, the annual rate on mortgages is assumed to be 9.00%, that is, it's a flat curve for the first 6 months. As examples, the 8-month annual rate is derived as $(8-6)(9.41-9.00)/12+9.00$. The 17-month annual rate is $(17-12)(9.72-9.41)/12+9.00$. A similar linear interpolation for other months is used.

left-hand side so as to produce the equality. The coupon bias for a mortgage with M months to maturity is then $h(0,M)-r'$.

Tables 10–3 and 10–4 illustrate the calculation of the bias. In Table 10–3 exactly the same term structure is used as derived from the par bond yield curve in Table 10–2. This term structure gives the annual yields on a 6-month compounding basis. Linear interpolation is used to transform it to one that is applicable to a monthly compounding basis. This interpolation is illustrated in Figure 10–1. In this diagram, the 6-month yields, as in Tables 10–2 and 10–3, are illustrated as the solid points on the curve. Yields for months

Figure 10–1. Linear Interpolation of Six-Month Yields

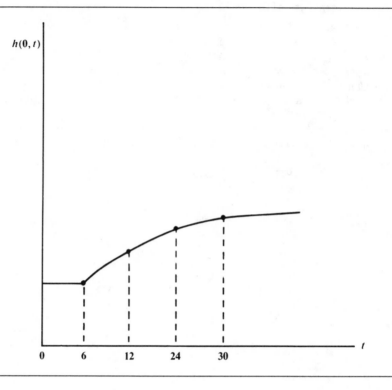

in between are drawn from the straight line connecting them. For example, the first 6-month yield is 9% (on an annual basis), and the 12-month yield is 9.41%. The 7-month yield (on an annual basis) is then

$$9.00 + (1/6)(9.41 - 9) = 9.068\%,$$

and so forth. To transform these annual yields into monthly yields, we simply divide by 12. Thus, the 7-month yield, on a monthly basis is $9.068/12 = 0.756\%$ and the value of the monthly flow occurring in the seventh month is then $F/(1.00756)^7$, and so forth for monthly flows at other dates. The yields on the mortgages as derived from this term structure are illustrated in Table 10–3 for maturities that are 6 months apart. Again, we find that the yield curve lies entirely beneath the term structure. The difference is the coupon bias which is expressed in basis points in the fourth column. A comparison with the coupon biases for bonds in Table 10–2 shows that the coupon biases for mortgages are much larger. However, the coupon bias for mortgages also reflects the monthly compounding whereas the bias for bonds reflects only 6-month compounding. A direct comparison between the coupon biases on the two securities necessitates that the flows on both securities be compounded in the same way. The last column in Table 10-3 shows the coupon bias for mortgages that have flows every 6 months just as the bonds have. The monthly compounding accounts for only a small portion of the coupon bias, and it is very clear that the coupon bias for mortgages is larger than the bias for bonds.

For very steep term structures, the coupon bias on mortgages can be very large. Table 10-4 illustrates this very well. Here the term structure increases linearly from 9% to 12.8% over a 10-year period. The coupon bias is 161 basis points for a 10-year mortgage promising monthly cash flows, and 156.7

Table 10-4. Coupon Biases for Mortgages Given a Monthly Term Structure

Term to Maturity (in 6-Month Periods) t	Annual Term Structure Rates 2h(0, t)	Annual Yield to Maturity; Mortgage; Monthly Cash Flows r	Coupon Bias; Mortgages; Monthly Cash Flows (in Basis Points)	Coupon Bias; Mortgages; 6-Month Cash Flows (in Basis Points)
1	.0900	.0900	0	0
2	.0920	.0909	11	6.9
3	.0940	.0921	19	13.9
4	.0960	.0934	26	21.0
5	.0980	.0947	33	28.3
6	.1000	.0959	40	35.6
7	.1020	.0972	48	43.1
8	.1040	.0984	56	50.7
9	.1060	.0996	64	58.6
10	.1080	.1008	72	66.5
11	.1100	.1020	80	74.7
12	.1120	.1032	88	83.0
13	.1140	.1043	97	91.5
14	.1160	.1055	105	100.2
15	.1180	.1066	114	109.1
16	.1200	.1077	123	118.2
17	.1220	.1088	132	127.5
18	.1240	.1098	142	137.0
19	.1260	.1108	152	146.7
20	.1280	.1119	161	156.7

See notes, Table 10-3.

basis points for mortgages promising 6-month cash flows. Morgan (1978) also shows that the mortgage coupon bias also increases with the *level* of the term structure. That is, if we raise the term structure in column 2 by a fixed number of basis points for every maturity, the coupon bias in column 4 would also increase.

IMPLICATIONS OF COUPON BIAS

In the financial markets, the yield to maturity is the most commonly used indicator of the earning power of a security. The coupon bias distorts this measure of earning power. A positive (negative) coupon bias implies that the earning power is greater (smaller) than the yield to maturity. For example, in Table 10-4 the term structure shows that the rate of return on a 10-year zero coupon bond is 12.8% per annum (compounded monthly) whereas the yield to maturity is 11.19% per annum (compounded monthly). If all of the monthly cash flows from the mortgage are reinvested when they occur at the current forward rates, then after 10 years the mortgage will have grown in value at the rate of 12.80% per annum (compounded monthly). In equilibrium under certainty all securities are perfect substitutes. This means that the continual reinvestment of the mortgage cash flows must provide a value of an investment fund at every future date that is exactly equivalent to the value of a zero coupon bond at the same date if equivalent amounts were initially invested in both securities. The yield to maturity does not indicate the growth rate of an investment fund unless the term structure is flat. For steeply increasing term structures the yield to maturity, as shown in Table 10-4, can be considerably less than the true rate of return if current forward rates become actual future rates. To show this difference in dollars and cents, suppose $1,000,000 is invested in a 12.8% zero coupon bond. In 10 years at monthly compounding this grows to a value of

$$1,000,000(1+.128/12)^{120} = \$3,572,342.$$

On the other hand, if $1,000,000 is invested in an 11.19% zero coupon bond, in 10 years it grows in value to

$$1,000,000(1+.119/12)^{120} = \$3,267,870.$$

This difference in accumulation, $304,472, is strictly due to the coupon bias and shows clearly that the yield to maturity may substantially understate the potential growth in the value of a mortgage investment fund.

MEASURING THE TERM STRUCTURE

Acquiring observations on the term structure rates, $h(0, t)$, is no simple matter. Except for U.S. Treasury bills, maturing at most within a year of their issue, there are very few zero coupon default-free bonds outstanding. Default-prone bonds such as corporate bonds contain a default premium that may be viewed as added to the default-free rate so that, in effect, to determine the yield $h(0, t)$, one must first estimate the premium in any case which also is not a simple matter. On the other hand, yields to maturity on outstanding government securities can be calculated from the closing bid price quotations; these are regularly published in the *New York Times,* the *Wall Street Journal,* and in many other newspapers and financial publications. Figure 10-2 shows a scatter diagram of the yields to maturity on U.S. Treasury securities, as calculated from closing bid quotations on March 31, 1986, and published in the *Treasury Bulletin*. A first glance shows that these yields do not lie on a single smooth curve, although the Treasury has drawn a freehand curve to suggest where the term structure is. There are many reasons why the yields do not lie on a single curve. This is primarily because (1) the coupon bias is present; (2) there is differential taxation – ordinary income tax rates for most taxpaying investors exceed the long-term capital gains tax rate; (3) some bonds are "callable"; and (4) some bonds are "flower" bonds.

Coupon Bias

From the previous two sections, we know that the coupon bias is larger (in absolute value) the larger the coupon rate, ceteris paribus. Thus, in the absence of other effects that would counter the bias, we would expect premium bonds to have lower yields to maturity than discount bonds for upward sloping term structures. The scatter of points in Figure 10-2 suggests that just the opposite is true. Yields on premium bonds appear to be higher than the yields on discount bonds. Other effects have apparently swamped the coupon bias.

Differential Taxation

The federal government taxes interest income on securities at ordinary income tax rates. These rates can vary substantially among taxpaying investors. However, the federal government taxes long-term capital gains from

Figure 10-2. Yields of Treasury Securities, March 31, 1986 (based on closing bid quotations)

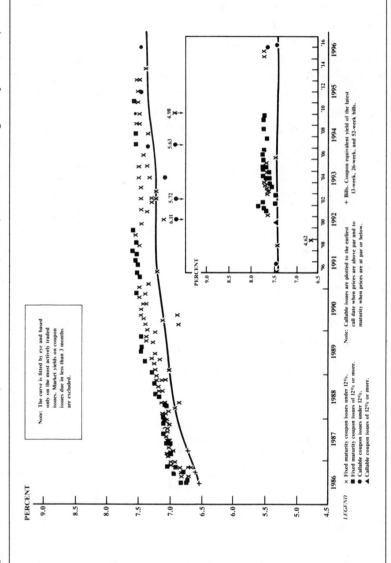

Source: *Treasury Bulletin*, 2nd Quarter, Fiscal 1986 Spring Issue, U.S. Department of Treasury.

the purchase and sale of securities at the long-term capital gains rate. This latter rate, for most taxpaying investors, is lower than the ordinary income tax rate. This difference in tax rates means that discount bonds have a preferential advantage over par bonds because the portion of the discount constituting the return is taxed at a lower rate to most taxpayers. Taxpaying investors are therefore willing to accept a lower pretax yield to buy them. As shown in Chapter 2, and illustrated in Figure 2-1, if the yield to maturity does not change over time, the price of a discount bond increases as time passes until it is equal to its face value at maturity. Regardless of interest rate changes over time, if such bonds are held until maturity, a portion of the earned return is in the form of price appreciation. This appreciation is taxed at the capital gains tax rate, whereas any coupon income received as time passes is taxed at the ordinary income tax rate. Taxpaying investors are interested in their after-tax returns. In an equilibrium, from the perspective of the "marginal" taxpayer, the yields on different securities having the same maturity will tend to equilibrate until the after-tax returns per dollar invested are the same.[3] Appendix 10B shows how this equilibrium procedure works. If the marginal taxpayer's income tax rate exceeds the long-term capital gains tax rate, then the pretax yield to maturity on par bonds must exceed the pretax yield to maturity on discount bonds of the same maturity.

Premium bonds have a similar preferential advantage over par bonds. As also shown in Chapter 2, and illustrated in Figure 2-1, the price of a premium bond decreases as time passes until it is equal to its face value at maturity. Under current tax laws, the investor can deduct (or amortize) this depreciation from the coupon return to calculate the return that is taxable at ordinary rates. Moreover, the amount of the deduction permitted by law exceeds the depreciation of the asset in the market when interest rates do not change. Consider a premium bond that matures in m 6-month periods. The coupon return over the first 6 months is $100(c/2)$ and the permitted deduction is $(P-100)/m$, where P is the price. If t is the ordinary tax rate, then the tax paid is $t[100(c/2) - (P-100)/m]$. The after-tax cash return is then $100(1-t)(c/2) + t(P-100)/m$. The latter amount, $t(P-100)/m$, is a tax saving due to the amortization permitted by law. This tax saving is so great that there is an advantage to buying premium bonds rather than par bonds, and taxpaying investors are, therefore, willing to accept a lower pretax yield to maturity. However, this advantage is tempered by two other considerations. First, the cash flows per period per dollar initially invested are higher on premium bonds than on discount or par bonds. The reinvestment of these larger cash flows may thus involve a higher reinvestment risk. Hence, the acceptable pretax yield on premium bonds may not be very much lower (if

Figure 10-3.   Pre-Tax Yields for Equivalent After-Tax Yields

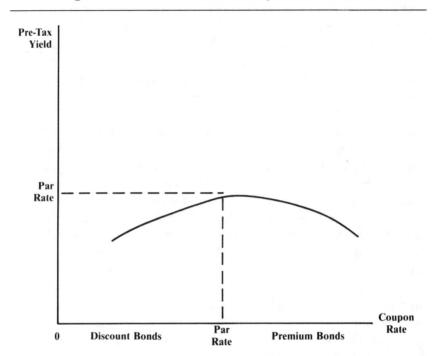

at all) than the par bond pretax yield. Second, the more that must be reinvested at different future dates, the higher the anticipated transactions cost of doing so. This may also imply that the acceptable pretax yield on premium bonds may not be lower on premium bonds than on par bonds.

Figure 10-3 illustrates the pretax yield as a function of the coupon rates on bonds having the same maturity. In this diagram, the yields are determined so that the bonds will have equal after-tax rates of return. The mathematics of this curve is developed in Appendix 10B. The portion of the curve ascribed to premium bonds, of course, may be upward sloping in view of the two considerations on risk and transactions cost noted above.

These variations in yields on bonds of the same maturity can help to explain the yield differentials in the scatter diagram of Figure 10-2.

Callability

Some U.S. Treasury bonds are callable at par after some particular future date known as the *call date*. These call dates are usually 5 to 10 years prior to the bond's maturity. If a bond is callable, this means that the Treasury can "call" or redeem the bond at face value on or after the call date. If, for example, a callable bond is selling at the premium price of $110 in the market and it is past or on the call date, the Treasury can call the bond and pay only $100 for it. The Treasury could then reissue a par bond that would have a lower coupon rate and thus save the Treasury some interest costs. However, it would be foolish for an investor to pay $110 for such a bond because there would be an immediate danger of a capital loss of $10. Consequently, bonds in danger of being called soon will not sell in excess of par. If noncallable bonds of the same maturity are selling at a premium, it follows that the yields on the imminently callable bonds must be higher in order that they sell at par or less. As such bonds approach the call date, their yields must tend, therefore, to be such that they sell at either par or at a discount. If the bonds are in no danger of being called because the call date is still far into the future, these bonds can sell at a premium. However, the Treasury routinely regards these bonds as having a maturity equal to the call date, because if interest rates remain unchanged, these bonds most likely would be called on the call date at 100 just as though the call date were the maturity date. The call feature on a bond is an option that has value to the U.S. Treasury because it can potentially save the Treasury some interest costs if interest rates should fall. The Treasury could then refinance some of the debt at a lower interest cost. However, since the call option creates uncertainty with regard to the implied future income stream, investors must be compensated for this additional risk if they are to hold these bonds. Thus, the yields on callables, ceteris paribus, will tend to exceed the yields on bonds having identical coupon rates and maturities. In the scatter diagram, the yields on callables tend to be less than the yields on other securities of the same maturity. This can be so because the coupon rates on the noncallables are different, and it can also imply that the effects due to the coupon bias and to differential taxation swamp the callability effect.

Flower Bonds

Some very-long-term U.S. Treasury securities, issued 20 years ago or so, have extremely low coupon rates relative to other bonds. This means that these bonds most certainly sell at a discount. Most of these bonds can also be used *at par* to pay off Federal estate taxes if owned by a decedent at time of death. For example, suppose an estate owes taxes of $1,000,000 to the federal government and that the decedent owned some of these low coupon bonds at time of death. Suppose these bonds were selling in the market at $85 and that the market value of these securities held was $850,000. These bonds could then be used to defray the entire estate tax obligations to the federal government thus saving the estate $150,000 were the tax money to be raised elsewhere. Since these bonds have an additional value to investors who anticipate imminent death, these investors are willing to pay more for them than for other like bonds even though they earn a smaller yield. Thus, the prices of these bonds are bid up by this special group of taxpaying investors and the bonds tend to sell at very low yields. In the diagram, this explains the low yields of 6.11, 6.72, 5.63, 4.98, and 4.62 percent on these few deep discount bonds.

The above aspects of U.S. Treasury securities make it difficult to derive explicitly the implied term structure from a scatter diagram of yields. The attempts to do so range from extremely crude methods to very sophisticated methods. Often the methods used depend on the use to which the derived data is to be put. If fine detail is required so as to avoid measurement errors in the tests of intricate hypotheses, sophisticated techniques ought best to be used. Otherwise very crude measurements may be sufficient.

Consider some of the less sophisticated methods. Bradley and Crane (1973) simply fit the equation

$$\ln(1+R_m) = a + b_1 M + b_2 \ln(M) \tag{10.20}$$

by ordinary least squares regression procedures. Here, $\ln(1+R_m)$ is the natural logarithm of one plus the yield to maturity M, $\ln(M)$ is the natural logarithm of maturity, and a, b_1, and b_2 are parameters. Of course, this curve does not account for the coupon bias, differential taxation, callability, or flower bonds. It gives only a rough relationship between yield and maturity. Instead of applying this equation to the scatter in Figure 10-2, it is always best to apply it to special sets of data in which some of the special effects noted above have already been eliminated. For example, if one applied it to the Salomon Brothers par yield data, we know already that coupon bias is restricted to that which can be ascribed to par bonds. Salomon Brothers in constructing their data for various maturities has attempted to utilize its expertise to determine the yields at which noncallable par bonds would sell at various maturities. The Bradley–Crane equation is a method to smooth that relationship and to extend it to all maturities. Although Bradley and Crane did not do it, one can then use this estimated par yield curve to derive the term structure as was done in the example earlier in this chapter. Echols and Elliot (1976) use the following equation:

$$\ln(1+R_i) = a + b_1(1/M_i) + b_2(M_i) + b_3 C_i, \tag{10.21}$$

where R_i is the yield to maturity, M_i is maturity, and C_i is the coupon rate on the ith bond. This equation can be applied to all bonds, not just par bonds.

The added effect of the coupon rate allows for the yield, ceteris paribus, to reflect just variation in the coupon rate. This is intended to capture the effects of coupon bias and differential taxation. Having estimated this regression to obtain values for a, b_1, b_2, and b_3, one can let C_i be zero and then the regression gives us the term structure. The relationship does not include effects due to callability, differential taxation, or estate taxes. Hence, this equation is best applied to data that has already had these effects removed by one method or another. Cohen, Kramer, and Waugh (1966) fit a variety of equations to scatter diagrams like those in Figure 10–2. They were the first to suggest the use of regression techniques in deriving a yield curve. Their equations consisted of specifying the yield to maturity or the logarithm of it as a function of maturity, maturity squared, and the square of the logarithm of maturity. Of the various regressions considered, the equation

$$R_m = a + bM + c(\log M)^2 \qquad (10.22)$$

generally fits the data best. They made no effort to extract special effects.

More sophisticated approaches to the measurement of the term structure include principally the work of McCulloch (1971, 1975), Carleton and Cooper (1976), and Houglet (1980).

McCulloch. McCulloch's general methodology is spelled out in his 1971 paper, and extended to include the effects of differential taxation in his 1975 paper. A full technical development of McCulloch's methodology is not included here, but his original papers are very easily understood by students who have a good background in econometrics. McCulloch estimates the discount function, $\delta(t) = 1/[1 + h(0, t)]$, under the assumption of continuous compounding, and then he transforms the estimated function into a term structure. The general form of the discount function is specified in advance. In the 1971 paper, he specifies that $\delta(t)$ should be a continuous piecewise quadratic relationship in t. Thus, in the interval specified a priori, $t_0 \leq t \leq t_1$, he would specify that $\delta(t) = a_{01} + b_{01}t + c_{01}t^2$. The estimation process consists of estimating the parameters for the function within this interval. For the adjoining interval, $t_1 \leq t \leq t_2$, in which the parameters are a_{12}, b_{12}, and c_{12}, he requires the parameters to be such that $\delta(t)$ has the same value at t_1. The intervals are smallest in length on the maturity axis where there are the largest number of observations. This gives the best fit (or "resolution") to maturity intervals within which we have the greatest information about the term structure. This piecewise quadratic curve representing the discount function is called a quadratic *spline*. Having specified the discount function in this manner, it can then be substituted into the price equation for any bond.

Then the price of any bond will depend upon the parameters in the discount function. Each of these parameters will be multiplied by an appropriate cash flow and the time (or the square of the time) at which it occurs. If no cash flow occurs at the time specified then the appropriate parameters will be multiplied by zero. By specifying this relationship for all bonds (possibly excluding callable or flower bonds), one can run a regression that allows estimation of the parameters of the discount function.

Example.[4]   Consider a discount function defined simply as

$$\delta(t) = \begin{cases} a_{01} + b_{01}t + c_{01}t^2; & 0 \le t \le 2, \\ a_{11} + b_{11}t + c_{11}t^2; & 2 \le t \le \infty. \end{cases} \quad (10.23)$$

When $t = 0$, let $\delta(0) = 1$ indicating a zero rate of interest at $t = 0$. Therefore, assume $a_{01} = a_{11} = 1$. We also want $\delta(t)$ to be continuous at $t = 2$. Therefore, $2b_{01} + 4c_{01} = 2b_{11} + 4c_{11}$, or $c_{11} = b_{01}/2 - b_{11}/2 + c_{01}$. This means the discount function can be written, after substituting for c_{11}, as

$$\delta(t) = \begin{cases} 1 + b_{01}t + c_{01}t^2; & 0 \le t \le 2, \\ 1 + b_{11}(t - t^2/2) + (b_{01}/2 + c_{01})t^2, & 2 \le t \le \infty. \end{cases} \quad (10.24)$$

There are three parameters in the function to estimate, b_{01}, c_{01}, and b_{11}. Assume $\delta(t)$ gives the discount function for t measured in 6-month periods. The price of a 6-month zero coupon bond is then

$$p_1 = 100\delta(1) = 100 + b_{01}100 + c_{01}100. \quad (10.25)$$

The price of a 1-year bond with coupon rate c_2 is

$$\begin{aligned} p_2 &= 100(c_2/2)\delta(1) + 100\delta(2) \\ &= 100(c_2/2)(1 + b_{01} + c_{01}) + 100(1 + 2b_{01} + 4c_{01}) \\ &= 100(c_2/2) + b_{01}100(c_2/2 + 2) + c_{01}100(c_2/2 + 4). \quad (10.26) \end{aligned}$$

The price of an *m*-period bond where $m > 2$ is

$$p_m = 100\left(\frac{c_m}{2}\right) \sum_1^m \delta(t) + 100\delta(m). \quad (10.27)$$

Now,

$$\sum_1^m \delta(t) = m + b_{01}\left(1 + \sum_2^m \frac{t^2}{2}\right) + b_{11} \sum_2^m \left(t - \frac{t^2}{2}\right) + c_{01}\left(1 + \sum_2^m t^2\right), \quad (10.28)$$

and

$$\delta(m) = 1 + b_{11}\left(m - \frac{m^2}{2}\right) + \left(\frac{b_{01}}{2} + c_{01}\right)m^2. \quad (10.29)$$

Substituting (10.28) and (10.29) into (10.27) gives

$$p_m = 100\left(\frac{c_m}{2}\right)m + b_{01}\left(1 + \sum_2^m \frac{t^2}{2}\right) + b_{11}\sum_2^m \left(t - \frac{t^2}{2}\right) + c_{01}\left(1 + \sum_2^m t^2\right)$$

$$+ 100\left[1 + b_{11}\left(m - \frac{m^2}{2}\right) + \left(\frac{b_{01}}{2} + c_{01}\right)m^2\right]. \tag{10.30}$$

Collecting terms on the parameters, this reduces to

$$p_m = \frac{mc_m 100}{2} + b_{01}\left\{\frac{100c_m}{2}\left(1 + \sum_2^m \frac{t^2}{2}\right) + 100\frac{m^2}{2}\right\}$$

$$+ b_{11}\left\{\frac{100c_m}{2}\sum_2^m \left(t - \frac{t^2}{2}\right) + 100\left(m - \frac{m^2}{2}\right)\right\}$$

$$+ c_{01}\left\{\frac{100c_m}{2}\left(1 + \sum_2^m t^2\right) + 100m^2\right\}. \tag{10.31}$$

Finally, one can redefine the variables in the following way. For equation (10.25), we have

$$y_1 = b_{01}X_{11} + c_{01}X_{21} + b_{11}X_{31}, \tag{10.25'}$$

where $y_1 = p_1 - 100$, $X_{11} = 100$, $X_{21} = 100$, and $X_{31} = 0$. For equation (10.26) let

$$y_2 = b_{01}X_{12} + c_{01}X_{22} + b_{11}X_{32}, \tag{10.26'}$$

where

$y_2 = p_2 - 100(c_2/2)$, $X_{12} = 100(c_2/2 + 2)$, $X_{22} = (c_2/2 + 4)$, and $X_{32} = 0$.

For equation (10.31), let

$$y_m = b_{01}X_{1m} + c_{01}X_{2m} + b_{11}X_{3m}, \tag{10.31'}$$

where

$$y_m = p_m - \frac{m100c_m}{2}$$

$$X_{1m} = 100\left(\frac{c_m}{2}\right)\left(1 + \sum_2^m \frac{t^2}{2}\right) + 100\frac{m^2}{2},$$

$$X_{2m} = 100\left(\frac{c_m}{2}\right)\left(1 + \sum_2^m \frac{t^2}{2}\right) + 100m^2, \quad \text{and}$$

$$X_{3m} = 100\left(\frac{c_m}{2}\right)\sum_2^m \left(t - \frac{t^2}{2}\right) + 100\left(m - \frac{m^2}{2}\right).$$

Together the equations (10.25'), (10.26') and (10.31') can be expressed as

$$y_j = b_{01} X_{1j} + c_{01} X_{2j} + b_{11} X_{3j}, \quad j = 1, 2, \ldots. \tag{10.32}$$

Given the price of a security, its coupon rate, and its maturity, the variables $y_j, X_{1j}, X_{2j}, X_{3j}$ are particular numbers. For a set of many different bonds (no fewer than three) we can run an ordinary least squares regression on (10.32) to estimate b_{01}, c_{01}, and b_{11}. This is the essence of McCulloch's idea.

In effect the idea is to regress the bond's price on modified cash flow variables so as to estimate the discount function. In fact, however, the actual transactions price of the bond may not be known. Regularly published data only gives the bid and asked price quotations as provided by a government bond dealer. Actual prices at which trades are consummated may be in between these quoted prices. McCulloch uses the mean of the bid and asked prices; that is, $p_j = (p_j^a + p_j^b)/2$, where p_j^a and p_j^b are respectively the asked and bid prices on the jth security. This means that the actual price may differ from this by as much as one half of the difference, $p_j^a - p_j^b$. Noting that the difference between the asked and bid prices tends to increase with maturity, McCulloch takes this into account by using a weighted least squares technique. McCulloch's regressions have very high R^2's and the estimated variances of the prices tend to be quite small. In his 1975 paper, the bond prices are specified as functions of the tax rates. The discount function is then estimated as a cubic spline. This is an after-tax discount function that can be transformed into an after-tax term structure useful for discounting after-tax cash flows. The marginal income tax rate is that rate which minimizes the error in the price estimates and hence provides the best fit. The optimal marginal tax rates for data of the 1960s varied between .22 and .30. The discount function for most years fit the data extremely well. Callable bond yields were not always estimated, and, of course, the yields on flower bonds were not well predicted at all but one could estimate the portion of the bond's price that constituted the value of the bond for estate purposes.

Carleton–Cooper. Carleton and Cooper (1976) noted that U.S. Treasury bonds pay interest on only four annual dates: February 15, May 15, August 15, and November 15. Also Federal Home Loan Bank securities bearing a U.S. government guarantee pay interest only on the days 25 to 27 of each month. They proposed to estimate the discount function directly from the cash flows using an equation for the ith bond,

$$p_i = b_1 X_{1i} + b_2 X_{2i} + \cdots + b_n X_{ni}, \tag{10.33}$$

where b_t is the discount factor, $(1 + h(0, t))^{-t}$, for discounting the cash flow X_{ti} occurring at time t on the ith bond. For some bonds, of course, $X_{ti} = 0$

because t is a date beyond the bond's maturity. With a large population of bonds, one could then run ordinary regressions to estimate the discount factors $b_1, b_2, ..., b_n$. Transformation of the discount factors into term structure rates is then a simple matter. Use of this method requires no a priori statement as to the functional form of the discount function as required in McCulloch's approach, and the fixed dates during the year at which interest payments are made keeps down the number of independent variables, X_{ti}, that are required in the equation in order to estimate the discount function fairly accurately at least for the short-term end of the term structure. However, this method can only estimate points on the term structure, as can McCulloch's procedure. Thus, unless one interpolates or fits another curve through the term structure points, one cannot use this estimated term structure to evaluate flows that may occur on other instruments that have cash flows occurring in between the interest paying dates specified in the model. A derivation of the forward rates from the estimated points on the term structure shows that these rates fluctuate wildly as a function of maturity. Very small changes in the term structure rates that occur as maturity changes can have dramatic effects on the derived forward rates. Carleton and Cooper suggest caution in the use of this estimated term structure in models where forward rates must play a prominent role. Recall that forward rates involve the ratio of discount functions as in equation (10.10), for example. Any small error in estimating the discount function can be dramatically exaggerated in calculating the forward rates because of this.

The estimation procedure does not explicitly take into account the effect of differential taxation. However, if one views the estimated term structure as the appropriate one for evaluating pretax cash flows, the tax effects need not be explicitly included. Alternatively, the cash flows X_{ti} could be modified so that they represent after-tax cash flows and the resulting term structure would then be the after-tax term structure comparable to McCulloch's (1975). Conceivably, one could then transform this after-tax term structure into a pretax term structure and compare it with the pretax structure directly estimated by Carleton and Cooper. There is no reason to believe, however, that this would produce a smooth pretax term structure from which the derived forward rates would also be smooth functions of maturity.

Recently, Chambers, Carleton, and Waldeman (1984) extended the estimation technique so as to estimate the parameters of a discount function. This new technique effectively smooths the discount function and provides for estimates of yields at all points. They assume that the term structure is a polynomial so that in continuously discounting cash flows, the bond prices are exponential polynomials. The technique is the same as McCulloch's except for the fact that McCulloch utilizes polynomial splines and considers cash flows at all future dates. The Chambers–Carleton–Waldeman technique can be extremely computer intensive, especially if heteroskedasticity or other dependencies among residuals are taken into account.

Houglet.   Houglet (1980) combines attributes of McCulloch and the Carleton–Cooper approach, and, in addition, Houglet attempts to account for differential tax effects and coupon bias, callability, and the flower bond effects. These latter effects are estimated by specifying that an adjustment factor in the term structure rate at any date be a linear function of the measure of these effects. Thus, in effect, there exists a term structure for callable bonds, bonds subject to the same tax rates, and for flower bonds. To move from one term structure to another only requires the appropriate specification of the parameters in this linear function. Yet, the information given on each bond in the data set may be relevant to the estimation of the parameters in this linear relationship. To put it formally, the price of bond j can be specified as

$$p_j = \sum_{t=1}^{m} \frac{X_{jt}d(t)}{(1+K_v)^t}, \qquad (10.34)$$

where m is maturity, X_{jt} is the cash flow, and K_v is the relevant adjustment rate in the term structure for bonds of type v if bond j is of that type and $(1+K_v)^t$ is the adjustment coefficient. Thus

$$d(t)(1+K_v)^{-t} = (1+h(0,t))^{-t}(1+K_v)^{-t} = (1+h_v(0,t))^{-t}$$

represents the discount factor appropriate for evaluating bonds of type v. The adjustment rate K_v is expressed as

$$K_v = b_{v0} + b_{v1}Z_1 + \cdots + b_{vq}Z_q \qquad (10.35)$$

where Z_s, $s = 1, 2, \ldots, q$, is a measurable property of the bond, and $(b_{v0}, b_{v1}, \ldots, b_{vq})$ are parameters to be estimated. Some of the parameters b_{vs} may be the same for bonds of different types. For example, callable bonds may have some coefficient that is the same for both discount and premium bonds but there may be other coefficients that differ as between premium and discount bonds, and, moreover, some of the coefficients may indicate an interaction effect between characteristics. Some of the Z variables may be dummy variables. For example, it might be specified that $Z_1 = 1$ if the bond is callable and $Z_1 = 0$ otherwise. One of the objectives of the Houglet approach is to estimate the parameters b_{vs}, $s = 0, 1, 2, \ldots, q$. In order to use the Carleton–Cooper method of direct estimation Houglet fixes the points in time, t, at which the points $d(t)$ are estimated. These points are chosen a priori so as to maximize the "resolution" of the estimate in the region where there are the most observations — the short-term region of the term structure. This is similar to McCulloch's approach. However, since the cash flows X_{jt} may occur at dates in between the prespecified points it is necessary to modify them and move them appropriately. This is accomplished by use of forward rates that are implicit in the discount factors, the $d(t)$'s. If the cash flow X_{jt} occurs between dates t_0 and t_1, for example, a portion of X_{jt} is moved to t_0 and a portion to t_1. If X_{jt}^* is the portion moved to t_0, then $X_{jt}^*(1+h_v(t_0, t))^{-(t-t_0)}$ is the amount added to the flows occurring at t_0; a similar method allocates the remainder of X_{jt} to t_1.[5] In this way the present value of the bond's cash flows remains the same and the price of the bond is unaltered. Finally Houglet introduces some "smoothness" conditions on the forward rates so that they do not jump wildly as in the Carleton–Cooper procedure. This is accomplished by a technical procedure beyond the scope of this volume.

The Houglet method utilizes some of the best attributes of the Carleton-Cooper-McCulloch methodology. The work, although completed in 1980, has not received wide scrutiny by the profession because it is only available in dissertation form and in a brief undated working paper.

Vasicek and Fong (1982) recently introduced a method of estimating the discount function using exponential spline functions. Applications of their procedures have not been published. Langetieg and Smoot (1981), also in an unpublished paper, have reviewed the spline methodology. The work of Houglet and Vasicek and Fong represents frontier efforts to acquire term structure estimates that have minimal measurement errors. It remains to be seen whether these procedures are more accurate than the methods already well known.

APPENDIX 10A
YIELD CURVES AND THE TERM STRUCTURE:
COUPON BIAS

The price of an n-year bond can be expressed as

$$p = 100\left(\frac{c}{2}\right) \sum_{t=1}^{2n} (1+h(0, t))^{-t} + 100(1+h(0, 2n))^{-2n}, \quad (10A.1)$$

where $h(0, t)$ is the 6-month rate for discounting a flow to occur in t 6-month periods and c (>0) is the annual coupon rate. Similarly, the price p can be expressed as

$$p = 100\left(\frac{c}{2}\right)\sum_{t=1}^{2n}(1+r')^{-t} + 100(1+r')^{-2n}, \tag{10A.2}$$

where r' is the 6-month yield to maturity. Subtracting equation (10A.2) from (10A.1) imples that

$$F = \left(\frac{c}{2}\right)\sum_{t=1}^{2n}[(1+h(0,t))^{-t} - (1+r')^{-t}] + [(1+h(0,2n))^{-2n} - (1+r')^{-2n}]$$

$$= 0, \tag{10A.3}$$

which enables us to see how the yield to maturity r' is related to the term structure: $h(0,1), h(0,2), h(0,3), \ldots, h(0,2n)$.

Suppose the term structure is upward sloping so that $h(0,1) < h(0,2) < \cdots < h(0,2n)$. Consider various possible values that r' might take so as to make equation (10A.3) hold. Suppose $r' > h(0,2n)$. It must then follow that $(1+h(0,t))^{-t} > (1+r')^{-t}$ for all t. Hence $F > 0$. Consequently for $F = 0$, it must follow that $r' \leq h(0,2n)$. Next, suppose that $r' < h(0,1)$. It must then follow that $(1+h(0,t))^{-t} < (1+r')^{-t}$. Hence, $F < 0$ in equation (10A.3). It must now follow that $h(0,1) \leq r' \leq h(0,2n)$. Now, suppose that $n > (1/2)$ so that the bond is not a zero coupon bond. If $r' = h(0,2n)$, it follows for $t < 2n$ that $(1+h(0,t))^{-t} > (1+r')^{-t}$; hence, some terms in (10A.3) are positive and none are negative so that $F > 0$. If $r' = h(0,1)$, it follows for $t > 1$ that $(1+h(0,t))^{-t} < (1+r')^{-t}$ so that $F < 0$. From this process of elimination, we can observe that $h(0,1) < r' < h(0,2n)$ because only in this way can positive and negative terms in (10A.3) cancel so that $F = 0$.

Proceeding with the same development for other maturities (other values of n) allows us to show r' as a function of n. This produces the yield curve. A very similar development is appropriate for mortgages.

It immediately follows that $h(0,2n) - r'$, the coupon bias, is positive when the term structure is upward sloping. A development similar to that above for a downward sloping term structure implies that the coupon bias is negative. A very similar development of the coupon bias, among other results, is contained in Buse (1970), Khang (1975), Bierwag (1977), and Hawawini (1982).

APPENDIX 10B
BOND PRICES AS FUNCTIONS OF
AFTER-TAX YIELDS

In the cases considered below, we assume semiannual discounting, and we define the discount function as $\delta^*(t) = (1+h(0,t))^{-t}$ where $h(0,t)$ is the 6-month rate per period for t periods.

Discount Bonds (Nonzero Coupon Rates)

The ordinary coupon income on a discount bond is subject to the ordinary income tax in the year that it is received. The coupon income for a 6-month period is $100(c/2)$, where c is the annual coupon rate. Let the ordinary income tax rate be T. The after-tax coupon cash flow for the 6-month period is then $(1-T)100(c/2)$. At maturity the bond will be worth its face value of 100. If p (<100) was the price paid, the capital gain is $100-p$ at maturity. This gain received at maturity is taxed at the capital gains tax rate of T_g. Hence, at maturity the after-tax redemption value for the bond is $100-T_g(100-p)$.[6] The taxpaying investor views the income stream as

$$(1-T)100\left(\frac{c}{2}\right),\ (1-T)100\left(\frac{c}{2}\right),\ ...,\ (1-T)100\left(\frac{c}{2}\right),$$

$$(1-T)100\left(\frac{c}{2}\right)+100-T_g(100-p).$$

If we think of $\delta(t)$ as the after-tax discount function, it must be such that discounting the terms in the after-tax income stream will be equal to the price paid. Hence,[7]

$$p=(1-T)100\left(\frac{c}{2}\right)\sum_{t=1}^{n}\delta(t)+(100-T_g(100-p))\delta(m). \qquad (10B.1)$$

This expression can be solved for p so as to express the price as a function of the other variables. On the other hand, as is done throughout this book, the price can be expressed in terms of a pretax discount rate as

$$p=100\left(\frac{c}{2}\right)\sum_{t=1}^{m}\delta^*(t)+100\delta^*(m), \qquad (10B.2)$$

where now pretax cash flows are discounted at pretax term structure rates.

Premium Bonds

Not all of the coupon income received on premium bonds is subject to the income tax. Recall that the premium bond price will fall to its face value at maturity. The taxpaying investor has the option of taking this as a capital loss at maturity or amortizing the loss linearly and deducting it from the current coupon income and paying the income tax on the remainder. Taxpayers for whom T exceeds T_g, which is usually the case, find it advantageous to amortize the loss, and this is the way it is treated here. If p is the initial price and T is the ordinary income tax rate, the after-tax cash flow on the bond over a 6-month period is

$$100\left(\frac{c}{2}\right)-T\left[100\left(\frac{c}{2}\right)-\frac{p-100}{m}\right]=(1-T)100\left(\frac{c}{2}\right)+T\left(\frac{p-100}{m}\right), \qquad (10B.3)$$

where m is the maturity in 6-month periods. In this expression for the after-tax cash flow the amount $T(p-100)/m$ can be regarded as the tax saving due to amortization.[8] Letting $\delta(t)$ be the after-tax discount function, the price of the bond is

$$p=\left[(1-T)100\left(\frac{c}{2}\right)+T\left(\frac{p-100}{m}\right)\right]\sum_{t=1}^{m}\delta(t)+100\delta(m). \qquad (10B.4)$$

In terms of the pretax term structure the price is calculated as in (10B.2).

Treasury Bills

Treasury bills are zero coupon bonds. These bonds are typically of very short term (up to 1 year in maturity). However, unlike other discount bonds, the entire appreciation before maturity is taxed at the ordinary income tax rate. Thus, if the face value is 100 and p is the price, the redemption value at maturity after taxes is $100-T(100-p)=100(1-T)+Tp$, and the price is

$$p=[100(1-T)+Tp]\delta(m). \qquad (10B.5)$$

Relative Yields to Maturity

In the text it is argued that the pretax yield to maturity on par bonds exceeds the pretax yield to maturity on discount or premium bonds in order for the bonds to have the same after-tax rate of return. However, it is argued that due to the greater reinvestment risk and higher reinvestment transactions costs, the yields may be higher on premium bonds than suggested by the equality of the after-tax yields.

To show the implication of equal after-tax yields, let r_p and r_d be the respective pretax 6-month yields to maturity for premium and discount bonds. The price of a discount bond can be specified as

$$p_d=\frac{100(c_d/2)}{r_d}[1-(1+r_d)^{-m}]+100(1+r_d)^{-m} \qquad (10B.6)$$

as shown in Chapter 2, where c_d is the annual coupon rate, and m is the maturity in 6-month periods. Multiplying (10B.6) by r_d, the 6-month pretax dollar return is

$$r_d p_d = 100(c_d/2) + 100(r_d - c_d/2)(1 + r_d)^{-m}. \tag{10B.7}$$

The first term is the coupon return in dollars and the second is the appreciation of the bond in 6 months. The income tax is $T(100)(c_d/2)$, where T is the tax rate. The present value of the capital gains tax to be paid in m 6-month periods is $T_g(1 + r_d)^{-m}100(r_d - c_d/2)$. This latter tax may not be paid immediately as a cash flow but it is a tax obligation that reduces the 6-month return on the bond even though it may not reduce current cash flows. Let r_a be the after-tax rate of return. Then

$$r_a p_d = (1-T)100\left(\frac{c_d}{2}\right) + (1+r_d)^{-m}100\left(r_d - \frac{c_d}{2}\right)(1-T_g). \tag{10B.8}$$

Let

$$B = \frac{100c_d/2}{100(c_d/2) + 100(1+r_d)^{-m}(r_d - c_d/2)} = \frac{100c_d/2}{r_d p_d} \tag{10B.9}$$

be the proportion of the return, $r_d p_d$, subject to the income tax. Then $(1-B)$ is the proportion of $r_d p_d$ subject to the capital gains tax. Substituting (10B.9) into (10B.8), we have

$$r_a p_d = (1-T)Bp_d r_d + (1-T_g)(1-B)r_d p_d. \tag{10B.10}$$

Hence,

$$r_a = [(1-T)B + (1-T_g)(1-B)]r_d. \tag{10B.11}$$

Note that when $T = T_g$, then $r_a = (1-T)r_d$. It will be convenient to write (10B.11) as

$$r_a = r_d - [TB + T_g(1-B)]r_d = (1-T^*)r_d, \tag{10B.12}$$

where $T^* = BT + (1-B)T_g$, a weighted average of the two tax rates.

The price of a premium bond is similarly calculated as

$$p_p = \frac{100(c_p/2)}{r_p}[1 - (1+r_p)^{-m}] + 100(1+r_p)^{-m}, \tag{10B.13}$$

and

$$r_p p_p = 100\left(\frac{c_p}{2}\right) + 100(1+r_p)^{-m}\left(r_p - \frac{c_p}{2}\right). \tag{10B.14}$$

The first term is the coupon income and the second is the depreciation in the value of the premium bond over the first 6 months. Note that $r_p - c_p/2 < 0$ for premium bonds. The tax owed the government can then be written as

$$\text{Tax} = T\left(\frac{100c_p}{2} - \frac{p_p - 100}{m}\right). \tag{10B.15}$$

Hence, the after-tax rate of return on premium bonds is

$$r_a = r_p - \text{Tax}/p_p = (1 - T^\Delta)r_p, \qquad (10\text{B}.16)$$

where

$$T^\Delta = \text{Tax}/p_p r_p. \qquad (10\text{B}.17)$$

For par bonds, the only tax paid is that on the coupon return; there is no capital gains tax and no tax savings resulting from amortization. Hence, the after-tax rate of return on par bonds can be written as

$$r_a = (1 - T)\bar{r}, \qquad (10\text{B}.18)$$

where $\bar{r}$ is the pretax yield on par bonds.

The pretax yield on discount bonds is less than that on par bonds if their after-tax yields are the same. That is, using (10B.18) and (10B.12), we have

$$(1 - T^*)r_d = (1 - T)\bar{r}. \qquad (10\text{B}.19)$$

Since $(1 - T^*) > (1 - T)$, it follows that $r_d < \bar{r}$. This occurs because $T^* < T$, which follows because T^* is a weighted average of T and T_g, and $T_g < T$.

Similarly the pretax yield on premium bonds is less than that on par bonds if their after-tax yields are the same, but here the proof of it is more difficult. From (10B.18) and (10B.16), we have

$$(1 - T^\Delta)r_p = (1 - T)\bar{r}. \qquad (10\text{B}.20)$$

Then, if $(1 - T^\Delta) > (1 - T)$ or $T - T^\Delta > 0$, it follows that $r_p < \bar{r}$. To prove that $r_p < \bar{r}$, we need to show that $T - T^\Delta > 0$. Using the definition of T^Δ in (10B.17),

$$T - T^\Delta = T - T\left[\frac{100c_p/2}{r_p p_p} - \frac{p_p - 100}{m r_p p_p}\right] = T - \frac{\text{Tax}}{p_p r_p} \qquad (10\text{B}.21)$$

or

$$\frac{T - T^\Delta}{T} = 1 - \frac{100c_p/2}{r_p p_p} + \frac{p_p - 100}{m r_p p_p}, \qquad (10\text{B}.22)$$

or

$$\frac{T - T^\Delta}{T}(r_p p_p) = r_p p_p - \frac{100c_p}{2} + \frac{p_p - 100}{m}. \qquad (10\text{B}.23)$$

Using (10B.14) to eliminate $r_p p_p$, we have

$$\frac{T - T^\Delta}{T}(r_p p_p) = 100(1 + r_p)^{-m}\left(r_p - \frac{c_p}{2}\right) + \frac{p_p - 100}{m}. \qquad (10\text{B}.24)$$

Next, using (10B.13) to calculate $p_p - 100$, we can write

$$p_p - 100 = 100\left(\frac{c_p/2 - r_p}{r_p}\right)[1 - (1 + r_p)^{-m}]. \qquad (10\text{B}.25)$$

Substitution of (10B.25) into (10B.24) gives us

$$\frac{T-T^{\Delta}}{T}(r_p p_p) = 100(1+r_p)^{-m}\left(r_p - \frac{c_p}{2}\right)$$

$$+ 100\left(\frac{c_p/2 - r_p}{r_p m}\right)[1 - (1+r_p)^{-m}]. \qquad (10B.26)$$

Factoring $c_p/2 - r_p$ from the right-hand side,

$$\frac{T-T^{\Delta}}{T}(r_p p_p) = 100\left(\frac{c_p}{2} - r_p\right)\left[\frac{1}{r_p m} - (1+r_p)^{-m} - \frac{(1+r_p)^{-m}}{r_p m}\right]$$

$$= 100\left(\frac{c_p}{2} - r_p\right)\frac{(1+r_p)^{-m}}{r_p m}[(1+r_p)^m - 1 - r_p m]. \qquad (10B.27)$$

The right-hand side is positive because $c_p/2 > r_p$ for premium bonds, and $(1+r_p)^m > 1 + r_p m$ because $1 + r_p m$ is the first two terms in the binomial expansion of $(1+r_p)^m$ and the other terms are excluded on the right. Therefore, $T - T^{\Delta} > 0$, and hence, $r_p < \bar{r}$.

NOTES

1. See Salomon Brothers, *An Analytical Record of Yields and Yield Spreads,* New York. Salomon Brothers gives only selected yields for some maturities in this class of par bonds, but interpolation is often sufficient and useful for estimating yields on missing maturities.
2. An historical note: A. Buse (1970) and C. Khang (1975) appear to have been the first to point out the existence of the coupon bias for bonds; and Weingartner (1966) appears to have been the first to distinguish between yield curves and the term structure of interest rates.
3. Since taxpaying investors may fall into different income tax brackets, the equilibration in which the after-tax returns per dollar are identical for any maturity can occur for only a single income tax rate. This tax rate corresponds to the "marginal" tax rate. Taxpayers with income tax rates below the marginal rate will prefer par bonds to discount bonds, and those with tax rates above the marginal tax rate will prefer discount bonds. These latter taxpaying investors are called *intramarginal* taxpayers. Marginal taxpayers would be indifferent between par bonds and discount bonds.
4. In this example, semiannual compounding is assumed. McCulloch actually assumed continuous compounding.
5. The division of X_{jt} between t_0 and t_1 is a simultaneous equation procedure, the details of which are not fully presented here. Houglet utilizes continuous compounding.
6. If short-term capital gains taxes apply, then $T_g = T$.
7. F.J. Fabozzi (1983) is an excellent source on the tax laws that relate to financial securities.
8. If the bond is sold at a capital gain prior to maturity, then the basis on the premium bond is reduced by the tax saving, $T(p - 100)/m$.

REFERENCES

Bierwag, G.O. 1977. "Immunization, Duration, and the Term Structure of Interest Rates." *Journal of Financial and Quantitative Analysis* (December): 725–42.

Bradley, Stephen P., and Dwight B. Crane. 1973. "Management of Commercial Bank Government Security Portfolios: An Optimization Approach under Uncertainty." *Journal of Bank Research* (Spring): 18–30.

Buse, A. 1970. "Expectations, Prices, Coupons and Yields." *Journal of Finance* (September): 809–18.

Carleton, Willard T., and Ian A. Cooper. 1976. "Estimation and Uses of the Term Structure of Interest Rates." *Journal of Finance 31*, no. 4 (September): 1067–83.

Chambers, Donald R., Willard T. Carleton, and Donald W. Waldeman. 1984. "A New Approach to Estimation of the Term Structure of Interest Rates." *Journal of Financial and Quantitative Analysis* (September): 233–51.

Cohen, Kalman J., Robert L. Kramer, and W. Howard Waugh. 1966. "Regression Yield Curves for U.S. Government Securities." *Management Science 13*, no. 4 (December): B-168–B-175.

Echols, Michael E., and Jan Walter Elliott. 1976. "A Quantitative Yield Curve Model for Estimating the Term Structure of Interest Rates." *Journal of Financial and Quantitative Analysis* (March): 87–114.

Fabozzi, Frank J. 1983. "Federal Income Tax Treatment of Fixed Income Securities." Chapter 3 in *The Handbook of Fixed Income Securities,* edited by F.J. Fabozzi and Irving M. Pollack (Homewood, Ill.: Dow Jones–Irwin), pp. 33–52.

Hawawini, G. 1982. "The Mathematics of Macaulay's Duration." In *Bond Duration and Immunization,* edited by G. Hawawini (New York: Garland).

Houglet, M. 1980. Estimating the Term Structure of Interest Rates for Non-Homogeneous Bonds. Dissertation, School of Business Administration, University of California, 1980. (A sketchy summary is contained in undated working paper of the same title.)

Kaufman, George G., and George E. Morgan, 1980. "Standardizing Yields on Mortgages and Other Securities." *Journal of American Real Estate and Urban Economics Association* (Summer): 163–79.

Khang, Chulsoon. 1975. "Expectations, Prices, Coupons and Yields: Comment." *Journal of Finance* (September): 1137–40.

Langetieg, Terence C., and Stephen J. Smoot. 1981. "An Appraisal of Alternative Spline Methodologies for Estimating the Term Structure of Interest Rates." Working Paper, University of Southern California, December.

Livingston, M., and S. Jain. 1982. "Flattening of Bond Yield Curves for Long Maturities." *Journal of Finance 37:* 157–167.

McCulloch, J. Huston. 1971. "Measuring the Term Structure of Interest Rates." *Journal of Business 44,* no. 1 (January): 19–31.

———. 1975. "The Tax-Adjusted Yield Curve." *Journal of Finance 30,* no. 3: 811–30.

Morgan, George E. 1978. "Coupon Bias and the Level of Interest Rates: A Note." Working Paper, University of Texas, Austin.

Vasicek, Oldrich A., and H. Gifford Fong. 1982. "Term Structure Modeling Using Exponential Splines." *Journal of Finance* (May).

Weingartner, Martin. 1966. "The Generalized Rate of Return." *Journal of Financial and Quantitative Analysis* (June): 1–29.

11 DURATION AND STOCHASTIC PROCESSES OF THE TERM STRUCTURE

The development and measurement of the term structure in Chapter 10 forms the background for modern applications of duration in the formulation of investment strategies for fixed-income securities. This modern approach began with Fisher and Weil (1971). They developed the first bond immunization strategy that explicitly took nonflat term structures into account. This necessitated a new definition of duration. Later, Bierwag (1977) and Bierwag and Kaufman (1977) showed that many definitions of duration were possible. It was pointed out that appropriate definitions or measures of duration depended on the assumed manner in which the term structure shifted from period to period. The way in which the term structure shifted was called the *stochastic process*. Hence, the duration-based formation of fixed-income portfolios to implement an investment strategy depended upon some explicitly assumed stochastic process.

STOCHASTIC PROCESSES

Suppose an investor initially observes the term structure $h(0, t)$, $t = 1, 2, 3, \ldots$. Instantly after allocating an investment fund, suppose the term structure randomly shifts to $h^*(0, t)$, $t = 1, 2, 3, \ldots$, and that, thereafter, the forward rates in $h^*(0, t)$ become the actual future rates. This simple statement of the shift in the term structure forms the basis for a large class of stochastic processes. Each stochastic process in this class is made explicit when the difference $h^*(0, t) - h(0, t)$, $t = 1, 2, 3, \ldots$, is explicitly specified as a function of one or more random variables. This approach to a random shifting term structure of interest rates is very comparable to the random shifting interest rate that formed the basis for the applications in Chapters 6–9. There it was assumed that the currently observed interest rate was r and that instantly after an allocation of investment funds the interest rate shifted to r^* and remained at that level thereafter. Here, it is assumed the *term structure* shifts from $h(0, t)$ to $h^*(0, t)$, $t = 1, 2, 3, \ldots$, and that the forward rates become the actual future rates thereafter. This is illustrated in Figure 11–1. There $h(0, t)$ is the term structure observed now. Instantly after an investment is made, the structure shifts to $h^*(0, t)$. At the start of the next period the forward term structure, $h^*(1, t)$, becomes the set of actual rates. If there are no further shifts in the term structure, thereafter, the forward term structure to this structure, given as $h^*(2, t)$ then gives the term structure at the start of the second period, and so forth through time. One can diagrammatically trace the evolution of the T-period rate through time. At time zero, this rate

Figure 11–1.   Sequence of T-Period Rates

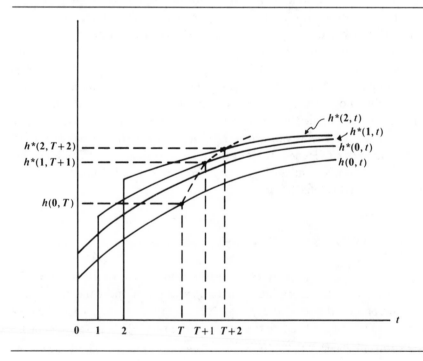

is $h(0, T)$ as indicated. At the start of the next period the term structure is $h^*(1, t)$. The T-period rate on this structure is $h^*(1, T+1)$, again as indicated. At the start of the next period, the term structure is $h^*(2, t)$ and the T-period rate is $h^*(2, T+2)$, and so forth. The T-period rate is always found by moving to the appropriate term structure for the period and finding the rate relevant for discounting a flow to occur T periods later. The evolution of the T-period rate is given by the dashed line in the diagram. It first starts at $h(0, T)$, then instantly moves to $h^*(0, T)$, and thereafter in successive periods it becomes $h^*(1, T+1)$, $h^*(2, T+2)$, $h^*(3, T+3)$, ... If there had been no initial random upward shift, the successive T-period interest rates would have been $h(0, t), h(1, T+1), h(2, T+2), ...$, where the rates starting with the period after time zero would be taken from the forward rates calculated from the initial term structure. Since the initial shift is a random one, it is possible that a great variety of future interest rate scenarios can evolve. In other words, there exists a future scenario of all interest rates that corresponds to each initial random shift. If the initial shift is related to a single random variable, the entire sequence of future interest rates depends on the value of that random variable. In this way we can associate an entire sequence of rates over time with a single random variable, or, in more advanced versions of the process, we can associate an entire sequence of rates over time with a single vector of random variables.

Contrast this evolution of rates, above, with the special case in which the initial term structure is flat. If the flat structure shifts additively by some random amount λ as in Figure 11-2, the rates $h^*(1, T+1)$, $h^*(2, T+2)$, ..., are read off the flat curves because the forward term structure is always the same structure by definition (as shown in Chapter 10). In this case we can represent the initially observed rate by r $(= h(0, t)$ for all $t)$ and the ensuing rates by r^* $(= h^*(0, t)$ for all $t)$. This is exactly what we did in the first nine chapters of this book. The idea here is simply a generalization of that concept to nonflat term structures.

Some of the previous equilibrium concepts are present in this more general approach to a randomly shifting term structure. Under certainty conditions in Chapter 10, it was shown that

$$[1 + h(0, 2)]^2 = [1 + h(0, 1)][1 + h(1, 2)] \tag{11.1}$$

was the way to define the forward rate, $h(1, 2)$. This is an equilibrium notion. It says that \$1.00 invested in a one-period zero coupon security grows to $1 + h(0, 1)$ dollars in one period. If this amount is reinvested in another one-period security at the one-period rate then, $h(1, 2)$, it must grow to $[1 + h(0, 1)][1 + h(1, 2)]$; and this must be equivalent to the return from in-

Figure 11-2.   Sequence of T-Period Rates: Flat Term Structures

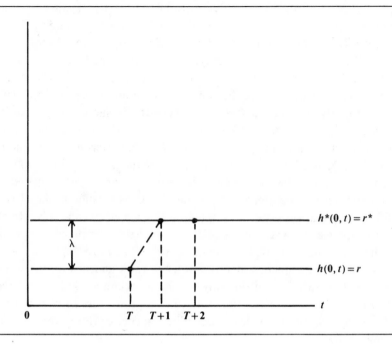

vesting \$1.00 initially in a two-period security, $[1+h(0,2)]^2$, so that the equality in (11.1) results in order that the returns from the two strategies are equivalent. Uncertainty is now introduced only for the first period. Although $h(0,t)$ is currently observed, and forward rates can be derived from it, the term structure shifts randomly to $h^*(0,t)$ instantly after an initial investment. Thereafter, certainty is assumed to prevail so that the forward term strucures become the actual term structures later on, and actual rates can be read from them as described in Figure 11-1.

The initial uncertainty has an effect in later periods that can be described as the difference

$$h^*(\tau,\tau+T)-h(\tau,\tau+T), \quad T=1,2,\dots. \tag{11.2}$$

Here, $h^*(\tau,\tau+T)$ is the T-period rate read from the actual term structure at date τ and $h(\tau,\tau+T)$ is the forward rate in the initially observed structure, $h(0,t)$. This difference can be decomposed in a variety of ways. One can write the actual rate $h^*(\tau,\tau+T)$ as

$$h^*(\tau,\tau+T)=h(\tau,\tau+T)+[h^*(\tau,\tau+T)-h(\tau,\tau+T)]. \tag{11.3}$$

Under the so-called pure expectations hypothesis of the term structure, this is equivalent to saying that the actual rate, $h^*(\tau, \tau+T)$ is equal to the expected rate, $h(\tau, \tau+T)$, plus an unexpected component, $[h^*(\tau, \tau+T) - h(\tau, \tau+T)]$. The uncertainty involved in the shift that produced $h^*(0, t)$ now becomes embedded in an unexpected component of future rates. On the other hand, if we wish to allow for a so-called liquidity premium, we can contend that the expected rate is $h(\tau, \tau+T) - L(\tau, \tau+T)$, where $L(\tau, \tau+T)$ is the liquidity premium. The future rate can then be decomposed as

$$h^*(\tau, \tau+T) = h(\tau, \tau+T) - L(\tau, \tau+T)$$
$$+ [h^*(\tau, \tau+T) - h(\tau, \tau+T) + L(\tau, \tau+T)], \quad (11.4)$$

so that the last term in brackets becomes the unexpected component of the future rate. One can also decompose the difference (11.2) using the inertia hypothesis of expectations. That is, let $h(0, T)$, the current T-period rate, be the expected T-period rate τ periods later. Then, of course, we can write the actual future T-period rate as

$$h^*(\tau, \tau+T) = h(0, T) + [h^*(\tau, \tau+T) - h(0, T)], \quad (11.5)$$

where now $[h^*(\tau, \tau+T) - h(0, T)]$ becomes the unexpected component. The difference in (11.2), of course, can be decomposed in an infinitely large number of ways because expressions like (11.3), (11.4), and (11.5) are essentially identities. These decompositions take on no particular meaning unless we are willing to specify the form of the decomposition by some explicitly asserted hypothesis that has behavioral implications in the markets for securities.

Portfolio strategies that are appropriate or optimal for moving and ever-changing nonflat term structures depend on the specification of the stochastic process of the term structure. This specification explicitly stipulates how $h^*(0, t)$ is formed as a function of one or more random variables. This is sufficient to establish the difference, $h^*(\tau, \tau+T) - h(\tau, \tau+T)$, for all T, as a function of relevant random variables. Some of these explicit specifications and their implications for duration-based models are developed in this chapter.

A major point of this chapter is that there are many different measures of duration. Duration has been defined as a weighted average of the dates at which future cash flows occur: $D = \sum w_t t$. Using a flat term structure, the appropriate weights at time t consisted of the value of the cash flow occurring at time t relative to the total value of the income stream. A different measure of duration results if the weights are differently defined. Each stochastic process of the term structure implies a duration measure. Different stochastic processes may imply different duration measures.

SPECIFYING THE STOCHASTIC PROCESS

In this section four very simple stochastic processes are considered. Each of these processes, considered at one time or another in the literature, is a one-factor process. Each instantaneous random shift of $h(0, t)$ to $h^*(0, t)$, $t = 1, 2, 3, \ldots$, is a function of a single random variable or factor. In each process this random factor plays the same role as the yield to maturity in the first nine chapters. The random factor is an index of an entire term structure just as yield to maturity is an index of the discount rate applicable to particular future periods. A one-factor stochastic process applicable to nonflat term structures is a natural generalization or extension of a random shifting of a flat term structure.

Additive Shifts

A very simple way to specify the difference, $h^*(0, t) - h(0, t)$, is to contend that this difference is random and independent of the term to maturity t. Thus,

$$h^*(0, t) = h(0, t) + \lambda, \quad t = 1, 2, 3, \ldots, \tag{11.6}$$

where λ is a random variable. This is a very natural extension of the procedure of the first nine chapters in which $r^* = r + \lambda$ for flat term structures. Having obtained $h^*(0, t)$ in this way, the future rates simply evolve as the forward rates derived from $h^*(0, t)$. The difference, $h^*(\tau, \tau + T) - h(\tau, \tau + T)$, is then an explicit function of λ. This is an additive process because λ is simply added to the current term structure in order to compute the new *instantaneous* term structure. In the literature this is sometimes called a *parallel* shift, even though adding a constant to $h(0, t)$ does not produce a line, $h^*(0, t)$, that is parallel to $h(0, t)$ if $h(0, t)$ is nonflat. The value of the random variable, λ, is sometimes called the instantaneous *shock*. For reasonable ranges of interest rates (for example, $0 < h(0, t) < .2$ for all t), the difference $h^*(\tau, \tau + T) - h^*(\tau, \tau + T)$, will be almost constant for all T. Consequently, if the stochastic process is additive, the future rate $h^*(\tau, \tau + T)$ is found by essentially adding a random variable to $h(\tau, \tau + T)$, and the added variable will be a function of λ, the instantaneous shock. The additive shock to nonflat term structures was first specified and discussed in Bierwag (1977).

Multiplicative Shifts

Staying within the realm of simplicity, one might alternatively specify the process as

$$h^*(0, t) = \lambda h(0, t), \quad t = 1, 2, 3, \dots, \tag{11.7}$$

where λ is a positive random variable. Thus, if $\lambda = 1$ the term structure does not shift; if $\lambda > 1$, the term structure shifts upward; and, if $\lambda < 1$, the term structure shifts downward. If the term structure is initially upward sloping and $\lambda > 1$, then the term structure shifts upward *and* long-term rates instantaneously shift more than short-term rates. Similarly, if the term structure is upward sloping and $\lambda < 1$, long-term rates decreases instantaneously more than short-term rates. This is illustrated in Figure 11–3a. On the other hand, if the term structure is downward sloping, the short-term rates change instantaneously more than the long-term rates as shown in Figure 11–3b. It should be kept in mind, however, that these are comparisons of instantaneous interest rate changes. It doesn't follow that *over time* the same results prevail. That is, the difference, $h^*(\tau, \tau + T) - h(0, T)$, may not always get larger with T for $\lambda > 1$ when $h(0, t)$ is upward sloping. A simple example will demonstrate this fact. Let $h(0, 1)$, $h(0, 2)$, and $h(0, 3)$ be given as

$$(.083, .084, .0847).$$

Let $\lambda = 1.015$. Then $h^*(0, 1)$, $h^*(0, 2)$, and $h^*(0, 3)$ will be given as

$$(.08425, .08526, .08628).$$

One can calculate the forward rates from this term structure as $h^*(1, 2) = .08628$ and $h^*(1, 3) = .08683$. Then, $h^*(1, 2) - h(0, 1) = .0033$ and $h^*(1, 3) - h(0, 2) = .0028$. The 1-year rate rises by 33 basis points and the 2-year rate rises by 28 basis points after the passage of 1 year. The multiplicative process may be consistent with the observed empirical regularity in which, over time, short rates fluctuate more than long rates. The multiplicative stochastic process was first specified and discussed in Bierwag (1977).

Fisher–Weil Shifts

As noted earlier, Fisher and Weil (1971) were the first to devise immunization strategies based on fluctuations in the term structure rather than on fluctuations in the yield to maturity. They worked within a framework of continuous compounding and assumed an additive stochastic process within that framework. Here, we have not been assuming continuous compounding, but there is an analogous term structure shift. The stochastic process with noncontinuous compounding can be specified as

$$1 + h^*(0, t) = \lambda[1 + h(0, t)], \quad t = 1, 2, 3, \dots, \tag{11.8}$$

where λ is again some positive random variable with a range that always implies that $h^*(0, t) > 0$. We can rewrite (11.8) as

Figure 11-3.   Multiplicative Term Structure Rates

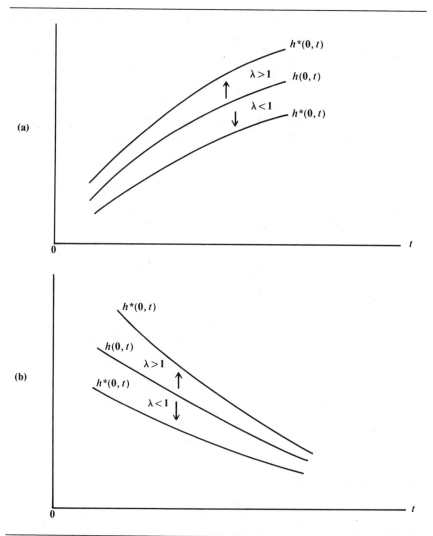

$$h^*(0, t) = (\lambda - 1) + \lambda h(0, t), \quad t = 1, 2, 3, \ldots, \tag{11.9}$$

so that this process is a combination of an additive shift and a multiplicative shift and where the two shifts are related to the single random variable λ. It is easy to see that this process produces a pattern similar to that exhibited in Figure 11-3 for multiplicative shocks. Again, it should be noted that *over time* short rates may change more than long rates.

Log Shifts

None of the above stochastic processes allow for short term rates to fluctuate instantaneously more than long-term rates for both downward and upward sloping term structures. Khang (1979), noting this, devised two processes that allow for this feature.[1] His log-additive process was specified as

$$h^*(0, t) = \frac{\lambda \ln(1+\alpha t)}{\alpha t} + h(0, t), \quad t = 1, 2, 3, \ldots, \qquad (11.10)$$

where λ is a random variable, and α is a positive parameter. It may be noted
that $\ln(1+\alpha t)$, which is positive, increases with t at a slower rate than αt so
that the ratio $\ln(1+\alpha t)/\alpha t$ decreases as t increases. Thus, for a given value
of α, short-term rates are instantaneously shocked by larger increments than
long-term rates. The given positive value of α regulates the degree to which
short-term rates fluctuate more than long-term rates. The larger the value
of α the greater the ratio of short-term changes to long-term changes. As α
goes to zero, $\ln(1+\alpha t)/\alpha t$ goes to unity. Thus, if α is made small enough
the log-additive process behaves like the additive process.

The Fisher–Weil analogue to this process can be specified as

$$1 + h^*(0, t) = \left[1 + \frac{\lambda \ln(1+\alpha t)}{\alpha t}\right][1 + h(0, t)], \qquad (11.11)$$

so that

$$h^*(0, t) = \frac{\lambda \ln(1+\alpha t)}{\alpha t} + \left[1 + \frac{\lambda \ln(1+\alpha t)}{\alpha t}\right]h(0, t), \quad t = 1, 2, 3, \ldots,$$

and is called the *log-multiplicative* shock. It is a combination of an additive
and a multiplicative shock, and it preserves the feature of short rates fluctuating instantaneously more than long-term rates. Both of these log processes
involve *term-dependent* shocks. The additive and multiplicative components
are functions of the term to maturity. This is a way by which the term structure shock can vary with term to maturity, t. As α goes to zero, the log-multiplicative shock tends toward the Fisher–Weil shock. The larger the value
of α, the greater the ratio of short-rate changes to long-rate changes.

DURATION AS AN ELASTICITY

In previous chapters, duration was used in two major ways. First, it was
used as an elasticity. Second, it was used in a planning period context to determine whether and to what extent an investor was going long or short; and

the degree of risk of an investment strategy was accordingly related to duration. In this section, duration is redefined so as to correspond properly to the assumed underlying stochastic process and still retain an elasticity interpretation. The use of this new duration in the formulation of an investment strategy is discussed in Appendix 12A.

Let us briefly review how duration was devised as an elasticity concept in previous chapters. The price of a security was specified as

$$p = \sum_{t=1}^{m} F_t(1+r)^{-t}, \tag{11.12}$$

where r was the yield to maturity, m was maturity, and F_t was the cash flow promised on date t. Taking the derivative of p with respect to r yields

$$\frac{dp}{dr} = -\sum tF_t(1+r)^{-t-1}. \tag{11.13}$$

Multiplying this expression by $(1+r)$ and dividing by p gives us

$$\frac{1+r}{p}\frac{dp}{dr} = -\sum tF_t(1+r)^{-t} \Big/ p = -D, \tag{11.14}$$

where D is the duration. Multiplying by r and dividing by $1+r$ implies that

$$\frac{r}{p}\frac{dp}{dr} = \frac{-Dr}{1+r}, \tag{11.15}$$

which is the elasticity of p with respect to r. Alternatively, the elasticity of p with respect to the discount factor $\beta = (1+r)^{-1}$, is the duration and can be expressed as

$$\frac{\beta}{p}\frac{dp}{d\beta} = D. \tag{11.16}$$

The formulation in (11.15) was used to approximate the percentage change in price for an instantaneous change in interest rates. This was written as

$$\frac{\Delta p}{p} \cong \frac{-D}{1+r}\Delta r, \tag{11.17}$$

where Δp and Δr are finite changes that have been substituted for dp and dr, respectively.

In the context of a shifting term structure as opposed to a shifting yield to maturity, we are interested in producing an equation like (11.17) to show the percentage change in the security price corresponding to a random change in the term structure. Initially we observe that the price of the security can be expressed as

$$p = \sum_{1}^{m} F_t[1 + h(0, t)]^{-t}. \tag{11.18}$$

Instantly after the shock to the term structure this price changes to

$$p(\lambda) = \sum_{1}^{m} F_t[1 + h^*(0, t)]^{-t}. \tag{11.19}$$

Here the price is expressed as a random function of the shock λ because the new term structure, $h^*(0, t)$, is a function of λ. For example, if the Fisher-Weil process is in effect, then (11.19) becomes

$$p(\lambda) = \sum_{1}^{m} F_t \lambda^{-t}[1 + h(0, t)]^{-t}, \tag{11.20}$$

by substituting from equation (11.8). Taking the derivative of (11.20) with respect to λ yields

$$p'(\lambda) = \frac{dp}{d\lambda} = -\sum_{1}^{m} t F_t \lambda^{-t-1}[1 + h(0, t)]^{-t}. \tag{11.21}$$

Then, evaluating this function at the point where $\lambda = 1$, we have

$$p'(1) = \frac{dp}{d\lambda}\bigg|_{\lambda=1} = -\sum_{1}^{m} t F_t[1 + h(0, t)]^{-t}. \tag{11.22}$$

Dividing through by the original price, $p(1)$, gives

$$\frac{p'(1)}{p(1)} = \frac{1}{p}\frac{dp}{d\lambda}\bigg|_{\lambda=1} = -\sum_{1}^{m} t F_t[1 + h(0, t)]^{-t}\bigg/p. \tag{11.23}$$

If now we define duration for this Fisher-Weil process as

$$D_{\text{FW}} = \sum_{1}^{m} t F_t[1 + h(0, t)]^{-t}\bigg/p, \tag{11.24}$$

we can write (11.23) as

$$\frac{1}{p}\frac{dp}{d\lambda}\bigg|_{\lambda=1} = -D_{\text{FW}}. \tag{11.25}$$

Using this equation to approximate the percentage change in price we can write

$$\frac{\Delta p}{p} \cong -D_{\text{FW}} \Delta\lambda. \tag{11.26}$$

where Δp and $\Delta\lambda$ have been substituted respectively for dp and $d\lambda$. In (11.26) Δp represents an approximation of $p(\lambda) - p(1)$, the new price less the original price; and $\Delta\lambda$ is the change $\lambda - 1$, the new value of λ less its original value.

This formulation of the percentage price change now involves a new definition of duration, given in (11.24). To distinguish this measure of duration from others, the subscript FW is appended to indicate that it is derived from the Fisher–Weil stochastic process. Similarly, let the prior measure of duration used in (11.14) be written with the subscript M for Macaulay, who was among the first to invent it. Thus,

$$D_M = \sum_1^m t F_t (1+r)^{-t} \Big/ p, \qquad (11.27)$$

where r is the yield to maturity.

The duration D_{FW} has many of the same properties previously ascribed to D_M. If the security is a zero coupon bond, then there is only one nonzero cash flow, F_m, the price of which is $F_m[1+h(0,m)]^{-m}$ so that $D_{FW} = m$, the maturity. If we let $w_t^{FW} = F_t[1+h(0,t)]^{-t}$ be a weight and substitute it into (11.24), we observe that D_{FW} is a weighted average of the maturity dates at which cash flows occur, and $\sum_1^m w_t^{FW} = 1$. Similarly, for D_M, $w_t^M = F_t(1+r)^{-t}$ is a weight such that $\sum_1^m w_t^M = 1$. The major distinction between (11.24) and (11.27) is then simply that the weights are different. If the term structure is upward sloping so that r, the yield to maturity exceeds $(0,1)$ but is less than $h(0,m)$, we observe that $w_t^M < w_t^{FW}$ for small values of t and $w_t^M > w_t^{FW}$ for large values of t. This means that more weight is given to the early cash flow dates in D_{FW} and less weight is given to the later cash flow dates, and hence this must imply that $D_{FW} < D_M$ for upward sloping term structures and $D_{FW} > D_M$ for downward sloping term structures.

There are two major points to understand in this development. First, the new approximation to the percentage price change, as in equation (11.26), is in terms of the random shock, λ. It is not expressed in terms of a change in the yield to maturity. Second, the random shock in equation (11.26) has an impact on the term structure that differs with the stochastic process assumed, and the duration in (11.26) may also be dependent on the stochastic process.

Formulation of measures of duration for the other stochastic processes noted in the previous section is more difficult and the durations can only be derived implicitly. As shown in Appendix 11A, these durations and the approximating equations for the percentage changes in prices may be tabulated in the following way.

Additive Stochastic Processes

The duration D_A is implicitly defined by

$$\frac{D_A}{1+h(0,D_A)} = \sum_1^m F_t \left\{ \frac{t}{1+h(0,t)} \right\} [1+h(0,t)]^{-t} \Big/ p, \qquad (11.28)$$

and the percentage price change is approximated as

$$\frac{\Delta p}{p} \cong \frac{-D_A}{1+h(0, D_A)} \lambda. \qquad (11.29)$$

To derive D_A from equation (11.28), it may be necessary to know the term structure $h(0, t)$, at points t in between the cash flow dates. However, to use (11.29) only requires that the calculation of the right-hand side of (11.28). The value of λ in (11.29) is also the change in λ because the initial value of λ is zero.

Multiplicative Stochastic Processes

The duration D_{MS} is implicitly defined by

$$\frac{D_{MS}h(0, D_{MS})}{1+h(0, D_{MS})} = \sum_{1}^{m} F_t \left\{ \frac{th(0, t)}{1+h(0, t)} \right\} [1+h(0, t)]^{-t} \bigg/ p, \qquad (11.30)$$

and the percentage price change is approximated as

$$\frac{\Delta p}{p} \cong \frac{-D_{MS}h(0, D_{MS})}{1+h(0, D_{MS})} (\lambda - 1). \qquad (11.31)$$

Here, $\lambda - 1 = \Delta\lambda$ because the initial value of λ is unity. Similarly, to utilize (11.31) we do not need to compute D_{MS}; the right-hand side of (11.31) is sufficient.

Log-Stochastic Processes

The duration for the log-additive process is $D_{LA}(\alpha)$, and is implicitly defined in

$$\frac{\ln[1+\alpha D_{LA}(\alpha)]}{1+h[0, D_{LA}(\alpha)]} = \sum_{1}^{m} F_t \left\{ \frac{\ln(1+\alpha t)}{1+h(0, t)} \right\} [1+h(0, t)]^{-t} \bigg/ p \qquad (11.32)$$

and the approximating equation is

$$\frac{\Delta p}{p} \cong \frac{-\ln[1+\alpha D_{LA}(\alpha)]}{\alpha[1+h(0, D_{LA}(\alpha))]} \lambda. \qquad (11.33)$$

The duration for the log-multiplicative process is $D_{LM}(\alpha)$, implicitly defined as

$$\ln(1+\alpha D_{LM}(\alpha)) = \sum_{1}^{m} F_t \ln(1+\alpha t) [1+h(0, t)]^{-t} \bigg/ p, \qquad (11.34)$$

and the approximating formula is

$$\frac{\Delta p}{p} = -\frac{\ln(1+\alpha D_{LM}(\alpha))}{\alpha}\lambda. \qquad (11.35)$$

EXAMPLES

The Macaulay duration, D_M, is always applicable in the approximation formula for the percentage price change. To utilize the formula, equation (11.17),
all one needs to know is the current yield, the duration, and the yield change.
The approximation formulas corresponding to the specific stochastic processes can be correctly used only for shocks that correspond to those stochastic processes. Moreover, to compute each of these durations, one must
know explicitly the entire term structure, and in the case of the log processes
one must additionally know the value of α.

Table 11-1. Two Term Structures Used to Illustrate
Shock-Specific Duration Calculations and the Percentage
Price Change Formulas

t	Upward Sloping Term Structure $h(0,t)$	Downward Sloping Term Structure $h(0,t)$
1	8.00%	11.00%
2	8.50	10.50
3	8.90	10.10
4	9.20	9.90
5	9.60	9.60
6	9.90	9.40
7	10.20	9.20
8	10.40	9.00
9	10.60	8.80
10	10.80	8.60
11	10.95	8.45
12	11.10	8.30
13	11.25	8.15
14	11.35	8.05
15	11.45	7.95
16	11.50	7.85
17	11.55	7.75
18	11.60	7.70
19	11.62	7.68
20	11.65	7.65

To illustrate the computations involved, let us begin with two particular term structures, one upward sloping and the other downward sloping. Then each of these term structures will be shocked according to each of the stochastic processes, and the approximation formulas used. Table 11-1 gives the two initial term structures. The upward sloping structure rises quickly and then tends to level off. The downward sloping structure falls quickly and then tends to level off. For simplicity, assume the cash flows are $100 in every period. Utilizing these term structures, the prices of these flows are

$$p_u = 100 \sum_{t=1}^{m} [1+h(0,t)]^{-t} = \$814.96, \quad \text{and}$$

$$p_d = 100 \sum_{t=1}^{m} [1+h(0,t)]^{-t} = \$944.60,$$

(11.36)

respectively for the upward and downward sloping term structures. For the upward sloping term structure, the yield to maturity is 10.65%. For the downward sloping term structure the yield to maturity is 8.53%. Although the cash flows are the same for both term structures, the downward sloping structure gives a higher value for the income stream. This implies that the yield to maturity must be lower for the downward sloping structure in order to obtain this higher price. The Macaulay duration is inversely related to the yield to maturity because a smaller yield gives greater weight to the earlier cash flow dates. Thus, we would expect the Macaulay duration to be larger, here, for the downward sloping term structure. Table 11-2, which gives all the durations for these two term structures, shows that the Macaulay duration ($D_M = 7.8942$ years) is indeed larger for the downward sloping term structure. It was previously noted that the Fisher–Weil duration, D_{FW}, exceeds the Macaulay duration for downward sloping term structures and that it is vice-versa for upward sloping term structures. Table 11-2 shows that this is indeed the case. The durations for the log-stochastic processes tend to be less than the other durations as Table 11-2 shows. This occurs because the logarithms in the duration formulas increase very slowly with the cash flow dates and this places greater weight on the earlier cash flow dates. The log-stochastic processes in Table 11-2 are calculated using a value of $\alpha = .1$. Interpolation is necessary in Table 11-2 to calculate the durations for the additive, multiplicative, and log processes. This was accomplished by assuming the term structure rates between cash flow dates are given by a linear relation. It may be instructive to illustrate this interpolation. For the upward sloping term structure, the additive duration is given implicitly by

$$6.3721 = \frac{D_A}{1+h(0,D_A)}.$$

Table 11-2. Calculation of Durations from the Term Structure of Table 11-1

---

a. Upward Sloping Term Structure

$D_M = 7.3452$ years.

$D_{FW} = 7.0485$ years.

$\dfrac{D_A}{1+h(0,D_A)} = 6.3721; \ D_A = 7.0221$ years.

$\dfrac{D_{MS}h(0,D_{MS})}{1+h(0,D_{MS})} = .67638; \ D_{MS} = 7.2723$ years.

$\dfrac{\ln(1+.1D_{LA})}{1+h(0,D_{LA})} = .445346; \ D_{LA} = 6.2922$ years.

$\ln(1+.1D_{LM}) = .4920; \ D_{LM} = 6.3561$ years.

b. Downward Sloping Term Structure

$D_M = 7.8942$ years.

$D_{FW} = 8.1956$ years.

$\dfrac{D_A}{1+h(0,D_A)} = 7.5538; \ D_A = 8.2301$ years.

$\dfrac{D_{MS}h(0,D_{MS})}{1+h(0,D_{MS})} = .6418; \ D_{MS} = 7.7309$ years.

$\dfrac{\ln(1+.1D_{LA})}{1+h(0,D_{LA})} = .5089; \ D_{LA} = 7.4244$ years.

$\ln(1+.1D_{LM}) = .5527; \ D_{LM} = 7.6380$ years.

Some calculations show that

$$6.352 = \frac{7}{1+h(0,7)} < 6.3721 = \frac{D_A}{1+h(0,D_A)} < \frac{8}{1+h(0,8)} = 7.246. \quad (11.37)$$

For the upward sloping term structure, $h(0,7) = .102$ and $h(0,8) = .104$. Assuming linearity, it follows that $h(0,t) = h(0,t) + .002(t-7)$ for $7 \le t \le 8$, or $h(0,t) = h(0,7) + .002\delta$ where δ is the increment added to 7 to obtain t. Using (11.37) we simply determine this increment so that

$$\frac{7+\delta}{1+h(0,7+\delta)} = \frac{7+\delta}{1.102+.002} = \frac{D_A}{1+h(0,D_A)} = 6.3721 \quad (11.38)$$

and then solve for δ and let $D_A = 7+\delta$. A similar procedure can be used for the multiplicative and log processes.

In Tables 11-3 through 11-7, each of the term structures of Table 11-1 is shocked according to the additive, Fisher–Weil, multiplicative, log-additive, and log-multiplicative processes. The shocks are specified so that the term structures increase by 50 basis points or so. For the additive process the increase is exactly 50 basis points, but for the others it varies because of the nature of the shock; and sometimes the short rates increase by more than 50 basis points and the long rates increase by less or vice versa. For each new term structure obtained by this shocking procedure, the new price and yield to maturity for the security is computed. The percentage change in the security price is then approximated using the Macaulay and the shock-specific formulas. For almost all of the cases, the Macaulay formula more closely approximates the true percentage change in the security price. The Macaulay formula is very valuable for purposes of these approximations. It is a formula that neither depends on the slope of the term structure nor upon the stochastic process; and it gives no worse an approximation than the shock-specific formulas on average.

MULTIVARIABLE RANDOM SHIFTS

The random shift of the term structure from $h(0, t)$ to $h^*(0, t)$ can be very complex. The stochastic processes so far specified involve a single random variable. Given the functional form of the process, once the random variable λ was determined, the new term structure $h^*(0, t)$ was revealed. If the shift or shock is a function of more than one random variable, however, a greater variety of new term structures can be created. In this section, the random shock is represented as a function of two or more random variables.

One of the simplest multivariable random shocks consists of a simple combination of the additive and multiplicative processes. Let

$$h^*(0, t) = \lambda_1 + \lambda_2 h(0, t), \quad t = 1, 2, 3, \ldots, \qquad (11.39)$$

where λ_1 and λ_2 are random variables that are not perfectly correlated.[2] This stochastic process, noted in Bierwag (1977), permits the term structure to shift so that some of the rates in $h^*(0, t)$ may increase and some may decrease. If $\lambda_1 > 0$ and $\lambda_2 < 1$ (or $\lambda_1 < 0$ and $\lambda_2 > 1$), the additive and multiplicative components work in opposite directions so that the term structure may move in a variety of twisting motions. As shown in Appendix 11B, the percentage price change of a security can be approximated by

$$\frac{\Delta p}{p} = \frac{-D_A}{1 + h(0, D_A)} \lambda_1 - \frac{D_{MS} h(0, D_{MS})}{1 + h(0, D_{MS})} (\lambda_2 - 1). \qquad (11.40)$$

Table 11-3. Additive Shocks

t	Upward Sloping Term Structure $h^*(0, t)$	Downward Sloping Term Structure $h^*(0, t)$
1	8.50%	11.50%
2	9.00	11.00
3	9.40	10.60
4	9.70	10.40
5	10.10	10.10
6	10.40	9.90
7	10.70	9.70
8	10.90	9.50
9	11.10	9.30
10	11.30	9.10
11	11.45	8.95
12	11.60	8.80
13	11.75	8.65
14	11.85	8.55
15	11.95	8.45
16	12.00	8.35
17	12.05	8.25
18	12.10	8.20
19	12.12	8.18
20	12.15	8.15
Yield change	.0048	.0051

Price change approximations
Upward sloping term structure

Macaulay: $\dfrac{\Delta p}{p} \cong \dfrac{-D_M \Delta r}{1+r} = \dfrac{-7.3452}{1.1065}(.0048) = -.0319.$

Shock-specific: $\dfrac{\Delta p}{p} \cong \dfrac{-D_A \lambda}{1+h(0, D_A)} = -6.3721(.0050) = -.0319.$

Downward sloping term structure

Macaulay: $\dfrac{\Delta p}{p} \cong \dfrac{-D_M \Delta r}{1+r} = \dfrac{-7.8942}{1.0853}(.0051) = -.0371.$

Shock-specific: $\dfrac{\Delta p}{p} \cong \dfrac{-D_A \lambda}{1+h(0, D_A)} = -7.5538(.0050) = -.0378.$

Actual price changes
Upward sloping term structure: $\Delta p/p = -.0310.$
Downward sloping term structure: $\Delta p/p = -.0367.$

Note: Each of the term structures of Table 11-1 is shocked by a 50 basis point increase. The new term structures and the approximation formulas are given in this table.

Table 11-4. Fisher–Weil Shocks

t	Upward Sloping Term Structure $h^*(0, t)$	Downward Sloping Term Structure $h^*(0, t)$
1	8.50%	11.51%
2	9.00	11.01
3	9.40	10.61
4	9.70	10.41
5	10.10	10.10
6	10.41	9.90
7	10.71	9.70
8	10.91	9.50
9	11.11	9.30
10	11.31	9.10
11	11.46	8.95
12	11.61	8.80
13	11.76	8.65
14	11.86	8.55
15	11.96	8.45
16	12.01	8.35
17	12.06	8.25
18	12.11	8.20
19	12.13	8.18
20	12.16	8.15
Yield change	.0049	.0051

Price change approximations
Upward sloping term structure

Macaulay: $\dfrac{\Delta p}{p} \cong \dfrac{-D_M \Delta r}{1+r} = \dfrac{-7.3452}{1.1065}(.0049) = -.0325.$

Shock-specific: $\dfrac{\Delta p}{p} \cong -D_{FW}(\lambda - 1) = -7.0485(.0046) = -.0324.$

Downward sloping term structure

Macaulay: $\dfrac{\Delta p}{p} \cong \dfrac{-D_M \Delta r}{1+r} = \dfrac{-7.8942}{1.0853}(.0051) = -.0371.$

Shock-specific: $\dfrac{\Delta p}{p} \cong -D_{FW}(\lambda - 1) = -8.1956(.0046) = -.0377.$

Actual price changes
Upward sloping term structure: $\Delta p/p = -.0316.$
Downward sloping term structure: $\Delta p/p = -.0366.$

Note: Each of the term structures of Table 11–1 is shocked by a value of $\lambda = 1.0046$. The new term structures and the approximation formulas are given in this table.

Table 11-5.   Multiplicative Shocks

t	Upward Sloping Term Structure $h^*(0, t)$	Downward Sloping Term Structure $h^*(0, t)$
1	8.38%	11.52%
2	8.90	10.99
3	9.32	10.57
4	9.63	10.37
5	10.05	10.05
6	10.37	9.84
7	10.68	9.63
8	10.89	9.42
9	11.10	9.21
10	11.31	9.00
11	11.46	8.85
12	11.62	8.69
13	11.78	8.53
14	11.88	8.43
15	11.99	8.32
16	12.04	8.22
17	12.09	8.11
18	12.15	8.06
19	12.17	8.04
20	12.20	8.01
Yield change	.0050	.0041

Price change approximations
  Upward sloping term structure

Macaulay: $\dfrac{\Delta p}{p} \cong \dfrac{-D_M \Delta r}{1+r} = \dfrac{-7.3452}{1.1065}(.0050) = -.0332.$

Shock-specific: $\dfrac{\Delta p}{p} \cong \dfrac{-D_{MS} h(0, D_{MS})}{1 + h(0, D_{MS})}(\lambda - 1) = -.67638(.047) = -.0318.$

  Downward sloping term structure

Macaulay: $\dfrac{\Delta p}{p} \cong \dfrac{-D_M \Delta r}{1+r} = \dfrac{-7.8942}{1.0853}(.0041) = -.0298.$

Shock-specific: $\dfrac{\Delta p}{p} \cong \dfrac{-D_{MS} h(0, D_{MS})}{1 + h(0, D_{MS})}\Delta\lambda = -.6418(.047) = -.0302.$

Actual price changes
  Upward sloping term structure: $\Delta p/p = -.0309.$
  Downward sloping term structure: $\Delta p/p = -.0295.$

Note: Each of the term structures of Table 11-1 is shocked by a value of $\lambda = 1.047$. The new term structures and the approximation formulas are given in this table.

Table 11-6.   Log-Additive Shocks

t	Upward Sloping Term Structure $h^*(0, t)$	Downward Sloping Term Structure $h^*(0, t)$
1	8.57%	11.57%
2	9.05	11.05
3	9.42	10.62
4	9.70	10.40
5	10.09	10.09
6	10.37	9.87
7	10.65	9.65
8	10.84	9.44
9	11.03	9.23
10	11.22	9.02
11	11.35	8.85
12	11.49	8.69
13	11.63	8.53
14	11.73	8.43
15	11.82	8.32
16	11.86	8.21
17	11.90	8.10
18	11.94	8.04
19	11.96	8.02
20	11.98	7.98
Yield change	.0040	.0042

Price change approximations
Upward sloping term structure

Macaulay:
$$\frac{\Delta p}{p} \cong \frac{-D_M \Delta r}{1+r} = \frac{-7.3452}{1.1065}(.0040) = -.0266.$$

Shock-specific:
$$\frac{\Delta p}{p} \cong \frac{-\ln(1+.1D_{LA})\lambda}{.1(1+h(0, D_{LA}))} = \frac{-.44536}{.1}(.006) = -.0267.$$

Downward sloping term structure

Macaulay:
$$\frac{\Delta p}{p} \cong \frac{-D_M \Delta r}{1+r} = \frac{-7.8942}{1.0853}(.0042) = -.0305.$$

Shock-specific:
$$\frac{\Delta p}{p} \cong \frac{-\ln(1+.1D_{LA})\lambda}{.1(1+h(0, D_{LA}))} = \frac{-.5089}{.1}(.006) = -.0305.$$

Actual price changes
Upward sloping term structure: $\Delta p/p = -.0262.$
Downward sloping term structure: $\Delta p/p = -.0299.$

Note: Each of the term structures of Table 11-1 is shocked by a value of $\lambda = .006$, when $\alpha = .1$. The new term structures and the approximation formulas are given in this table.

Table 11-7. Log-Multiplicative Shocks

t	Upward Sloping Term Structure $h^*(0, t)$	Downward Sloping Term Structure $h^*(0, t)$
1	8.62%	11.63%
2	9.09	11.10
3	9.47	10.68
4	9.75	10.45
5	10.13	10.13
6	10.42	9.91
7	10.70	9.70
8	10.89	9.48
9	11.07	9.27
10	11.26	9.05
11	11.40	8.89
12	11.54	8.73
13	11.68	8.57
14	11.77	8.46
15	11.86	8.35
16	11.90	8.24
17	11.94	8.13
18	11.98	8.07
19	12.00	8.04
20	12.02	8.00
Yield change	.0044	.0045

Price change approximations
Upward sloping term structure

Macaulay: $\dfrac{\Delta p}{p} \cong \dfrac{-D_M \Delta r}{1+r} = \dfrac{-7.3452}{1.1065}(.0044) = -.0292.$

Shock-specific: $\dfrac{\Delta p}{p} \cong \dfrac{-\ln(1+.1D_{LM})\lambda}{.1} = \dfrac{-.4920}{.1}(.006) = -.0295.$

Downward sloping term structure

Macaulay: $\dfrac{\Delta p}{p} \cong \dfrac{-D_M \Delta r}{1+r} = \dfrac{-7.8942}{1.0853}(.0045) = -.0327.$

Shock-specific: $\dfrac{\Delta p}{p} \cong \dfrac{-\ln(1+.1D_{LM})\lambda}{.1} = \dfrac{-.5527}{.1}(.006) = -.0332.$

Actual price changes
Upward sloping term structure: $\Delta p/p = -.0289.$
Downward sloping term structure: $\Delta p/p = -.0324.$

Note: Each of the term structures of Table 11-1 is shocked by a value of $\lambda = .006$, when $\alpha = .1$. The new term structures and the approximation formulas are given in this table.

Two terms are now exhibited on the right-hand side of the equation. There is a term corresponding to each of the random variables contained in the stochastic process of equation (11.39). Moreover, each of these terms corresponds to the implicit function (for example, $-D_A / [1 + h(0, D_A)]$) for determining the duration that would exist were the corresponding random variables the only one shocking the term structure.

Table 11–8 illustrates this case of a combined additive and multiplicative random shock. The values of the random variables are chosen so that the term structures twist into shapes quite different from the initial ones. Again the shock-specific percentage price approximation can be compared with the Macaulay approximations. These shock-specific approximations are not better. However, one can identify the separate impact of each of the component shocks.

In Appendix 11B, the concept of a random shock to the term structure is extended so as to involve any number of random variables. Equations comparable to (11.40) result. The implicit duration functions appear additively on the right-hand side of the approximating equation. Because of this additivity property, it is always easy to create new stochastic processes by combining the simple ones of the last section and perhaps others.

SOME GENERAL FEATURES OF STOCHASTIC PROCESSES

There are essentially two ways to view a stochastic process of the term structure of interest rates. First, one can take the view that the financial markets are efficient in the sense that available information on the value of securities is already contained in the current term structure so that, regardless of how expectations are formed, the future term structure in a general equilibrium setting depends on information yet to be revealed but which is not currently anticipated. In this context the stochastic process is a way to represent the uncertain impact of future information on future term structures for purposes of optimal current portfolio construction. Second, regardless of market efficiency or the manner in which information past or present affects the future term structures, the investor finds it reasonable, and perhaps less costly than acquiring more information, to regard future fluctuations in the term structure as determined by a stochastic process. This is comparable to the case of the gambler who bets on coin tosses. He may simply find probability distributions very easy and inexpensive to use in determining his betting behavior. Hence, even though we may concur with Einstein that "God does

Table 11-8. Combined Additive and Multiplicative Shocks

t	Upward Sloping Term Structure $h^*(0, t)$	Downward Sloping Term Structure $h^*(0, t)$
1	8.16%	10.62%
2	8.57	10.21
3	8.90	9.88
4	9.14	9.72
5	9.47	9.47
6	9.72	9.31
7	9.96	9.14
8	10.13	8.98
9	10.29	8.82
10	10.46	8.65
11	10.58	8.53
12	10.70	8.41
13	10.83	8.28
14	10.91	8.20
15	10.99	8.12
16	11.03	8.04
17	11.07	7.96
18	11.11	7.91
19	11.13	7.90
20	11.15	7.87
Yield change	$-.0030$	$.0007$

Price change approximations
Upward sloping term structure

Macaulay: $\dfrac{\Delta p}{p} \cong \dfrac{-D_M \Delta r}{1+r} = \dfrac{-7.3452}{1.1065}(-.0030) = .0199.$

Shock-specific: $\dfrac{\Delta p}{p} \cong \dfrac{-D_A}{1+h(0, D_A)}\lambda_1 - \dfrac{D_{MS} h(0, D_{MS})}{1+h(0, D_{MS})}(\lambda_2 - 1)$

$$= -6.3721(.016) - .67638(-.18) = .0198.$$

Downward sloping term structure

Macaulay: $\dfrac{\Delta p}{p} \cong \dfrac{-D_M \Delta r}{1+r} = \dfrac{-7.8942}{1.0853}(.0007) = -.0051.$

Shock-specific: $\dfrac{\Delta p}{p} \cong \dfrac{-D_A}{1+h(0, D_A)}\lambda_1 - \dfrac{D_{MS} h(0, D_{MS})}{1+h(0, D_{MS})}(\lambda_2 - 1)$

$$= -7.5538(.016) - .6818(-.18) = -.0053.$$

Actual price changes
Upward sloping term structure: $\Delta p/p = -.0203.$
Downward sloping term structure: $\Delta p/p = -.0052.$

not throw dice," it may be useful to assume He does. Both of these two views justify the specification of stochastic processes that generate future term structures.

There are many ways to specify a stochastic process. Those considered in this chapter were very simple, and therein lies their appeal. Whether or not any of these processes are "good enough" to explain the motion of the term structure depends on (1) the purpose to which the process is put and on (2) the user's subjective criterion of what is "good enough." It is already clear that shock-specific durations for approximating percentage price changes are not generally more accurate than the Macaulay approximation, which is easier to utilize. However, these simple stochastic processes may be more useful and good enough for other purposes, some of which are surveyed in Chapter 12.

The simple stochastic processes with one random variable can be used as building blocks for more sophisticated processes. The case, above, in which additive and multiplicative processes are combined is an example. Here, a more flexible process that produced far more complex shifts and twisting motions was possible. The most extreme form of this procedure consists simply of specifying the stochastic process as

$$h^*(0, t) = \lambda_t + h(0, t), \quad t = 1, 2, 3, \ldots, \tag{11.41}$$

where λ_t, $t = 1, 2, 3, \ldots$, is a set of random variables no one of which is perfectly correlated with any set of the others. In this process there are as many random shifts as there are new rates in the term structure to determine. In this extreme form of term-dependent random shocks, additivity may always be sufficient to specify the process. Even if $h^*(0, t)$ was more complex and specified as

$$h^*(0, t) = f[h(0, t), \theta_1, \theta_2, \ldots, \theta_n], \quad t = 1, 2, \ldots, n, \tag{11.42}$$

where θ_j, $j = 1, 2, 3, \ldots, n$ are the random variables, it may be possible to transform the θ_j's into the λ_t's so as to produce equation (11.41) in the form of additivity with new random variables, λ_t, that are functions of the θ_j's.[3] This extreme form of the stochastic process with term dependence breaks down the functional connection between $h^*(0, t)$ and $h^*(0, \tau)$, for $\tau \neq t$. In effect, this is an extreme form of the segmentation hypothesis in which it is contended that the rates for each maturity are functionally independent of

---

Notes to Table 11-8

Each of the term structures in Table 11-1 is shocked additively by $\lambda_1 = .016$ and multiplicatively by $\lambda_2 = .82$. The new term structures and the approximation formulas are given in this table.

the rates on other maturities because there are separate unrelated bond markets for each maturity. As a general rule, the larger the number of term-dependent random variables included the greater the degree of functional segmentation. The smaller the number of random variables, as in the cases of a single random variable, the greater is the degree of functional dependence between rates of different maturities. Thus, the more inclined we are to believe that rates in the term structure are functionally related the fewer the number of random variables that need to be specified. Brennan and Schwartz (1982), for example, utilize a stochastic process involving just two term-dependent random variables. Although they develop their model within the context of continuous stochastic processes, the flavor of their process can be described in the discrete framework used here. We might specify their process in the following form:

$$h^*(0, t) = \beta_t \lambda_1 + (1 - \beta_t)\lambda_n + h(0, t), \quad t = 1, 2, 3, \ldots, \qquad (11.43)$$

where λ_1 and λ_n are random variables that affect respectively the short rate, $h^*(0, 1)$, and the long rate, $h^*(0, n)$, and where β_t is a term-dependent parameter with the property that $\beta_1 = 1$ and $\beta_n = 0$. Here, every rate in the term structure is shocked by some combination of a short-rate shock and a long-rate shock. The underlying notion is that the intermediate maturities behave in a manner that reflects a combination of short-term and long-term properties. In effect there is functional independence between the shortest short-term market and the longest long-term market; and one can argue that this may reflect the traditional distinction between money markets (short-term securities that are very liquid and represent money substitutes) and capital markets (long-term instruments issued primarily to finance the real capital of the economy). The Brennan–Schwartz process has never been applied in the discrete context.

Although the specification of a stochastic process constitutes something of an arbitrary procedure, and the primary concern is with empirical validity and the usefulness of the process for particular purposes, there are guidelines that can be utilized in the specifications. Simplicity and the degree of functional dependence between maturities are major ingredients that we would wish those guidelines to include.

CONCLUDING REMARKS

Uncertainty and the resulting sequence of future term structures was introduced in this chapter in a way that was analogous to the method used in earlier chapters (Chapter 1–9). Immediately after the investor allocates an investment fund at time zero, the term structure shifts from $h(0, t)$, $t = 1, 2,$ 3, ..., to $h^*(0, t)$, $t = 1, 2, 3, \ldots$. Thereafter, it was assumed that forward term structures became the actual term structures and that there were no further random term structure shifts as time passed. This is exactly the same methodology used in the first nine chapters where it was assumed that all term structures were flat.

In the first nine chapters, the random shift in the interest rate (the flat term structure) was always stated as an additive shift. As soon as it is assumed that the term structure is not flat then the variety of possible random shifts becomes endlessly large. The specification of the form of the random shift, or random shock, was called the *stochastic process*. Several examples of very simple stochastic processes were considered. It was shown that there existed a measure of duration that corresponded to each stochastic process. Hence, the concept of duration was generalized and associated with specific stochastic processes. These new measures of duration can be used like the Macaulay duration to devise shock-specific approximations to the percentage change in the price of a security. In the examples considered, the Macaulay duration formula provided generally more accurate approximations to the percentage price changes.

This generalized duration concept plays exactly the same role in the formation of duration-based strategies as when the term structure was flat. As shown in Appendix 12B, for example, a portfolio is immunized when the portfolio is chosen so that its duration is equal to the planning period length. Similarly, active strategies can be constructed just as before. The investor "goes long" when he sets the portfolio duration longer than the planning period and the investor "goes short" when he sets the portfolio duration shorter than the planning period. The contingent immunization strategy, the gap analysis, and futures markets operations can all similarly be redefined in terms of these new "durations."

Which stochastic process should be assumed in developing an investment strategy? It is conceivable that an investor could assume an incorrect stochastic process and, as a consequence, the perceived durations would be different from the actual ones. The investor faces *stochastic process risk*. Bierwag, Kaufman, and Toevs (1983) show that stochastic process risk is not a trivial concern. Losses from misestimation (or misguesstimation) of the correct process can be substantial. It may be reasonable to assume a particular process, or use of particular duration estimation procedure, as one that minimizes stochastic process risk. The determination of the "best" process from some appropriate class of processes has yet to be considered as a formal theoretical problem. Some empirical evidence in Chapter 12 suggests that the Macaulay duration is a good one to use in the absence of further evidence.

APPENDIX 11A
DERIVATION OF DURATION MEASURES

Additive Stochastic Processes

With this process in effect, the price of a security instantly after the shock to the term structure can be written as

$$p(\lambda) = \sum_{1}^{m} F_t [1 + \lambda + h(0, t)]^{-t}. \tag{11A.1}$$

The derivative with respect to λ is then

$$\frac{dp}{d\lambda} = p'(\lambda) = -\sum_{1}^{m} t F_t [1 + \lambda + h(0, t)]^{-t-1}. \tag{11A.2}$$

Evaluating this function at the value of $\lambda = 0$ (the value that gives the original price at which the security may be purchased) we have

$$\frac{dp}{d\lambda}\bigg|_{\lambda=0} = p'(0) = -\sum_{1}^{m} F_t \{t[1 + h(0, t)]^{-1}\}[1 + h(0, t)]^{-t}. \tag{11A.3}$$

Dividing through by the original price, $p(0)$, we can write

$$\frac{p'(0)}{p(0)} = \frac{1}{p}\frac{dp}{d\lambda}\bigg|_{\lambda=0} = -\sum_{1}^{m} F_t \left\{\frac{t}{1 + h(0, t)}\right\}[1 + h(0, t)]^{-t}\bigg/ p(0). \tag{11A.4}$$

We are now in a position to define the duration measure that is appropriate for this stochastic process. Unfortunately, it must be defined by the implicit function

$$\frac{D_A}{1 + h(0, D_A)} = \sum_{1}^{m} F_t \left\{\frac{t}{1 + h(0, t)}\right\}[1 + h(0, t)]^{-t}\bigg/ p \tag{11A.5}$$

in order that it should have the properties we desire. To calculate D_A, we may need to know the value of $h(0, t)$ for values of t between the cash flow dates in order to compute $h(0, D_A)$. Expressing D_A in this manner gives it an interpretation comparable to other duration measures. If it is a zero coupon bond so that F_m is the only nonzero cash flow, then $D_A = m$, the maturity. If the term structure is flat the duration is exactly the same as D_M. This will be generally true for all of the duration measures. That is, when the term structure is flat, the duration reduces to the Macaulay duration. Using (11A.4) to approximate the percentage price change, we have

$$\frac{\Delta p}{p} \cong \frac{-D_A}{1 + h(0, D_A)}\lambda. \tag{11A.6}$$

Notice, though, that we do not need actually to calculate D_A in order to use (11A.6). The term $D_A/(1+h(0, D_A))$ can be computed directly from the right-hand side of (11A.5).

Multiplicative Stochastic Processes

With this process in effect, the price of a security instantly after the shock to the term structure can be written as

$$p(\lambda) = \sum_1^m F_t[1+\lambda h(0, t)]^{-t}. \tag{11A.7}$$

The derivative with respect to λ can be written as

$$p'(\lambda) = \frac{dp}{d\lambda} = -\sum_1^m F_t\left[\frac{th(0, t)}{1+h(0, t)\lambda}\right]\{1+\lambda h(0, t)\}^{-t}. \tag{11A.8}$$

Similarly, we can implicitly define the corresponding duration as

$$\frac{D_{MS}h(0, D_{MS})}{1+h(0, D_{MS})} = \sum_1^m F_t\left\{\frac{th(0, t)}{1+h(0, t)}\right\}[1+h(0, t)]^{-t}\bigg/p, \tag{11A.9}$$

where D_{MS} is the duration for the multiplicative stochastic process. Then evaluating $p(\lambda)$ at $\lambda = 1$ and dividing it by $p(1)$, we can write

$$\frac{p'(1)}{p(1)} = \frac{1}{p}\frac{dp}{d\lambda}\bigg|_{\lambda=1} = \frac{-D_{MS}h(0, D_{MS})}{1+h(0, D_{MS})}, \tag{11A.10}$$

and the approximation equation becomes

$$\frac{\Delta p}{p} \cong -\frac{D_{MS}h(0, D_{MS})}{1+h(0, D_{MS})}\Delta\lambda. \tag{11A.11}$$

Log-Stochastic Processes

With the log-additive stochastic process in effect, the price of a security instantly after the shock to the term structure can be written as

$$p(\lambda) = \sum_1^m F_t\left[1+\frac{\lambda \ln(1+\alpha t)}{\alpha t} + h(0, t)\right]^{-t}. \tag{11A.12}$$

Taking the derivative with respect to λ and evaluating it at $\lambda = 0$ gives

$$\frac{dp}{d\lambda}\bigg|_{\lambda=0} = p'(0) = -\sum_1^m F_t\left\{\frac{1}{\alpha}\frac{\ln(1+\alpha t)}{1+h(0, t)}\right\}[1+h(0, t)]^{-t}. \tag{11A.13}$$

We can then define the duration implicitly by

$$\frac{\ln[1+\alpha D_{\text{LA}}(\alpha)]}{1+h[0, D_{\text{LA}}(\alpha)]} = \sum_{1}^{m} F_t \left\{ \frac{\ln(1+\alpha t)}{1+h(0, t)} \right\} [1+h(0, t)]^{-t} \bigg/ p, \qquad (11\text{A}.14)$$

where $D_{\text{LA}}(\alpha)$ is the log-additive duration corresponding to a specific value of α. Dividing (11.A.13) by p implies the approximation formula

$$\frac{\Delta p}{p} \cong \frac{-\ln[1+D_{\text{LA}}(\alpha)]}{\alpha[1+h(0, D_{\text{LA}}(\alpha)]} \Delta \lambda. \qquad (11\text{A}.15)$$

Under the log-multiplicative process that is analogous to the Fisher–Weil process,

$$p(\lambda) = \sum_{1}^{m} F_t \left[1 + \frac{\lambda \ln(1+\alpha t)}{\alpha t} \right]^{-t} [1+h(0, t)]^{-t}. \qquad (11\text{A}.16)$$

The derivative with respect to λ evaluated at $\lambda = 0$ is

$$\frac{dp}{d\lambda}\bigg|_{\lambda=0} = p'(0) = -\sum_{1}^{m} F_t \left\{ \frac{\ln(1+\alpha t)}{\alpha} \right\} [1+h(0, t)]^{-t}. \quad (11\text{A}.17)$$

The duration is defined implicitly by

$$\ln[1+\alpha D_{\text{LM}}(\alpha)] = \sum_{1}^{m} F_t \ln(1+\alpha t)[1+h(0, t)]^{-t} \bigg/ p. \quad (11\text{A}.18)$$

Dividing (11A.17) by $p(0)$ implies the approximation formula

$$\frac{\Delta p}{p} \cong -\frac{\ln(1+\alpha D_{\text{LM}}(\alpha))}{\alpha} \Delta \lambda. \qquad (11\text{A}.19)$$

APPENDIX 11B
MULTIVARIATE RANDOM SHOCKS

The Case of Two Random Variables

One of the simplest two-variable random shocks is one having additive and multiplicative components, as noted in the text. In this case, the new instantaneous term structure becomes

$$h^*(0, t) = \lambda_1 + \lambda_2 h(0, t), \quad t = 1, 2, 3, \ldots, \qquad (11\text{B}.1)$$

where λ_2 and λ_2 are the random variables. It is assumed (1) that λ_1 and λ_2 are not perfectly correlated, and (2) that $h(0, t)$ is not flat. If the variables are perfectly correlated so that $\lambda_1 = g(\lambda_2)$, an explicit function of λ_2, then substitution of $g(\lambda_2)$ for λ_1 reduces the shock to one expressed as a function of a single random variable. If $h(0, t) = r$ for all t so that the term structure is flat then $h^*(0, t) = \lambda_1 + \lambda_2 r$ and does not vary with t. In this case the variable $\lambda_1 + \lambda_2 r = r^* = r + \lambda_3$, where $\lambda_3 = \lambda_1 + (\lambda_2 - 1)r$ and this implies that the combination $\lambda_1 + \lambda_2 r$ can itself be expressed as a single random variable. Thus, this two-variable process reduces to a single-variable process and as with the other stochastic processes the duration reduces to the Macaulay duration. Viewing this random shock in the elasticity context, we can show how the percentage change in the price of a security can be approximated. The price of a security immediately after the random shock can be expressed as

$$p(\lambda_1, \lambda_2) = \sum_1^m F_t [1 + \lambda_1 + \lambda_2 h(0, t)]^{-t}, \tag{11B.2}$$

where F_t is the cash flow promised by the security at time t. Taking the differential of (11B.2) with respect to the random variables, we have

$$dp(\lambda_1, \lambda_2) = - \sum_1^m t F_t [1 + \lambda_1 + \lambda_2 h(0, t)]^{-t-1} [d\lambda_1 + h(0, t)d\lambda_2]. \tag{11B.3}$$

As in the case of a single random variable, we can divide both sides by $p(\lambda_1, \lambda_2)$ and evaluate it at the values $\lambda_1 = 0$ and $\lambda_2 = 1$, the values at which we secure the original price paid for the security. This produces

$$\frac{dp(0,1)}{p(0,1)} = - \sum_1^m t F_t [1 + h(0, t)]^{-t-1} [d\lambda_1 + h(0, t)d\lambda_2] \Big/ p(0,1)$$

$$= \frac{-D_A}{1 + h(0, D_A)} d\lambda_1 - \frac{D_{MS} h(0, D_{MS})}{1 + h(0, D_{MS})} d\lambda_2, \tag{11B.4}$$

using the prior definition for the durations D_A and D_{MS}.[4] One can then approximate the percentage change in price by substituting Δp, $\Delta \lambda_1 = \lambda_1$, $\Delta \lambda_2 = (\lambda_2 - 1)$ for dp, $d\lambda_1$, and $d\lambda_2$, respectively. This produces the approximation equation

$$\frac{\Delta p}{p} \cong \frac{-D_A}{1 + h(0, D_A)} \lambda_1 - \frac{D_{MS} h(0, D_{MS})}{1 + h(0, D_{MS})} (\lambda_2 - 1), \tag{11B.5}$$

which can be compared with the Macaulay approximation as in Table 11–8.

Generalizing to Any Number of Random Variables[5]

As a general funtion, one can describe the new instantaneous term structure as

$$h^*(0, t) = f(\theta_1, \theta_2, ..., \theta_n), \tag{11B.6}$$

where θ_j is the jth random variable. In this expression we assume that no single random variable is perfectly correlated with any group of others. This means that it is not possible to reduce the function (11B.6) to a simpler expression containing fewer random variables because of perfect correlation somewhere among the variables. The form of the function f describes the way in which the random variables collectively determine the new structure. The "no shock" case in which $h^*(0, t)$ becomes $h(0, t)$ — so as to reproduce the original price as done in equation (11B.4) — can be expressed as

$$h(0, t) = f(\theta_{10}, \theta_{20}, ..., \theta_{n0}), \tag{11B.7}$$

where θ_{j0}, $j = 1, 2, ..., n$, represents that set of values which reproduces the original term structure for all t. In order for it not to be possible to reduce (11B.6) and (11B.7) to a function of fewer random variables, the set of values θ_{j0}, $j = 1, 2, 3, ..., n$, must be unique so that the equation (11B.7) holds for all t. If the term structure, for example, is flat before and after the shock, then (11B.7) and (11B.6) can be reduced to a single random variable process and many different sets of θ_j's can produce the same shock. In another example, suppose there are more random variables, n, than there are values of $h^*(0, t)$ to evaluate for different t's, then the process can be reduced to one in which there need be no more random variables than values of $h^*(0,t)$ to determine.

The price of a security after the shock is

$$p(\theta_1, \theta_2, ..., \theta_n) = \sum_1^m F_t[1 + f(\theta_1, \theta_2, ..., \theta_n)]^{-t}. \tag{11B.8}$$

Taking the total differential as before gives us

$$dp(\theta_1, \theta_2, ..., \theta_n) = -\sum_1^m tF_t[1 + f(\theta_1, \theta_2, ..., \theta_n)]^{-t-1}[f_1 d\theta_1 + \cdots + f_n d\theta_n], \tag{11B.9}$$

where f_j is the partial derivative of the function f with respect to θ_j. Proceeding as before, we divide both sides of equation (11B.9) by $p(\theta_1, \theta_2, ..., \theta_n)$ and evaluate the function at the original values of the θ_j's. Let us do this in steps. First, let f_j^* be the value of the jth partial derivative evaluated at the point where $\theta_j = \theta_{j0}$ for all j. It follows that

$$(f_1 d\theta_1 + f_2 d\theta_2 + \cdots + f_n d\theta_n) \mid_{\theta_j = \theta_{j0} \text{ for all } j} = \sum_{j=1}^n f_j^* d\theta_j. \tag{11B.10}$$

Next, dividing both sides of (11B.9) by $p(\theta_1, \theta_2, ..., \theta_n)$ and evaluating at θ_{j0} for all j gives us

$$\frac{dp(\theta_1, \theta_2, \ldots, \theta_n)}{p(\theta_1, \ldots, \theta_n)} \bigg|_{\theta_j = \theta_{j0} \text{ for all } j} = \frac{-\sum_{t=1}^{m} tF_t [1 + h(0, t)]^{-t-1} \sum_{j=1}^{n} f_j^* d\theta_j}{p(\theta_{10}, \theta_{20}, \ldots, \theta_{n0})}.$$

(11B.11)

We are now in a position to define a duration for each of the n random variables comprising the shock. Let

$$\frac{f_j^* D_j}{1 + h(0, D_j)} = \sum_{t=1}^{m} F_t \frac{t f_j^*}{1 + h(0, t)} \bigg| p,$$

(11B.12)

where D_j is the duration corresponding to the jth random variable. Equation (11B.12) gives us the implicit duration function that would result if only the jth random variable were to occur while the others remain fixed at θ_{j0}. Substituting (11B.12) into (11B.11) gives us the approximating equation

$$\frac{\Delta p}{p} \cong -\sum_{j=1}^{n} \frac{f_j^* D_j (\theta_j - \theta_{j0})}{1 + h(0, D_j)},$$

(11B.13)

where $(\theta_j - \theta_{j0})$ approximates $d\theta_j$. In general (11B.13) can be used as an approximation equation for the percentage price change, and it can be compared to the Macaulay approximation. Also, if the function f can be reduced to a function of fewer random variables, the effect is to reduce the number of terms in (11B.13).

NOTES

1. Khang also works in a framework of continuous compounding. Here, we present the analogues in the case of noncontinuous compounding.
2. If they are perfectly correlated the process is reduced to a process having a single random variable because λ_1 and λ_2 move together in a perfectly predictable manner.
3. This necessitates that the function f and the probability distribution over the θ's satisfy particular properties the analysis of which need not detain us here. We assume these properties as necessary so as to obtain (11.41) in the extreme additivity form as shown. The implications of this extreme form are the object of the analysis here and not the methodology by which it may be obtained from a non-additive specification.
4. If the term structure is flat then $D_A = D_{MS} = D_M$ and the approximation reduces to the Macaulay approximation.
5. This section may be too advanced for some readers and may be safely omitted without spoiling the intuitive basis for understanding the multivariable stochastic process.

REFERENCES

Bierwag, G.O., 1977. "Immunization, Duration, and the Term Structure of Interest Rates." *Journal of Financial and Quantitative Analysis* (December): 725–42.

Bierwag, G.O., and George G. Kaufman. 1977. "Coping with the Risk of Interest Rate Fluctuations: A Note." *Journal of Business* (July): 364–70.

Bierwag, G.O., George G. Kaufman, and Alden L. Toevs. 1983. "Bond Portfolio Immunization and Stochastic Process Risk." *Journal of Bank Research* (Winter).

Brennan, M.J., and Eduardo S. Schwartz. 1982. "An Equilibrium Model of Bond Pricing and a Test of Market Efficiency." *Journal of Financial and Quantitative Analysis 18,* no. 3 (September).

Fisher, Lawrence, and Roman L. Weil. 1971. "Coping with the Risk of Interest Rate Fluctuations: Returns to Bondholders from Naive and Optimal Strategies." *Journal of Business 44* (October): 408–31.

Khang, Chulsoon. 1979. "Bond Immunization when Short-Term Rates Fluctuate More Than Long-Term Rates." *Journal of Financial and Quantitative Analysis* (December): 1035–90.

12 EMPIRICAL RESEARCH

The empirical research on duration analysis can be divided into two groups of studies. In the first of these groups, immunization and other duration-based investment strategies are simulated utilizing term structures estimated with a variety of data bodies. The objective of these studies is to show that an immunization strategy works better (more closely immunizes) than other easily constructed and sometimes appealing strategies. The second group of studies consists of regression-based models that are designed to show the characteristics of an underlying stochastic process. The objective of these studies is to show the extent to which changes in term structures can be explained by the motion of a single factor or variable through time. If a single-factor model adequately explains term structure changes, then it is implicitly understood that duration-based investment strategies should work well as intended. This chapter surveys most of the empirical studies in each of the two groups.

IMMUNIZATION STUDIES

In Chapter 4, a portfolio was immunized when its duration was set equal to the remaining time in the planning period. Duration was calculated as the "Macaulay" duration, computed using the yield to maturity. When the stochastic process is complex and the term structure is not necessarily flat, the immunization procedure remains essentially the same; only the duration measure changes. As shown in Appendix 12A immunization still requires that duration be set equal to the remaining time in the planning period, but the duration measure should now be computed as implied by the underlying stochastic process generating changes in the term structure of interest rates. This form of the immunization strategy is extensively used in the following sections.

Fisher and Weil (1971)

L. Fisher and R. Weil conducted the first simulations of a portfolio immunization strategy. They used the Durand interest rate data collected for the period 1925–1968.[1] Each of these term structures is constructed as a curve that represents the lower bound on the interest rates on corporate bonds at a point in time. Each term structure is intended to measure a default-free term structure. Fisher and Weil consider planning periods of 5, 10, and 20 years. They construct a number of hypothetical bond portfolios based upon the so-called Fisher–Weil stochastic process, as analyzed in previous chapters. Immunizing portfolios are constructed by acquiring two bonds, one with a maturity equal to the planning period length and the other is the one with the largest possible duration. The coupon on each bond is assumed to be 4%. In the period 1925–1968 there are 39 overlapping 5-year planning periods, 34 overlapping 10-year planning periods, and 24 overlapping 20-year periods. At the end of each year during the planning period, the investor reinvests the accumulated assets and coupon income in a new portfolio having a duration equal to the remaining time in the planning period. At the end of the planning period, r_i is the annual rate of return from the immunization strategy, r_m is the rate of return from holding a bond with maturity always equal to the planning period (and reinvesting all coupon income in such a bond), and r_p is the rate of return promised at the beginning of the planning period and given by the term structure as the applicable rate on a zero coupon bond having a maturity equal to the planning period. If the immunization strategy works precisely correctly at all time, then $r_i = r_p$ for each planning period. Some of Fisher and Weil's results are shown in Table 12-1. Over the period 1925–1968 the immunization strategy tends to get closer to the promised return more frequently than the maturity strategy. From these simulations, Fisher and Weil conclude that an immunization strategy is more likely to "lock in" or get closer to the promised rate of return than a maturity strategy.

Table 12-1.   Fisher and Weil's Immunization Results, 1925–1968

Planning Period Length (Years)	Percentage of Time $\|r_i - r_p\| < \|r_m - r_p\|$	Percentage of Time $r_i > r_p$
5	77	41
10	82	24
20	96	0

Note: Fisher and Weil's original presentation was in terms of wealth ratios rather than rates of return. Slight modifications are made here for purposes of comparability with other studies.

Bierwag, Kaufman, Toevs, and Schweitzer (1981)

In this study the authors update the Fisher–Weil results for 10-year planning periods with the Durand data, extended to 1978, and utilize several other duration measures corresponding to different stochastic processes. The results are exhibited in Table 12-2. Five different immunizing duration (ID) strategies are denoted. These durations correspond to the stochastic processes of Chapter 11:

ID1:   Macaulay duration; computed using the yield to maturity for each bond. Appropriate for flat term structures

ID2:   Additive stochastic processes

ID3:   Fisher–Weil stochastic processes

ID4(0.1):   Log-multiplicative process; $\alpha = 0.1$

ID4(1.0):   Log-multiplicative process; $\alpha = 1.0$

In addition to these five immunization strategies, the results were compared to the following "active" strategies:

Maturity Strategy: A single bond with maturity equal to the remaining planning period is held and all coupon income is reinvested in it.

Rollover Strategy: Portfolio is totally allocated to one-period bonds and rolled over at maturity.

Long-Bond Strategy: A 20-year bond is maintained so that its maturity declines with the planning period length and is a 10-year bond at the end of the planning period.

Table 12-2. Promised and Realized Returns for Alternative Portfolio Strategies: 10-Year Planning Periods, 1925–1978; Bierwag, Kaufman, Toevs, and Schweitzer (1981)

Strategy	Promised (Annual Average)	Realized (Annual Average)	Realized Minus Promised	Closer to Promised than Maturity Strategy	Within 5 Basis Points of Promised	Greater than Promised	Highest Realized	Lowest Realized
				Return (%)				
				1925–1978[a]				
Immunization[d]	3.364							
ID1		3.286	−.078	86	48	9	0	0
ID2		3.289	−.075	89	48	9	0	0
ID3		3.289	−.075	89	48	9	0	0
ID4(0.1)		3.270	−.094	82	27	2	0	0
ID4(1.0)		3.236	−.128	52	34	11	2	0
Maturity		3.329	−.035	—	16	41	0	0
Rollover		2.927	−.437	2	7	48	50	48
Long bond[b]	→	3.194	−.170	9	7	45	48	52
				1925–1949[c]				
Immunization[d]	3.697							
ID1		3.552	−.145	93	13	0	0	0
ID2		3.555	−.142	93	13	0	0	0
ID3		3.555	−.142	93	13	0	0	0
ID4(0.1)		3.595	−.102	93	20	0	0	0
ID4(1.0)		3.668	−.029	93	53	27	0	0
Maturity		3.465	−.232	—	0	0	0	0
Rollover		1.801	−1.896	0	0	0	0	100
Long bond[b]	→	4.749	+1.052	7	0	100	100	0

				1940–1963[a]				
Immunization[d]	2.257							
ID1		2.214	− .043	79	50	14	0	0
ID2		2.214	− .043	86	50	14	0	0
ID3		2.214	− .043	86	50	14	0	0
ID4(0.1)		2.214	− .043	86	50	7	7	0
ID4(1.0)		2.212	− .045	64	50	7	0	0
Maturity		2.214	− .043	—	36	29		
Rollover	→	2.074	− .183	7	14	43	50	43
Long bond[b]		1.987	− .270	21	21	36	43	57
				1954–1978[a]				
Immunization[d]	4.064							
ID1		4.026	− .038	87	80	13	0	0
ID2		4.027	− .037	87	80	13	0	0
ID3		4.027	− .037	87	80	13	0	0
ID4(0.1)		3.930	− .134	67	13	0	0	0
ID4(1.0)		3.759	− .305	0	0	0	0	0
Maturity		4.234	+ .170	—	13	93		
Rollover	→	4.848	+ .784	0	7	100	100	0
Long bond[b]		2.767	−1.297	0	0	0	0	100

a. The last portfolio in each period purchased 10 years before the last year in the period.

b. Maintained bond with initial maturity of 20 years.

c. 10-year yield-to-maturity at date of purchase.

d. Portfolio consists of initial 10- and 20-year bonds.

The immunizing portfolios consist of two bonds—a bond having a 20-year maturity and one with a maturity equal to the remaining length of the planning period. The proportions of each bond are such that the appropriate immunizing duration is set equal to the remaining length of the planning period.

The results show that immunization strategies invariably get closer to the promised rate of return than the maturity strategy. Moreover, with considerable frequency, an immunization strategy gets within 5 basis points of the promised rate. The results of the active strategies are very close to what one would expect. Short-duration strategies tend to produce their highest (lowest) returns in periods of generally rising (falling) rates, and long-duration strategies tend to produce their highest (lowest) returns in periods of falling (rising) interest rates. The more sophisticated immunization strategies, ID2 through ID4(1.0), do not appear to work consistently and substantially better than the duration strategies based on the yields to maturity, the Macaulay duration. The additive (ID2) and Fisher–Weil (ID3) stochastic processes appear to give results that are indistinguishable in all of the periods considered. For small shifts in the term structure these two processes are also theoretically close to one another. The log-multiplicative processes, ID4(0.1) and ID4(1.0), are clearly inferior except for the 1925–1949 period.

These empirical observations suggested three main conclusions:

1. Immunizing by use of Macaulay durations (ID1—computing durations of the financial instruments using yields to maturity) works as well as more sophisticated duration measures that are intended to account for term structure motion.
2. Duration strategies (except possibly for weird ones like the ID4's) tend to produce returns that are on average closer to initially promised returns than the maturity strategy. That is, the duration immunization strategies tend to approximate more closely a risk-free return over a planning period than the maturity strategy.
3. Little or no improvement in minimizing the error in realizing the promised return can be expected by using the log-stochastic processes.

Ingersoll (1983)

Ingersoll utilizes CRSP data in his simulations of some immunization strategies.[2] He estimates semiannual term structures with these data following the methodology of Houglet (1980), discussed in Chapter 10. All flower bonds and bonds callable within 10 years were excluded from the samples and the means of the bid/ask quotes were used as estimates of the transaction prices. The estimated term structures could then be utilized to evaluate any future cash flows and to compute prices of hypothetical securities.

Ingersoll considers three immunization strategies — "bullet," "barbell," and "ladder" portfolios — for 5-year planning periods. The *bullet* portfolio is one that mixes two bonds into a portfolio in which one bond has a duration just slightly greater than the planning period and one bond has a duration that is just slightly less. From the list of available bonds and their computed durations these two bonds for the bullet portfolio are easily identified. The *barbell* portfolio was a mixture of the two available bonds having the largest and smallest durations. The *ladder* portfolio was a diversified mixture of all available bonds in which as little of the portfolio value as possible was held in any single bond.[3] In this way no single bond could dominate the results. Each of the portfolios was chosen so that its duration was equal to 5 years. Ingersoll chose the portfolios both on the basis of Macaulay as well as the Fisher–Weil computations.

The performance of these immunizing portfolios is compared to the performance of three other strategies, two "naive" strategies and the maturity strategy. For "naive" strategies, the investor either holds 2-year or 10-year bonds and reinvests the proceeds in either 2- or 10-year bonds every 6 months. These "naive" strategies are thus simple short and long strategies. The maturity portfolio consists of a single bond whose maturity matches the planning period length. All coupon income is reinvested in the same bond at 6-month intervals. It is presumed that Ingersoll utilized only par bonds in his simulations.

Table 12–3 exhibits the results of these portfolio strategies for the overlapping 5-year planning periods contained in the period, 1950–1979. In this table the root mean squared differences (RMSDs) are computed as follows. Let r_{pt} be the "promised" return for the tth 5-year planning period; it is read off the estimated term structure as that rate corresponding to a 5-year maturity. Let r_{st} be the actual annual yield for the sth strategy over the same period. Then RMSD for strategy s is defined as

$$\text{RMSD} = \sqrt{\frac{1}{N} \sum_t (r_{st} - r_{pt})^2} \tag{12.1}$$

where $(r_{st} - r_{pt})$ is measured in basis points and there are N observations or planning periods. For the *index target*, the target yield to maturity is r_{pt} as measured from the term structure as estimated at the beginning of the planning period, and all durations are computed as Fisher–Weil durations using

Table 12–3. Root and Mean Squared Difference (in Basis Points) of Actual Yield and Target Yield for Six Portfolio Strategies over 5-Year Holding Periods, 1950–1979; Ingersoll (1983)

	Root Mean Squared Difference of Yields (Basis Points)	
	Index Target	Yield-to-Maturity Target
Naive strategies		
2-year bonds	58.7	65.0
10-year bonds	97.9	99.6
Maturity strategy	34.6	36.2
Duration strategies		
Bullet	35.1	32.3
Barbell	39.7	36.2
Ladder	28.7	34.8

the estimated term structures. For the yield to maturity target, the target (promised) yield is the yield on a bond having a 5-year Macaulay duration, and all durations for the duration strategies are computed as Macauly durations. Ingersoll found substantial differences between these measured target yields in some periods and has presented both results.[4]

It is clear that the maturity and duration strategies have substantially smaller RMSDs than the naive strategies. This indicates that the naive strategies are riskier for the 5-year planning period than the other strategies. Except possibly for the ladder duration strategy — using the index target — the maturity strategy appears to immunize as well as the duration strategies. Several explanations for this result have been suggested. Stochastic process risk is one of the strongest candidates for an acceptable explanation. Here it is argued that the true durations of the "immunized" portfolios were smaller than 5 years and that very likely the "true" durations of the maturity and immunized portfolios were very close together, and, therefore, performed similarly. Ingersoll considered some log-stochastic processes also and obtained even worse results. The exact nature of the process misspecification, if that is a reason for the failure of the immunized portfolios to perform better, is not clear. Sometimes it has been argued that the Houglet process doesn't smooth the data sufficiently and that it contains too much noise. Just exactly why more noise would affect the strategies differently is not clear. Ingersoll changed the Houglet procedure so as to obtain a smoother term structure and found that this reduced the RMSDs of *all* the strategies with that of the maturity strategy falling the most. This estimating procedure, nonetheless, still involved the Houglet methodology. Conceivably, an alternative estimation procedure may have produced different results. A smoother term structure may imply the same underlying stochastic process; only independent noise may be removed by smoothing, especially if the same basic methodology is employed. Estimation by a different procedure, McCulloch's for example, may imply not only a smoother curve but one consistent with a different stochastic process. No one else has found the maturity strategy to work so well, even with the CRSP data.

Efforts to explain Ingersoll's results have highlighted the problem of deriving estimates of the term structure from bid/ask price quotes. Different term structure curves that appear to explain equally well the average of the bid and ask quotes may imply quite different stochastic processes and hence different duration measures. The actual transaction prices may not be strongly related to the mean of the bid/ask quotes. There is very little published information on actual transactions prices. Attempts to infer precise performance characteristics of various portfolio strategies using the extant data on quotes may be futile.

Bierwag, Kaufman, and Toevs (1982b)

The authors of this paper (BKT) repeat some of the simulations of Bierwag, Kaufman, Toevs, and Schweitzer (1981). These simulations are developed using term structures estimated with the CRSP data, the same data that Ingersoll used. D. Babbel (1981) estimated some term structures using the CRSP data for the period 1947–1979. His results are reported later in this chapter. Bierwag, Kaufman, and Toevs (BKT) use Babbel's estimated term structures in this study. Babbel uses McCulloch's (1975) procedure for estimating the term structure. This procedure essentially accounts for yield biases induced by income taxes. Babbel used a cubic spline regression equation to fit discount functions to bond prices (the means of the bid/ask quotes).

In the BKT simulations, 5-year planning periods were assumed because the CRSP quotes do not allow for reliable estimation of the term structure for maturities beyond 13 years or so, and durations are often considerably less than maturity.

Table 12–4. Promised and Realized Returns for Alternative Portfolio Strategies; Babbel (1983)

Strategy	Average Promised Yield	Average Realized Yield	Average Excess Yield	Root Mean Squared Error	Within 5 Basis Points of Promised	Closer to Promised than Maturity	Greater than Promised
ID1	4.97	4.95	−.02	.045	77%	67%	28%
ID2	4.97	4.95	−.02	.044	72	67	44
ID3	4.97	4.95	−.02	.044	72	67	44
ID4(0.1)	4.97	4.94	−.03	.049	61	67	6
ID4(1.0)	4.97	4.91	−.06	.083	27	56	11
Maturity	4.97	4.98	+.01	.082	38	—	67

Note: Five-year planning periods. Periods start in each year, 1957–1974.

Table 12–4 exhibits the results of these simulations for the period 1957–1974. Clearly the five immunization strategies worked better than the maturity strategy. The RMSDs in basis points per annum are much smaller than those that Ingersoll obtained, indicating that the estimated term structures are very likely much smoother than the Houglet estimated curves and that the motion of the estimated structure is different. Table 12–5 shows the results as applied to the Durand data for the same period. The results are closely similar and suggest that the Durand data may be an appropriate data body for illustrating the results of simulations of this type.

Comparisons of these results with the 10-year planning period in the section on Fisher and Weil's (1971) simulations show that the precision of the immunization strategy tends to fall with shorter planning periods. This undoubtedly reflects the larger variance of short-term rates relative to long-term rates and it may also indicate that single-factor models tend to reveal any stochastic process error with greater probability in models with short holding periods. If a multifactor process is truly generating shifts in the term structure and if the correlation between short and long rates tends to be relatively small, then the precision of short-term immunization strategies will be more affected than long-term immunization strategies because the latter strategies will be far more concentrated in long-term bonds and not much affected by short-term fluctuations whereas immunization strategies over 5-year periods or less are likely to be affected by both the long- and short-term rate movements.

Brennan and Schwartz (1983)

In their study, Brennan and Schwartz also estimate term structures with the CRSP data. They estimate monthly term structures over the period December 1958 to December 1979 utilizing a quadratic spline as described in McCulloch (1971), and as described in Chapter 10 of this book. Brennan and Schwartz principally wish to compare the results from immunizing a portfolio to the results from hedging according to a two-factor model. Their work is also discussed in the next section of this chapter, on regression-related results. Their simulation of the immunization strategy for 5-year planning periods is reported here so that they can be compared with other simulation results.

Table 12–6 shows their results for the seventeen 5-year periods contained in the data body. Each immunized portfolio is a ladder portfolio constructed over the first twenty maturities. The portfolio weights are derived in the same

Table 12-5. Promised and Realized Returns for Alternative Portfolio Strategies; Durand Data

Strategy	Average Promised Yield	Average Realized Yield	Average Excess Yield	Root Mean Squared Error	Within 5 Basis Points of Promised	Closer to Promised than Maturity	Greater than Promised
ID1	4.99	4.96	−.03	.069	59%	65%	23%
ID2	4.99	4.96	−.03	.069	59	65	35
ID3	4.99	4.96	−.03	.069	59	65	35
ID4(0.1)	4.99	4.95	−.04	.077	53	58	18
ID4(1.0)	4.99	4.92	−.07	.101	35	35	18
Maturity	4.99	5.00	+.01	.089	53	—	65

Note: Five-year planning periods. Periods start in each year, 1957–1974.

Table 12–6.   Simulation of Immunization Results for
Conventional Duration Strategy, 5-Year Holding Periods;
Brennan and Schwartz (1983)

Starting Date of Holding Period	Realized Rate of Return per Annum	Promised Rate of Return per Annum	Difference (Basis Points)
Dec. 1958	.037310	.038344	− 10.34
″ 1959	.047141	.048137	− 9.96
″ 1960	.032955	.033832	− 8.77
″ 1961	.038344	.038688	− 3.44
″ 1962	.035403	.034880	5.23
″ 1963	.039375	.039546	− 1.71
″ 1964	.038516	.040059	− 15.43
″ 1965	.049130	.046475	26.55
″ 1966	.048964	.046808	21.56
″ 1967	.055490	.055973	− 4.83
″ 1968	.059806	.057896	19.09
″ 1969	.080099	.082294	− 21.95
″ 1970	.065142	.060755	43.87
″ 1971	.062801	.055168	76.33
″ 1972	.062958	.061544	14.14
″ 1973	.066073	.068078	− 20.05
″ 1974	.071134	.072649	− 15.15

Root mean squared error = 25.65 basis points.

Note: The original Brennan–Schwartz presentation was in terms of wealth ratios. The results are expressed here in rates of return per annum and basis points for comparability to other studies.

way as Ingersoll, above, had derived them. Fisher–Weil durations are used. Each simulated bond in the portfolio has an assumed coupon rate equal to the average of the coupon rates in the sample for that maturity. The root mean squared error (RMSE) is 25.65 basis points and is comparable to Ingersoll's RMSD for immunized ladder portfolios of 28.7 for 5-year planning periods covering roughly the same period (1950–1979). Unfortunately, Brennan and Schwartz do not simulate the maturity strategy. They show, however, that their results compare favorably to a more sophisticated method of hedging over 5-year planning periods, and that very little is to be gained by specifying a two-factor model.

REGRESSION STUDIES

Babbel (1983)

Babbel attempts to adjust the immunizing durations for stochastic process error as time passes. In this way information gleaned from the most recent shifts in the term structure can be incorporated into current rebalancing decisions. The Fisher–Weil stochastic process (in its original disequilibrium form) stipulates that $1 + h^*(0, t) = (1 + \lambda)[1 + h(0, t)]$, where h^* is the new term structure at time 0 and h is the old. In this process, λ is assumed to be uniformly the same for all terms to maturity, t. As a matter of realization, we can write $1 + h^*(0, t) \equiv (1 + \lambda_t)[1 + h(0, t)]$ as an identity and so compute the values of λ_t after the new structure is observed. Babbel writes $\beta_t = \lambda_t / \lambda_1$ and studies the patterns of β_t that have been observed in the past and attempts to derive stable estimates (forecasts) of them using information on shifts of the term structure in the recent past. He utilizes generalized least squares regressions and ARIMA procedures for obtaining these estimates. Having estimates (forecasts) of the β_t's, one can then modify the Fisher–Weil stochastic process so as to accommodate the embodiment of this new information. For example, let λ_1 behave as prescribed for the Fisher–Weil process; then $1 + h^*(0, t) = (1 + \lambda_1 \hat{\beta}_t)[1 + h(0, t)]$, where $\hat{\beta}_t$ is given by the estimation process. This modified process, as Babbel notes, implies a new and different single-factor stochastic process.

Babbel uses McCulloch's (1975) after-tax estimation procedure for measuring the term structure of interest rates. This procedure consists of fitting a cubic spline to the mean of the bid/ask quotes in the CRSP data. Babbel tests various strategies for 5-year planning periods taken from the study period 1947–1980. The strategies are divided into "no-look-ahead" and "look-ahead" strategies; the results are shown in Table 12-7. For the "look-ahead" strategies, the durations of the portfolios are set at values shorter than the planning period. They are set at smaller values so that at the end of the first 6 months, the portfolio duration will be exactly 4.5 years and so forth. This procedure tends to reduce the transaction costs of rebalancing but at the cost of having a duration that is a little short. In the "no-look-ahead" strategies the durations are set at their appropriate values. Babbel allows for transaction costs in the sense that all purchases are at ask prices and all sales are at bid prices. The "old duration strategy," as noted in the table, does not involve the β_t adjustments; it assumes, in effect, that $\beta_t = 1$ for all t. The "new duration" strategy involves the β_t adjustment. The "money market" fund

Table 12-7.   Portfolio Strategies over 5-Year Planning Periods, January 1947–January 1975; Babbel (1983)

	Average Return	Semistandard Error [a]
No-look-ahead strategies		
Maturity	4.837	.0163
Old duration	4.835	.0012
New duration	4.831	.0015
Look-ahead strategies		
Maturity	4.843	.0098
Old duration	4.849	.0015
New duration	4.820	.0016

a. Computed as the root mean squared error only over returns when the realized return was less than the promised return.

consists of investments in 6-month Treasury bills. The semistandard error, the most important statistic reported here, consists of the root mean squared error computed only from the cases of "failure" in which the realized return for the planning period fell below the promised or target return.

Two main conclusions can be drawn from Babbel's tests. First, the maturity strategy does not perform (immunize) as well as the duration strategies. The semistandard error in the no-look-ahead cases is over ten times larger, for example. Second, the new duration strategies do not appear to immunize any better than the older ones. Adjustments for stochastic process error do not appear to matter. Babbel notes that the maturity strategy failed to meet the target return less often than the new duration strategy, but that this was expected in a period of rising rates and, in any case, the magnitude of the failures in the new duration cases tended to be smaller.

Nelson and Schaefer (1983)

Nelson and Schaefer assume that the term structure of interest rates moves over time according to a multifactor equilibrium process that can be described in continuous time as an Ito process. In this model, they assume that K factors move through time according to a joint diffusion process. Then, given that the yield on any pure discount bond is a function of the K factors, one can describe the stochastic differentials of the bond price as a function of the derivatives of the discount rate or yield with respect to each factor. The coefficient of the random component of the bond price differential is a weighted linear function of these derivatives and bears a strong resemblance to a duration concept. These coefficients are called the *factor sensitivities* of the stochastic process. In the traditional duration model, an instantaneous shift in the term structure results in a bond price change that can be expressed as a coefficient (expressed as a function of duration) multiplied by a random shift in the term structure. In the Nelson–Schaefer framework, the coefficient that is multiplied by a random shift factor is a factor sensitivity coefficient. These factor sensitivities can be empirically estimated.

In an equilibrium context, any two securities having exactly the same factor sensitivities should have exactly the same returns and be statistically indistinguishable. From this basic tenet of modern portfolio theory, it follows that it should be possible (certainly in complete markets) to construct a portfolio of securities that will imitate or "track" the returns on some other specifically given security or portfolio. It is only necessary that the factor sensitivities of the constructed portfolio *match* those of the given security or portfolio to be tracked or imitated. Fundamentally, this is precisely what is involved in an immunization strategy. The immunizing portfolio has a duration that matches the maturity (or duration) of a zero coupon bond, and so it should track or behave like the zero coupon bond over a given planning period—whether or not a zero coupon bond exists and is traded in the market. Nelson and Schaefer estimate the factor sensitivities and attempt to show the extent of successful tracking.

They use term structures that have been estimated in two different ways. They utilize Schaefer's (1981) linear programming approach for estimating the term structure with CRSP data over the period 1925–1979. In addition, they obtain access to McCulloch's (1975) tax-adjusted estimates of the term structure using CRSP data for the period 1946–1971.

One- and two-factor models are devised. The short, 1-year rate is specified as one factor and the long, 13-year rate is specified as a second factor. The derivatives of the discount rates entering the factor sensitivity computations are estimated by regressing changes in the tth rate on changes in the short rate and separately on changes in the long rate. Factor sensitivities are then computed from an average of the estimated slope coefficients in these regressions over subperiods.

The strategies to be simulated are different from the strategies reported in previous simulations. Nelson and Schaefer want to see how well a particular strategy tracks the performance of some target security. They specify the 5-, 10-, and 15-year pure discount bonds as target bonds. The returns on these target bonds are then to be simulated by several portfolio strategies. The maturity strategy is specified as the naive strategy against which to compare the other ones. The maturity strategy consists of forming a portfolio whose average maturity is equal to that of the target security. The duration strategy consists of forming a portfolio having a Fisher–Weil duration equal to that of the target security. The short-rate strategy utilizes the short rate as a single factor (with factor sensitivities devised as noted above) and consists of forming a portfolio with a weighted average factor sensitivity equal to that of the target. A long-rate strategy is similarly designed as a single-factor model. Finally, a two-factor model is similarly designed using the short and long rates as factors.

Table 12–8 shows the results for the 5-year target bonds. The returns on the target bond and the immunizing portfolio are compared at the end of each month. The immunizing portfolio is reconstructed at the end of each month so that it will always match the relevant characteristics of the target bond. The target bond never declines in maturity as in other simulations. The conventional duration strategy invariably performs very well as measured by the standard deviation of the difference in returns and by the relatively smaller unexplained remaining target variance.[5] Except for the short-rate strategy, the differences between strategies appear to be very slight.

The two-factor model was applied only to the 10-year target bond and it performed worse than the conventional Fisher–Weil duration strategy (although probably not significantly worse). This is a startling result in view of the fact that the two-factor model of term structure motion must by definition explain the motion of the term structure better than a single-factor model. Nelson and Schaefer suggest that their two-factor model performs no better because more weight in the portfolio tends to be placed on short-term bonds the yields on which may not be well explained by the 1-year rate. This result is of considerable interest because of the apparent contradiction of intuition. Although a two-factor model may explain the evolution of observed yields better than a one-factor model, there is no assurance that a portfolio hedge based on the two factors will more closely track the target yield than a portfolio hedge based on one factor.

Brennan and Schwartz (1983)

Some of the Brennan–Schwartz simulations are noted above. Their study goes beyond these simulations, however, and involves regression estimates and a two-factor model. Although the Brennan–Schwartz model is very similar to Nelson and Schaefer's, it is more restrictive. Brennan and Schwartz

Table 12-8. Results from Tracking a Target Pure Discount Bond with Maturity of 5 Years; Nelson and Schaefer (1983)

Strategy	Mean Returns (% per Annum)			Std. Dev. of Diff.	Percentage of Target Variance Remaining[a]
	Target Bond	Port-folio	Diff.		
1930–1979					
Maturity	3.253	3.106	0.147	1.321	11.50
Duration	3.253	3.072	0.181	1.271	10.65
Short rate	3.253	3.270	−0.017	1.674	18.47
Long rate	3.253	3.097	0.156	1.277	10.75
1930–1946					
Maturity	2.648	2.137	0.511	0.780	11.36
Duration	2.648	2.187	0.461	0.757	10.71
Short rate	2.648	3.159	−0.511	0.930	16.16
Long rate	2.648	2.169	0.479	0.769	11.04
1946–1963					
Maturity	2.298	2.243	0.055	0.928	10.23
Duration	2.298	2.197	0.100	0.932	10.30
Short rate	2.298	2.343	−0.046	1.220	17.66
Long rate	2.298	2.235	0.062	0.925	10.15
1963–1979					
Maturity	4.854	4.992	−0.138	1.757	13.91
Duration	4.854	4.886	−0.033	1.658	12.39
Short rate	4.854	4.371	0.482	2.162	21.07
Long rate	4.854	4.939	−0.085	1.676	12.67

Note: Return differences are computed every 6 months. Maturity of target bond never declines over the time series, 1930–1979.

a. Computed as the variance of the difference in returns as a percentage of the variance of returns on the target bond.

also assume a short-rate factor and a long-rate factor, but they explicitly assume (1) the standard deviation of each interest rate is proportional to the interest rate level, (2) the short rate tends to regress toward the long rate, and (3) the instantaneously expected proportional change in the long rate is a linear function of the current levels of the long and short rates.[6] Given estimates of the parameters of their system, Brennan and Schwartz proceed in much the same way as Nelson and Schaefer. They match factor sensitivi-

Table 12-9.   Simulation of Immunization Results with
a Two-Factor Hedging Model, 5-Year Holding Periods;
Brennan and Schwartz (1983)

Starting Date of Holding Period	Realized Rate of Return per Annum	Promised Rate of Return per Annum	Difference (Basis Points)
Dec. 1958	.040572	.037828	27.44
" 1959	.049130	.048137	9.92
" 1960	.034880	.034182	6.98
" 1961	.038860	.039032	− 1.72
" 1962	.036445	.035924	5.20
" 1963	.039717	.040059	− 3.42
" 1964	.042611	.040742	18.68
" 1965	.046308	.047141	− 8.33
" 1966	.045472	.047141	− 16.69
" 1967	.055490	.057417	− 19.27
" 1968	.059171	.061859	− 26.88
" 1969	.078477	.079657	− 11.80
" 1970	.060597	.061859	− 12.61
" 1971	.055812	.057097	− 12.84
" 1972	.063740	.062644	10.96
" 1973	.068539	.068692	− 1.53
" 1974	.072800	.073403	− 6.03

Root mean squared error = 14.05 basis points.

Note: The original Brennan–Schwartz presentation was in terms of wealth ratios. The results are expressed here in rates of return per annum and basis points for comparability to other studies.

ties to produce a hedging strategy for a given planning period. Table 12-9 shows the result of this hedging strategy utilizing the two factors. These simulations are similar to previous simulations in which an initial investment fund is allocated and continuously rebalanced so that it matches the factor sensitivities of a pure discount bond whose maturity always matches the remaining time in a planning period. The hedging results in Table 12-9 can be compared with the results from a conventional duration hedge in Table 12-6 for the same planning period and using the same underlying CRSP data and term structure estimates. The two-factor hedge reduces the root mean squared error of the annual difference in the rate of return promised for the planning period and the realized rate by almost 50%. Although this is a substantial improvement, Brennan and Schwartz point out that the performance of the conventional duration model is most likely well within acceptable limits for practical purposes. In comparing Tables 12-9 and 12-6, we observe that the absolute difference between the realized and promised return is not always smaller for the two-factor hedge. In fact the large differences in the results for the planning periods ending in 1970 and 1971 for the duration model substantially account for the relatively larger root mean squared error. These results are mindful of Nelson and Schaefer's. Two-factor hedging simulation models need not always perform better than one-factor hedging simulation models.

Bierwag, Kaufman, and Toevs (1982b) and Bierwag and Roberts (1985)

A criticism that has nagged duration portfolio analysis almost since its inception has been the notion that immunization permits investors to earn more than a risk-free rate of return if interest rates change. Because the returns are "convex" functions of interest rates, any change in rates results in higher returns, a point developed thoroughly in Chapter 4 and well described in Figure 4-3. In an early criticism, Ingersoll, Skelton, and Weil (1978) vigorously denied that such convexities could conceivably exist in an equilibrium because these convexities allow investors to sell zero coupon bonds short (or issue them) and use the proceeds to buy the immunized portfolio. If interest rates change in any way, a sure profit is then made on a zero investment.[7] The difficulties of short-selling bonds, especially long-term bonds or of issuing zero coupon bonds in markets not accustomed to them (circa 1980) were never a serious consideration. Confining themselves to continuous stochastic processes, Ingersoll, Skelton, and Weil conclude that the durations and the underlying stochastic processes typically utilized in the formation of immunized portfolios are inconsistent with equilibrium (except when term structures are flat and shift additively).

Bierwag, Kaufman, and Toevs (1982a) introduce discrete stochastic processes of term structure motion and show that there is a very large set of equilibrium processes that one can choose in order to derive durations or sensitivity measures that are useful in devising hedges or in immunizing portfolios. Moreover, Bierwag (1987) shows that the duration measures utilized in the past are consistent with equilibrium processes. In other words, a particular duration measure may be derived from either equilibrium or disequilibrium processes; the question as to whether it is derived from an equilibrium or a disequilibrium process is irrelevant. The criticism by Ingersoll, Skelton, and Weil is without foundation in a more general context.

Appendix 12B contains a development of the discrete stochastic processes of term structure motion. For any particular single-factor stochastic process it is shown that the following time series relation is implied:

$$R_{t\tau} - R_{q\tau} = \beta_{tq}(D_t)(R_{k\tau} - R_{q\tau}), \quad t = 1, 2, \ldots, \quad \tau = 1, 2, \ldots, \quad (12.2)$$

where $R_{t\tau}$ is the return per dollar over the τth period on a zero coupon bond of maturity t, q and k ($k \neq q$) are the maturities of two reference securities, D_t is the duration of the t-period pure discount bond ($D_t = t$ for pure discount bonds) and is measured relative to an underlying equilibrium stochastic process, and where $\beta_{tq}(D_t)$, a function of D_t, measures the sensitivity of changes in $R_{t\tau} - R_{q\tau}$ to changes in $R_{k\tau} - R_{q\tau}$. Equation (12.2) is comparable to a CAPM (capital asset pricing model) equation in which $R_{k\tau}$ measures the "market" return and $R_{q\tau}$ measures the risk-free return. The function $\beta_{tq}(D_t) = 1$ when $t = k$ and $\beta_{tq}(D_t) = 0$ when $t = q$. These β's represent sensitivity factors and may be viewed very comparably to the sensitivity factors estimated by Nelson and Schaefer.

Empirically, there are a variety of ways to proceed, given equation (12.2). An assumed stochastic process implies that $\beta_{tq}(D_t)$ is a particular function. For example, if we assume an equilibrium stochastic process that gives rise to the Fisher–Weil duration, then $\beta_{tq}(D_t) = (D_t - q)/(k - q)$, where $D_t = t$ if $R_{t\tau}$ is the return on a zero coupon bond. In this case $\beta_{tq}(D_t)$ is linear in t. One can then devise tests to see if this (or some other) specification of the functional form of $\beta_{tq}(D_t)$ holds in equation (12.2). Alternatively, the stochastic process need not be specified at all. One can simply estimate the β's for each t by running a regression over the observations for a sample of time intervals. This produces estimates $\hat{\beta}_{1q}, \hat{\beta}_{2q}, \hat{\beta}_{3q}, \ldots$. One can then use these estimates as factor sensitivities analogously to Nelson and Schaefer, to construct a hedged portfolio that replicates the return on a t-period pure discount bond.

Bierwag, Kaufman, and Toevs (1982b) estimate the β's in equation (12.2) by utilizing Babbel's term structure estimates taken from the CRSP tapes for the period January 1942 to January 1980. Term structures are estimated at 6-month intervals and pure discount bonds are assumed to mature every 6 months. The returns over 6-month intervals for hypothetical zero coupon bonds were computed. Letting $q = 1$ (6 months) and $k = 17$ (8½ years), the β's were estimated for the entire sample period. Table 12–10 shows the regression results. Similar results were obtained for the regressions when alternative reference securities were specified. The estimated β's are monotonic in term to maturity; the R^2's are very high and approach unity as t approaches 17. The regression fit is worse for short-term securities than for long-term securities. To test for a structural shift in the β's, the sample period was divided

Table 12–10. Estimates of Factor Sensitivity Betas, January 1942–January 1980; Bierwag, Kaufman, and Toevs (1982)

Maturity of Pure Discount Bond (in 6-Month Periods)	Beta	t-Stat.	R^2
3	.128212	9.5471	.7462
4	.254667	11.5099	.8104
5	.359151	13.3413	.8517
6	.445533	15.6196	.8873
7	.518242	17.9153	.9119
8	.578979	20.1009	.9287
9	.631752	22.6364	.9430
10	.680159	25.9433	.9560
11	.726577	30.4686	.9677
12	.772401	36.9415	.9778
13	.818028	46.8093	.9860
14	.863527	63.4211	.9924
15	.908905	97.0940	.9967
16	.954438	198.4689	.9992
17	1.000000	–	1.0000
18	1.045820	210.5980	.9993
19	1.091949	108.5678	.9974
20	1.138466	74.5799	.9945
21	1.185617	57.5199	.9907
22	1.233372	47.0324	.9862
23	1.282139	39.6287	.9806
24	1.330902	33.8312	.9736
25	1.382813	28.9715	.9644
26	1.435478	24.7053	.9517
27	1.490237	20.9584	.9341

Note: Returns on pure discount bonds computed every 6 months using Babbel's term structure. Reference securities: a 6-month bond and a bond maturing in seventeen 6-month periods.

in half and the β's separately estimated in each half sample. Tests showed no strong evidence of a structural shift in the β's—that is, a change in the underlying stochastic process as between the two half-sample periods.

Bierwag and Roberts (1985) estimate equation (12.2) using raw data, thus eliminating some possible distortion caused by term structure smoothing. We use data on the bid/ask quotes on Canadian government bonds for the period January 1963 through December 1982. The data base consists of the average of bid and ask prices. The Macaulay durations on all bonds were computed in each month. Nine duration targets were specified: 6 months, 1 year, 2 years, ..., and 8 years. In each month a bond with a duration closest to each target duration was identified. The monthly returns on these targeted bonds were computed for each month in the sample period. The 6-month and 5-year durations were chosen as reference securities and regressions of equation (12.2) were run. Table 12–11 shows the results of these regressions. The intercept terms are not significantly different from zero as hypothesized and the R^2's are larger than 0.80 in all the regressions except for the shortest and the longest. The relatively low R^2 for the short-term regression was not unexpected. Short-term volatility and distorted shifts of the term structure at the short end have often resulted in such low R^2 regressions. The deterioration in the regression fit for long-duration securities is a mystery. Splitting the data into two half-sample periods showed that there

Table 12–11. Regression of Excess Returns per Dollar for Various Duration Categories on Excess Returns per Dollar on Reference Securities: the 6-Month Bond and the 5-Year Bond; Bierwag and Roberts (1985)

Duration in Years	Intercept Estimate	Slope Estimate (Beta)	Adjusted R^2	Durbin–Watson Statistic
1	−.1111 (−.5029)	.1284 (19.868)	.6849	2.2299
2	−.1323 (−.3597)	.4088 (30.004)	.8714	2.2418
3	−.2515 (−.4755)	.6947 (44.902)	.9044	2.0412
4	−.5337 (−.8225)	.8073 (42.544)	.8946	2.5297*
6	.5695 (.4951)	1.2705 (37.766)	.8699	2.2708
7	.7249 (.4925)	1.5960 (37.079)	.8657	2.0883
8	2.7357 (1.1698)	.6516 (9.5277)	.2965	2.1337

Note: Canadian Government Bond Data, 1963–1982. t-statistics in parentheses.
*Significant negative autocorrelation at the 1% level.

was clear evidence of a shift in the stochastic process between the periods. The regression fits were better in the second period than in the first. Monotonicity of the β's held throughout in the early period except that $\beta_4 < 1$ and $\beta_6 < 1$ when $\beta_5 = 1$ was expected. The second half of the sample period showed

Table 12–12. Regression of Excess Returns per Dollar for Various Maturity Categories on Excess Returns per Dollar on Reference Securities: the 6-Month Bond and the 5-Year Bond; Bierwag and Roberts (1985)

Maturity in Years	Intercept Estimate	Slope Estimate (Beta)	Adjusted R^2	Durbin–Watson Statistic
1	−.1484 (−.6477)	.1310 (14.2323)	.4982	2.0735
2	−.3158 (−.9385)	.4121 (30.2056)	.8171	1.9610
3	−.1115 (−.2443)	.6757 (37.3217)	.8760	2.4955
4	−.3439 (−.7642)	.7034 (38.8289)	.8817	2.1452
6	.1975 (.2783)	1.0093 (35.3830)	.8603	2.3354
7	−.5352 (−.0531)	1.3880 (34.2236)	.8522	2.5800
8	−.3865 (−.4235)	1.2173 (33.0349)	.8423	2.3239
10	.4493 (.4069)	1.2149 (27.3221)	.7893	2.3793
12	1.2604 (.9288)	1.7421 (31.7628)	.8323	2.2603
15	.5400 (.3123)	.8415 (12.0560)	.4131	1.7837
17	−.7198 (−.4168)	.7094 (10.2002)	.3356	2.0294
20	.0310 (.0165)	2.0883 (27.5425)	.7878	2.4355
25	1.0014 (.5224)	1.9548 (25.5258)	.7648	2.2681

Note: Canadian Government Bond Data, 1963–1982. *t*-statistics in parentheses.

monotonicity with $\beta_4 < 1$ and $\beta_6 > 1$ as expected but deterioration of the regression for the 8-year duration resulted. These results using raw data thus show mixed results with relatively good fits on the intermediate durations.

These regressions were compared to some similar maturity regressions. In these naive regressions we simply substitute maturity for duration and run the regressions. Table 12–12 exhibits these results. The adjusted R^2's show some strong relationships. The estimated betas are monotonic as expected for the maturities out to 7 years, but thereafter the betas show no clear pattern. We have argued that the durations in each maturity category are nearly constant across the time series so that the monotonicity of the betas actually reflects the durations as expected in equation (12.2). In these early maturity regressions the variance of the durations within each regression, although small, is larger than in the duration regressions. We would expect that the R^2's would decrease for these regressions if the duration models are in fact superior. They do not. This suggests that in the use of raw data, it may not be important to hit the durations exactly in the construction of a hedging strategy. There exists, in effect, a range on the durations such that any duration in the range may very likely work as well as another. These are speculative interpretations of very limited results, however. Much more thorough investigations are required to pin down or eliminate such hypotheses.

Gultekin and Rogalski (1984)

The Gultekin–Rogalski (GR) work is reported here because it has been cited widely and little criticism of it, although well-deserved, has been published. GR begin by using the linear approximation noted frequently in this book: $\Delta p/p \cong -D\Delta r$, where Δp is the change in the price p of a security induced by a change in the yield to maturity Δr and where D is Macaulay's modified duration (that is, the Macaulay duration divided by $1 + r$). GR argue that $\Delta p/p$ is a good measure of the rate of return per dollar over a month. Thus, one should expect the rate of return to be a linear function of duration. That $\Delta p/p$ is a measure of the rate of return is an imaginative leap. As customarily developed, $\Delta p/p$ is the instantaneous percentage change in price induced by a change in interest rates. Using $\Delta p/p$ in this equation as a measure of interest return over a time interval leads to some immediate absurdities. Suppose the bond is a pure discount bond. Then, over time $\Delta p/p$ is a measure of the rate of return if interest rates do not change. Thus, $\Delta p/p > 0$ when $\Delta r = 0$ contrary to the equation. Suppose the bond is a par bond and that interest rates do not change, then $\Delta p/p = 0$ and $\Delta r = 0$ thus implying that par bonds have a zero rate of return unless interest rates change! The point is clear. An instantaneous percentage change in price may have very little to do with the measured bond return over a time interval. GR, nonetheless, devise some very intensive (and expensive) computer routines based on this assumption.

GR propose to test the linearity of the relationship between the rate of return and duration. To do so, they specify the relationship:

$$\tilde{r}_\tau(m) = \tilde{\gamma}1_\tau + \tilde{\gamma}2_\tau Dk_{\tau-1}(m) + \tilde{\gamma}3_\tau Dk_{\tau-1}^2(m) + \tilde{\gamma}4_\tau C_\tau(m) + \tilde{e}_\tau(m), \qquad (12.3)$$

where $\tilde{r}_\tau(m)$ is the return on a security with maturity m during time interval τ, $Dk_{\tau-1}(m)$ is the duration corresponding to the kth stochastic process at date $\tau-1$ on the security with maturity m, $Dk_{\tau-1}^2(m)$ is that duration squared, and $C_\tau(m)$ is the coupon rate on that security. The coefficients $\tilde{\gamma}1_\tau$, $\tilde{\gamma}2_\tau$, $\tilde{\gamma}3_\tau$, and $\tilde{\gamma}4_\tau$ are free to vary with τ but not with maturity m. Finally $\tilde{e}_\tau(m)$ is the usual homoskedastic disturbance term. Over any month τ, one can then run the regression for bonds having different maturities. Over time one can then study the evolution of the estimated coefficients. GR hypothesize that $\tilde{\gamma}3_\tau = \tilde{\gamma}4_\tau = 0$, among other things.

As an ad hoc equation not derived from fundamental notions of behavior or equilibrium, the GR equation is obviously subject to the most severe criticisms. Justification of the measurement of $\tilde{r}_\tau(m)$ as the rate of return as derived from the approximation equation cannot be accomplished without admitting the noted absurdities. As already noted in the linear equations involving the β's, linearity of the return in duration is not a necessary aspect of duration analysis in or out of equilibrium. The coefficient $\tilde{\gamma}2_\tau$ has the interpretation of being a general change in interest rates and is assumed to be the same for all bonds regardless of maturity m. Yet, as noted in many studies [such as Yawitz and Marshall (1981) and Nelson and Schaefer (1983)] the change in rates tends to be larger for short-term securities than for long-term securities. Thus $\tilde{\gamma}2_\tau$ is a function implicitly of $Dk_{\tau-1}(m)$ and a major nonlinearity in the relationship is implied because replacing $\tilde{\gamma}2_\tau$ with a function of $Dk_{\tau-1}(m)$ must produce a nonlinearity. Moreover, this misspecification implies that the least squares estimates of other coefficients are biased and that the standard errors are biased downward so that no sensible tests can be conducted using these regression results. Further criticism of GR is contained in Bierwag, Kaufman, Latta, and Roberts (1987).

APPENDIX 12A
IMMUNIZATION: SINGLE-FACTOR
STOCHASTIC PROCESSES

As noted in the text, the immunization theorems of part II can be modified so as to be consistent with nonflat term structures that may randomly shift through time as single-factor stochastic processes. In this appendix, it is shown that the immunization results of Part II still hold in much the same form. In this more general context, the immunization condition may be stated as

Given a known single-factor stochastic process, designated as process p, *and a planning period of length* q, *a portfolio of fixed income securities is immunized if it is chosen so that*

$$D_p = q,$$

where D_p *is the portfolio duration corresponding to process* p.

To show this result, we assume as in Chapter 11 that the term structure shifts from $h(0, t)$ to $h^*(0, t)$, $t = 1, 2, 3, \ldots$, instantly after a portfolio has been formed. Let λ be a single random factor so that we can write

$$h^*(0, t) = f(t, \lambda) \qquad (12A.1)$$

with the property that $f(t, 0) = h(0, t)$. The functional form f takes on many possible forms for different processes. In general we assume that f and f' are continuous in t, where f' is the partial derivative with respect to λ. If it is an additive stochastic process, for example, we might simply write $f(t, \lambda) = h(0, t) + \lambda$, and if it's Fisher–Weil we might write $f(t, \lambda) = (1 + \lambda) \times [1 + h(0, t)] - 1$, and so forth. Let the successive cash flows for a chosen portfolio be represented as $F_1, F_2, F_3, \ldots$. The initial value of the portfolio is then

$$W = \sum_{t=1} F_t [1 + h(0, t)]^{-t}. \qquad (12A.2)$$

Immediately after the investment, the term structure shifts and its value becomes

$$W(\lambda) = \sum_{t=1} F_t [1 + f(t, \lambda)]^{-t}. \qquad (12A.3)$$

If the term structure does not subsequently shift, at date q the value of the accumulated investment becomes

$$W_q(\lambda) = [1 + f(q, \lambda)]^q \sum_{t=1} F_t [1 + f(t, \lambda)]^{-t}. \qquad (12A.4)$$

Taking the derivative with respect to λ, we get

$$W_q'(\lambda) = q[1 + f(q, \lambda)]^{q-1} f(q, \lambda) \sum_{t=1} F_t [1 + f(t, \lambda)]^{-t}$$
$$- [1 + f(q, \lambda)]^q \sum_{t=1} t F_t [1 + f(t, \lambda)]^{-t-1} f'(t, \lambda). \qquad (12A.5)$$

Letting $\lambda = 0$, equation (12A.5) reduces to

$$W_q'(0) = q[1 + h(0,q)]^{q-1} f'(q,0) W$$
$$- [1 + h(0,q)]^q \sum_{t=1} t F_t f'(t,0)[1 + h(0,t)]^{-t-1} \qquad (12A.6)$$

$$= [1 + h(0,q)]^q \left\{ \frac{q f'(q,0)}{1 + h(0,q)} - \sum_{t=1} \frac{F_t t f'(t,0)[1 + h(0,t)]^{-t-1}}{W} \right\}.$$

The duration corresponding to the stochastic process is then given implicitly by

$$\frac{D f'(D,0)}{1 + h(0,D)} = \sum \cdot \frac{F_t[1 + h(0,t)]^{-t}}{W} \left(\frac{t f'(t,0)}{1 + h(0,t)} \right). \qquad (12A.7)$$

Substitution into (12A.7) of some of the various forms of f used in Appendix 10A produces the same durations derived there. Equation (12A.6) can now be written as

$$W_q'(0) = [1 + h(0,q)]^q \left(\frac{q f'(q,0)}{1 + h(0,q)} - \frac{D f'(D,0)}{1 + h(0,D)} \right). \qquad (12A.8)$$

It is now clear that $W_q'(0) = 0$ if $D = q$.

Thus, if the stochastic process, $f(t,\lambda)$, is known, then the duration can be calculated as in (12A.7) and the investor may choose bonds so that $D = q$ and $W_q'(0) = 0$. In this way a necessary condition for immunization is established.[8] Small shifts in the term structure (that is, small changes in λ) result in only small departures of the terminal wealth accumulation from what it would have been had there been no shifts at all.

If the stochastic process is not known, then there is no way to calculate the corresponding duration. If one chooses the wrong stochastic process and uses the corresponding duration, there can be no assurance that $W_q'(0) = 0$. In this case, the wealth accumulation is subject to *stochastic process risk*. Bierwag, Kaufman, and Toevs (1983) have shown that the stochastic process risk can be substantial in some examples.

APPENDIX 12B
DISCRETE SINGLE-FACTOR EQUILIBRIUM MODELS

Bierwag, Kaufman, and Toevs (1982a) have shown that there is a large class of discrete single-factor equilibrium models. These are models in which one can identify a random factor λ such that $W_q(\lambda)$ is a linear function of λ. In this way, no "convexities" obtain and an equilibrium in which there are no opportunities for risk-free arbitrage results. These models correspond to stochastic processes having well-defined durations that can be utilized in the usual way. Bierwag (1987) has shown that a given duration measure can be derived from more than one stochastic process. For example, the Fisher–Weil duration D_{FW} which we know to be derived from "convex" processes — processes for which $W_q''(\lambda) > 0$ — can *also* be derived from an equilibrium stochastic process for which $W_q(\lambda)$ is linear. The Ingersoll–Skelton–Weil criticism, noted in the text, that the usual durations correspond only to "convex" disequilibrium processes is without foundation. In this appendix, it is shown how these single-factor equilibrium models can be constructed.

Let $P(0, t)$ be the current price (at time 0) of \$1.00 to be received at date t in the future. That is, $P(0, t)$ is the price of a pure discount bond (or zero coupon bond) paying \$1.00 in t periods. This pure discount bond does not promise any cash flows before or after date t. One period from now the price of the bond is assumed to move to $P_s(1, t)$ if state s occurs. Thus, $P_s(1, t)$ is the price in state s at time period 1 of receiving \$1.00 at date t. If $t = 1$, then by definition $P_s(1, 1) = 1$ because this is then the price of a bond at its maturity date and it must be the same regardless of state s, assuming there is no default.

The current forward price of a bond spanning the $(1, t)$ time interval can be expressed as $P(1, t) = P(0, t)/P(0, 1)$. The forward price, $P(1, t)$, must be the equilibrium price of the initial t-period bond one period from now in a world of certainty and equilibrium. To show this, we note that in this world of certainty, there are two ways, at least, in which an investment of $P(0, t)$ dollars now, can accumulate to \$1.00 t periods from now. One obvious way is to buy initially the t-period bond and to hold it for t periods. Another way is to buy X one-period bonds for which we now pay $X \cdot P(0, 1) = P(0, t)$ dollars. We choose X so that $X \cdot P(0, 1) = P(0, t)$ because in this way we initially invest the same number of dollars in pursuing either strategy. After one period we then have X dollars because each of these one-period bonds pays \$1.00 after one period. If $P(1, t)$ is the price one period from now of \$1.00 to be received at time t, then $X = P(1, t)$ in equilibrium under certainty. If $X > P(1, t)$, then $X/P(1, t)$ is greater than unity and is the number of dollars one can accumulate at time t by buying the one-period bond and reinvesting; and this amount exceeds the dollar earned by buying the t-period bond and holding it. Similarly, if $X < P(1, t)$, then $X/P(1, t)$ is less than unity and is the number of dollars one can accumulate at time t by buying the one-period bond and reinvesting; and this amount is less than the dollar earned by buying the t-period bond and holding it. Thus, in equilibrium $X \cdot P(0, 1) = P(0, t)$ or $X = P(1, t) = P(0, t)/(0, 1)$ for otherwise one strategy is favored over the other by all investors.

No loss of generality results if we assume that

$$P_s(1, t) = P(1, t) + g(s, t), \quad t = 1, 2, \ldots, \quad s = 1, 2, \ldots, \quad (12\text{B}.1)$$

so that $g(s, t)$ represents the extent of departure of next period's price $P_s(1, t)$ from the currently computable forward price $P(1, t)$. Of course, $g(s, 1) = 0$ in the absence of default risk. Dividing both sides of (12B.1) by $P(0, t)$ gives us the return per dollar over one period from investing $P(0, t)$ dollars initially in the t-period bond. Thus, we may write

$$
\begin{aligned}
R_s(1, t) &= P(1, t)/P(0, t) + g(s, t)/P(0, t) \\
&= 1/P(0, 1) + g(s, t)/P(0, t) \quad\quad\quad (12\text{B}.2) \\
&= R_F + g(s, t)/P(0, t), \quad t = 1, 2, \ldots,
\end{aligned}
$$

where R_F is the risk-free return per dollar over the period as is easily seen because the one-period bond is risk-free over one period in the absence of default risk.

Assuming complete markets and two states, $s = 1, 2$, it follows that the return per dollar over one period on any t-period bond can be expressed as the return per dollar from a portfolio containing two different bonds called reference bonds. Let v and m be the maturities of two possible reference bonds. It follows that

$$
\begin{aligned}
R_s(1, t) &= \beta_{vt} R_s(1, v) + (1 - \beta_{vt}) R_s(1, m) \\
&= R_s(1, m) + \beta_{vt}[R_s(1, v) - R_s(1, m)],
\end{aligned}
\quad (12\text{B}.3)
$$

where β_{vt} is the proportion of the initial investment allocated to the reference bond with maturity v.

Now, consider an initial investment in a portfolio, $\alpha_1, \alpha_2, \ldots, \alpha_t, \ldots,$ where α_t is the proportion invested in a t-period bond. The return per dollar from this portfolio can then be expressed as

$$R_s(\alpha) = \sum_t \alpha_t R_s(1, t) = R_s(1, m) + \left(\sum_t \beta_{vt} \alpha_t \right)[R_s(1, v) - R_s(1, m)]. \quad (12\text{B}.4)$$

Now, suppose that the return per dollar on this portfolio is the same as that on a τ-period bond. It must follow that

$$\sum_t \beta_{vt} \alpha_t = \beta_{v\tau}. \quad (12\text{B}.5)$$

A notion of duration can be derived from this equation. The portfolio behaves like a single pure discount bond of maturity τ. It is natural to suppose that the portfolio has a duration of τ. If β_{vt} is a monotonic function of t, then every pure discount bond is unique; no two such bonds can have the same return per dollar. Under this condition of monotonicity, the maturity of every pure discount bond can be utilized as a unique indicator of its beta, and by relating the notion of duration to maturity in this way, the duration of a portfolio indicates the zero coupon bond that is equivalent. Thus, equation (12B.5) provides an implicit definition of duration for a portfolio. It is possible that the left-hand side of (12B.5) may satisfy

$$\beta_{v\tau} < \sum_t \beta_{vt}\alpha_t < \beta_{v,\tau+1} \qquad (12B.6)$$

for some τ if β_{vt} is monotonic increasing in t. In this case, the return on the portfolio is equivalent to that which could be earned on some portfolio of pure discount bonds having maturities τ and $\tau+1$. In general, the return on any portfolio is equivalent to the return on either some pure discount bond or on some portfolio of two different pure discount bonds.

Explicit definitions of duration can be derived from explicit definitions of $g(s, t)$, which defines the stochastic process. For example, suppose $g(s, t) = k_s(t-1)P(0, t)$, where k_s is some parameter that is a function of state s.[9] Then $g(s, 1) = 0$ as required. Using (12B.3) and (12B.2), one can then define β_{vt} as

$$\beta_{vt} = \frac{R_s(1, t) - R_s(1, m)}{R_s(1, v) - R_s(1, m)} = \frac{k_s(t-1) - k_s(m-1)}{k_s(v-1) - k_s(m-1)}$$

$$= \frac{t-m}{v-m}, \quad t > 0, \qquad (12B.7)$$

which is a linear function of t. Substitution of this result in (12B.5) implies

$$\sum_t \alpha_t \frac{t-m}{v-m} = \frac{\tau-m}{v-m}, \qquad (12B.8)$$

or

$$\sum_t \alpha_t t = \tau. \qquad (12B.9)$$

If the portfolio $(\alpha_1, \alpha_2, ..., \alpha_t, ...)$ implies the cash flows $(F_1, F_2, ..., F_t, ...)$, then

$$\alpha_t = \frac{F_t P(0, t)}{V}, \qquad (12B.10)$$

where V is the value of the bond. If we define $P(0, t) = [1 + h(0, t)]^{-t}$, then in (12B.9) we have

$$\sum_t F_t t [1 + h(0, t)]^{-t}/V = \tau. \qquad (12B.11)$$

The expression on the left-hand side is the Fisher–Weil duration measure. Going back to (12B.1), we can now state that

$$P_s(1, t) = P(1, t) + k_s(t - 1)P(0, t), \quad t = 1, 2, \ldots, \qquad (12B.12)$$

is an equilibrium stochastic process giving rise to the Fisher–Weil duration measure. One may similarly define $g(s, t)$ so that other duration measures, like those in Chapter 11, can be derived as equilibrium durations.

When $s = 1, 2$, only one of two possibly different realizations of the returns can occur. In Bierwag, Kaufman, and Toevs (1982a), an incomplete market version is developed in which an infinitely large set of possible returns can occur, but yet the coefficient β_{vt} in (12B.3) remains unaffected and the duration measures remain the same. Only a slight modification of the stochastic process is necessary for this result.

A version of (12B.3) is easily devised in the usual way for testing purposes. A nonsystematic error term is added to the equation under the assumption that it represents "noise" or measurement error that is uncorrelated with the difference in return on the reference securities.

NOTES

1. Durand's (1942) initial paper estimates these yields only for the 1900–1942 period. Later yield estimates employing the same Durand procedures are kept up to date by Scudder, Stevens, and Clark, Inc., New York, and are published in the *Economic Almanac, Business Fact Book* published by the National Industrial Conference Board (New York: Macmillan).
2. These data are collected by the Center for Research on Security Prices (CRSP) at the University of Chicago. The data consist of the bid and asked quotations of a single government bond dealer on marketable U.S. Treasury securities for the last Friday of each month since 1925.
3. Ingersoll chooses the proportion w_i going into bond i by minimizing $\sum w_i^2$ subject to $\sum w_i = 1$ and to $\sum w_i D_i = 5$ years with $w_i > 0$.
4. There are two other columns that would also have been interesting to look at. Using the yield-to-maturity target, one could have computed the results for cases in which the Fisher–Weil durations were used, and using the index target, one could have computed the results for cases in which Macaulay durations were used.
5. Very similar results occurred when tracking the 10- and 15-year bonds.
6. An implicit restrictive component in the Nelson–Schaefer work is a constant variance-covariance matrix of the factors. Brennan and Schwartz make their assumptions explicit and attempt to estimate the parameters of the factor process.
7. There is ample evidence that many analysts accept the notion that these convexities actually exist — apart from the equilibrium or disequilibrium attributions.

Investment bankers and others have been attempting to devise ways to exploit them; see, for example, Klotz (1985).

8. If $W_q''(0) > 0$, then $D = q$ is a necessary and sufficient condition for local immunization. If $W_q''(\lambda) > 0$ for all λ and if $W_q'(0) = 0$ at $D = q$ then $D = q$ is a necessary and sufficient condition for global immunization.

9. In an equilibrium in which no single bond dominates another by having a higher return in both states, $k_1 k_2 < 0$.

REFERENCES

Babbel, David. 1983. "Duration and the Term Structure of Interest Rate Volatility." In *Innovations in Bond Portfolio Management,* edited by G. Kaufman, G. Bierwag, and A. Toevs (Greenwich, Conn.: JAI Press), pp. 239–65.

Bierwag, Gerald O. 1987. "Bond Returns, Discrete Stochastic Processes, and Duration." *Journal of Financial Research* (Autumn).

Bierwag, Gerald O., George G. Kaufman, Robert Schweitzer, and Alden Toevs. 1981. "The Art of Risk Management in Bond Portfolios." *Journal of Portfolio Management* (Spring): 27–36.

Bierwag, Gerald O., George G. Kaufman, and Alden Toevs. 1982a. "Single-Factor Duration Models in a Discrete General Equilibrium Framework." *Journal of Finance* (May): 325–38, reprinted in *Innovations in Bond Portfolio Management,* edited by G. Kaufman, G. Bierwag, and A. Toevs (Greenwich, Conn.: JAI Press, 1983).

———. 1982b. "Empirical Tests of Alternative Single Factor Duration Models." Working Paper, presented at conference of Western Finance Association, Portland, Ore., June.

———. 1983. "Bond Portfolio Immunization and Stochastic Process Risk." *Journal of Bank Research* (Winter).

Bierwag, Gerald O., and Gordon Roberts. 1985. "Single Factor Duration Models: Canadian Tests." Working Paper.

Bierwag, Gerald O., George G. Kaufman, Cynthia M. Latta, and Gordon S. Roberts. 1987. "Usefulness of Duration in Bond Portfolio Management: Response to Critics." *Journal of Portfolio Management* (Winter).

Brennan, Michael J., and Eduardo S. Schwartz. 1983. "Duration, Bond Pricing, and Portfolio Management." In *Innovations in Bond Portfolio Management,* edited by G. Kaufman, G. Bierwag, and A. Toevs (Greenwich, Conn.: JAI Press), pp. 3–36.

Durand, David. 1942. *Basic Yields of Corporate Bonds 1900–42.* National Bureau of Economic Research.

Fisher, Lawrence, and Roman Weil. 1971. "Coping with Risk of Interest Rate Fluctuations: Returns to Bondholders from Naive and Optimal Strategies." *Journal of Business 4,* (October): 408–31.

Gultekin, B., and R. Rogalski. 1984. "Alternative Duration Specifications and the Measurement of Basis Risk: Empirical Tests." *Journal of Business* (April): 243–62.

Ingersoll, Jonathan. 1983. "Is Immunization Feasible? Evidence from the CRSP Data." In *Innovations in Bond Portfolio Management,* edited by G. Kaufman, G. Bierwag, and A. Toevs (Greenwich, Conn.: JAI Press), pp. 163–82.

Ingersoll, Jonathan, Jeffrey Skelton, and Roman Weil. 1978. "Duration Forty Years Later." *Journal of Financial and Quantitative Analysis* (November).

Houglet, M.X. 1980. "Estimates of the Term Structure of Interest Rates for Non-Homogeneous Bonds." Unpublished Doctoral Dissertation, University of California, Berkeley.

Klotz, Richard G. 1985. "Convexity of Fixed-Income Securities." Bond Portfolio Analysis Group, Salomon Brothers, October.

McCulloch, J. Huston. 1975. "The Tax-Adjusted Yield Curve." *Journal of Finance 30,* no. 3 (June): 811–30.

Nelson, Jeffrey, and Stephen Schaefer. 1983. "The Dynamics of the Term Structure and Alternative Portfolio Immunization Strategies." In *Innovations in Bond Portfolio Management,* edited by G. Kaufman, G. Bierwag, and A. Toevs (Greenwich, Conn.: JAI Press), pp. 239–65.

Schaefer, S.M. 1981. "Measuring a Tax Specific Term Structure of Interest Rates in the Market for British Government Securities," *Economic Journal 91* (June): 415–38.

Yawitz, J., and W. Marshall. 1981. "The Shortcomings of Duration as a Risk Measure for Bonds." *Journal of Financial Reseasrch* (Summer): 91–101.

V NON–INTEREST RATE RISK

13 SOME CAVEATS ON CALLABILITY AND CREDIT RISK

All of the fixed-income securities considered so far in this volume have been option and default-free securities. However, investment fund managers often place callable securities or nongovernment securities into fixed-income portfolios. The interest rate sensitivity of the value of these funds is not the same as that of option and default-free securities. If immunization or other duration-based strategies are undertaken, a prudent investment manager will attempt to account for any distortion in the interest rate sensitivity that may stem from these alternative sources of interest rate risk. In this chapter, we review some of the consequences of not considering these sources of risk.

CALLABLE BONDS

Price Behavior

Most corporate bonds as well as many U.S. Treasury bonds contain callability provisions. Under these provisions the issuer may redeem or call bonds at prespecified prices after they have been outstanding for a prespecified number of years. Callability provisions enable issuers to retire such debt prior to maturity. An issuer may wish to retire debt early for several reasons. If interest rates decrease, it may be possible thereby to replace outstanding debt with new debt having lower interest costs. The issuer may wish in the future also to eliminate some covenants in the bond indenture which, although currently protecting the credit quality of the debt in the interest of the bondholders or providing other benefits, may not give sufficient overall management flexibility in future time periods to operate in the best interest of all concerned parties. In the future, the issuing entity may also wish to reorganize its capital structure because of mergers or for other reasons.

Callability provisions are in the form of an option to the issuer. That is, the issuer may, if eligible to do so, choose either to call the debt or not to call it. This *call option* has value to the issuer and he/she may be willing to pay for it. For example, if $P(c, n)$ is the price of a noncallable bond with maturity n and coupon rate c, and if $C(c, n, m)$ is the value of this same bond if callable after m years ($m < n$), then we'd expect $P(c, n) - C(c, n, m) > 0$. In other words, the yield must be higher on the callable bond in order to discount exactly the same income stream back to the lower value $C(c, n, m)$. This higher yield represents the extra interest cost paid by the issuer to acquire the call option. From another point of view, the issuer receives $C(c, n, m)$ dollars when issuing the callable bond rather than the larger amount $P(c, n)$ even though the issuer is liable for the same outgo stream. Moreover, investors must be compensated for the enhanced uncertainty of their holdings of callable bonds. That is another reason why the yield to maturity tends to be higher on callable bonds, ceteris paribus.

In order to illustrate how callability may affect the interest rate sensitivity of such a bond, let us make the strong assumption that the currently observed yields to maturity are expected to be exactly the same at all future dates. We can weaken this assumption later in order to be more realistic. Suppose a bond is callable at par, as is the case with U.S. Treasury securities. This means that the issuer can call the bonds at a prespecified date (or later) and so redeem them at the par value. Assume that the earliest call date is m years in the future where $m < n$, the years to maturity. If interest rates fall sufficiently, the issuer will plan to call the bonds for 100 (100% of face value—that is, par) at time m and will plan to acquire the funds to do so by issuing new debt. It is advantageous to the issuer to do this if the value of the new debt is less than the present value of the remaining income stream on the callable bond. For example, suppose the callable bonds have the income stream

($50, $1,050)

remaining to be paid, where $50 is paid in 6 months and $1,050 is paid in 1 year. This is equivalent to the income stream on a 10% 1-year par bond. If the bond is currently callable and interest rates are at 8%, say, the issuer can issue a new 1-year par bond for $1,000, thus obligating itself to the income stream

($40, $1,040)

and use the $1,000 to redeem (call) the old bonds. Clearly, the only effect of doing this is to replace the old income stream by the new one. The difference between the income streams is

($10, $10).

At 8 percent, the value of this income stream is $18.86, and this is a measure of the savings in interest costs. If the initial bond were not callable, its value would have been

$$\frac{50}{1.04} + \frac{1,050}{(1.04)^2} = \$1,018.86,$$

which is equivalent to the cost of the new bond plus the cost savings. Thus, an issuer always has an incentive to call a bond if the value of the noncallable equivalent security at the current yield to maturity is a premium bond. The issuer has no incentive to call the bond if the noncallable equivalent security is a discount bond. If (1) the call date has not been reached, (2) the callable bond currently sells at a discount, and if (3) the current yield to maturity is expected to remain the same in the future, then the bond will not be called. Such a bond behaves like a noncallable bond. If (1) the call date has not yet been reached, (2) the callable bond currently sells at a premium, and if (3) the current yield to maturity is expected to remain the same in the future, then most certainly the bond will be called. Such a bond behaves like a noncallable bond of maturity m. Consequently, under the assumption that the current yield to maturity will be constant through time, callable bonds are of two types — those that will be called at date m and those that will not. That is, they are bonds that are priced in the market as though they either have a maturity date m (the earliest call date) or maturity n. The price behavior of such bonds as a function of the yield to maturity is illustrated in Figure 13-1. When $r > r_0$, the bond is a discount bond that behaves as though its maturity were m. The curve in Figure 13-1 has a kink at r_0 reflecting the shift in effective maturities at r_0. When $r > r_0$ small changes in r have a bigger percentage change in price than when $r < r_0$. In other words, the duration of the callable bond abruptly shifts at r_0. Figure 13-2 illustrates this duration shift. When $r > r_0$, duration as a function of the interest rate is described by the curve $D(r, n)$, whereas when $r < r_0$, duration as a function of the interest rate is described by the curve $D(r, m)$. The discontinuity at r_0 reflects the kink in the price–yield relationship in Figure 13-1. The curves $D(r, n)$ and $D(r, m)$ represent duration as inverse functions of the yield to maturity, as shown in Figure 3-7 of Chapter 3.

The duration–yield relationship is drawn in Figure 13-2 under the assumption that the current yield to maturity will remain constant into the

Figure 13–1. Price-Yield Relationship for Callable Bonds

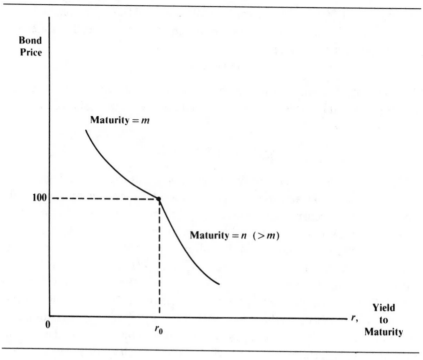

future. If this is not the case, we may expect that the discontinuity in Figure 13-2 is likely to be smoothed out to look more like the curve in Figure 3-3. If interest rates are above r_0, but close to r_0, investors may anticipate a drop in rates or they may regard a drop in rates as more probable. The bond then begins to behave as though its maturity were shortened. If interest rates are below r_0, but close to r_0, investors may anticipate an increase in rates or they may regard an increase as more probable. The bond then begins to behave as though its maturity were lengthened beyond the call date. These anticipatory or probabilistic features may be regarded as smoothing out the curve in Figure 13-2.

Some Implications

Recent experiences of some investment managers in the period January 1986 to May 1986 reveal some of the consequences of ignoring the duration shift on callable bonds. In this period, interest rates dropped precipitously. Using the formula

Figure 13-2. Duration–Yield Relationship for Callable Bonds: Fixed Expectations

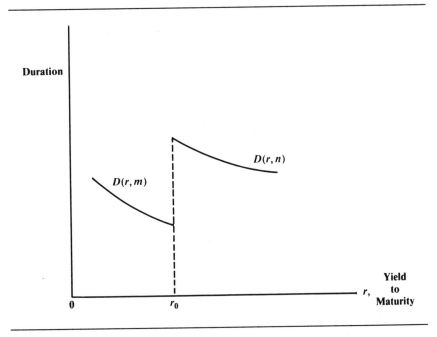

$$\frac{\Delta p}{p} \cong -D\Delta r, \qquad (13.1)$$

where D is duration and Δr is the change in interest rates, we observe that large percentage increases in a bond price correspond to large decreases in interest rates.[1] However, if the duration decreases as interest rates fall, the percentage increase in prices will not be as large. This is precisely what happened to many callable bonds in this 1986 period. In Figure 13-3, as rates dropped to critical levels, near but above r_0, the durations dropped rapidly also. Now, suppose an investment manager, seeking to lock in the high rates of 1983 or so, had failed to account for the duration shift that could occur on callable bonds, and had instead assumed their values behaved like noncallable bonds. As interest rates decreased, the percentage increase in bond prices represented insufficient increments to the bond portfolio values to offset the reduced future earnings from reinvesting at new lower rates. There was no way that the high rates of 1983 could then be locked in over 5-year planning periods or so. In effect, these investment managers had assigned to callable bonds durations that were too large. The durations of their port-

Figure 13–3. Duration–Yield Relationship for Callable Bonds: Variable Expectations

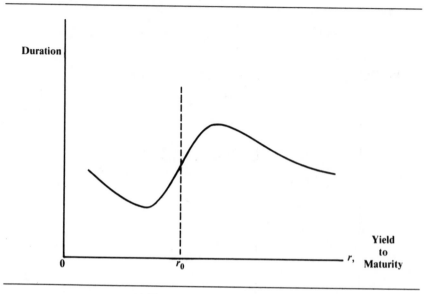

folios were, in fact, too short in order to immunize over such planning periods. The realized rates of return over such planning periods are thus likely to be less than many investment managers had projected for their clients.

A solution, akin to killing the messenger who brings bad news, consists of abandoning duration-based models and of utilizing an alternative investment strategy. A prudent use of duration-based models would require that the callability option either be evaluated or avoided. Some investment managers have avoided the issue of callability by investing only in noncallables (even if they are Treasury of Federal Agency securities) and/or investing in very low coupon discount bonds. These latter bonds, although they may be callable, must appreciate by very large amounts before their values are likely to be affected by callability provisions. Some successful managers during the 1986 period have emphasized that passive fixed-income investment management doesn't mean that monitoring is not required (Jansson 1986). Continued monitoring of callable bonds should reveal the extent to which current interest rates are in or near the critical region of Figure 13–3.

The extent to which one may invest in callable bonds without suffering the consequences of precipitous decreases in interest rates also depends on an investor's ability to forecast the direction of change of interest rates and upon the general investment environment. A reliance upon forecasting would clearly be a reliance upon the performance of an active strategy so that in the extreme there would be no reason to immunize. On the other hand, in an environment of accelerating inflation, there may be a general well-founded belief that interest rates will rise and that, therefore, interest rates are likely to remain above r_0 so that callability may be of little concern. As inflation or its rate of change subsides or is not expected to be a strong influence on interest rates, then callability becomes a more important feature to ponder. As callability becomes more important in the management of a portfolio — because rates are either in the vicinity of r_0 or expected to be — managers can consider swapping the callables for bonds having durations perceived to be more stable.

DEFAULT RISK

Unlike U.S. Treasury securities, corporate securities and other privately issued securities are subject to default or credit risk. Portfolio investment managers are often attracted to these default-prone securities because of the higher yields offered by them. However, investing in these securities involves many dangers. These are not securities to be managed in a strictly passive mode; there are many nonsystematic factors that can affect realized returns. The activities and financial affairs of each issuer can affect the realized return on its securities. Some monitoring of an issuer's activities and financial affairs thus may be necessary in order to move in and out of its securities on a timely basis. Monitoring only the durations of these securities may provide not only misleading information but insufficient information for prudent management. Moreover, given that the fluctuations in the returns on default-prone securities may be nonsystematic (that is, they stem from the issuer's activities and not from general market conditions), an investment manager may be well advised to undertake some diversification to reduce the non-systematic risk.

Defaults on corporate securities, although acknowledged to be rare, do occur and they can obviously affect realized returns. Although diversification can reduce default risk, this risk may still be very real and material. For example, suppose an investment fund is allocated evenly to the bonds of 100 corporations. Let $1,000,000 be invested in each of these 100 issues. Further, suppose the returns are to average 10% per annum. Now, suppose just one of the corporations goes bankrupt, so that there is a $1,000,000 loss. That loss represents 1% of the entire investment fund as well as a decline in earnings of 10 basis points in virtually every future year of the fund. This is the result if there is a total loss stemming from a single bankruptcy, but other losses may also result from corporate reorganizations and from reduced or postponed payments of interest and principal.

In modern portfolio theory, the risk of a loss that cannot be reasonably diversified away must involve a premium that is added to a risk-free rate of return on each security to compensate for such losses on the average; and those securities having a greater probability of default must pay a larger premium. Investment managers who are attracted to corporate and other private issues must also acknowedge a greater risk as well as the need to engage in a program of diversification or monitoring. Diversification may be necessary in order that the additional yield premium just cover expected losses; otherwise the premium may be insufficient or even unrealized. Monitoring may be a substitute for diversification and may allow the investor to avoid losses by timely movements in and out of the markets. The default premium can be expected to be close to the average monitoring costs. Over time, the investor's return, after all these costs, can be expected to be no larger than the risk-free return (assuming other risks are zero). It is understandable that investment managers would be attracted to high-yielding corporate securities and that they would acknowledge and perhaps accept or attempt to manage the attendent risks, but it is irresponsible to ignore them.

Fitting default-prone securities into a duration-based investment program may involve several problems. First, the computation of the appropriate durations may pose a problem. The easiest duration to compute is the Macaulay duration utilizing the promised future cash flows and the yield to maturity, but this may not be appropriate. The promised cash flows may not materialize because of default losses and the yield to maturity may not be consequently realized either. Adjustments for these default losses are possible in principle. If F_t is the promised cash flow at time t, one can replace it by an expected cash flow F_t^* which adjusts for expected default losses. We would expect that normally $F_t^* < F_t$ where $F_t - F_t^*$ is the default loss; but, in some cases a bond issue may be liquidated (perhaps by court order) so that we get the payoff $F_N^* > F_t$, but $F_t^* = 0$ for $t > N$. After accounting for expected default losses, we should have a risk-free rate of return (assuming no other risks). Letting r_F be the risk-free rate and r ($> r_F$) be the actual yield to maturity including the risk premium, discounting the adjusted flows at the adjusted rates should be equivalent to discounting the promised flows at the promised yield to maturity. Thus, if P is the price of such a security, we can write

$$P = \sum_t F_t^*(1+r_F)^{-t} = \sum_t F_t(1+r)^{-t}. \tag{13.2}$$

Two durations can now be calculated: one using F_t^* and r_F and the other using F_t and r. There is no reason to expect the durations to be equivalent. Which duration should be used in a duration-based investment program? That is a dubious, unanswered, and largely an unaddressed question. Duration adjusted for default may be the most appropriate from a long-term perspective in which an investment program is repeated many times. The unadjusted duration may be the most appropriate from a short-term perspective, but any default losses may then affect the degree of interest rate risk as well. In general, one would guess than an unknown interaction between default and interest rate risk is avoided by using the adjusted duration. There has been very little study of the default effects on the returns from duration-based strategies. The issue begs for analytic attention.

The appropriate duration to be used is not the only question posed by placing default-prone securities into a portfolio. The stochastic process governing the motion of the term structure of interest rates on default-prone securities may not be the same as the one for default-free securities. In other words, some part of the default premiums added to the risk-free rates may have an independent life of its own. Default risk, in addition to interest rate risk, may represent additional sources of risk so that only a multifactor model is appropriate for describing fluctuations in the return on default-prone securities. A better understanding of these multiple risk factors and their interactions may be particularly important in order to devise efficient forms of diversification.

NOTE

1. The duration here corresponds to the case of continuous compounding. For discrete compounding, we would have to divide D by one plus the interest rate for the length of the compounding period.

REFERENCE

Jansson, Solveig. 1986. "Is the Dedicated Bond Business Coming Unglued?" *Institutional Investor* (May): 119–25.

AUTHOR INDEX

SUBJECT INDEX

ABOUT THE AUTHOR

Gerald O. Bierwag is a Professor of Finance and Economics at the University of Arizona. He is president of the Western Finance Association, one of the most prestigious academic associations in finance in the United States. He has served on the Board of Editors of the *American Economic Review* and as an Associate Editor of the *Journal of Financial and Quantitative Analysis;* he continues to review articles for many finance journals. He has also been a project evaluator for the National Science Foundation. Bierwag has made numerous and important contributions to the relatively new and developing area of duration analysis, and is regarded as one of the world's foremost authorities on that subject.